Therapeutic Alliances in Couple and Family Therapy

Therapeutic Alliances in Couple and Family Therapy

An Empirically Informed Guide to Practice

Myrna L. Friedlander
Valentín Escudero
Laurie Heatherington

American Psychological Association | Washington, DC

Published by
American Psychological Association
750 First Street, NE
Washington, DC 20002
www.apa.org

To order
APA Order Department
P.O. Box 92984
Washington, DC 20090-2984
Tel: (800) 374-2721; Direct: (202) 336-5510
Fax: (202) 336-5502; TDD/TTY: (202) 336-6123
Online: www.apa.org/books/
E-mail: order@apa.org

In the U.K., Europe, Africa, and the Middle East, copies may be ordered from
American Psychological Association
3 Henrietta Street
Covent Garden, London
WC2E 8LU England

Typeset in Goudy by Stephen McDougal, Mechanicsville, MD

Printer: Sheridan Books, Ann Arbor, MI
Cover Designer: Naylor Design, Washington, DC
Technical/Production Editor: Genevieve Gill

Library of Congress Cataloging-in-Publication Data

Friedlander, Myrna L.
    Therapeutic alliances in couple and family therapy : an empirically-informed guide to practice / Myrna L. Friedlander, Valentín Escudero, and Laurie Heatherington.— 1st ed.
        p. cm.
    Includes bibliographical references and index.
    ISBN 1-59147-331-4
    1. Marital psychotherapy. 2. Family psychotherapy.
    [DNLM: 1. Family Therapy—methods—Case Reports. 2. Couples Therapy—methods—Case Reports. 3. Professional-Patient Relations—Case Reports. 4. Psychotherapeutic Processes—Case Reports. 5. Models, Psychological. WM 430.5.F2 F911t 2006] I. Escudero, Valentín, 1961- II. Heatherington, Laurie. III. Title.
    RC488.5.F7445 2006
    616.89'1562—dc22   2005021057

British Library Cataloguing-in-Publication Data
A CIP record is available from the British Library.

Printed in the United States of America
First Edition

If I keep from meddling with people, they take care of themselves,
If I keep from commanding people, they behave themselves,
If I keep from preaching at people, they improve themselves,
If I keep from imposing on people, they become themselves.

Lao-tse

CONTENTS

ACKNOWLEDGMENTS

We are grateful to many individuals who contributed to the conceptualization, development, and validation of the System for Observing Family Therapy Alliances (SOFTA) and Sistema de Observación de la Alianza Terapéutica en Intervención Familiar (SOATIF). Research on the instruments could not have been conducted without the aid of Marilyn Wheeler, executive director of Counseling Care and Services (Cohoes, New York) and the therapists there; the workers and therapists of the Fundación Meniños (La Coruña, Spain); and especially the parents and children who were clients in these two agencies' programs.

In the initial stages of the project, the following individuals were instrumental: Marsha Cutting, Nancy Field, Pamela Lehman, and Marilyn McKee. Jane Higham, Nathan Haar, Melissa Horn, and Jessica Lambert were project coordinators for the collection of data, and Adam Horvath, Laura Deihl, and Kristin Talka contributed to the validation of the measures. Manuel A. Linares developed the software for the observational measures, and Matthew Martens and Richard F. Haase contributed statistical expertise. Jianjun Wang and Roderick J. Beaton, both at the Williams College Office of Information Technology, provided invaluable technological help. Ana Martínez-Risco, Michael Beck, and Amanda Ferrier helped with the bilingual translations, and Elizabeth Mulligan, Janette Funk, and Justin Lavner assisted with the literature review and reference cataloguing. We especially appreciate the time and effort spent by the many graduate students who rated videotapes with the SOFTA–o and SOATIF–o and the numerous actors who helped create the training vignettes.

We also thank the researchers and supervisors in the University of La Coruña's Family Intervention Unit: Silvia López-Larrosa, Pepe Rodríguez-Arias, Lola and Manolo Romero, Marcela Santorum, and Nuria Varela. We are grateful to colleagues Emilio Gutiérrez (University of Santiago), Mark

Beyebach (Pontificia University of Salamanca), Miguel Garrido (University of Sevilla), and José A. Ríos (Complutense University of Madrid).

Finally, we are extremely grateful to our families for their loving support during the creation of this project.

Therapeutic Alliances in
Couple and Family Therapy

INTRODUCTION

How we conceptualize and publicize the work of psychotherapists has crucial implications for theory, research, practice, training, and public policy. In the 1990s, burgeoning support for the use of psychotropic medications to alleviate human suffering and well-reasoned arguments against the proliferation of inert, potentially harmful therapies prompted the call to identify sound psychosocial treatments. Answering the call, Division 12 (Society of Clinical Psychology) of the American Psychological Association commissioned a task force to develop a list of empirically validated treatments, that is, therapies of "proven" efficacy in randomized clinical trials (Nathan & Gorman, 1998), now known as *empirically supported treatments*. These treatments are being disseminated widely with actual and perceived imperatives to guide (or, as some fear, limit) practice and clinical training.

Some critics have argued that, in contrast to the real world of clinical practice, these trials are conducted with strict controls, exclusion criteria, and standardized time frames; thus, they cannot provide unequivocal answers to questions of effectiveness (Westen, Novotny, & Thompson-Brenner, 2004). Others have argued that by focusing on technique, we risk losing sight of the therapeutic relationship, insofar as empirically supported treatment "lists and most other practice guidelines depict disembodied therapists performing procedures on Axis I disorders" (Norcross, 2002, p. 4). In contrast to a strict medical model in which the person of the physician is secondary to the treatment, and the individual characteristics of the patient are less salient than symptoms and diagnoses, in psychotherapy "the person of the psychotherapist is inextricably intertwined with the outcome of therapy" (Norcross, p. 4). This point of view is amply supported by the empirical lit-

3

erature on common factors, such as installation of hope, acceptance and positive regard, catharsis, exploration of emotional issues, cognitive change, client involvement, and so forth, that cut across treatment approaches and modalities (Goldfried & Wolfe, 1996; Norcross, 2002; Wampold, 2001).

In virtually every account of common factors and principles of change, the working alliance between the therapist and the client takes center stage. The alliance is an essential feature of good therapy but not unique to any one approach, and the strength of the alliance predicts treatment success and explains treatment failure. However, compared with the burgeoning literature on the alliance in individual therapy, far less is known about developing and sustaining strong working alliances in conjoint treatment.

This book introduces our transtheoretical model of the therapeutic alliance in conjoint therapy, the System for Observing Family Therapy Alliances (SOFTA). As a model, the SOFTA is an elaboration of our ongoing empirical work to develop and validate a set of tools, observational (SOFTA–o; Appendix A) and self-report (SOFTA–s; Appendix B), for estimating the strength of the alliance in couple and family therapy.

As the product of a North American and Spanish collaboration, the SOFTA–o (Friedlander, Escudero, Horvath, et al., 2005) and its Spanish counterpart, the *Sistema de Observación de la Alianza Terapeútica en Intervención Familiar—observación* (SOATIF–o; Escudero & Friedlander, 2003), are observational tools that mirror the clinician's thinking process. When we created these tools, we assumed that effective therapists naturally monitor the strength of their relations with clients by taking note of particular kinds of client behavior as the process unfolds. Do the clients respond readily to questions? Initiate discussions? Disclose intimate information? Or do they refuse to talk, blame each other with hostility, or threaten to walk out? In session, does one spouse lean forward and joke around with the therapist while the other avoids eye contact, sitting defensively in stony silence? Do family members encourage each other to speak honestly, do they offer to compromise, or do they try to align with the therapist against one another?

Whereas the client SOFTA–o draws our attention to specific client behaviors that *reflect* clients' thoughts and feelings about the alliance, the therapist SOFTA–o focuses on therapists' behaviors that *contribute to* a strong or weak alliance. By drawing attention to specific behaviors, the SOFTA–o helps therapists reflect on their own behavior and consider how their interventions may be enhancing or damaging the alliance. "Did the angry son shut down after I complimented his mother's attempts to set limits?" "Did the father ask his daughter what she wanted from therapy after I pointed out how similar they were?" "Did my self-disclosure about my father's death give the mother permission to express her grief?"

We created the SOFTA to organize and synthesize the wealth of behavioral information that therapists should pay attention to in creating, nurturing, and sustaining alliances with family members who may be in conflict with one another or have highly variable motivations for treatment. Using the SOFTA, either formally as a rating tool or informally as a framework for thinking about couple and family therapy processes, therapists (and supervisors) can evaluate the strength of alliances with different family members, identify problematic behaviors that threaten the alliance, and figure out how to move the therapeutic process forward.

In this book, SOFTA serves as an organizing framework for integrating extant theory, research, and practice on the therapeutic alliance in couple and family therapy. Chapter 1 reviews the literature on the alliance in individual and conjoint treatment, focusing on the unique flavor of systemic couple and family therapy. As described in depth in chapter 2, the multidimensional SOFTA takes into account couple and family therapy's uniqueness as well as features common to all therapy modalities: client collaboration and affective bonds with the therapist (i.e., Bordin's, 1979, now-classic conceptualization of the working alliance). Chapter 2 presents a heuristic model of the SOFTA's role in each of four critical therapeutic processes (establishing relationships, negotiating goals, completing tasks and achieving change, and discharging the family from treatment). As summarized in detail in chapter 2, we created the SOFTA inductively, with the stipulation that it be transtheoretical, multidimensional, interpersonal, and reflected in observable behavior so as to be a resource for training and supervision.

In the second section of this book, we describe, with many short and extended actual examples, the SOFTA conceptual dimensions (*Engagement in the Therapeutic Process, Emotional Connection With the Therapist, Safety Within the Therapeutic System,* and *Shared Sense of Purpose Within the Family*), which reflect the in-session behavioral manifestations of between-systems alliances (i.e., each client with the therapist) and within-family alliances (chaps. 4–7). For example, *showing vulnerability* is a positive manifestation of Safety, *whereas refusing to respond to another family member* is a negative manifestation. *Showing indifference* is a negative manifestation of Engagement, whereas *introducing a problem for discussion* is a positive manifestation. Chapter 8 discusses the interrelations of the four dimensions as building blocks of the alliance, developing and evolving over time—both naturally and problematically.

In the third section, chapters 9 through 14, we present various challenging clinical situations, such as working with mandated clients who have little motivation to engage in therapy. The specific "challenges and opportunities" that we selected to highlight include multicultural diversity and problematic alliances between therapist and family (split alliances, unwilling clients, therapist countertransference), within the family itself (zero-sum presenting problems), and among professional helpers (e.g., therapists, supervisors, probation officers, guidance counselors) working with the family. Practical recommendations are offered for nurturing and maintaining strong, healthy alliances in these challenging situations.

We anticipate that therapists with different specialties and a broad range of theoretical orientations will find this book useful in their work with couples and families. Counseling, school, and clinical psychologists; social workers; psychiatrists and psychiatric nurses; school counselors; marriage and family counselors; as well as those who train and supervise therapists in public and private clinical settings can gain a better understanding of clients' behavioral manifestations of strong and weak alliances. With this understanding, therapists will be in a better position to select interventions to enhance a poorly developing, stalled, or faltering alliance. Moreover, experienced clinicians with little training in couple and family therapy will have their attention drawn to the alliance as a salient resource to meet the challenges of conjoint treatment, challenges that therapists who only work with individuals are likely to approach with trepidation.

We anticipate that aside from practicing clinicians, this book will appeal to academic faculty, who may use it as a text for graduate students learning about couple and family therapy. Supervisors of practicum students, interns, and postdoctoral fellows are likely to find the SOFTA–o particularly helpful for teaching supervisees to identify behaviors related to strong and weak alliances in conjoint sessions.

Although the SOFTA–o can be used with paper and pencil (Appendix A), a software version, e-SOFTA, is also available (free of charge from http://www.softa-soatif.net). As described in chapter 3, because actual video data can be loaded into the software program, therapists and supervisors can observe and analyze their own sessions using e-SOFTA directly from their computers. Using the time-stamped comments box within the software program, supervisors can record their impressions of events for their supervisees' consideration.

As an integration of theory, research, and practice, SOFTA advances knowledge on all three fronts. Thus, we anticipate that scholars interested in the therapeutic alliance will gain a broad understanding of its purpose and structure from reading this book. Researchers planning to use the SOFTA–o or SOFTA–s in their investigations are encouraged to read all the clinical material in this book, particularly chapters 4 through 8, as background. Psychometric information on the SOFTA–o and SOFTA–s is presented in chapter 3, along with recommendations for training raters on the observational measures. (The training manual is available at http://www.softa-soatif.net.) As described in chapter 3, e-SOFTA's 16 training vignettes allow multiple raters to be trained independently to an acceptable interrater criterion. Then, by loading their video data into the software program, trained raters can analyze research sessions directly from their computers.

Whether your interest is practical, scientific, or both, we hope that this introduction to the SOFTA has piqued your interest.

I

OVERVIEW

1

THERAPEUTIC ALLIANCE
IN PSYCHOTHERAPY

What makes "good therapy" good? According to many clients, a good relationship with the therapist is the most important element of successful therapy. What then makes a good relationship with the therapist?

A colleague of ours posed this question to one of his clients as their therapeutic work together was coming to an end. The therapist had been treating her for nearly 2 years; she had made significant improvement. Thinking the information might be helpful in his work with future clients, he asked her during their last appointment, "What was it about the therapy that was helpful to you?" "Do you remember the time the bumblebee flew in the window?" she countered. "Yes," he replied, with considerable embarrassment. He was both allergic to and deathly afraid of bees, and her question brought back a vivid image of cowering under the desk while his client chased the bee out of the window. "That was the turning point for me," she continued, "because until that time I saw you as a perfect person, but distant and unapproachable. I didn't trust that you could really help or understand me. But when I saw that you had fears and flaws too, that's when I decided I could relate, I opened up. After that, I began to really work in our sessions. It all started to fall into place."

For purposes of confidentiality, all names in this book are fictitious, and clinical material is significantly disguised or loosely based on actual cases.

9

Her answer was not one the therapist expected, nor was diving under a desk an intervention that he learned in graduate school! Nonetheless, this story is instructive. First, the relationship with the therapist is crucial for successful therapy. It is the foundation on which everything else is built. Whether clients listen or tune out, cooperate or resist, persevere or give up—indeed, whether they keep their appointments—depends on whether they have a sense that the therapist cares about them. Research across a variety of therapy approaches (e.g., psychoanalysis, process–experiential therapy, cognitive–behavioral therapy) has demonstrated that the therapeutic alliance, particularly as measured early in the treatment, is a significant predictor of successful therapy outcome (Horvath & Bedi, 2002; Horvath & Symonds, 1991). Second, we know from research and clinical experience that it is often the client's assessment of the alliance that matters the most and that the client's and therapist's perceptions of the alliance do not always match. Many a beginning (and sometimes even a more experienced) therapist has had a client leave therapy "because it's just not working for me," even though the therapist believed the treatment was progressing well.

Finally, the bumblebee story reminds us that every client and every therapeutic relationship is unique. Granted, there is a science of psychotherapy, and therapists in training learn all sorts of relationship-building skills, therapeutic strategies, and empirically supported interventions for specific disorders. Yet in the therapy room, the application of technique in the moment-to-moment interaction with the client is an art. When it comes to the alliance, the challenge is to take what we know—about building it, assessing it, and repairing it—and apply it to each individual case. However, as we discuss in the next section, the individual case is much more complex when that "case" is a family.

To lay the foundation for the remainder of the book, we use this chapter to review the history, measurement, and major research findings related to the therapeutic alliance in both individual psychotherapy and conjoint couple and family therapy. Before doing so, however, we comment briefly on the uniqueness of conjoint treatment.

UNIQUE FLAVOR OF CONJOINT TREATMENT

Amy and Lisa Ng, 14-year-old twins, were "dragged" to family therapy after their father caught them smoking marijuana with friends in the storeroom of his gift shop. As their father explained to the therapist, his daughters were ruining not only their lives but also his own. For Amy and Lisa, therapy was punishment. For their father, it was the last resort. For their mother and immigrant grandmother, it was a nearly unendurable shame.

Thus starts many a family treatment, with an accuser, an accused, and one or more bystanders. When there are conflicting motives (M. Beck, Friedlander, & Escudero, in press) and a large number of people in attendance, establishing an alliance with each individual, and with the whole, can be a formidable task.

When there are only two clients—a couple or a single parent and child, for example—the motivations for seeking help can at first appear identical or at least congruent. For example, both wife and husband may want to strengthen their marriage, or both father and daughter may come to complain about the girl's court-mandated visits with her mother. Over time, however, the therapist can get wind of hidden agendas. In the first case, when the husband was not looking, his wife found a lover. She thought of marriage counseling as a way to get her husband connected with a therapist before she left him. In the other case, the 14-year-old girl feared her father as much as she missed her absentee mother. Counting the days until those court-mandated visits, she secretly wanted the therapist to help her get more time with her mother. If not, she would escape, too, as soon as she turned 16 and could drop out of school.

In other words, it is not only the sheer number of people involved but also the complexity of motives that make establishing therapeutic alliances in couple and family therapy challenging. Conflicting motives are not restricted to the family itself. When there is an intrusion on the family from the outside, such as Child Protective Services, Family Court, or the school system, the alliance can be in jeopardy even before the first session (see chap. 11). In one case with which we are familiar, a Family Court judge mandated therapy to force Jim and Stephanie Hillmans to parent their children more effectively, but the Hillmans—all eight of them—denied having any problems other than poverty. Because the therapist was seen as the mouthpiece for the judge, Jim and Stephanie showed up for the first session united in their contempt of the therapist, the clinic, and indeed the rest of the world. The second oldest child, Tony, 13, sat through the session in stony silence, refusing to answer the therapist's questions, all the while staring daggers at the floor. The therapist felt defeated by the family and became even more so when she was told, 2 days after the first visit, that Tony had run away. His last hope for help was dashed after witnessing the therapist's impotence.

This sad example illustrates two additional points about the difficulty of establishing alliances in family treatment. First, the family's power structure makes some people vulnerable to other people, and the degree of vulnerability can be extreme if those in power are cunning as well as abusive. Second, more often than not, families come for help when their members are in acute conflict with one another. The individual seeking therapy alone often presents a conflict that is strictly internal. When in conflict with significant others, it is his or her choice what to reveal about the nature and extent of that conflict. However, when the client brings family members along to therapy, there are real-life consequences to what takes place in session (Friedlander, 2000). Young Tony Hillman had to choose between telling a stranger what really went on in his home, risking the wrath of two angry paranoid parents, or remaining silent, less vulnerable but desperate and helpless.

Along with conflict come secrets (Imber-Black, 1993). In individual therapy, the client chooses what to disclose and what not to disclose. In couple and family therapy, however, there is no hiding from what others choose to reveal. In a therapy session, a mother tells her children that she is divorcing their father because he gambled away the family home. A woman tells her boyfriend that she knows he shook the baby and that she is leaving him because of it. In individual therapy, a client can dismiss what the therapist says as irrelevant, off the mark, or simply wrong. There is no such dismissal when a family member lets a shameful secret out of the bag.

The Thompson family is a case in point. The secret in this family was the grandmother's recent suicide. For a long time she had lived alone but marginally, in chronic poor health and perpetual pain, until she could take it no longer. Nancy Thompson developed an agitated depression after her mother's suicide, which she hid from Tricia, 13, and emotionally vulnerable. However, Nancy's husband, Bill, believed in facing unpleasantness head on. In the first session when the topic of the grandmother's death was brought up, Bill told the truth. Tricia, who had felt closer to her grandmother than to either parent, blamed Nancy and stomped furiously out of the room.

The point is safety. The need for safety within the therapeutic environment is a unique feature of conjoint couple and family treatment (Friedlander, Lehman, McKee, Field, & Cutting, 2000). Although clients in individual therapy also need to feel safe, they (and the therapist) have more control over what is said and the pace at which disturbing material is faced. When family members have conflicting motives for seeking help, are in conflict among themselves, and are at different developmental levels, making the context safe for everyone can be a daunting task, particularly when the situation is defined from the outset as win–lose or victim versus victimizer.

The curious thing about safety is that, although too little safety can drive people from therapy, too much comfort can signal an inert treatment. Just as clients in individual therapy must experience some discomfort in order to discover new aspects of themselves, face their fears, or try out new behavior, clients in couple and family therapy need to take risks with each other—risks that, at times, can make them feel anxious and threatened. The therapist's task is to calibrate the degree of anxiety in the system so that no one feels overwhelmed in the session or afraid of repercussions when the session is over. If the right balance can be achieved, clients move from feeling individually vulnerable to giving each other support, acceptance, and understanding.

One of the most precarious moments in therapy is the initial session, when family members first come together to expose what is not right in their world. Wondering how the therapist will construe the story being told, some clients can be tremendously frightened. Their thoughts might run something like this: "Can I tell my side in the right way?" "Will I be believed?" "Who will get the blame?" "Is there any hope for us?" Naturally, many clients in individual therapy have similar fears at the outset of treatment, but they can usually choose to continue with the therapy or to leave if they are dissatisfied with what takes place. The most vulnerable clients in family therapy often do not have that option.

When clients wonder who will be blamed, they are naturally concerned with how the therapist will construe the problem. Often, however, they are less interested in the therapist's view than in how other family members will tell the story. In families in which communication is poor or absent, people have little idea how their husbands, wives, children, or siblings see them. Thus, when therapy begins, what is foremost on everyone's mind is what the *others* will say. When there are secrets—or humiliating facts known to all— anticipating how the tale is told can engender great anxiety.

This is not to say that clients have little interest in the therapist's perspective or in who she or he is as a person. Indeed, the therapist's responsiveness to family members' concerns tends to determine their willingness to commit to treatment beyond the first session (Shapiro, 1974). The complicating feature of conjoint treatment, though, is that each client takes stock not only of his or her own feelings and reactions to the therapist but also of the feelings and reactions of everyone else in the room (Pinsof & Catherall, 1986; Rait, 1998). In fact, the evidence suggests that women tend to be more sensitive to others' perceptions of the therapist, particularly their husbands', than they are to their own (Quinn, Dotson, & Jordan, 1997).

In individual therapy, as discussed earlier, the therapeutic or working alliance is traditionally conceptualized as a strong emotional bond between client and therapist and their mutual agreement on the goals and tasks of treatment (Bordin, 1979; Horvath & Greenberg, 1989). These processes are essential components of the alliance in couple and family therapy as well, but they take on a unique significance.

The therapist's bond must be strong with all family members, not only those who come to every session (Pinsof, 1995). When one family member feels much more strongly about the therapist than another, a split alliance can occur (see chap. 9). Splits happen when some family members are neutral about the therapist and others are positive, but the more pernicious splits happen when some clients' feelings are juxtaposed with others' intense antagonism (Pinsof, 1995).

Various factors can make establishing a bond between therapist and client easier with some family members than with others. Age and gender are two such factors. Therapists are automatically perceived by children as allies of their parents. Working with a heterosexual couple, the therapist is the same gender as one of the partners. If there are within-family differences in race, ethnicity, or religion and the therapist shares a salient characteristic with some family members, this can make a difference relationally (see chap. 10).

When family members have conflicting motives, hidden agendas, and different developmental needs, therapist–client agreements on the goals and tasks of therapy may not come about simply through negotiation, as they do in individual therapy. Validating the goal of one party can alienate another. Indeed, even agreeing with one family member on the need for therapy can alienate another family member who may have come to the session unwillingly, perhaps as a "hostage" (see chap. 11).

To work effectively with couples and families, therapists must simultaneously pay attention to individual needs and to system needs, weaving them together in a way that makes sense to everyone. Doing so may involve reframing the presenting problem, pointing out everyone's good intentions (Pittman, 1987), and emphasizing common values and family strengths (Coulehan, Friedlander, & Heatherington, 1998). When this process is effective, hope rises and the person "on the spot" knows that she or he has an ally in the therapist. In other words, navigating alliances among family members involves transforming individual goals to group goals and nurturing the family's shared sense of purpose about the therapy.

Just as in individual therapy, alliances in couples and family therapy are fluid, shifting in strength, direction, and importance over time. Early in therapy, it is important to create a safe space, get everyone involved, and identify some common ground to which all can agree. At the beginning, the family only needs to click with the therapist to commit to treatment, but over time, as the going gets tough, the emotional bond takes on more significance (Pinsof, 1995). More than any cognitive understanding of the therapeutic process, trust in the therapist gives family members the strength to take interpersonal risks, face hard truths, and chart a new course.

Because changes are always taking place in people's lives, both within and outside the family, even the most secure therapeutic alliance can become strained. For example, Donna and Leo Stevenson were finally getting their marriage back on track as Leo began to recover from a cocaine addiction. The first phase of treatment had moved along by fits and starts, as Donna and the therapist worked as a team to motivate Leo to overcome his addiction. Numerous times Leo had threatened to walk out, but eventually he began to attend Narcotics Anonymous meetings and got "clean." Then Donna's 23-year-old daughter, Shawna, from her first marriage was arrested for shoplifting, and Donna invited her to move back home. Leo was outraged because he felt shoved into the background as a result of Donna's shift in attention. The therapist's alliance with the couple faltered at this juncture. When he suggested that the Stevensons explore the impact of this decision on their marriage, Donna was adamant that her decision to support Shawna was hers alone to make. Nonverbally, she walled herself off, feeling as abandoned by the therapist as by her husband.

Gently redirecting, the therapist pointed out that now that Leo had begun pulling his weight in the family for the first time, Donna could turn to him for comfort in the crisis with Shawna, something she had never before been able to do. The problem was reframed, from a potential conflict about Shawna moving back home to an opportunity for the couple to begin experiencing mutual support and shared decision-making. Challenging Leo to "step up to the plate," the therapist suggested that he speak to his wife from his heart. Taking the hint, Leo sincerely pleaded with Donna to let him be there for her. Hearing this, she tearfully relaxed into his embrace.

It was a rocky road for the Stevensons. The second phase of therapy had faltered when Donna, angry at the shift in the focus, felt a loss of support from the therapist. Earlier in the process she had seen herself as a quasi-cotherapist, seeing her husband as the one with the problem. Now the therapist was implying that her attitude was problematic. In the end, the strong connections of each spouse individually with the therapist as well as with each other made the alliance strain short-lived, and the treatment got back on track with renewed vigor.

The therapeutic process is not always rocky, however. Some couples and families seek help willingly, having discussed their concerns with each other at length and well before the first session. They come united and ready to work. As Pittman (1987) put it, "Often all that is required of the therapist is an awareness of the process, a gentle guidance back onto the path, good humor and good manners, and meticulous reality testing. Technique is unnecessary" (p. 42).

NATURE, EVOLUTION, AND
IMPORTANCE OF THE THERAPEUTIC ALLIANCE

In this section we provide an overview of the theory and research on the alliance in individual psychotherapy.

Construct

Like many psychological terms, the word *alliance* is used differently in professional parlance than in common parlance. The dictionary definition denotes strategic maneuvering or goal-driven coalitions, as in business or war. In therapy, by contrast, *alliance* refers to

> [the] quality and strength of the collaborative relationship between client and therapist . . . [it] is inclusive of: the positive affective bonds between client and therapist, such as mutual trust, liking, respect and caring . . . consensus about, and active commitment to, the goals of therapy and to the means by which these goals can be reached . . . a sense of partnership. (Horvath & Bedi, 2002, p. 41)

Furthermore, the term *alliance* has historically been used in a variety of ways, even among theorists and practitioners. It was originally discussed by

Freud (1912/1940), who distinguished *alliance* from *transference*. In contrast to the patient's real feelings about the analyst, transference was the patient's displacement of feelings, impulses, and needs toward significant others on the analyst, that is, conflicting material that could become "grist" for the analytic "mill." According to Freud (1912/1940), the "unobjectionable" or "positive" transference was something different—it was the patient's basic affection for and trust in the therapist, not to be analyzed, providing the foundation and motivation for the therapeutic work (Muran & Safran, 1998).

For several decades, the alliance was exclusively associated with psychoanalysis, its definition shaped by the perspectives of theorists who wrote about it. One fruitful conceptualization was put forth by ego psychologists Bibring (1937) and Sterba (1934), who raised objections to the object relations tenet that *everything* a client feels toward a therapist is transference. Instead, ego psychologists focused attention on the patient's reality-oriented adaptations and the "real" aspects of the therapeutic relationship, not only the transference. The person of the therapist came into play, not merely as a blank slate for the patient's distortions. Credited with elevating the status of the working alliance to the level of the transference, Greenson (1967) opened the door for analysts to make interventions other than transference interpretations and take a therapeutic stance other than strict neutrality (Muran & Safran, 1998).

In the working alliance, both intrapersonal (i.e., client and therapist introjects) and interpersonal (i.e., dynamics arising from their interaction) elements are present. Strupp (1973) first articulated this point and argued that the alliance is crucial not only in psychoanalytic psychotherapy but in all therapies. Strupp described the alliance as a pantheoretical construct that accounts for the effectiveness of technical interventions of any type (e.g., interpretations, behavior modification, Gestalt techniques). Therapy is about learning, Strupp argued, and learning involves identification and imitation, both of which require the client's openness to and influence from an important, trusted figure, much like a good parent (Henry & Strupp, 1994).

From the debut of the alliance in the literature of the 1930s, and well into the 1970s, various proposals have been put forth about which elements— the patient's capacity to connect with the therapist, the therapists' personal characteristics, the client being on board with the tasks of treatment, the emotional bond between therapist and client, and so forth—are most critical. As theories of the alliance developed, various modifiers were attached to the term, including *ego* alliance, *working* alliance, and *therapeutic* alliance. In the late 1970s Bordin (1979) suggested a pantheoretical definition that incorporated several of these elements. To date, this conceptualization has been the most heuristically rich and influential model of the alliance in conjoint as well as individual psychotherapy. The working alliance, Bordin proposed, includes three components: (a) agreement between therapist and client about the goals of treatment, (b) agreement about the therapy tasks needed to accomplish those goals, and (c) affective bonds, necessary to sustain the hard work of therapeutic change.

The heuristic value of Bordin's (1979) thinking and the intuitive appeal of the alliance as an explanatory construct can be seen in its application across diverse schools of therapy. Despite its roots in psychoanalysis, theorists, researchers, and practitioners working from virtually every treatment model are now intensely interested in the alliance.

A considerable amount of writing has been done, for example, on the alliance in humanistic and experiential therapies (Watson & Greenberg, 1988). Traditionally, the therapeutic relationship was a central feature in Carl Rogers's (1951) thinking about the therapist characteristics and relationship conditions—empathy, unconditional positive regard, genuineness, and congruence—deemed necessary (and sufficient) for client change. Gestalt therapists, as well, unabashedly championed the importance of genuineness, directness, and mutuality in the therapeutic relationship. In contrast to some psychoanalytic and behavioral theorizing, humanists saw relationship factors as central, curative elements of therapy rather than as merely the backdrop for other mechanisms of change (Friedman, 1985).

In more recent humanistic models, such as process-experiential therapy (Watson & Greenberg, 1988), clients experience emotions and symbolize them in conscious awareness. A strong alliance facilitates this process, whereas a weak one detracts from it (Watson & Greenberg, 1988). In the moment, therapists must listen carefully, understand their clients' inner experience and communicate understanding, be aware of markers that signal opportunities (for deeper experience, resolution of affective splits, etc.), and intervene to help clients more fully access their internal world. This kind of attunement, argued Watson and Greenberg, is what Bordin (1979) meant by collaboration on therapeutic goals and tasks giving rise to strong emotional bonds.

Even behavioral and cognitive–behavioral therapists, traditionally more interested in specific change mechanisms than in the therapeutic relationship, recognize the alliance as critical for successful outcomes. Indeed, cognitive–behavioral therapies are inherently and explicitly collaborative, and integral to their protocols is providing clients with a persuasive rationale for treatment goals and the tasks involved in achieving those goals. In the language of social-learning theory, for example, affective bonds increase the reinforcement value of the therapist, facilitate modeling, and promote positive expectancies (Raue & Goldfried, 1994). Like an anesthetic used during surgery, a strong alliance stays in the background, allowing the procedures (therapy techniques) to be applied in ways that benefit the patient (Goldfried, 1982).

Undoubtedly, the therapeutic alliance as written about in the literature is theoretically and clinically compelling. To what extent does it really matter in psychotherapy? The answer to this question, essentially an empirical one, first requires a discussion of the construct's operationalization.

Measures

Alliance measures are critically important, as *de facto* conceptual definitions as well as operational ones (Horvath & Bedi, 2002). In 2002, Horvath and Bedi counted 24 measures of the alliance in individual therapy research, including four sets of instruments used in multiple studies and different research sites. The most well known for adults are the Penn Helping Alliance Scales (L. B. Alexander & Luborksy, 1987; Luborsky, Crits-Cristoph, Alexander, Margolis, & Cohen, 1983), the Vanderbilt Therapeutic Alliance Scale (Hartley & Strupp, 1983; Suh, O'Malley, & Strupp, 1986), the Working Alliance Inventory (Horvath & Greenberg, 1986, 1989), and the California–Toronto Scales (Marmar, Gaston, Gallagher, & Thompson, 1989).

The Penn Helping Alliance Scales reflect Luborsky et al.'s (1983) psychodynamic formulation of the alliance as strong affective bonds and a sense of mutual collaboration between the therapist and the client. Observational items assess Type 1 signs of the alliance (behaviors reflecting the client's experience of the therapist as helpful and supportive) and Type 2 signs (behaviors reflecting a sense of collaboration). In addition to the observer rating scale, there is a therapist rating scale and a questionnaire for clients, with items paralleling the behavioral signs (Luborsky, 1994). The Vanderbilt Scale, similarly based in psychodynamic theory and Bordin's (1979) conceptualization of the alliance, uses clinical observers to rate therapy segments. Also derived from Bordin's model, Horvath and Greenberg's (1986, 1989) Working Alliance Inventory is by far the most widely used and cited instrument in the literature. The original inventory has therapist and client self-report versions; an observer form was created by Tichenor and Hill (1989), and a shortened form was developed by Tracey and Kokotovic (1989). Finally, the California–Toronto Scales were derived from psychoanalytic theory, focused on affective dimensions, and yielded several spin-offs. A popular one is the California Psychotherapy Alliance Scale, which taps four dimensions that are said to be relatively independent: (a) the working alliance (the client's contribution to the therapeutic work), (b) the therapeutic alliance (affective aspects of the relationship), (c) the therapist's involvement and understanding, and (d) client–therapist agreement on goals and strategies. This scale has self-report versions for therapist and client, as well as an observer-rated version (Gaston & Marmar, 1994).

Clearly, these instruments are conceptually similar; they are also statistically intercorrelated, some at the subscale level (Horvath & Symonds, 1991). Although not completely overlapping either conceptually or empirically, most measures reliably estimate the strength of affective bonds and collaboration (agreement on goals and bonds, a commitment to the therapy process). In a meta-analysis, Horvath and Symonds found a consensus among alliance researchers on two core themes: collaboration and an ongoing negotiation between therapist and client about the therapeutic contract.

Research

Measurement issues notwithstanding, what is the relationship between the alliance and treatment outcome? An extended review of the literature is beyond the scope of this chapter, although the following brief summary has an important conclusion: The alliance is predictive of outcome across a variety of (individual) therapeutic approaches when measured early in treatment, and much of the research suggests that the client's perspective is paramount (Horvath & Symonds, 1991).

The National Institute of Mental Health Treatment of Depression Collaborative Research Program provided a valuable opportunity to study the alliance in relation to treatment outcome in a large-scale comparison of interpersonal therapy, cognitive–behavioral therapy, and pharmacotherapy (Krupnick et al., 1996). In fact, 21% of the variance in therapy success was accounted for by the client contribution to the therapeutic alliance, across treatment approaches. More important perhaps, follow-up analyses showed that for clients who completed treatment, those who expected therapy to be helpful were more actively engaged in the process and more likely to change (Meyer et al., 2002).

Three meta-analyses of the alliance–outcome relation found similar, significant effect sizes. The first analysis (Horvath & Symonds, 1991), with 20 different data sets and fairly experienced therapists (primarily psychodynamic, experiential, and cognitive), showed a combined effect size of .26, "moderate but reliable" (p. 139). Horvath and Symonds concluded that the alliance can be reliably measured by observers, therapists, and clients, although the latter source had the strongest relationship to outcome, followed by observers' ratings. It is interesting to note that clients' reports converged more with observers' ratings than with therapists' reports. A subsequent, larger meta-analysis (D. J. Martin, Garske, & Davis, 2000), with 79 studies of diverse outpatient therapies and a wide variety of clinical problems, found a slightly lower but still significant effect size of .22. In contrast to Horvath and Symonds's results, however, the alliance–outcome relation did not vary by the source of the measure (i.e., client, therapist, or observer). Finally, in an updated review, Horvath and Bedi (2002) reported a median effect size of .25 and some evidence contradicting previous conclusions. This meta-analysis included six studies of substance abuse treatment, contributing more variation to the sample. Like Martin et al., Horvath and Bedi found that the relationship between outcome and alliance was slightly stronger when clients' and observers' (vs. therapists') ratings of the alliance were used. Notably, the alliance seems to be a somewhat better predictor of treatment success when it is measured early in therapy than midway. Reports of the alliance late in treatment tend to be highly associated with outcome, but clients' (and therapists') perceptions at that point are likely to be influenced by the already experienced benefits of therapy. In fact, some authors (DeRubeis &

Feeley, 1990; Feeley, DeRubeis, & Gelf, 1999) have cautioned that to assert that a strong alliance *causes* client improvement, therapy gains need to be assessed at a point in time well after the alliance is measured.

ALLIANCE IN COUPLE AND FAMILY THERAPY

Work on the alliance in couple and family therapy lags behind (Sexton, Robbins, Hollimon, Mease, & Mayorga, 2003). With a few notable exceptions, such as Carl Whitaker (Whitaker & Keith, 1981) and Virginia Satir (1964), early family theorists focused uniquely on technique. Traditional systemic theories emphasize analyses of family interaction patterns by therapists who are cautioned to stand back and take a meta-perspective and then to intervene incisively and strategically to unbalance family homeostasis, reframe clients' misguided views on their problems, and plant the seeds of solution-focused thinking. When one-way mirrors are used, sometimes the "treatment team" is not even in the room with the family.

Family therapists' traditional roles have emphasized the need to be a conversational "traffic cop" or apply theory-specific techniques, rather than to establish warm, vital relationships with overwhelmed clients. The need for a traffic cop is understandable, given the complexities and pitfalls of managing multiple alliances when, more often than not, one family member does not want to be present.

However, as work on the alliance in individual therapy has proliferated, demonstrating its power to make sense of the therapeutic process and predict treatment success and failure, and as family therapy theories and practice have matured, there is now a burgeoning interest in the alliance in conjoint psychotherapy. The following sections summarize the theory, measurement, and outcome research on the alliance in couple and family therapy.

Construct

Several unique features are involved in developing and sustaining working alliances in couple and family therapy (Pinsof, 1995; Rait, 1998). Collaboration begins with the establishment of a safe atmosphere by limiting negative family interchanges and clarifying confidentiality limits, treatment objectives, and participants' roles (Snyder, 1999). From there, the therapist must figure out how to nurture alliances with multiple clients whose working capacities, personalities, developmental needs, and clinical issues are likely to differ. The process is further complicated by the fact that when several people are present, what goes on between the therapist and any one family member is observed by—and likely to affect—all the others.

When working in a conjoint treatment format, the therapist must rapidly analyze and manage emotional triangles (Bowen, 1976), so that tension within a dyad does not draw him or her in and unbalance the developing alliance. In couple therapy in particular, the therapist–couple triangle is salient. Arguably, developing a collaborative alliance between two partners and a therapist, and between the partners themselves (Jacobson & Margolin, 1979), is the most fundamental step in couple treatment (Snyder, 1999). The success of techniques, from the most didactic (e.g., building communication skills) to the most emotionally intense (e.g., examining historical sources of relationship distress), depends on and also has an influence on the developing alliance.

Rait (1998) described a continuum of theoretical stances on the alliance in couple and family therapy. At one end are experiential therapies (e.g., Satir, 1964), in which the "person" of the therapist is salient and warmth, support, and mutual collaboration are central features. At the other end of the spectrum are multigenerational therapies (e.g., Bowen, 1976), in which the therapist stays out of the transference to remain objective and differentiated, and Milan systemic therapy (Selvini-Palazzoli, Boscolo, Cecchin, & Prata, 1978), in which an observing team, strict neutrality, and prescriptive interventions (delivered in an authoritative manner) keep therapists out of the quagmire. According to Rait, each theoretical model, from one end of the continuum to the other, requires attention to and strengthening of alliances.

Moreover, each model pays attention to alliance ruptures—repairing them directly or indirectly, depending on the approach (Rait, 1998). Ruptures in the alliance in family therapy may occur with one, more than one, or all family members (Pinsof, 1995). As noted earlier, split or unbalanced alliances (see also chap. 9) are a special case in conjoint therapy (Heatherington & Friedlander, 1990b; Pinsof, 1995; Pinsof & Catherall, 1986). These may or may not be detrimental to the treatment, depending on their intensity and the person (or subsystem) with whom the therapist has the most and least favorable alliance (Pinsof, 1995). In many families, the mother gets the others to therapy, but the father's opinion about whether to commit to treatment is pivotal. In other families, the roles may be reversed. Regardless of who has the power, therapists must ensure a positive alliance with the most influential individual to keep the family in treatment (Pinsof, 1995).

Clients as well as therapists are continually sizing each other up, but research in couple and family therapy and clinical experience suggests that the client's experience of the alliance is critical, arguably more important than the therapist's experience (Barnard & Kuehl, 1995; Horvath & Symonds, 1991). Clients have valuable information that can help shape good outcomes, but when therapists are overly focused on technique and do not assess the clients' experience of what is taking place, failures can ensue. As therapy progresses, therapists must repeatedly evaluate their relationships with clients, periodically inquiring, "Is there anything I (we) haven't done that you were expecting and are wondering about?" or "How does what I'm offering/

suggesting fit for you and what you're hoping to accomplish here?" (Barnard & Kuehl, 1995, p. 169).

A father leaving a therapy session was overheard commenting, "I have no idea what the %$#(*& just happened in there, but I don't like it one bit!" Although we do not know what happened either, it is possible that when the therapist pushed down a resistance "bubble" in one area of the alliance, another "bubble" got pushed up for the father. Reciprocal causality in the alliance was first described by Pinsof (1994, 1995; Pinsof & Catherall, 1986), who argued convincingly for a systemic perspective on the alliance in work with couples and families. Noting that no simple formula for summing each individual client's relationship with the therapist can account for the overall alliance, Pinsof and Catherall described how individual client–therapist alliances, therapist–subsystem (e.g., parental, sibling) alliances, and therapist–family alliances affect one another in a mutually reinforcing dance. In subsequent writings, Pinsof (1994, 1995) added a fourth interpersonal dimension, the *within-system alliance*, which refers to alliances within the family (individuals and subsystems) as well as alliances within the therapeutic system (e.g., cotherapists, therapist and supervisor, or therapist and other professionals involved with the family).

Pinsof's (1994, 1995) conceptualization is based on interpersonal (individual, subsystem, within-system, and whole system) and content factors (strong emotional bonds and an agreement on therapy goals and tasks; Bordin, 1979), but this view of the alliance is more detailed and holistic than expressed by the interaction of these components. In his writings, Pinsof emphasized the clients' psychic investment in the treatment, which goes well beyond bonds, goals, and tasks. For example, changes in the alliance occur over time, in the interpersonal realm or the content realm, and are reflected in different "alliance profiles" (1995, p. 75). In his integrative problem-centered therapy, Pinsof (1995) postulated a gradual deepening of the emotional connection between and within subsystems over time, facilitated by (a) enhancing the "relational focus of the therapy," (b) increasing session frequency, (c) decreasing the number of people seen as therapy progresses, and (d) time in treatment (p. 79).

Influenced by several trends in the literature, we wanted to develop a multidimensional model of the alliance that would reflect both the uniqueness of systemic couple and family work and features common to all therapy modalities: client collaboration and affective bonds with the therapist (i.e., Bordin's, 1979, classic conceptualization of the alliance). Three trends guiding the creation of the System for Observing Family Therapy Alliances (SOFTA) were (a) the transtheoretical applicability of the alliance, (b) the importance of client behavior, specifically within-family alliances (Pinsof, 1994, 1995), and (c) the conceptual and empirical overlap between therapy goals and tasks (Horvath & Bedi, 2002). As described in detail in chapter 2, the SOFTA dimensions (Engagement in the Therapeutic Process, Emotional

Connection With the Therapist, Safety Within the Therapeutic Context, and Shared Sense of Purpose Within the Family), which reflect both between-systems alliances (i.e., each client with the therapist) and within-family alliances, play a role in four critical therapeutic processes: establishing relationships, negotiating goals, completing tasks and achieving change, and discharging the family from treatment.

Measures

Until the SOFTA (Friedlander, Escudero, Haar, & Higham, 2005; Friedlander, Escudero, Horvath, et al., in press; Friedlander, Lehman, et al., 2000, 2001; Friedlander et al., 2003), all systems-based measures of the alliance in couple and family therapy were based on Bordin's (1979) tripartite conceptualization. Self-report instrumentation began with Pinsof and Catherall's (1986) integrative Couple and Family Therapy Alliance Scales. Within each of three content subscales, items representing Bordin's model tapped client–therapist (a) emotional bonds, (b) agreement on goals, and (c) agreement on therapeutic tasks. Three interpersonal subscales reflected bonds, goals, and tasks in terms of the therapist's alliance (a) with each individual family member, (b) with the family as a whole, and (c) with subsystems (e.g., parental or sibling). Thus, the three content scales and three interpersonal scales made up a nine-cell matrix with parallel but reverse-scored items, such as "The therapist cares about me as a person," "The therapist does not care about my partner as a person," and "The therapist cares about the relationship between my partner and myself."

The Couple Therapy Alliance Scale and Family Therapy Alliance Scale have high internal consistencies (Heatherington & Friedlander, 1990b) and rate–rerate reliabilities, as well as predictive validity based on associations with therapists' ratings of client progress (Pinsof & Catherall, 1986). In an outpatient sample, Heatherington and Friedlander found the Tasks and Bonds subscales to be highly intercorrelated, although the couple and family versions of the measure had somewhat different patterns of associations with therapist-rated session evaluations. It is interesting to note that whereas agreement on tasks was closely associated with the perceived depth or value of sessions for couples, a strong emotional bond was paramount for clients (children included) in family therapy.

Concerned about the within-family alliance (Pinsof, 1994, 1995), Pinsof (1999) revised the Couple Therapy Alliance Scale and Family Therapy Alliance Scale to address this important dimension. In the revised versions, subscales assess the degree to which the partners or family members are in agreement with each other about the therapeutic goals and tasks and the quality of the bonds (e.g., "My partner and I care about each other in this therapy") between them. Confirmatory factor analyses have validated the theoretical structures of the revised instruments (Knobloch-Fedders, Pinsof, & Mann, in press).

A couple's alliance can also be assessed using the Working Alliance Inventory—Couples (Symonds, 1998; Symonds & Horvath, 2004) from either the therapist's or the clients' perspective. Like Pinsof's (1999; Pinsof & Catherall, 1986) measures and the Working Alliance Inventory for individual therapy (Horvath & Greenberg, 1986, 1989), the inventory for couples is based on Bordin's (1979) model of goals, tasks, and bonds. In addition, like the Couple Therapy Alliance Scale—Revised, the measure assesses the individual's perspective on (a) his or her own alliance with the therapist, (b) the partner's alliance with the therapist, and (c) the partners' alliance with each other (e.g., "She and I have an understanding about what we are trying to accomplish in therapy"). Reliabilities are high for both client and therapist versions, and scores on the Working Alliance Inventory—Couples predict treatment outcome (Symonds & Horvath, 2004). In contrast to most research on individual psychotherapy (Horvath & Symonds, 1991), the inventory's alliance–outcome association is reportedly stronger from the therapist's perspective than from the clients' perspectives (Symonds & Horvath, 2004).

As described in detail in chapter 2, we created the SOFTA tools from the ground up, that is, inductively and empirically, with the stipulation that they be transtheoretical, multidimensional, and interpersonal. The observer rating scales for client and therapist behavior (the SOFTA–o in English and the SOATIF–o in Spanish) are designed to be a resource for training and supervision as well as research. In these measures, client (and therapist) behaviors contributing to strong and weak alliances are noted; then their frequency, intensity, and clinical meaningfulness are used to make a rating, from –3 (*extremely problematic*) to +3 (*extremely strong*), on Engagement in the Therapeutic Process, Emotional Connection With the Therapist, Safety Within the Therapeutic System, and Shared Sense of Purpose Within the Family. (Each client receives a rating on Engagement, Emotional Connection, and Safety, and the couple or family as a unit is rated on Shared Purpose.) Operational definitions of the scales appear in Appendix A and are illustrated in numerous clinical examples throughout this book.

In addition to the observer scales, there are two 16-item self-report questionnaires for clients and therapists (SOFTA–s and SOATIF–s), reproduced in Appendix B. Research on the SOFTA–o and SOFTA–s, although not extensive as of this writing, supports the reliability of the measures and face, content, concurrent, and predictive validity (M. Beck et al., in press; Friedlander, Escudero, Haar, & Higham, 2005; Friedlander, Escudero, Horvath, et al., in press; Friedlander, Talka, et al., 2003; see chap. 3 for a summary). Notably, in four case studies postsession interviews with individual family members about their own and the within-family alliance were more congruent with SOFTA–o ratings of early sessions than with self-reported perceptions of the alliance on the Family Therapy Alliance Scale—Revised (M. Beck et al., in press).

Research

Three decades ago, a study of nearly 4,000 cases identified 11 factors associated with good outcomes in couple and family therapy, and the therapist–client relationship topped them all (D. F. Beck & Jones, 1973). The relationship was a stronger predictor of outcome (indeed, twice as strong) than all client characteristics combined. In 1978, Gurman and Kniskern comprehensively reviewed the literature and concluded that

> the ability of the therapist to establish a positive relationship with his or her clients, long a central issue of individual therapy, receives the most consistent support as an important outcome-related therapist factor to marital and family therapy. (p. 875)

Twenty years later, in a comprehensive review of "what works" and "what doesn't work" in couple and family therapy, Friedlander, Wildman, Heatherington, and Skowron (1994) found evidence that session effectiveness, continuation in treatment, and outcome could be predicted by self-reported therapeutic alliances or other aspects of the therapeutic relationship.

Overall, positive feelings about the therapist have been identified as important in a number of couple and family therapy studies (e.g., Christensen, Russell, Miller, & Peterson, 1998; Firestone & O'Connell, 1980; Green & Herget, 1991). In open-ended interviews, couples indicated, among other things, that a felt sense of safety and a belief that the therapist was impartial were preconditions for change (Christensen et al., 1998). In Milan-style systemic therapy, supervisors' ratings of therapist warmth were significantly associated with clients' self-rated improvement at 1-month and 3-year follow-up assessments (Green & Herget, 1991), a fascinating finding because systemic therapists value neutrality and technique over warmth and other relationship factors.

With respect to the alliance, positive correlations with treatment retention or outcome have been observed in multidimensional family therapy for substance-abusing adolescents (Shelef, Diamond, Diamond, & Liddle, 2005), in a couples group treatment for partner abuse (P. D. Brown & O'Leary, 2000), in a structured group marital skills training program (Bourgeois, Sabourin, & Wright, 1990), in integrative problem-centered therapy with couples (Knobloch-Fedders, Pinsof, & Mann, 2004), in functional family therapy for delinquent youth (Robbins, Turner, Alexander, & Perez, 2003), in emotionally-focused couple therapy (S. M. Johnson & Talitman, 1997), in home-based family therapy (L. N. Johnson, Wright, & Ketring, 2002), and in couple therapy "as usual" in private practice (Symonds & Horvath, 2004). However, couple and family therapy research with systemically based measures (Couple Therapy Alliance Scale or Family Therapy Alliance Scale,

Working Alliance Inventory—Couples, or SOFTA–o), or with instruments developed for individual therapy but used in a family setting (e.g., Shelef et al.'s [2005] research with the Working Alliance Inventory and Vanderbilt scales), suggest a complex relationship between each client's alliance with the therapist and treatment outcomes. Split alliances, common in both couple and family therapy (Heatherington & Friedlander, 1990b), tell only part of the story. Shelef et al., for example, found that the degree to which adolescents overcame marijuana abuse was partially related to an interaction between the teen's alliance with the therapist and his or her alliance with the parent. In another recent study, Symonds and Horvath (2004) found that when partners agreed about the strength of the alliance, the alliance–outcome relationship was much stronger than when they disagreed, regardless of the absolute quality of the alliance. The authors suggested that a couple's alliance with the therapist is affected by the historical and ongoing allegiance between the partners, what in the SOFTA is called the couple's *shared sense of purpose*.

To date, much of the research on couples has treated marital satisfaction as the sole outcome variable. A recent study of integrative problem-centered therapy (Knobloch-Fedders et al., 2004), however, included individual progress on self-reported well-being, symptoms, and functioning as well as marital satisfaction. Both sets of variables were assessed midway through treatment. Clients who continued in treatment had stronger first session alliance scores than those who terminated earlier. Knobloch-Fedders et al. (2004) cautioned, however, that for some couples, early termination may have been due to the accomplishment of treatment goals rather than premature drop out. Moreover, the combined alliance scores (Session 1 + Session 8) predicted improvement in marital distress, but more so for wives than for husbands. When men's Session 8 alliances were stronger than those of their wives, there was a greater reduction in marital distress. Furthermore, women's ratings of the couple's alliance was significantly correlated with treatment response by Session 8, though their own alliance with the therapist was not. (Gender issues in the alliance are treated in more depth in chap. 10.)

As noted earlier, the distinguishing feature of couple and family therapy is that multiple alliances develop simultaneously and systemically. Conceptual issues are also measurement issues: How (and whether) to combine family members' self-reports of the alliance, how to interpret and analyze split alliances, and whether some family members' alliances are more important than others'. As experienced family therapists well know, the angry adolescent who keeps her parents on their toes at home can derail the treatment if the therapist is unable to connect with her early on. Similarly, the spouse who sees no value in improved communication skills can hamper the couple therapy, despite the other spouse's eagerness to follow any and all of the therapist's suggestions.

The detrimental effects of split alliances are highlighted in two studies. In research on good- and poor-outcome families (Bennun, 1989), mothers' and fathers' perceptions of the therapists' positive regard, activity–directiveness, and competence–experience differed more in the less successful than in the more successful cases. In a study of functional family therapy for adolescent behavior problems (Robbins et al., 2003), observer-rated individual alliances (i.e., parent with therapist, or teen with therapist) did not predict retention. In fact, *greater* parent alliances with the therapist were a risk factor for drop out, particularly when the father's alliance with the therapist was much higher than the teen's. Interpreting these results, Robbins et al. (2003) suggested that the "therapists in dropout cases may have inadvertently validated parental negativity about the adolescent without adequately responding to the adolescent's needs or concerns" (p. 541), contributing to an overall climate of negativity.

The clinical and research importance of understanding each client's perception of the family–therapist alliance is underscored by a study of home-based conjoint therapy (L. N. Johnson et al., 2002). The alliance–outcome relationship varied greatly for mothers, fathers, and adolescents. Furthermore, on the self-report Family Therapy Alliance Scale (Pinsof & Catherall, 1986), the tasks (for mothers and adolescents) and goals (for fathers), not the bonds, predicted treatment outcome. Johnson et al. (2002) explained that clients had difficulty assessing other family members' emotional connections with the therapist (i.e., the Other-Alliance Bond subscale). For many clients, observing others' agreements on tasks and goals is likely to be far easier.

It is interesting to note that the multiple and indirect alliances that characterize the family therapy context can work in fortuitous ways. Establishing strong family alliances and making progress with the families of delinquent adolescents can have important reverberating effects, such as a dramatic decrease in the younger siblings' becoming juvenile offenders (N. C. Klein, Alexander, & Parsons, 1977). Whole families may also benefit from strong therapeutic alliances with one parent. In a large prevention program for child aggression (Hanish & Tolan, 2001), for example, strong parent–provider alliances, and the alliances' improvements over time, were predictive of gains in parenting skills.

Not only large-sample, quantitative studies but also intensive, qualitative studies of clients' experiences support the importance of the alliance in continuance and outcome in couple and family therapy. Moreover, the qualitative studies highlight aspects of the alliance that are of particular importance to clients. In Christensen et al.'s (1998) study of couples, clients were asked to reflect on the treatment, the therapist interventions, and the turning points that facilitated change. Five contextual factors were common to clients' perceptions. One factor was *fairness*, which clients described as therapists' understanding both partners' points of view and not taking sides. Another factor was *safety*. Clients commented, for example, "[The therapists] make it safe for us to say things to them and to each other," "I just feel really safe with her . . . she's not devious or anything . . . she stays on our level and doesn't try to use a bunch of big words." Safety also played a major role in clients' postsession discussions of the alliance in a recent qualitative study of four Spanish families (M. Beck, Friedlander, & Escudero, in press). Moreover, poorer outcomes characterized the two families in which client Safety ratings on the SOFTA–o were highly negative early in treatment.

The revelations of a different sample of couple and family therapy clients were also quite informative (Kuehl, Newfield, & Joanning, 1990). Clients said they really did not know what to expect in the first session. They were "turned off" by having to fill out forms and speak to an intake worker rather than to a therapist. In the early-to-middle phase of therapy, they often felt stuck and impatient with a lack of progress; they also considered dropping out if they (or other family members) were misunderstood or "picked on" by the therapist. Some adolescents felt "scared" and chose to stay quiet, partly to figure out how to avoid being put on the spot. If they did not see the therapist as interested in them as people, they were less likely to be open and honest (pp. 314–316).

In summary, there is solid empirical evidence that the "common factor" status of the alliance in individual therapy extends to couple and family therapy as well (Sprenkle & Blow, 2004). We know less, however, about the issue of most concern to practitioners: What makes for good alliances with couples and families (J. F. Alexander, Robbins, & Sexton, 2000)?

Process studies addressing this question in couple and family therapy are sparse but highly informative. One investigation, for example, focused on resolving impasses in family therapy related to (in SOFTA language) a shared sense of purpose (G. S. Diamond & Liddle, 1996). G. S. Diamond and Liddle intensively compared a small sample of successfully and unsuccessfully resolved impasse events in multidimensional family therapy. Results suggested that delinquent teens can become more engaged and cooperative when parents move from trying to control them to trying to understand them. Specifically, the therapist begins by blocking the parent's blaming and helplessness by noting, "It must be disappointing that you don't get along with your child." To the teen, "Did you know that your mother misses you?" (pp. 483–484). This question pulls for regret. When the teen expresses doubt, the therapist prevents the parent from responding defensively and focuses on the teen's disbelief and feelings of "missing" the parent. The point is to attempt to

> resuscitate that part of the adolescent that still desire[s] a relationship with his or her parent. This shifts clients to a more vulnerable stance, and to a focus on their relationship vs. control, "Did you know why your son was so angry? Would you like to know why?" (pp. 484–485)

Listening empathically and not blaming, the therapist hopes the teen's vulnerability and reduced negativity will soften the parents' stance, resulting in a more productive family dialogue and increased cooperation in therapy.

Process research on attachment-based family therapy (G. S. Diamond, Siqueland, & Diamond, 2003) with depressed teens also underscores the importance of balanced alliances with teens and their parents. Effective therapists show interest in the teen's interests and strengths and define therapy goals that are important to him or her, simultaneously joining with parents on the difficulties of raising a depressed child. By refraining from criticism and instead teaching listening skills, the therapist aligns with the parents, eventually strengthening within-family relationships. In this treatment model, the SOFTA alliance dimensions of Engagement (i.e., Will the adolescent get involved in treatment?), Safety (Does the teen feel safe enough to be vulnerable?), Emotional Connection With the Therapist (Do the parents trust the therapists not to blame them?), and Shared Sense of Purpose Within the Family (Can family members work together productively?), all of which are essential, are buttressed by the therapist's "re-attachment" interventions. These kinds of investigations get to the heart of concerns most dear to practitioners.

CONCLUSION

Despite many permutations in conceptualization and operationalization of the therapeutic alliance, remarkable common elements stand out. The alliance is a mutual collaboration of therapist and client or clients on shared goals and tasks. However, it is not merely a behavioral contract—the alliance has a strong emotional component as well. Research shows that when assessed early in therapy, especially observationally and from the client's perspective, it robustly predicts success in treatment across diverse therapeutic approaches. Although there are unanswered questions about causality, there is good reason to believe that a strong alliance is partially responsible for favorable treatment outcomes.

When it comes to couple and family therapy, the picture is much more complicated, just as it is with many other factors that weather the translation between individual and conjoint therapy contexts. Each person's alliance, as well as the couple's or family's alliance with the therapist *and* within the couple or family unit, must be considered—conceptually, methodologically, and clinically. In developing the SOFTA to advance knowledge and effective practice, we wanted to capture not only each client's involvement in therapy and feelings about the therapist but also two unique, interrelated features: the degree to which clients feel safe working in therapy with other family members, and the degree to which family members agree among themselves on the need, purpose, goals, and value of conjoint treatment.

In chapter 2 we describe the development and conceptual foundation of the SOFTA, introduce the SOFTA–o and SOFTA–s, and lay the groundwork for the subsequent, clinically focused chapters. Chapter 3 provides details on using the SOFTA–o and summarizes the research to date on the measures.

2

INTRODUCING THE SYSTEM FOR OBSERVING FAMILY THERAPY ALLIANCES

The System for Observing Family Therapy Alliances (SOFTA) is a set of tools, both observational (SOFTA–o; Escudero, Friedlander, & Deihl, 2004; Friedlander, Escudero, & Heatherington, 2001) and self-report (SOFTA–s; Friedlander & Escudero, 2002), to evaluate the strength of the therapeutic alliance in the context of conjoint couple and family therapy. These measures were developed inductively and refined empirically. We thus arrived at a multidimensional conceptual model reflecting the complexity and unique features of couple and family therapy. Elaborating the SOFTA model and conducting research with its measurement tools, we trained our lenses on clinical work with couples and families in a fresh way, prompting the writing of this book, which integrates theory, science, and practice related to the alliance in conjoint treatments.

As discussed in chapter 1, the therapeutic alliance has received far less attention in the couple and family therapy field than it has in the theory, research, and practice of individual psychotherapy, even though many approaches view strong relationships between therapists and clients as essential to their success and couple and family therapy has many elements that challenge the development of these relationships. The glaring lack of attention to this crucial construct among couple and family therapy theorists is reflected in a paucity of instruments to evaluate the strength of the alliance in conjoint treatment. Two major exceptions are self-report measures developed by Pinsof (1999; Pinsof & Catherall, 1986) and Symonds (1998; Symonds & Horvath, 2004). In both instruments, clients report on their own alliance with the therapist as well as their perceptions of the therapist's alliance with their spouse or other family members participating in the treatment. However, self-reported perceptions, such as "I trust the therapist," offer little information about clients' behavioral manifestations of trust. Without knowledge of the kinds of verbal and nonverbal behaviors that reflect clients' feelings of trust, therapists are left to rely on intuition and guesswork—a precarious position to be in when the risks are great or families drop out of treatment.

We began by creating an observational tool, SOFTA–o, for researching the process of couple and family therapy and guiding the work of clinicians, trainers, and supervisors. Subsequently, we developed the self-report version, SOFTA–s, with versions for both clients and therapists. In contrast to Pinsof's (1999; Pinsof & Catherall, 1986) and Symonds and Horvath's (2004) questionnaires, which are extrapolations to couple and family therapy of individual therapy measures derived from Bordin's (1979, 1994) pantheoretical conceptualization of the alliance, the SOFTA–s questionnaires have two scales that reflect Bordin's model (Engagement in the Therapeutic Process and Emotional Connection to the Therapist) and two that reflect elements unique to couple and family treatment (Safety Within the Therapeutic System and Shared Sense of Purpose Within the Family).

CHARACTERISTICS OF THE SOFTA

Our project to develop and apply the SOFTA to clinical work with couples and families evolved from a collaboration between United States (Friedlander and Heatherington) and Spanish (Escudero) family therapy researchers, nurtured by a Spain–U.S. exchange program in family interventions and counseling psychology for graduate students (described in Friedlander, Escudero, & Guzmán, 2002). As a product of this collaboration, the SOFTA and its instruments were created simultaneously in English and Spanish (called *Sistema de Observación de la Alianza Terapéutica en Intervención Familiar* [SOATIF]; Escudero & Friedlander, 2003). In our thinking and research with the SOFTA/SOATIF, assuring the appropriateness of the constructs in both Spain and North America was a prime consideration.[1]

---

[1]In this book, our comments about the SOFTA model and instruments apply equally to the Spanish SOATIF. In Appendixes A and B, the measures are presented in both languages. The software version of the observational measure, e-SOFTA (available at http://www.softa-soatif.net), is also available in both languages.

The SOFTA–o was originally written in English and translated into Spanish, whereas the opposite process was undertaken for the SOFTA–s. In each step of the development process, the constructs, items, operational definitions, and training manual were translated and back-translated to ensure accuracy. Validation studies conducted in both North America and Spain were highly congruent.

Transtheoretical

The SOFTA, both as a set of tools for evaluating the alliance in couple and family therapy and as a conceptual model, was developed inductively. We began by stipulating that the SOFTA not be limited to a single theoretical approach (e.g., systemic, psychoanalytic, experiential, cognitive) nor constrained by the tenets of any one school of couple and family therapy (e.g., structural, strategic, multigenerational, solution-focused). Thus, we selected SOFTA–o behaviors that would be meaningful across therapies and therapists. Client items, for example, reflect processes from emotion-focused (e.g., "Client shows vulnerability"), structural (e.g., "Client complies with therapist's request for an enactment"), behavioral (e.g., "Client agrees to do homework assignments"), solution-focused (e.g., "Client expresses optimism or indicates that a positive change has taken place"), and constructivist (e.g., "Family members ask each other for their perspective") couple and family therapy approaches.

We recognize that the nature of our training, experience, and professional development; our cultural and work contexts; and the kinds of videotaped therapies used to develop the SOFTA inevitably influenced its design. Hence, some therapists may consider, from the perspective of their particular work and theoretical approach, that important aspects of the therapeutic alliance are not sufficiently represented in the model and its measures. This caveat notwithstanding, when we describe the SOFTA as *transtheoretical*, we do so to emphasize our view of the alliance as a common, nonspecific factor in family therapy (Asay & Lambert, 1999; Sexton, Ridley, & Kleiner, 2004). The SOFTA thus reflects previous literature on the alliance in couple and family therapy (e.g., Pinsof, 1994, 1995; Rait, 1998) and within the broad field of psychotherapy (e.g., Horvath, 1994; Safran & Muran, 2000), especially Bordin's (1979, 1994) conceptualization of the alliance and the contributions of Pinsof (1999; Pinsof & Catherall, 1986) and Symonds and Horvath (2004) to its analysis and measurement within the specific context of couple and family therapy.

As presented in the following sections, the operational definitions of the four dimensions that constitute the SOFTA, as well as their behavioral descriptors, reflect a thorough review of the literature on couple and family therapy—not limited by theoretical allegiances—and the diverse clinical and scholarly experiences of all those who collaborated in the SOFTA's creation and validation.

Observable

We assume that social behaviors, in general, are manifestations of underlying thoughts and feelings about interpersonal relations. In specific terms, the client behaviors we identified, clustered, and defined in the SOFTA–o manifest clients' underlying thoughts and feelings about the alliance. Thus, SOFTA–o indicators, such as "Client describes or discusses a plan for improving the situation," "Family members validate each other's point of view," "Client expresses trust in the therapist," and "Client reveals a secret or something other family members didn't know" are behaviors that reflect clients' feelings and thoughts about the alliance, such as "We're working together with the therapist," "We're all in this together," "The therapist is here for us," and "In here, our conflict can be handled without harm." Likewise, the SOFTA–o therapist behaviors are manifestations of therapists' cognitive and emotional contributions to engagement, connection, safety, and fostering a shared sense of purpose within the family about the therapy.

In creating the measures, we began with client behavior, for two reasons. First, research on individual therapy has consistently shown that the client's perception of the alliance is the strongest predictor of therapeutic success (e.g., Horvath, 1994; Horvath & Symonds, 1991). Second, we found extraordinarily little in the theoretical and clinical literature about client behavior, thoughts, or feelings in couple and family therapy (cf. Friedlander, Wildman, et al., 1994).

Building the SOFTA from the ground up, we wanted to ensure that the behaviors we included were indeed meaningful reflections of clients' thoughts and feelings about their participation in treatment with other family members. Thus, the SOFTA–o descriptors were retained from a validation test of a large pool of items obtained from (a) our clinical experiences and those of colleagues who collaborated in the initial phase of the measure's development; (b) descriptions of therapeutic relationships and behavior in the couple and family therapy clinical, theoretical, and empirical literature; and (c) an intensive analysis of videotaped family therapy sessions. Although the items do not constitute the universe of alliance-related behaviors, they are nonetheless representative, meaningful, and common to most couple and family therapy approaches.

A similar process was used to develop the behavioral indicators of therapist contributions to each of the four SOFTA dimensions. Like the client behaviors, the therapist behaviors include both positive and negative contributions to the alliance, and many have parallels in the client SOFTA–o. For example, the item "Client encourages another family member to 'open up' or tell the truth" is paralleled by the item "Therapist helps clients to talk truthfully and nondefensively with each other."

Throughout the development process, we required that all client and therapist descriptors be observable behaviors, verbal as well as nonverbal (although the latter are far fewer). Thus, for example, rather than "Family members are interested in the points of view of other family members," the SOFTA–o item is behavioral: "Family members ask each other for their perspective." Moreover, each behavioral description has an operational definition to focus the evaluator on observable behavior and thereby minimize subjective inferences. For example, in the training manual (http://www.softa-soatif.net) the negative descriptor, "Client expresses feeling 'stuck,' questions the value of the therapy, or states that therapy is not or has not been helpful" is operationally defined as follows:

> This negative item is checked when the client explicitly mentions dissatisfaction with the way the therapy is going, the need for it, or the direction it is taking. This expression of negative attitude or emotion may or may not be in response to the therapist's question or to the question of some other family member. This item is *not* checked if the client's response is vague, such as "I don't know," or "Okay, I guess," even if a negative attitude is suspected. Such vague expressions might be indicators of another negative item, i.e., showing indifference. That is, for this item to be checked the expression of dissatisfaction must be clear and overt. (Friedlander, Escudero, Heatherington, Deihl, et al., 2004, p. 14)

How do behaviors like this one add up to a weak alliance? Clearly, it is not merely a matter of simply counting behaviors, when some are more influential than others. The item discussed previously is a stronger indicator of a poor alliance than the item "Client avoids eye contact with the therapist," for example. Thus, in making inferences about the strength of the alliance, the researcher, therapist, or supervisor needs to weigh the frequency, intensity, and meaningfulness in context of all the behaviors exhibited in a given therapy session. Essentially, the SOFTA–o judgment process mirrors the clinician's thought process—making inferences about clients' thoughts and feelings from their observable behavior.

As described in detail in chapter 3, the SOFTA–o training manual (http://www.softa-soatif.net) provides guidelines for making inferences about the strength of the four underlying dimensions (Engagement in the Therapeutic Process, Emotional Connection With the Therapist, Safety Within the Therapeutic System, and Shared Sense of Purpose Within the Family) from observations of client and therapist behaviors. On the basis of the kind, frequency, and intensity of the observed items in a given session, each dimension is then scored on a 7-point scale, ranging from –3 (*extremely problematic*) to +3 (*extremely strong*). To aid this process, the software version of the measures, e-SOFTA, allows the evaluator to record qualitative comments while looking for alliance-related behaviors. Dimensional scores can be used to profile contributions to the alliance for comparative purposes, as illustrated in chapter 8.

The central score on the dimension scales (0 = *unremarkable/neutral*) indicates either (a) that there are no behaviors in the session that suggest exceptionally strong or weak engagement, connection, safety, or shared purpose or (b) that the frequency and nature of both positive and negative client behavior cancel each other out, so to speak, resulting in a neutral rating. For example, a 0 on the Engagement scale means that the client's in-session behavior indicated neither particularly good engagement nor significant difficulty or reluctance to engage in the procedures or tasks of the therapy. The highest possible score (+3) indicates an optimal level of alliance contribution in a given dimension, whereas the lowest possible score (–3) indicates extreme stress in the alliance on that dimension. For a client to receive a –3 on Emotional Connection With the Therapist, for example, he or she must have exhibited many or highly intense negative behaviors, such as "hostile or sarcastic interactions with the therapist." Chapter 3 describes in detail the observational and rating procedures of SOFTA–o, as well as suggestions for training judges to use the instrument in process research.

The client and therapist self-report measures (SOFTA–s; Appendix B) were directly derived from the observational instrument. Our reasoning was that if, in fact, the behavioral manifestations of the alliance reflect clients' and therapists' covert experiences, there should be significant associations between observable behaviors like "responds defensively to another family member" and self-reported perceptions ("At times I feel on the defensive in therapy"). Preliminary work with the SOFTA–s suggests that the scales are internally consistent (i.e., reliable), predictive of session evaluations, and significantly associated with the respective SOFTA–o scales behaviors by the midpoint of brief family treatments (Friedlander, Escudero, Haar, & Higham, 2005; Friedlander, Talka, et al., 2003).

Interpersonal

The observational descriptors in the SOFTA–o refer to interactive behaviors among family members and between each client and the therapist. Therapy sessions are by definition an interpersonal context of high communicative value. The importance of the communicative context in the therapist–client relationship is reflected in the expression "You cannot not relate" (Speed, 1996, p. 103), a paraphrase of Watzlawick, Beavin, and Jackson's (1967) classic axiom, "You cannot not communicate" (p. 49). By considering the therapeutic relationship as a vehicle for conveying the content of the therapy, and by recognizing that the "real" relationship with the therapist (Greenson, 1967) is in itself therapeutic, we acknowledge that all behaviors produced by session participants have implications for the strength of the alliance. Hence the therapist item, "Therapist praises client motivation for engagement or change," for example, may be directed to one family member, but because the comment is heard by everyone present, it may affect the therapeutic alliance with other family members.

Because the SOFTA–o was designed to measure the strength of the alliance in conjoint couple or family treatments, in its creation we used videotaped therapy sessions with multiple family members. However, with the exception of Shared Sense of Purpose Within the Family, which explicitly evaluates the alliance among family members, the SOFTA is also applicable to individual and group therapies. However, the SOFTA was inspired by the need for instruments that reflect both the complexity and the uniqueness of couple and family therapies.

Multidimensional

Just as the Working Alliance Inventory (Horvath & Greenberg, 1986, 1989) is a multidimensional measure of a higher order construct (i.e., the alliance), so too is the SOFTA. The SOFTA is multidimensional in two ways: (a) Both the client system and the therapist system (Pinsof, 1994) are represented and (b) the descriptors reflect four underlying dimensions of the alliance construct. Each dimension consists of items, both positive and negative, that exemplify favorable and unfavorable contributions to the alliance. In Table 2.1, we present the operational definitions of the four dimensions and examples of positive and negative items, and in Table 2.2, we illustrate the correspondence of items across the measures (i.e., SOFTA–o and SOFTA–s). In the actual instruments (Appendixes A and B), all items composing each dimension are listed.

In our conceptualization of the alliance, the four SOFTA dimensions are meaningful ways to understand the uniqueness of conjoint work. Safety Within the Therapeutic System and Shared Sense of Purpose Within the Family reflect processes unique to therapy formats with multiple clients, whereas Engagement in the Therapeutic Process and Emotional Connection With the Therapist are common features in all forms of treatment, that is, collaboration on therapy goals and tasks and a bond with the therapist (Bordin, 1979, 1994). Moreover, the dimensions reflect client–therapist relations (Engagement, Emotional Connection) and within-family relations (Safety, Shared Purpose), as well as cognitive–behavioral (Engagement, Shared Purpose) and affective (Emotional Connection, Safety) areas of functioning.

Furthermore, we view the four SOFTA dimensions as dynamic and fluid processes. The importance of any one of these dimensions can wax and wane over the course of a session as over the course of treatment. It is reasonable to assume, for example, that a client's sense of safety is a product of his or her emotional connection with the therapist. At the same time, feeling safe helps the client to be engaged in the therapeutic process, and engagement strength-

TABLE 2.1
Dimensions and Illustrative Behaviors in the SOFTA–o (Client)

Dimension	Definition	Examples of behavioral descriptors
Engagement in the Therapeutic Process	The client views treatment as meaningful; has a sense of being involved in therapy and working together with the therapist; that therapeutic goals and tasks in therapy can be discussed and negotiated with the therapist; that taking the process seriously is important, that change is possible.	Positive: Client describes or discusses a plan for improving the situation. Negative: Client shows indifference about the tasks or process of therapy (e.g., paying lip service, "I don't know," tuning out).
Emotional Connection to the Therapist	The client views the therapist as an important person in his or her life, almost like a family member; has a sense that the relationship is based on affiliation, trust, caring, and concern; that the therapist genuinely cares and "is there" for the client; that he or she is on the same wavelength with the therapist (e.g., similar life perspectives, values); that the therapist's wisdom and expertise are valuable.	Positive: Client expresses interest in the therapist's personal life. Negative: Client has hostile or sarcastic interactions with the therapist.
Safety Within the Therapeutic System	The client views therapy as a place to take risks, be open, vulnerable, flexible; has a sense of comfort and an expectation that new experiences and learning will take place; that good can come from being in therapy; that conflict within the family can be handled without harm; that one need not be defensive.	Positive: Client reveals a secret or something that other family members didn't know. Negative: Client refuses or is reluctant to respond when directly addressed by another family member.
Shared Sense of Purpose Within the Family	Family members see themselves as working collaboratively in therapy to improve family relations and achieve common family goals; have a sense of solidarity in relation to the therapy ("we're in this together"); value their time with each other in therapy; essentially, a felt unity within the family in relation to therapy.	Positive: Family members validate each other's point of view. Negative: Family members blame each other.

Note. SOFTA–o = System for Observing Family Therapy Alliances—observational.

ens rapport with the therapist. These three dimensions are also likely to be strong when the entire family agrees on the reasons for being in treatment and has similar goals and expectations. Thus, although the four dimensions are interrelated (i.e., not mutually exclusive), each dimension offers specific

TABLE 2.2
Correspondence Among Items on the SOFTA–o and SOFTA–s

Dimension	SOFTA–o	SOFTA–s
Engagement in the Therapeutic Process	Client: Client indicates agreement with the therapist's goals. Therapist: Therapist encourages client(s) to articulate goals for therapy.	Client: The therapist and I work as a team. Therapist: The family and I are working as a team.
Emotional Connection With the Therapist	Client: Client expresses interest in the therapist's personal life. Therapist: Therapist expresses interest in the client(s) apart from the therapeutic discussion at hand.	Client: The therapist has become an important person in my life. Therapist: I have become an important person in this family's life.
Safety Within the Therapeutic System	Client: Client encourages another family member to open up or speak honestly. Therapist: Therapist helps client(s) talk truthfully and nondefensively with each other.	Client: The therapy sessions help me open up (share my feelings, try new things, etc.). Therapist: The therapy sessions are helping family members to open up (share feelings, try new things, etc.).
Shared Sense of Purpose Within the Family	Client: Family members argue with each other about the goals, value, or need for therapy. Therapist: Therapist does not intervene when family members argue with each other about the goals, value, or need for therapy.	Client: Some members of my family don't agree with others about the goals of therapy. Therapist: Some members of the family don't agree with others about the goals of therapy.

Note. Each dimension has both positive and negative items, although in the above examples only those in Shared Sense of Purpose Within the Family are negative. SOFTA–o and SOFTA–s are the observational and self-report versions of the System for Observing Family Therapy Alliances, respectively.

and nonredundant information about the strength of the therapeutic alliance for a given client or family (see Figure 2.1). In fact, research on the SOFTA–o and SOFTA–s has revealed moderate but significant correlations between the scale dimensions (Friedlander, Escudero, Haar, & Higham, 2005; Friedlander, Escudero, Horvath, et al., in press).

In therapy sessions, there is an interaction between what Pinsof (1995) called the *direct system of the therapist* and the *direct system of the client*, that is, the actual participants in the therapy (p. 5). There are two sources of direct influence on the observed, in-session behaviors: relationships between the therapist or therapists and clients who are present, and relationships among

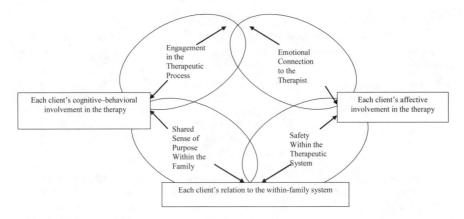

Figure 2.1. Interrelations of SOFTA dimensions. SOFTA = System for Observing Family Therapy Alliances.

the family members themselves. Interactions in both relationships influence interactions between them. Thus, for example, a highly conflicted family may generate mistrust and defensiveness among members; if there are secrets or covert threats, these affect the relationship that each member of the family establishes with the therapist. However, when a therapist has agreeable interactions with one spouse but unpleasant ones with the other, this imbalance will undoubtedly have a negative influence on the couple's relationship (see chap. 9 on split alliances).

There is, however, an important influence on the therapy from the *indirect systems* of both the therapist (e.g., supervisors, consultants, reflecting team members) and the family (influential family members or other individuals who are not taking part in the therapy). As Pinsof (1994) explained, there is a mutual and recursive influence among these four subsystems (the two direct and the two indirect systems). Thus, when we speak of the therapy alliance in couple and family therapy, we refer to the product of all between-systems relationships (i.e., interactions of therapist and client systems) and all within-system relationships (within the family system and within the professional system). Influences from the indirect therapist system (professional helpers at a distance, such as probation officers, clergy, guidance counselors, or caseworkers) can have a profound effect on the family's collaboration with and trust in the therapist. (This subject is discussed at length in chap. 14.)

Among the four SOFTA dimensions, two (Engagement and Emotional Connection) have a pronounced between-systems orientation, both by definition and in the items that compose the dimension: One dimension (Shared Purpose) refers entirely to within-systems relationships, and the remaining dimension (Safety) represents the individual client's relation to the entire (direct) therapeutic system (i.e., therapist and other family members). Nevertheless, as mentioned earlier, behaviors located within each dimension can have reverberating effects on the entire therapeutic system. For example, when a client "describes or discusses a plan for improving the situation" (Engagement), this behavior influences within-family relations because the client's "plan to improve the situation" is likely to involve (or at least affect) other family members. Similarly, behaviors in the Safety dimension, such as "Client reveals a secret or something that other family members didn't know," can have a significant effect on the indirect family system if the revelation involves some influential person who is not participating in the therapy.

DEVELOPMENT OF THE SOFTA INSTRUMENTS

We began with the client version of the SOFTA–o because research has repeatedly shown that the client's perspective on the alliance is most closely associated with therapeutic outcomes (Horvath & Symonds, 1991). Our decision to begin by creating observational measures, rather than self-reports, was based on several factors. First, a primary consideration was to provide information about clients' alliance-related behavior that would inform practice. Second, little has been written about *any* client behaviors that are important in couple and family therapy processes (Friedlander, Wildman, et al., 1994). Finally, although self-reports are useful in research, they are burdensome for clients and therapists in practice, especially because repeated administrations are necessary to observe fluctuations over time (referred to by Pinsof, 1994, as "tears and repairs in the alliance"; p. 186), and young children cannot reliably complete questionnaires. We reasoned that information about which behaviors signal clients' favorable and unfavorable perceptions of the alliance would help therapists redirect their efforts in the face of a strained, faltering, or split alliance.

SOFTA–o

Our construction of the client SOFTA–o began with a search of the theoretical, clinical, and empirical literature for information about the therapeutic relationship in couple and family therapy. This process, complemented by our own extensive clinical experience, resulted in a set of behavioral descriptors of both positive and negative therapeutic alliances. These descriptors were used to create an initial pool of items illustrating different aspects and levels of client involvement and collaboration in conjoint family therapy. As mentioned previously, guiding the item construction was the requirement that each item be an observable behavior.

To add to and modify the initial item pool, the research team (four individuals) observed 12 videotaped family sessions in which clients had provided their self-reported perceptions on the alliance using Pinsof and Catherall's (1986) integrative alliance scales. Knowing each family member's view on the alliance, the team searched for interpersonal behaviors that might indicate their positive or negative feelings and cognitions about what was taking place in the session. Item editing was done through repeated comparisons and negotiations of each team member's ratings of the 12 videotaped family sessions. The analysis of discrepancies allowed us to clarify items and discard those that were difficult to rate.

To create the four SOFTA dimensions (Table 2.1), the research team began by inductively clustering similar items and naming the resulting clusters. Next, each member of the team independently wrote definitions of the constructs reflected by each cluster. Comparing and integrating the definitions, we decided which items were logically related to each dimension. As described earlier, the rating procedure involves using the presence or absence of specific SOFTA behaviors to rate the strength or weakness of family members' contributions to the alliance on the four dimensions. A test of this rating procedure with six different videotapes showed that the process was feasible and resulted in good interrater agreement.

To assess the face validity of the instrument, we used a sorting task. The 44 initial items were randomly ordered, and 24 family therapy process researchers in the United States, Canada, and Spain (17 English-speaking and 7 Spanish-speaking) were asked to read the 4 dimension definitions and indicate which underlying construct was best reflected in each item. This method allowed us to test whether experts saw the item "Family members ask each other for their perspective," for example, as we did, reflecting a shared sense of purpose within the family.

The decision rule was as follows: If at least three fourths (75%) of our experts selected the same dimension for a given item, the item was retained; if not, it was eliminated or moved to a different cluster. The instructions for the sorting task allowed the experts to select more than one dimension per item but to indicate the most closely associated dimension. The experts were also asked to comment on the items and, to improve on the measure's content validity, to suggest additional items that, in their opinion, were important behavioral indicators of the four underlying alliance dimensions. The Spanish experts were additionally invited to comment on the appropriateness of the items and dimensions for Spanish-speaking clients.

Results indicated a high consistency across the two samples of experts, and the majority of items were viewed as behavioral exemplars of the four dimensions as originally clustered, κs = .81 (English) and .71 (Spanish; Friedlander, Escudero, Horvath, et al., in press). Indeed, most items were viewed similarly by 75% or more of the judges in both samples. Using the decision rule, we moved several items from one dimension to another or modified their wording. Using our experience with a new data set, we added a few new items to the Safety and the Shared Sense of Purpose dimensions. In addition, each behavioral item was operationally defined for purposes of training and enhancing reliability (as illustrated in the "Observational" subsection previously discussed).

A similar process was followed to develop the therapist version of the SOFTA–o (Escudero, Friedlander, & Deihl, 2005). That is, from the literature, our clinical experience, and the many sessions we had observed when developing and testing the client measure, we constructed items and asked family therapy researchers to sort them into the four SOFTA dimensions. Roughly half of the therapist items were written to parallel the client items (Table 2.2 and indicted by an asterisk in Appendix A), for example, "Therapist encourages client(s) to articulate their goals for therapy" and "Client agrees with the therapist's goals."

Notably, the SOFTA–o has few negative therapist items, and indeed in our investigations we found few instances of negative therapist behavior, even among relatively inexperienced therapists. This is not to say that therapists invariably behave in ways that enhance the alliance. Rather, therapists' negative contributions to the alliance tend to be subtle (such as failures to intervene when a client shuts down emotionally) rather than observably harmful acts. The failure to do something cannot reliably be judged, however. We recognize that research with the SOFTA–o is influenced by this methodological limitation because therapists do make mistakes, and these mistakes are important to identify. Many of the clinical illustrations throughout this book draw attention to therapists' missed opportunities, errors, and countertransferential reactions to clients.

SOFTA–s

After creating the observational instruments, we developed client and therapist self-report measures, SOFTA–s (Appendix B). Our purpose was twofold: to create brief questionnaires that could feasibly be used in field research on the alliance and to investigate the degree to which clients' and therapists' reported thoughts and feelings about Engagement, Emotional Connection, Safety, and Shared Sense of Purpose are associated with their observed behavior.

Using the conceptual definitions of the SOFTA dimensions (Table 2.1), we constructed four items per dimension. Thus, each version (client and therapist) of the SOFTA–s has 16 positive and negative items to be rated on a 5-point Likert scale (1 = *not at all*, 5 = *very much*). Client examples include "The therapist and I work together as a team" (positive Engagement) and "All my family members who come for therapy want the best for our family and to resolve our problems" (positive Shared Purpose); therapist examples include "I have become an important person in this family's life" (positive Emotional Connection) and "There are some topics that the family members are afraid to discuss in therapy" (negative Safety). Both instruments provide a total score (reflecting the alliance in general) ranging from 16 to 80 and 4 subscale scores (on Engagement, Emotional Connection, Safety, and Shared Purpose) ranging from 4 to 20.

CLINICAL APPLICATIONS OF THE MODEL

Although the SOFTA was created for use in research on the process of conjoint couple and family therapy, we have found it to be invaluable in the training and supervision of novice family therapists. Using the behavioral descriptors within each dimension, a therapist or supervisor can analyze the strength of the therapeutic alliance in one session or across sessions. The analysis can be focused on one or more alliance dimensions, on one member of the family, or on the family as a group. With the e-SOFTA (described in chap. 3), the observer can create a file (essentially a diary of the session) with qualitative notes, automatically arranged in chronological order by the program to accompany each behavioral descriptor as it is detected and marked. In this way, the SOFTA–o can be a useful aid in training, supervision, and self-supervision.

Considering SOFTA as an instrument for clinical research and a tool for practice, one can ask how each of the four dimensions contributes to the creation of favorable therapeutic alliances. In other words, questions relating to the model are interesting from both scientific and clinical points of view. For example, is strength in all four dimensions necessary for the creation of a solid, overall alliance with couples and families? Alternately, is there a specific sequence or pattern in the developing alliance that optimally structures the contribution of each dimension? That is, is one dimension indispensable or of higher priority than the others early in treatment?

Aside from these theoretical questions, the SOFTA can help practitioners conceptualize their ongoing work with clients. Because the SOFTA emphasizes the dynamic aspects of the therapeutic process (see chap. 8), it is reasonable to expect that, for any one family, the way in which different SOFTA dimensions contribute to therapeutic progress depends on diverse factors, among which are the following:

- *Characteristics of the family system:* Different dimensions of the alliance may be more salient for couples than for families (Heatherington & Friedlander, 1990b) and for nuclear versus divorced, remarried, single parent, or three-generation families (see chap. 10). The importance of the various SOFTA dimensions will also differ if the clients are self-referred or mandated to treatment (see chap. 11). In terms of family organization, facilitating a shared sense of purpose, for example, takes on a different meaning with enmeshed and highly cohesive families versus highly disengaged or chaotic families.
- *Therapeutic approach:* Different orientations to family therapy vary in the ways they require the participation of family members. Because the tasks, goals, and procedures in some therapies are more behaviorally oriented than others, it is reasonable to

expect that Emotional Connection With the Therapist plays a different role in brief solution-focused therapy than in emotion-focused or insight-oriented couple therapy, for example. Similarly, other SOFTA dimensions may vary in intensity depending on the therapist's approach or theoretical orientation.

- *Nature of the presenting problem:* The problem or complaint in the client system influences which dimension is of highest priority for the development and maintenance of the alliance. For a high-conflict family that has endured multiple episodes of violence or psychological abuse, safety within the therapeutic system is likely to be indispensable. For a family coping with a parent's chronic or terminal illness, however, safety is unlikely to have the same significance.

- *Gender and other therapist characteristics:* On the basis of the general literature on therapeutic relationships (Asay & Lambert, 1999; Bachelor & Horvath, 1999) and specific literature on the influence of gender in these relationships (Gehart & Lyle, 2001), gender and other personal characteristics of the therapist are likely to influence the relative importance of various SOFTA dimensions for a given couple or family (see chap. 10). The therapist's gender is likely to be a factor in safety, for example, when couples discuss sexual or other intimate matters. When there is a racial or religious difference between clients and therapist, emotional connection with the therapist may take precedence.

Optimally, guidelines for creating favorable alliances should result from empirical research as well as theory and clinical experience. To advance this goal, we propose a heuristic model for understanding the contribution of the SOFTA dimensions to four generic aspects of the therapy process (see Exhibit 2.1). In the model, these four tasks are viewed as fundamental to all conjoint family therapy (arguably, to all therapy):

1. Establish appropriate conditions for a therapeutic relationship, including defining the context and conditions for treatment, as well as other aspects that affect the initial relationship between therapist and clients.
2. Elaborate therapeutic goals that are acceptable to the couple or family, including the needs and expectations of each client (or subsystem) in relation to the presenting problem or problems.
3. Use techniques congruent with a theoretical model to achieve the goals negotiated with the family.
4. Ensure sufficient change so that the client system can become "emancipated," that is, to function well without therapeutic help.

	Conjoint couple and family therapy process tasks			
	Establish favorable conditions for therapeutic relationships	Negotiate goals with the couple or family system	Complete therapeutic tasks and achieve change	Generalize change (termination)
SOFTA dimensions expected to play a central role	Emotional connection with the therapist and Safety within the therapeutic system	Shared sense of purpose within the family and Engagement in the therapeutic process	Engagement in the therapeutic process	Shared sense of purpose within the family and Safety within the family
Expected results (in terms of the alliance)	Creation of trust and openness	Collaboration with the therapist and within the family	Active participation in therapy procedures and tasks, recognition of change	Assurance that changes can be maintained and new problems solved without therapy
Systemic focus	Between-systems (therapist–client) and within-systems	Between-systems (therapist–client) and within-systems	Between-systems (therapist–client) and within-systems	Within-systems
Examples of therapist contributions	Contains, controls, or manages overt hostility between clients Expresses interest in the client(s) apart from the therapeutic discussion at hand	Encourages client(s) to articulate their goals for the therapy Emphasizes communalities among clients' perspectives on the problem or solution	Praises client motivation for engagement or change Expresses optimism or notes that a positive change has taken place or can take place	Draws attention to family's shared values, experiences, needs, or feelings Praises clients for respecting each other's point of view

Note. SOFTA = System for Observing Family Therapy Alliances.

Depending on one's theoretical perspective, other tasks could be included in this general scheme, but we propose that successful couple and family therapy must address these four essential processes, irrespective of theoretical orientation or the importance placed on any one of these. Furthermore, the tasks are not approached rigidly or in chronological order as sequenced "phases" of the process. With the exception of the fourth, termination, the tasks can occur and reoccur throughout the process. After a rupture in the alliance, for example, the first task (establishing therapeutic conditions) should be revisited.

In this schematic, Safety Within the Therapeutic System is considered a "precondition," that is, necessary for establishing an adequate therapeutic relationship. In this sense, safety plays a central role at the start of treatment (see chap. 6). Nonetheless, Safety (as any of the other SOFTA dimensions) can be placed at risk at any time, depending on events within and outside the therapy. When this happens, re-establishing safety takes precedence over any other therapeutic goal. Assuring safety within the family is particularly vital in deciding when and how to terminate treatment.

The dimension Shared Sense of Purpose Within the Family (chap. 7) is basic for keeping the format of treatment conjoint and the focus systemic. In our view, this dimension is so vital that it may well be a mediator of treatment outcome (Heatherington, Friedlander, & Greenberg, 2005). When this dimension has negative values (i.e., when the goals, values, or needs for therapy are not shared), to continue treatment at all, individual sessions may need to be held with different family members, or parallel therapies may need to be established for various family subsystems (cf. M. Beck et al., in press). As with Safety, assuring a shared sense of purpose about maintaining the attained goals is an integral part of the termination process.

The dimension Emotional Connection With the Therapist (chap. 5) is central to establishing solid therapeutic relationships and maintaining them throughout treatment, especially when family conflicts arise or difficulties are experienced in the process of making changes. In some theoretical models, the therapeutic relationship is itself the "healing" element. In other models, the emotional bond between client and therapist is said to be an important common or nonspecific factor that "mediates" or "facilitates" the specific, technical elements in the therapy.

Finally, the dimension Engagement in the Therapeutic Process (chap. 4), regardless of theoretical model and techniques (e.g., paradoxical prescriptions, enactment, circular questioning, hypnosis), requires that clients accept and actively collaborate in treatment. To the degree that the changes produced in the therapy result from specific techniques and procedures, the family must experience these procedures as their own, not as something imposed on them (chap. 11). Indeed, in a comprehensive review of psychotherapy outcome research, Wampold (2001) concluded that it is not the specific method of treatment per se that produces a successful outcome but rather the therapist's ability to make the theorized goals and tasks meaningful to the client so that he or she will become actively involved in the process.

CONCLUSION

After observing a family session with a novice therapist, the supervisor comments, "Your relationship with the teenage girl in this family is a strong one—she likes and admires you—but you'll need to work hard to avoid alienating her mother, who's feeling upstaged, I think." This comment underscores the complex, systemic nature of therapeutic relationships in couple and family therapy. Without meaning to do so, the therapist has brought about a "split" alliance—the mother feels alienated in a therapy she voluntarily sought out to help her daughter.

Clearly, the therapist must rebalance the alliance before the mother discontinues treatment. How does one do so? Without knowledge of (a) what, specifically, the supervisor observed in the stream of behavior that suggested a split alliance and (b) what, specifically, can be done to repair this particular split alliance, the therapist has little to go on.

In creating the SOFTA, we wanted to provide the kind of information that would be most useful in clinical situations like this one. After pointing out the alliance problems in a general way, it would be helpful for the supervisor to say the following:

> In watching your session, I noticed the girl leaning forward every time she answered one of your questions, and she joked around with you a bit at the beginning [*positive Emotional Connection*], but she avoided all contact with her mother [*negative Safety*]. At one point in the session, the mother whispered, "This is hopeless," [*negative Engagement*] but you may not have heard her. And by not responding to this comment, you may unwittingly have damaged her desire to work together with you.

From here, supervisor and supervisee could go on to discuss various ways to engage the mother in treatment while making the process safer for the daughter. In talking over the goals for treatment, the supervisee may realize that mother and daughter have very different perspectives on the therapy (i.e., a weak Shared Sense of Purpose) and that the failure to address this gap has contributed to the split alliance.

The therapist now has a plan. In the next session she will begin by encouraging mother and daughter to ask each other for their perspective on the problems between them. As another way to enhance their shared sense of purpose, the therapist may find a way to point out similarities between mother and daughter and their common values (e.g., their feminist views). Toward the middle of the session, the therapist may engage the mother in planning a fun mother–daughter "homework assignment." Somewhere along the way, the therapist may express confidence in the daughter's ability to share more of her private self with her mother.

This brief illustration captures the essence of SOFTA—identifying behavioral manifestations of clients' perceptions of the alliance and therapists' contributions to it. As different aspects of this central therapy construct, the four dimensions carry practical, meaningful information about important processes in couple and family treatment. To enhance the engagement of one family member, the therapist can improve the safety of another. To nurture a shared sense of purpose about treatment, the therapist can create individual bonds with each family member and encourage everyone to participate and get involved.

In the next chapter, we summarize the psychometric properties of the SOFTA–o and offer instructions on using the instrument in research and practice. The remaining sections of this book offer in-depth discussions and clinical illustrations of the SOFTA in practice.

3

OBSERVING THE ALLIANCE

The ancient Greek philosopher Heraclitus is credited with the saying, *You can't step into the same river twice*. Like a stream of water, the psychotherapy "stream" is ever changing. A husband's complaint about his wife's disinterest in sex may have a different impact in Session 15, when the therapeutic alliance is robust, than it would have had in Session 1, when the alliance was new. Despite context, however, many behaviors predictably reflect strong or weak therapeutic alliances. Shouting or cursing at other family members (if it occurs) is likely to reflect a weak shared sense of purpose. Expressing painful feelings is likely to reflect some measure of safety whenever the feelings surface, whether they are elicited by the therapist or by another family member, and whether they have to do with loneliness, addiction, abuse, or sexual inadequacy.

In other words, many behaviors are common in couple and family therapy; they occur frequently and reflect the strength of the alliance, either contributing to it or detracting from it, regardless of the therapeutic approach, setting, or treatment context. As described in chapters 1 and 2, the System for Observing Family Therapeutic Alliances (SOFTA) directs our attention to specific behaviors that reflect clients' and therapists' contributions to four dimensions of the therapeutic alliance in couple and family therapy: Engagement in the Therapeutic Process, Emotional Connection With the Therapist, Safety Within the Therapeutic System, and Shared Sense of Purpose Within the Family. The SOFTA is not only a conceptual model but also a set of instruments, an observational rating system (SOFTA–o; Appendix A), and parallel self-report questionnaires (SOFTA–s; Appendix B) for clients and therapists.

In this chapter we describe the paper-and-pencil and software methods for using the SOFTA–o (or its Spanish version, the SOATIF–o). Because the measure can be used in research as well as in practice, training, and supervision (discussed in chap. 15), we summarize the training of raters and the measure's psychometric properties on the basis of process studies conducted in the United States, Spain, and Canada.

USING THE PAPER-AND-PENCIL SOFTA–O

Observers can analyze either a taped therapy session or a live one. Although rating live sessions can be useful for supervision, they obviously cannot be stopped and rewound for careful analysis. Videotapes are preferable to audiotapes because a number of SOFTA–o behaviors are nonverbal. (Rating of audiotapes is possible, however; the user simply needs to recognize that all of the alliance-related behavioral evidence is not available with this medium.)

To rate sessions with the paper-and-pencil SOFTA–o, the user needs the instrument itself, the guidelines for converting behavioral tallies to dimensional ratings, and the list of operational definitions for each item. The instrument and guidelines appear in Appendix A, and the operational definitions are included in the training manual, available at http://www.softa-soatif.net. Training in the correct use of these materials is described in the section Training SOFTA–o Users.

As seen in Appendix A, there are separate instruments for client behavior and therapist behavior. Although it is often desirable to rate both therapist and clients, reliable observation requires that the observer focus on one or the other at a time. Each instrument defines the four alliance dimensions first and then lists a series of positive and negative (in italics) behavioral items under each dimension title. On the client measure, raters fill in the roles (e.g., mother, father, daughter, son) or clients' names at the top of each column.

Ratings based on an entire session provide the most valid assessment of that session, but depending on the rater's purpose, portions of the session may be rated instead. In practice settings, for example, it may be of interest to observe the client behaviors leading up to a peak emotional exchange or a pivotal event, such as when a client declares that therapy is not helpful.

As discussed in chapter 2, the assumption underlying the SOFTA–o is that clients' thoughts and feelings about each alliance dimension are revealed by specific, relatively low-inference behavioral indicators, positive as well as negative—for example, "Client brings up a problem for discussion" (Engagement) or "Client avoids eye contact with other family members" (Shared Purpose). Likewise, the therapist's contribution to each dimension is reflected in the frequency and contextual meaning of his or her positive and negative alliance-related behaviors. As the observer views the session, tallies are recorded in the columns to the right of each behavior whenever it occurs. Observers are free to note whatever is needed (e.g., verbatim material, check marks, question marks, plus marks) to help them recall the importance, frequency, or impact of a given behavior.

When in doubt, the user should refer to the operational definitions in the training manual (see http://www.softa-soatif.net). In the Engagement dimension, for example, the operational definition of the behavioral item, "Client indicates agreement with the therapist's goals" is as follows:

> After the therapist has explicitly identified or described the purpose for therapy or the goals for the treatment, the client says something that indicates acceptance of the therapist's perspective. The client might explicitly ("Yes, that's good") or more implicitly agree (e.g., "Well, that makes sense because . . ." or "Let's get started then").

All client and therapist items are clarified in the training manual. Because nonverbal behaviors (e.g., leaning forward or avoiding eye contact) can occur off and on throughout a session, these items are tallied only once if they occur for the entire session or for a prolonged period of time. They also can be checked each time they occur in clear response to an ongoing discussion. For example, when a client moves from a relaxed sitting position to a forward lean when directly asked a question, the item "Client leans forward" (positive Safety) is checked. As another example, each time a client avoids eye contact after being directly addressed by the therapist, that item (negative Emotional Connection) is checked.

Some items require inferences, but the inferences simply require good social sense rather than clinical sophistication. Consider for example the item, "Client states or implies that therapy is a safe place." The operational definition of this item is as follows:

> The client might not necessarily use the word "safe," but the implication in his/her words is that he/she feels safe. This item requires some kind of verbal indicator; nonverbal indicators are *not* sufficient for this item to be checked. Implicit examples are when someone says he/she decided to wait until the therapy session to discuss something with a family member or says something like, "It's okay to cry in here" or "I didn't know whether I would have the courage to tell you, but . . ." or "I'm glad we finally made it here." The point is that the client suggests that the therapeutic environment is valued for its safety, not only as a place to solve problems. At times the indicator may be quite subtle, as "I don't know quite how to say

this, but I'll just take the plunge," or "I hope you [*other family member*] don't mind my saying this, but . . ."

The second task in the rating process involves going from the behavioral tallies to global ratings of the clients' Engagement, Emotional Connection, Safety, and Shared Purpose (or the therapist's contributions to the alliance on these dimensions). After watching the session, the observer considers the frequency, context, and importance of the checked behaviors to make dimensional ratings on a –3 (*extremely problematic*) to +3 (*extremely strong*) ordinal scale, where 0 = *unremarkable/neutral*. In the client measure, each family member is rated on Engagement, Connection, and Safety; the entire family is rated on Shared Purpose. The rating guidelines (Appendix A) require the observer to begin with the family member who seems to be the least engaged, connected, or "safe," followed by the next most engaged, connected, or safe, and so on. This method facilitates the rating process and is important because, invariably, the rating given to one family member influences the rating given to all the others.

In brief, a rating of 0 is given either when no positive or negative behaviors are present or when the number or the nature of both positive and negative behaviors cancel each other out, so to speak. Thus, a 0 rating suggests that the alliance is neither particularly positive nor particularly negative. When there are only positive behaviors, the score must be +1, +2, or +3. Similarly, when there are only negative behaviors, the score must be –1, –2, or –3. Subjectivity enters in when considering the context, content, and meaningfulness of the observed behaviors, and the rating requires more inference when a client's (or therapist's) behaviors in a session are both positive and negative. In these cases, the rating must be –1, 0, or +1. (Note that ordinal scales like this one do not assume strict equivalence between points.)

In making the global ratings, content needs to be considered in context. An offer to compromise (a Shared Sense of Purpose behavior) has a different meaning if the compromise is directly related to the problem under discussion or is more peripheral to the family's main concerns. For a couple that has spent many sessions arguing about the division of labor, a compromise about doing the laundry may be as meaningful as another couple's compromise about when to start a family.

Consider, for example, one of the vignettes in the training software. A young boy is almost in a fetal position, hiding his entire head and upper body from view. He is reluctant to respond to either the therapist or his grandmother, who is speaking to him softly and lovingly. At one point, however, the boy discloses something painful: "My father beat me." A few moments later, he starts to cry. In this 2-minute (role-played) vignette, the negative Safety behaviors are (a) the boy's extreme defensive posture and (b) his reluctance to respond when directly addressed by his grandmother. The positive indicators of Safety are his expressions of vulnerability (i.e., disclosing painful material and crying). Because the extreme negative behavior out-weighed the positive, the correct rating is –1. If the boy had not cried or mentioned the abuse (i.e., no positive Safety behavior), the rating would be –3 and would be based solely on his nonverbal behavior. However, if he had been reluctant to respond but was not sitting so defensively, the rating would be +1, given the sensitive nature of his disclosure. If he had cried, mentioned the abuse, and not been defensive or reluctant (i.e., only displaying positive Safety behaviors), the rating would be +3.

USING THE E-SOFTA

The SOFTA–o/SOATIF–o software application (e-SOFTA) allows for a fine-grained, time-stamped analysis of the therapeutic alliance in sessions of conjoint family therapy. The e-SOFTA facilitates training on the measure for clinicians and researchers by allowing for a direct comparison of two us-ers' work. That is, built into the computer program is the ability to directly compare two users' qualitative impressions and ratings of the same session.

The e-SOFTA can be ordered free of charge (i.e., as a CD-ROM) or downloaded at http://www.softa-soatif.net. The software includes 16 brief training vignettes (8 client, 8 therapist) in English and 16 in Spanish. These actor-simulated sessions illustrate various behavioral indicators of high and low client and therapist contributions to Engagement, Emotional Connec-tion, Safety, and Shared Sense of Purpose. After training with these sample sessions, users can load their own videos into the program for rating. In other words, e-SOFTA is useful for practice, supervision, and research, because users can (a) learn the SOFTA–o by rating a series of brief training vignettes and comparing their ratings to the correct ones, and then (b) load their own videos into the program for rating.

Figure 3.1 shows the software screen for a training vignette, set to the Safety dimension of the SOFTA–o. (Note that although the figure is in black and white, the e-SOFTA is in color.) At the left is the video screen, under which is a time bar with *start* and *stop* buttons. At the top right are tabs for each of the four SOFTA alliance dimensions. In this screen, the Safety tab is lit. Underneath the row of tabs is a list of (abbreviated) Safety behaviors; the list of behaviors is color-coded to differentiate positive from negative items. To the right of this list are columns, one for each client in the session. Tallies listed in the cells show how many times the husband and wife displayed each SOFTA–o behavior. At the bottom of each list are the clients' global Safety ratings.

When the user clicks on a behavioral item (e.g., *reluctant to respond* in the wife's column), the item is time stamped. When the user is uncertain about whether a given behavior should be marked, a click on the item will open a small window showing the operational definition of that item. Users

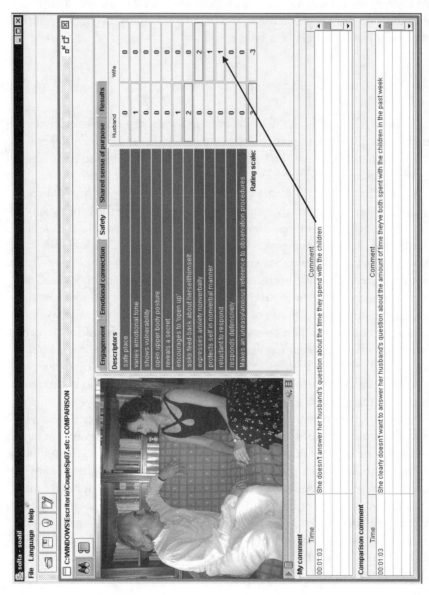

Figure 3.1. A training vignette screen in the e-SOFTA. e-SOFTA = System for Observing Family Therapy Alliances, software version.

can also go to the Help tab to read the operational definitions of all items from the training manual.

The screen shown in Figure 3.1 is set for "Solution" (note the binocular icon in the upper left corner), which the user clicks on after rating the entire training vignette. The program automatically compares the user's ratings with the correct ratings. Some tallies are surrounded by green rectangles. A green rectangle means that the user's tally for that item (including 0) is correct. A tally surrounded by a red rectangle indicates an incorrect mark. That is, a red rectangle appears if (a) the user clicked on a behavior that the client did *not* actually display in the vignette or (b) the user did not click on a behavior that the client *did*, in fact, display. In the latter case, the user can click on the red rectangle. The program automatically shows the time (in minutes and seconds) when the behavior occurred. Then a simple click on the time indicator will replay the video at the exact moment in the stream of interaction when the client displayed the behavior. By clicking any item, users can immediately revise their observations (e.g., from "1" [*present*] to "0" [*not present*] or from "1" to "2," etc.).

While observing the video, the user can pause at any point and record (in the box at the bottom of the screen) qualitative impressions of specific behaviors, the entire session, or anything of interest that is occurring. In this training vignette, for example, the user wrote about the item, *reluctant to respond*: "She doesn't want to answer her husband's question about the time they spend with the children." The "Solution" comment (i.e., titled *Comparison Comment* within the computer program), which shows why the item *reluctant to respond* is tallied at this precise moment in the session, is almost identical: "She clearly doesn't want to answer her husband's question about the amount of time they've both spent with the children in the past week."

Comparing one's own comments with the Solution comments is useful for learning the SOFTA–o (i.e., with the 16 training vignettes) or with the observer's own videos. When a user's own tapes are being rated, the two boxes beneath the video allow comments to be made independently by two observers—supervisor and supervisee, for example, or two individuals rating the same research data.

After the entire video is observed and rated, the user makes dimensional ratings (on the –3 to +3 scale) at the bottom of each column, guided by the software program. After the user has made these ratings, the program automatically assesses their concordance with the SOFTA–o guidelines. If there is an error, a message automatically appears, such as "If *only positive* items are checked, the score *must* be above 0." This message would appear if the user had checked one positive behavior but then given a Safety rating of 0.

Profiles in the form of graphs are generated by e-SOFTA from the dimensional ratings of family members and therapists. (An example is depicted in Figure 3.2.) In addition, a file is created with the behavioral indicators and

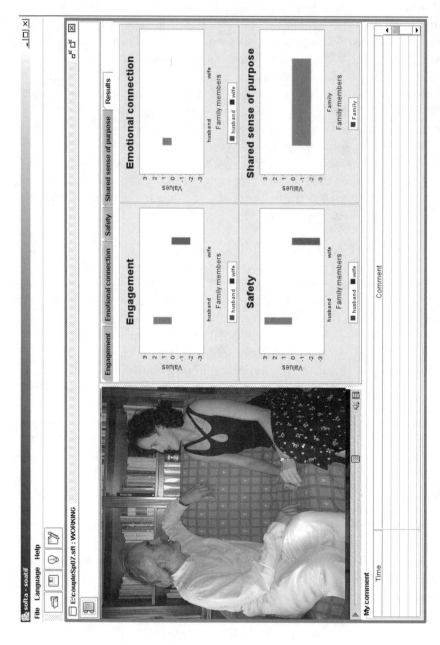

Figure 3.2. An alliance profile screen in an e-SOFTA training vignette. e-SOFTA = System for Observing Family Therapy Alliances, software version.

qualitative impressions, ordered chronologically. This file can be accessed by clicking on the parchment icon in the left corner above the video screen.

When rating their own videos, users need to switch back and forth between the four SOFTA dimensions as behaviors are observed. (Each training vignette focuses on a single dimension.) Before beginning, the user must choose whether to rate the therapist or the family members, inasmuch as the behavioral items differ. In other words, a user can first rate the clients' behaviors on all four dimensions, followed by the therapist's contributions, or vice versa.

A user's ratings can be saved for viewing later on or for comparison with another user's ratings. For research purposes, a therapy session can first be rated by the SOFTA–o trainer. Next, the individuals being trained can rate the same session, using the time-stamped items and qualitative comments by the trainer (i.e., the Solution) to understand differences between their own results and those of the trainer. In the context of supervision, a supervisee can rate his or her own sessions after (or before) the supervisor has independently done so.

TRAINING SOFTA–O USERS

Training is essential for accurate use of the SOFTA–o. Naturally, training methods differ depending on whether e-SOFTA or the paper-and-pencil version is used. However, some aspects are common to both training procedures. In this section we describe these common aspects and the distinct ones, which also depend on whether users are learning the SOFTA–o for purposes of research or as part of their education in couple and family therapy.

Regardless of the user's purpose, the first task is to gain a solid understanding of the SOFTA model. Before proceeding to the next step, all users should have a thorough understanding of the model. By this we mean the conceptual basis (i.e., similarities and differences between the alliance in individual and conjoint therapy; see chap. 1) as well as the SOFTA dimensions and their respective behavioral indicators, the operational definitions, and the research evidence (summarized in the following section). The case illustrations provided throughout this book are valuable for applying SOFTA to clinical situations; a close reading of chapters 4 through 8, which focus on the four dimensions, is essential for a thorough understanding of the model. Group discussions with the trainer (course instructor, supervisor, or investigator) should be held to clarify any questions or concerns about the rating process. If training in the SOFTA is solely for educational purposes, role-playing high and low levels of Engagement, Emotional Connection, Safety, and Shared Purpose can be used to bring the model "to life."

The second task is to learn which behaviors relate to each dimension of the alliance. Although it is unnecessary to memorize the behavioral indicators, the user should be familiar enough with them to quickly recall in which dimension a given behavior belongs. When the SOFTA–o is being used for research, group discussions with the trainer should focus on the operational definitions of each behavior and its discriminating features; for example, what is and is not considered "defensive behavior" (Safety), when to rate nonverbal behaviors (Emotional Connection, Safety, Shared Purpose), the distinction between a "goal" and a "positive change" (Engagement), and so on. Such a discussion can also be highly useful in supervision.

When the raters have a good working knowledge of the behavioral items and dimensions, the next step is to work with the training vignettes, which are a part of e-SOFTA or available for downloading separately at http://www.softa-soatif.net. As mentioned before, these vignettes are very brief illustrations with several behaviors, both positive and negative, from each dimension. The user should rate each vignette and then compare his or her ratings with the "Solution" and with the ratings of other individuals being trained. If e-SOFTA is being used, raters should use the time stamps to replay the video at the precise moments any errors were made. The training manual should be consulted whenever the raters' results are inconsistent with each other or with the training "solution."

In our experience, the training vignettes are easily rated because users only need to focus on a single dimension at a time. When a rater's results compare favorably with the training "solutions," the individual who is learning the SOFTA–o for clinical purposes can go on to rate his or her own videotapes.

Training for Research

When using the SOFTA–o for research, good interrater reliability is essential. To work toward this goal, the next step is to select 6 to 12 practice videotapes that are representative of the investigator's data. These training tapes should have few clients and good sound and video quality. If possible, it is desirable to select sessions that are clearly positive or negative examples of alliance-related behavior. In other words, our recommendation is to start with easy material, gradually increasing the level of difficulty as raters become comfortable with the system.

During this phase of training, we recommend working with a single dimension at a time. Either a VCR or DVD can be used or videos can be loaded directly into e-SOFTA. It is desirable for raters to work together on the first couple of tapes, sharing their impressions and jointly deciding on the ratings. The next step is to begin rating all four dimensions simultaneously. After practicing together on a few more tapes, the raters should work independently and compare their results frequently. During training (and during the actual rating of research tapes), it is essential that raters observe the same sessions independently and then meet (preferably at least weekly) to compare results and negotiate a consensus whenever ratings differ.

In these meetings, raters should closely compare their behavioral tallies as well as their global dimension ratings. Typically, we do a statistical assessment of reliability after the dimension ratings differ by no more than a single scale point at least 90% of the time. Reliabilities are assessed separately for each SOFTA dimension. Because reliabilities are more accurate when a substantial amount of data is rated, at least 5 practice therapy sessions should be used to assess reliability on the client SOFTA–o (i.e., a minimum of 10 clients). At least 10 practice sessions should be rated for the therapist measure. To lighten the burden and increase the sample, half sessions can be used for the reliability assessment (e.g., 10 half-sessions for clients, 20 half-sessions for therapists). Reliability also must be assessed on the actual research data.

Raters do not need clinical experience to use this instrument. In fact, most of our SOFTA–o research has been conducted with graduate students, some with no clinical experience at all. Conscientiousness, attention to detail, and good interpersonal skills are necessary qualities for raters. Whenever possible, we use both male and female raters because women and men tend to view social behavior somewhat differently. In our experience, good reliability can be reached after 10 to 15 hours of training, spread out over 4 to 5 weeks.

During training, sometimes one rater may consistently have different results from the others'. This individual's reliability can easily be checked by omitting his or her scores from the intraclass correlation analysis and recomputing the reliability values (assuming at least two other raters). When one individual's ratings on the practice tapes lower the group's reliabilities by .10 or more, remedial training is necessary. If, after analyzing the basis for the consistent discrepancies, this individual's ratings still do not improve, he or she should not participate in the actual research investigation.

At least two raters should be used; more than two is preferable. In our large data set, which spans several years, we have had rotating teams of raters. All raters must demonstrate good reliability on the same 5 to 10 practice tapes and subsample of research tapes before proceeding. We use consensus ratings in the data analysis because negotiating to a consensus on a weekly basis keeps raters from drifting too far apart over time. In the past, we have also averaged ratings when the training results were rarely more than 1 point apart.

During training, the reliability analysis may show that raters have more difficulty with one dimension than the others. In our experience, the two affect-related dimensions, Emotional Connection and Safety, tend to pose somewhat greater problems. Reliabilities can be affected by the clinical material itself or by the frequency with which raters meet to compare and negotiate their results. We cannot overemphasize the importance of frequent, regular meetings during the rating of practice and research data.

Training for Clinical Training and Supervision

Beyond the utility of the SOFTA–o for research, training with the measure can efficiently sensitize novice therapists to the complexities of the alliance in couple and family therapy. Students can learn to use the SOFTA–o, both the client system and the therapist system, as a way to recognize the behavioral manifestations of Engagement in the Therapeutic Process, Emotional Connection With the Therapist, Safety Within the Therapeutic System, and Shared Sense of Purpose Within the Family. Students can use either the paper-and-pencil version or e-SOFTA to rate their own videotaped sessions or those of "master" therapists (i.e., examples that faculty frequently use to demonstrate therapy techniques from different schools of couple and family therapy).

Although it is not as essential to learn the operational definitions of the SOFTA–o items for training purposes as it is for research purposes, a discussion of the nuances in the items can be worthwhile for clinical practice. Consider the negative therapist Engagement item, "Therapist defines therapeutic goals or imposes tasks or procedures without asking the client(s) for their collaboration." The operational definition of this item in the training manual is as follows:

> For this item to be checked, there must *not* be a direct question from the therapist asking for the client's input. The essence of this item is that in giving instructions for an assignment at home, for an enactment in session, or for some other proceeding in the treatment, the therapist imposes his/her will without considering the opinion or well being of the client. For this item to be checked, the therapist must not explain his/her reasoning, not ask if clients understand, and not use a questioning tone of voice. Examples: "Next session I'll see you separately. I want one of you to come in the morning and one in the afternoon" would be marked, but "Next session, could I see each of you separately?" would *not* be marked. Other examples: "Good, after consulting with the team, here is the assignment for you this week: You go pick up John every day at work and after . . . "; "In what remains of this session you'll take turns answering me, and I don't want you to speak to one another." An important precaution to keep in mind: the failure to ask for collaboration may be based on a prior agreement with the clients that allows the therapist to use his/her discretion in imposing tasks and procedures. In these cases, the item should *not* be marked. That is, on occasion, a previous conversation or some understanding established earlier in the session (or in a prior session) has given the therapist permission to offer directives or instructions without consulting the clients. As an example, working with a highly conflictual, troubled couple a therapist and couple agreed that if the level of conflict seemed untenable to the therapist, s/he would see them individually. Thus, when s/he informs the clients that they will be seen separately in the next session, there is no need to consult them because a previous agreement to do so was already in force.

Essentially, this descriptor refers to moments or episodes in which the therapist references the goals of therapy in a unilateral or highly assertive (or even aggressive) manner. As an example, a therapist working with an adolescent and his parents says, "What we have to achieve in therapy is increase your ability to discipline [*child*] around his study habits, so he doesn't fail in school." In this case, the therapist asserted the goal of treatment without asking for the opinion or for confirmation from the clients. When, however, the therapist has already actively negotiated the goals of therapy with the clients and finally asserts a summary of what will be accomplished, this item is *not* marked, as in "Okay, I understand that you all want this therapy to eliminate the conflicts you're having over [*client's*] education."

As this lengthy example shows, we are endeavoring to be as specific and behavioral as possible in writing these operational definitions. By doing so, in addition to maximizing interrater reliabilities for research purposes, the SOFTA–o provides a common language for therapists, students in training, and supervisors.

RELIABILITY AND VALIDITY

In this section we summarize the psychometric support for the SOFTA–o and SOFTA–s in research to date.

Reliability

SOFTA–o

As previously explained, it is important for raters to learn the operational definitions of the items and dimensions and refer to them for clarification as needed during the rating process. For best results, raters observe the same sessions and meet at least weekly to negotiate results to minimize "rater drift." When this process is followed, even clinically inexperienced raters can achieve moderate to high interrater reliabilities. In three reliability tests under these conditions (in both Spanish and English), intraclass correlations rated from .72 to .95 on the SOFTA–o.

SOFTA–s

The internal consistency reliability of the 16-item SOFTA–s is $\alpha = .87$ (client; English) and .95 (therapist; English), $\alpha = .83$ (client; Spanish) and .84 (therapist; Spanish). Engagement, Emotional Connection, and Shared Purpose reliabilities vary from .62 (client; English), .88 (therapist; English), .52 (client; Spanish), and .82 (therapist; Spanish; Friedlander, Escudero, Haar, & Higham, 2005). Although some of these values are not high, the reliabilities are adequate for subscales with only 4 items, and research supports the subscales' concurrent and predictive validity, as described in the following section.

Validity

Face Validity

The SOFTA–o was developed inductively and empirically, as described in chapter 2. As part of that process, we conducted face validity tests with English- and Spanish-speaking family therapy researchers. Specifically, we asked these experts to sort a large pool of items into the four operationally defined clusters (i.e., Engagement, Emotional Connection, Safety, and Shared Purpose) and to suggest any additional alliance-related items that occurred to them. Separate sorting tasks were conducted for the client and therapist SOFTA–o. Additions, deletions, and modifications were made on the basis of the sorting results.

Known-Groups Validity

To determine whether the SOFTA–o behaviors within each dimension are clinically meaningful and discriminate between strong and weak alliances, we conducted two known-groups validity tests (Suen, 1988), one in the United States and one in Spain (Friedlander, Escudero, et al., in press). For each experiment, eight brief role-played therapy vignettes were video-taped. The vignettes were constructed to depict high and low Engagement, Emotional Connection, Safety, and Shared Purpose. Each vignette had several (3–5) SOFTA–o client behaviors. As an example, one vignette depicted a family whose behaviors reflect a positive Shared Sense of Purpose (offering to compromise, sharing a joke, validating each other's perspective), and one vignette depicted a different family with negative Shared Purpose behaviors (exchanging blame and sarcasm, arguing about the need for therapy, avoiding eye contact). Participants—graduate students in family therapy classes—watched the vignettes (in random order) and rated both families on four 7-point semantic differential scales reflecting the conceptual definition of Shared Sense of Purpose (i.e., *collaborative* vs. *divisive, divided* vs. *unified, willing to negotiate* vs. *unwilling to negotiate*, and *blaming* vs. *accepting*). The semantic differential scales for the other three SOFTA dimensions were also derived from their respective definitions (Appendix A).

Statistically significant comparisons of participants' ratings on these "known groups" (i.e., the vignettes with the high vs. the low alliance stimuli) supported the construct validity of each dimension of the SOFTA–o (all ps .0001). Moreover, consistent results across the English and Spanish experiments (which used different actors, presenting problems, and SOFTA–o behaviors) indicate that the measure accurately reflects clinically meaningful alliance-related behavior (Friedlander et al., 2003; Friedlander, Escudero, Horvath, et al., in press).

Factorial Validity

Using five data sets from diverse couples and families in the United States, Spain, and Canada, we conducted an exploratory factor analysis to identify any higher order factors in the client SOFTA–o. To avoid redundancy, we randomly selected one client from each of 120 families. Entered into the factor analysis were clients' global ratings on Engagement, Emotional Connection, Safety, and Shared Purpose. Results indicated a single factor that accounted for roughly half the variance, suggesting that the four SOFTA dimensions are various aspects of a single construct (i.e., the therapeutic alliance).

Given these findings, it is reasonable to question the meaningfulness of conceptualizing the alliance using four dimensions. From a methodological perspective, however, intercorrelations among the dimensions were variable, from a low of .18 (Safety and Shared Purpose) to a high of .75 (Engagement and Emotional Connection) and, as demonstrated throughout this book, the four dimensions are useful constructs for practice.

Concurrent Validity

Concurrent validity is supported in three ways (Friedlander, Escudero, Haar, & Higham, 2005; Friedlander, Escudero, Horvath, et al., in press):

1. Significant associations were found between some observational and self-report scales. For example, clients' Emotional Connection and Shared Purpose-related behaviors (SOFTA–o ratings) in Session 6 were significantly associated with their self-reported perceptions of the family's Shared Sense of Purpose (SOFTA–s), obtained immediately after that session. These findings support the assumption that alliance-related behaviors in the SOFTA–o reflect clients' thoughts and feelings about the alliance with the therapist.
2. A significant association was found between client- and therapist-rated SOFTA–s Shared Purpose scores after Session 6.
3. Significant associations were found between some SOFTA–o ratings and SOFTA–s scores with (a) Luborsky et al.'s (1983) Penn Helping Alliance Questionnaire and (b) Symonds and Horvath's (2004) Working Alliance Inventory—Couples (Horvath, Friedlander, Symonds, & Gruter-Andrews, 2003).
4. Qualitative themes in postsession interviews about the alliance with individual family members were congruent with their SOFTA–o ratings, and the families' SOFTA–o Shared Purpose ratings were consistent with clients' self-reported within-system alliances on Pinsof's (1999) Family Therapy Alliance Scale—Revised (M. Beck et al., in press).

Predictive Validity

Predictive validity is supported in four ways (Friedlander, Escudero, Haar, & Higham, 2005; Friedlander, Escudero, Horvath, et al., in press):

1. Significant positive associations were found between the SOFTA measures and postsession scores on Stiles and Snow's (1984) Session Evaluation Questionnaire in two studies, one in Canada and one in the United States. For example, Canadian couples rated Session 3 as deeper and more valuable when their observed Engagement was high; men in particular saw the session as deeper when their ratings on Emotional Connection and Shared Purpose were higher. In the U.S. study, family members' observed Safety in Session 6 were significantly associated with their self-reported perceptions of the depth and value of that session on the Session Evaluation Questionnaire, and Shared Purpose was related to greater smoothness. In the same study, therapist-rated Engagement (SOFTA–s) was associated with therapists' perceptions of a deeper, more valuable session, and therapist-rated Emotional Connection was associated with therapists' perceptions of a smoother, easier session. More interesting still, client-rated Engagement was positively associated with therapist-rated depth and value.

2. Significant positive associations were found with therapist-rated (SOFTA–s) scores on all four dimensions after Session 6 and their "estimate of improvement so far" on the Penn Helping Alliance Questionnaire (Luborsky et al., 1983).

3. Significant and meaningful associations were found between SOFTA–o ratings and adolescent–therapist interactions reflecting verbal relational control. For example, more frequent competitive symmetry (reflecting conflict) was associated with lower adolescent Engagement ratings, whereas more frequent complementarity (reflecting mutual understanding) was associated with higher client Engagement, Emotional Connection, and Safety.

4. In four case studies, low SOFTA–o Safety and Shared Purpose ratings early in therapy were observed only in the two less successful families (as rated by therapists on Kiresuk, Smith, & Cardillo's [1994] Goal Attainment Scaling); the two more successful families had notably more favorable ratings on all four SOFTA–o dimensions early in treatment (M. Beck et al., in press).

CONCLUSION

We based our development of the SOFTA–o on the assumption, supported by empirical evidence, that observable behaviors in couple and family therapy are positively and negatively associated with participants' subjective experience of the alliance. Our transtheoretical, multidimensional model of the alliance includes two aspects common to individual and conjoint therapy (engagement, connection with the therapist) and two aspects unique to conjoint treatment (safety in the presence of other family members, shared sense of purpose within the family). Consequently, behaviors in the SOFTA–o include both between-systems and within-systems interactions, that is, interactions between each individual family member and the therapist (e.g., "Client agrees to do homework assignments"), interactions among family members ("Family members ask each other for their perspective"), and interactions within the entire therapeutic system—that is, therapist + family ("Family members try to align with the therapist against each other").

Useful for clinical practice and supervision as well as research, the SOFTA–o training manual and video illustrations minimize the level of inference needed for reliable assessment, thus providing a common language for therapists and a basis for comparing results across research studies. Chapter 15 provides specific recommendations for using the SOFTA–o in practice and research contexts. Although, to date, research on the alliance in couple and family therapy is sparse, the SOFTA–o and SOFTA–s are practical, reliable, and valid instruments for conducting future studies on important couple and family therapy processes and outcomes.

II

SOFTA DIMENSIONS

4

ENGAGEMENT IN
THE THERAPEUTIC PROCESS

Generally, people try to solve their problems in ways that reflect their idiosyncratic interpretation of those problems. They make attributions about the causes of the problems and have preconceived ideas about how problems like theirs should be addressed. Moreover, their worldview helps them make sense of proposed solutions. Indeed, a person's response to psychosocial problems reflects a complex set of influences: education, culture, experience in problem solving, family traditions, personality, and so forth.

By the time clients seek professional help, they believe that despite their best efforts to resolve their difficulties, the problems may even have worsened. Prior to considering therapy, clients frequently seek advice from friends, family members, teachers, clergy, or people they know in similar circumstances. Thus, when clients arrive at a therapist's door, they expect to be provided with an analysis of the problem and the tools to solve it—they expect answers that are beyond the reach of nonprofessionals.

Despite this expectation, therapy is not a simple application of prescriptions, with the client as a passive participant. Just as treatment compliance is essential for success in pharmacological therapy, in psychotherapy the client's cooperation is indispensable. To be an active partner in treatment, the client must first become engaged in the therapeutic process.

In the system for observing family therapy alliances (SOFTA), we define *Engagement in the Therapeutic Process* as follows:

> the client viewing treatment as meaningful; a sense of being involved in therapy and working together with the therapist, that therapeutic goals and tasks in therapy can be discussed and negotiated with the therapist, that taking the process seriously is important, that change is possible. (Friedlander, Escudero, Heatherington, Diehl, et al., 2004, p. 5)

Thus, we see engagement as a between-systems factor reflecting two components of Bordin's (1979) conceptualization of the alliance: agreement with the therapist on the goals and tasks of treatment. The degree to which an individual family member sees the treatment as meaningful depends on the views of the other participating clients. For this reason, Engagement in the Therapeutic Process is closely associated with the SOFTA within-systems alliance dimension, Shared Sense of Purpose Within the Family (see chap. 7).

In this chapter, we discuss one SOFTA dimension, Engagement in the Therapeutic Process, and specifically, theoretical perspectives on the construct and some client characteristics that can hinder engagement. Case examples are used to illustrate therapist techniques and strategies for fostering engagement with reluctant clients.

THEORY AND RESEARCH

Among the numerous common factors repeatedly found to account for success in individual therapy, the client's active involvement in the treatment ranks among the top (e.g., Wampold, 2001). In conjoint therapy, client involvement or engagement is just as essential, although arguably much more difficult to achieve. When a client voluntarily seeks individual help, he or she can choose what to disclose to the therapist, what to keep hidden, and the pace at which the therapy moves. If the therapist is "off the mark," the client can choose to drop out or get help elsewhere. However, even when family members seek treatment together willingly—which is not always the case—each individual has less "say" about the treatment objectives and procedures and indeed less "say" over what others reveal about her or him. It is not surprising, then, that client cooperation can be more challenging to achieve and sustain in a conjoint treatment format.

Resistance Versus Cooperation

Despite looking to therapy as a way to make changes, some or all family members may perceive the therapeutic process as a threat (to their relationships or, more generally, to the way they see the world) rather than as an opportunity. Thus, the concept of *resistance* has been central in family systems therapy, and techniques espoused by many different theoretical schools reflect the expectation that someone in the family is likely to be resistant. In fact, in the more influential treatment models of the 1960s and 1970s the concept *resistance to change* was fundamental. In structural family therapy (Minuchin, 1974; Minuchin & Fishman, 1981), for example, the family's resistance to changes in boundaries and hierarchy was said to be an important consideration for assessment and intervention. In terms of technique, the Milan group's paradoxical approach to therapy (Selvini-Palazzoli et al., 1978) and the paradoxical interventions inspired by the hypnotist Milton Erickson and adopted by therapists at the Mental Research Institute (Watzlawick, Weakland, & Fisch, 1974) and other strategic therapists (Haley, 1973) used the client's resistance to change as the impelling force to bring about that change.

A related concept is *homeostasis*—the idea that all systems have a tendency to return to the status quo to protect their structures, transactions, and relationships (Watzlawick, Beavin, & Jackson, 1967). The tendency toward stability has been used to explain why, despite having serious problems—even crises that demanded action—families often seem resistant to the very changes that would benefit them. From this theoretical perspective, difficulties related to engagement (by all or some family members) are seen as expressing the system's resistance to change. One client's disagreement with the therapist's proposed goals for treatment, reluctance to participate in sessions, or failure to complete "homework assignments" is a manifestation of the entire family's resistance.

Despite the intuitive appeal of this explanation, the concept of resistance was challenged by theorists in the 1980s. De Shazer (1984), for example, boldly proclaimed the "death of resistance" (p. 79). Indeed, solution-focused therapists have been the most vocal critics of the notion (de Shazer, 1985, 1988; O'Hanlon & Weiner-Davis, 1989). Focusing instead on cooperation, solution-focused theorists maintain that change could come about only when therapists assume that their clients always want to change. According to this view, the therapist's responsibility is to find the best way to facilitate change. In fact, resistance is reinterpreted as cooperation, pointing the way for shifts to occur. When a therapeutic process seems stuck, it is due to faulty calibration between what is taking place in session and the ways in which the family wants to change.

Whether from the perspective of resistance or from the perspective of cooperation (or from any other theoretical possibility, for that matter), the therapist must address poor engagement to facilitate progress. Thus, when a family member indicates that the therapy is not useful, implies that the process is blocked, or shows indifference to what is being discussed or proposed, the therapist must recognize the threat to the alliance and redirect his or her efforts. To enhance engagement, therapists can change focus or change strategies, moderate the pace of the therapy, or work through the motivational impasse. Direct confrontation of clients who show indifference, lack motivation, or clearly express their alienation is generally contraindicated (e.g., Patterson & Forgatch, 1985); it is only to be used when all other attempts to elicit collaboration have failed.

Family Engagement

There has been far more research on family engagement than on any other aspect of the therapeutic alliance in couple and family therapy, although the focus has been more on ensuring retention and avoiding dropout (e.g., Prinz & Miller, 1994) than on facilitating clients' in-session collaboration with the therapist. Studies that do focus on the technical aspects of engagement underscore the importance of clients' actively defining the problem. Research has shown, for example, that at the start of therapy, circular questioning (exploring the problem by juxtaposing different family members' perspectives) tends to prompt a greater sense of collaboration than either linear or strategic questioning (evaluating individual behavior or suggesting changes; Dozier, Hicks, Cornille, & Peterson, 1998; Ryan & Carr, 2001).

Research on families' perceptions of therapists suggests that clients commit to the therapeutic process when they believe that the therapist understands their situation and can make suggestions or give advice that seems relevant. In a study of 12 families who were asked to describe their experiences in therapy (Kuehl et al., 1990), those who had dropped out doubted that the therapist understood their problem and their personal situation. Some families that did not complete therapy were nonetheless satisfied with the outcome; they described their therapists as caring but unable to offer viable solutions for their concerns. One particularly interesting finding emphasized the importance of the initial phase of therapy. Family members who did not perceive their therapist as caring or genuinely interested in their problems found it difficult to contribute relevant information. In another qualitative study, Sells, Smith, and Moon (1996) reported that, for both clients and therapists, treatment effectiveness was related to the perceived clarity of goals and the adequacy of therapeutic tasks. It is interesting to note that whereas therapists were primarily concerned with the technical aspects of their work, the clients appreciated the therapists' trustworthiness, rapport, and caring. Indeed, the clients valued directness and caring over the therapist's formal, "professional" approach to their problems.

Consistent with this finding, our research with the SOFTA–o shows that clients' behavior related to Emotional Connection With the Therapist is substantially associated with their observable levels of Engagement in the Therapeutic Process (Friedlander, Escudero, Horvath, et al., in press; Friedlander, Talka, et al., 2003). As one way to connect with clients in the first session, therapists can counteract demoralization by showing respect for the family's resourcefulness. When family members explain that solutions that had been effective in the past no longer work, the therapist needs to help them find "new" solutions, all the while showing respect for their perspective and making suggestions that build on the family's existing resources. Asking clients to radically change their point of view to follow the therapist's directives can result in decreased engagement and, potentially, early termination. Typically, strong engagement is easily attained when the therapist's interventions are connected with the clients' own solutions—ones that worked in the past or new ones that are consistent with their worldview.

Arguably, the strength of a client's Engagement in the Therapeutic Process is the easiest dimension of the alliance to observe. Three behavioral aspects of engagement are represented in the SOFTA–o (see Appendix A): (a) client participation in defining therapeutic goals, that is, active collaboration and willingness to bring up problems for discussion, propose solutions, and articulate the anticipated outcomes of treatment; (b) client participation in specific therapeutic tasks (e.g., enactments, expressing feelings, working out compromises, carrying out homework assignments, filling out questionnaires) and in setting the pace for the therapy (e.g., the frequency of sessions and duration of treatment); and (c) motivation for change, that is, the client's expressed recognition of small improvements, of positive results from homework assignments, and of the efforts made by other family members. The therapist's contribution lies in stimulating these three aspects of client engagement—by explaining how therapy works, by actively asking clients for their input in defining goals and tasks, by exploring clients' willingness to try out new behavior during or after the sessions, by inquiring about clients' reactions to various therapeutic events, by engaging the attention and participation of everyone attending the sessions, and by praising and amplifying each small change as it is achieved.

CASE ILLUSTRATION:
REASONING WITH "REASONABLE" PARENTS

As an example of the therapist's role in initiating family engagement, take the case of Melanie and Paul Blayne, desperate about their 12-year-old daughter, Hilary, and what they described as her lack of discipline and behavior problems at home and at school. When the therapist asked about how the Blaynes had tried to solve these problems, Melanie's answer reflected the desperation commonly expressed by parents:

> all kinds of things, for the past year we've done everything imaginable
> . . . Hilary has always been a very reasonable girl, and we've always spent
> all the time and effort we can to explain things to her. Hilary has always

appreciated our talking to her, that we give her explanations of how and why things should be done. . . . In our family we've always solved problems through dialogue and reasoning, so we've always tried to talk things out with Hilary. Since her rebellion started, we tried to talk to her, all of us together, or just me and her, or just Paul . . . He even took her on a weekend fishing trip, the two of them alone, just to try to talk about her behavior at school. Nothing worked! We asked her grandfather to talk to her because they used to have an excellent relationship . . . but she totally rejected the idea . . . she became very aggressive . . .

The therapist investigated further, asking about the parents' reaction to finding out that Hilary had been skipping school. Paul answered, "We went into her room and explained our point of view and tried to reason with her—to make her see how damaging her behavior is, on her and on the whole family."

How cooperative would Melanie and Paul be if the therapist were to immediately set the therapeutic goal as "learning to be more authoritarian" and "forgoing 'reason' and 'dialogue'"? Would the Blaynes agree to punish Hilary whenever she violates basic rules of good behavior? Parents like Paul and Melanie might go along with the therapist's plan, at least at first. They might well decide that because they had been unable to influence their daughter's behavior on their own, the only thing left to do was to trust the therapist's wisdom and follow every suggestion. Frequently, however, parents reject suggested changes when they feel that the therapist's perspective on the problem challenges or disqualifies everything they've done in the past.

Family members' willingness to be active participants in therapy depends on a sense of working together with an understanding therapist on a mutually negotiated goal or set of goals. Paul and Melanie, like many parents, needed explanations at a slow, progressive pace (about the value of limit setting) before changing the problem-solving attitude that, to them, was a logical approach to parenting. Reasoning, "having a conversation," reaching consensus, and so forth had been effective in the past with Hilary; it also worked well for solving other problems in their lives. For the Blaynes to be fully engaged in the therapeutic process, they first needed to believe that what they were doing in therapy made sense, that is, that the steps being suggested to them would effect change in the problems that brought them to this impasse.

In other cases, some ways of solving problems do not work, not because they are misguided but because they contradict or are diametrically opposed to other ways of approaching problems. Unlike Melanie and Paul, who both tried to "reason with" their daughter, in many families one parent tries to convince a child to change his or her behavior, whereas the other parent uses every means to impose limits and discipline the child in a top-down manner. Having such contradictory strategies produces disagreements between parents, adds to an already acute conflict with their children, and makes it chal-

lenging to negotiate a common therapeutic goal. Typically, one parent understands that having failed in every attempt to redress the situation, they
need to follow the therapist's advice. Having opposing views on the solution,
however, the parents are unlikely to collaborate willingly. When they have
different expectations of what therapy should entail, it is not unusual for one
parent (or both) to think, "I hope the therapist will be able to make my
spouse understand that his (or her) attitude is wrong and needs to change."

SOME COMMON CHALLENGES TO ENGAGEMENT

Difficulties related to engagement and cooperation can arise from a
family's lack of resources—intellectual, emotional, or socioeconomic. In the
following sections we highlight a few specific challenges to engagement:
working with adolescents, multi-stressed families, and men. Before doing so,
however, we must acknowledge that therapists can unwittingly compromise
their clients' level of engagement. Countertransference (see chap. 13) or a
simple lack of understanding or skill can lead to mistakes, such as overlook-
ing the expressed concerns of one family member or not recognizing or rebal-
ancing a split alliance (see chap. 9). The therapist's personal history and
background can also affect his or her ability to create an atmosphere that
resonates with the family's ethnic, religious, or other cultural beliefs or values (see chap. 10).

Adolescents

An exploratory study (G. M. Diamond, Liddle, Hogue, & Dakof, 1999)
addressed the question: How can a therapist improve an alliance that starts
off on the wrong foot? The treatment context was multidimensional family
therapy with delinquent adolescents. Selecting families with an initially poor
teen–therapist alliance, G. M. Diamond et al. (1999) compared five cases in
which the alliance had improved by Session 3 with five cases in which it had
not. Several alliance-building strategies were present only in the improved
cases, including (a) paying attention to the adolescent's experience, (b) presenting oneself as an ally, and (c) helping the teen identify personally meaningful goals for therapy.

Alliance research conducted on adolescent inpatient units is also informative. In one study, the client's inaccessibility (i.e., isolation and alienation) was the greatest single barrier to the formation of a therapeutic alliance, far greater than angry defiance (Colson et al., 1990). In another
investigation, Eltz, Shirk, and Sarlin (1995) found that the client's prior
maltreatment seemed to hinder his or her initial emotional connections with
treatment providers, but having a history of abuse was not a factor in the
strength of later alliances or the degree of treatment success. Rather, poor

therapeutic progress was related to the severity of the teen's current interpersonal problems. However, in yet another study of adolescent inpatients (Florsheim, Shotorbani, Guest-Warnick, Barratt, & Hwang, 2000), strong early alliances were in fact associated with poorer outcomes than weak early alliances, possibly because a short "honeymoon period" dissipated as staff set more limits and expected greater interpersonal investment. However, a subgroup of patients resisted treatment initially but stuck it out and eventually established very strong therapeutic alliances. Perhaps these clients had a kind of "wait and see" attitude, just as some adolescents in outpatient family therapy describe (Kuehl et al., 1990).

These research findings are pertinent because they underscore the importance of developmental considerations in the alliance. The pacing of successful relationship-building work seems to differ between adolescents and adults. Moreover, children and adolescents are typically not self-referred, and so they are more likely to enter therapy in a precontemplative state of change (DiGiuseppe, Linscott, & Jilton, 1996). With reluctant teens, staying close to the client's concerns and supporting self-efficacy are likely to be more successful strategies than using silence or pushing for vulnerable feelings when parents are present.

In one case, Oksana, a 19-year-old whose family had immigrated from Eastern Europe 4 years previously, was depressed and isolated at home. At the urging of their parish priest, the parents sought help from a therapist. Engaging Oksana in treatment was challenging, not because she was unwilling, but because she knew that what she had to say would pain her parents. Intuiting the teen's acculturation dilemma, the therapist commented on Oksana's love and respect for her parents, her fear of disappointing them, and the tough place she found herself in, caught between two cultures. Then, by encouraging Oksana's parents to give their daughter permission to speak frankly, the therapist was able to engage the reluctant teen in a dialogue. Oksana courageously took the invitation. Speaking directly to the therapist, her eyes averted from her parents, Oksana disclosed that her love for an American boy had resulted in an unwanted pregnancy.

As this example shows, it would be inaccurate to characterize all teens as resistant to authority. However, adolescents often require special attention before they will collaborate actively in therapy with their parents. A number of treatment models have designed specific interventions to engage reluctant adolescents. As previously mentioned, multidimensional family therapists (Liddle, 2002; Liddle & Schwartz, 2002) use specific adolescent engagement interventions to show teens that they can gain something worthwhile from therapy, that their feelings will be respected, that therapy can help restore relationships, and that their participation is needed for change to occur. In this approach, a secure and comfortable relationship with the therapist comes about from showing genuine interest in the adolescent's personal goals and clearly stating that his or her participation in the process is valued. An important part of the process involves using specific parental reconnection interventions to address the adolescent–parent bond. According to Liddle and Schwartz (2002), active participation of the parents in the therapeutic process can be achieved by "reestablishing parental feelings of love toward, commitment to, and influence over their adolescents" (p. 465).

In working with adolescents, it is particularly important to adapt interventions to the individual client's developmental level (Oetzel & Scherer, 2003), which varies widely from one person to the next. Evaluation of the adolescent's maturity and characteristic attachment style are primary considerations for increasing levels of engagement. Adolescents with severe behavioral problems, for example, typically have less cognitive and social maturity than their peers, affecting their interpretation of the therapy and the therapeutic relationship. When clients (at any age) misinterpret the purpose of treatment, their motivation to cooperate is strained. Engagement is difficult, and the risk of dropping out of therapy is high.

Multistressed Families

Many low-income, multistressed families find it difficult to engage in the therapeutic process, despite a pressing need for help. Often these families come to therapy at the insistence of Child Protective Services or Family Court after a charge of child abuse or neglect has been reported or investigated. Because in most cases these referrals are mandated, the clients come to treatment under duress (see chap. 11).

To reduce resistance and facilitate the engagement of hard-to-reach Hispanic families with drug-abusing adolescents, researchers in Miami (Santisteban et al., 1996; Szapocznik et al., 1988) developed a specific intervention, strategic structural systems engagement (SSSE), which begins with the family's first telephone contact to the therapist. SSSE involves joining the family by demonstrating concern, interest and empathy, reframing the problem, and even visiting the reluctant client's home to forge alliances and facilitate engagement before treatment begins.

Difficulties in engaging multiproblem families arise in part from the clash between the clients' sociocultural context and that of the professionals involved in their case. Reframing is essential when the family and therapist have opposing views on the nature of the problem, on how it should be approached, on the therapeutic relationship, and on the family's relation to the agency where the therapist is working. According to one author, therapy with multistressed families is essentially "a cross-cultural negotiation in which the two parties act in a mutually influencing relationship" (Madsen, 1999, p. 97).

> [F]amily and helper can be seen as distinct micro-cultures with their own beliefs and preferred styles of interaction. . . . Therapy proceeds better

when both micro-cultures (helper and family) are on the same wave-length (i.e., hold similar beliefs about what the problem is, what should be done about it, and who should do what in addressing the problem or are aware and respectful of differences in those beliefs). (p. 97)

Many of the difficulties therapists encounter in trying to engage multi-stressed families are associated with a lack of safety (see chap. 6). When a Child Protective Services- or court-ordered family feels safe in the therapeutic system, it is because the "cross-cultural" context integrates the therapist's and clients' perspectives on the nature of the problems and potential ways to go about addressing them. To enhance safety and facilitate the family's engagement, the therapist must pay close attention to how his or her suggestions and interventions (including the role played by the institution or agency) are being interpreted. Using the client's language to explain how therapy works is the first step (see chap. 11).

Men

A woman in marital therapy described her husband as "a hard nut to crack." Not in any way defensive, he came to sessions without complaint. However, although willing to listen to his wife's complaints about him, he saw the problem strictly as her unhappiness. Despite a good relationship with the therapist, in 3 months of therapy he never identified a problem for discussion, never offered a different point of view, never proposed a course of action.

Although engagement in couple therapy is facilitated when both partners jointly search for a therapist (Slipp, Ellis, & Kressel, 1974), it is typically the female partner who initiates the process. Traditional gender role expectations can make therapy a trying ordeal for some men. Indeed, for many, the context of therapy is simply alien. Particularly when the process focuses on expressing feelings and analyzing relationships, many men feel out of their depth. If they do take part in treatment, it is because they see their marriage deteriorating or their children headed for a fall.

It is not surprising, then, that research on gender in couple and family therapy has consistently shown that treatment outcomes are enhanced when the therapist's alliance with the husband or father is strong (see chap. 10 for a review). Presumably, this is so because of the stereotypical reluctance of men to engage in "talk therapy." Although there are no data on the topic, in our experience the setting plays a role—building alliances with men in couple and family therapy is far easier in private practice than in public agencies, possibly because of the higher proportion of mandated clients in these settings. Moreover, in many communities the vast majority of family therapists are women, and some men refuse treatment if they feel outnumbered.

Cultural values also play an important role in this gender imbalance. In Latin cultures, for example, many men believe that talking about family problems is humiliating because it means they have been unable to solve those problems on their own (Santiago-Rivera, Arredondo, & Gallardo-Cooper, 2002). Sometimes both father and mother view men as incapable of handling the emotional involvement of therapy, even when the concerns involve their marriage, their children, or their extended family.

Arguably, engaging reluctant men in treatment requires different strategies for male and female therapists. Female therapists need to walk a fine line between supporting the husband or father to involve him in treatment, on the one hand, and not alienating the wife or mother, on the other. A woman client may feel in competition with or betrayed by a female therapist whom she expected to confirm her point of view. Male therapists may have an easier time relating to the man in the family, but their attention to the wife may be misinterpreted or even used as an excuse for the husband to drop out.

Levant and Philpot (2002) summarized four approaches to couple therapy that reflect a "gender-aware" philosophy (p. 319). Each of these approaches involves avoiding triangulation with the couple in a "who's right?" battle by validating, educating, and empowering both clients simultaneously. Just as culture can be framed as the culprit in acculturation-based family conflicts, in gender-aware approaches the source of the couple's problems is attributed to gender-based misunderstandings. By defining the problem in this way, the therapist is able to engage the couple in a dialogue about the degree to which destructive stereotypes and messages about appropriate behavior are negatively affecting their relationship. From there, it is a short jump to engagement in treatment.

In family therapy, finding creative ways to engage reluctant fathers is essential because their absence from treatment threatens the remaining family members' involvement and willingness to change. This priority was the early focus of therapy with William Ryerson, the father of an adolescent who was referred for aggressive behavior and attempts to molest a neighbor's preschooler. The boy, Matthew, lived with William, his stepmother (Nicole), and her daughter from a previous marriage, who was away at college. For the first 5 years of William and Nicole's marriage, Matthew's relationship with Nicole was fine until his behavioral problems came to a head. Although the therapist asked both parents to attend the first session, only Nicole and Matthew showed up. Asked about William's absence, his wife said, "He's distraught by the whole situation. It's hard for him to stay calm enough to talk about these things, especially if Matthew is here. . . . He never knows how to handle Matthew's teachers or school counselors either."

The therapist kindly but firmly insisted on William's involvement in future sessions. The father did, in fact, attend the second session, but his participation was minimal; he turned to his wife to answer every question posed by the therapist. Despite his promise, William did not attend the third appointment. Nicole made an excuse—something had come up at work at the last moment, making it impossible for William to get away. In response to the therapist's questions about progress over the past week, Nicole explained that William had told them "to do everything the therapist asked." William, however, had not done his part of the assigned homework; in fact, he was even more distant from the family and tied himself up with work.

It would be simple in a case like this for the therapy to continue without the father's participation. If the other family members cooperate and do not view the father's absence as problematic, the therapist's choice to ignore it may even be interpreted as a sign of respect for the father's decision. However, capitulating to the father's withdrawal could affect the engagement of other family members. Indeed, the father's lack of involvement in therapy could well affect other aspects of the family's life, such as his participation in raising and caring for the children.

Because the therapist in this case considered the father's participation to be essential, she contacted him by phone. After relating the important points of the last therapy session, she requested a meeting with William and Nicole to evaluate the success of the three initial sessions and discuss a treatment plan. Emphasizing the fact that she was requesting a "meeting, not another therapy session," the therapist asked William to choose a time and date when he could be sure to attend.

During the meeting, the therapist laid out the treatment plan and her initial assessment of the problem. Then she asked what she could do to facilitate William's participation. It came out that the sticking point was William's belief that his contribution would be minimal and that, in fact, his failure to discipline Matthew was the cause of all his son's behavior problems. In response, the therapist began by reframing the father's attributions positively:

> I understand what you want to do—whatever's best for your son—and you think that your contribution is to not interfere in the therapy. I know you have the best intentions, and really that honors you. But your family and I need your help. What we need is for you to come—your participation is important.

Next, the therapist elicited William's promise to attend biweekly sessions with his wife; sessions on the opposite weeks would be held with Nicole and Matthew together or with Matthew alone. William agreed to do so, and in fact his engagement in the therapy and with his son progressed nicely from that point on.

This example shows how engagement can be increased with modifications in strategy, such as having a meeting to inform and plan with an individual family member who is reluctant to be involved in the process. Some clients can eventually become influential participants in the treatment when they receive special attention from a therapist who is willing to work at their pace and applaud their efforts to make small changes in their behavior.

SENSITIVITY TO CHANGE

For engagement to be strong, clients must be sensitive to the changes that are slowly taking place and attribute them to their participation in the therapeutic process. When problems are serious and change is slow going, clients often dismiss small improvements as insufficient or not meaningful. Feelings of frustration and despair can easily inundate the mood of the session, bringing everyone down.

Thus, the therapist's task is to sensitize the family to small shifts in behavior or attitude that emerge from therapeutic conversations and from trying out new behavior. For example, the therapist can optimistically point out that a change is likely or that a change has already taken place. Alternatively, the therapist can propose simple homework tasks whose aim is merely to sensitize the family to change. In these change sensitivity interventions, each client is asked to make a slight change in routine that is absolutely unpredictable and keep it secret from the others. It is important that this change not be monumental or even related to therapy: "You might change your hairstyle, the place where you normally sit at the table, go fishing, ride a bike, whatever." Each family member is asked to figure out what the others have done, but without discussion. Typically, clients object: "If we're supposed to change something that doesn't have anything to do with X [*the problem*], what good will it do?" The therapist's response should be simply to explain the importance of practicing small changes and detecting them in each other before trying to make more important changes in their behavior. This strategy can be particularly effective when the problem has a long trajectory, leaving pessimism and demoralization in its wake. In our experience, when "training" in small changes is successful, family members enjoy it and quickly become more engaged in the therapy and more optimistic about their future.

Aside from declaring optimism, therapists can praise clients for their motivation and willingness to try new behavior, to compromise, to talk about feelings, and so forth, even if the behavioral change is not substantial. Structural therapists (Minuchin & Fishman, 1981), who work with in-session enactments, recommend "punctuating" change in a family interaction before it disintegrates to the old, familiar patterns of blame, criticism, or withdrawal. To do so, the therapist stops the action and praises the differences that did occur. When clients become aware that small changes add up to bigger ones, they often make comments like, "The truth is, we feel more encouraged just being able to come here" or "My daughter said she missed coming to therapy when we skipped a week."

CASE ILLUSTRATION: BEAUTY AND THE BEAST

The following case illustrates many points in the previous discussion, the personal and contextual challenges to client engagement and suggested therapeutic interventions to enhance engagement or unblock disengagement. Ronald and Caryn Jacobs sought couple therapy at an agency that specializes in substance abuse. A young couple, Ronald was 30 and Caryn 31, had been married for only 2 years. They had known each other since adolescence, however, and had always been close, first in a group of friends and later on their own, until they finally became a couple. After a year of heavy partying every weekend, Ronald voluntarily began an outpatient alcohol rehabilitation program. Before that, Caryn would go to bars with him, but eventually she stopped doing so in the face of his increasingly compulsive drinking. The rehabilitation program recommended conjoint treatment when it became clear that Ronald's alcoholism was destroying the couple's relationship.

From the first moments of couple therapy, differences in the two clients were striking. Caryn was active and positive, providing relevant information without being asked, offering ideas and suggestions to help Ronald and their marriage; she was positively disposed to trying anything. Ronald, however, was shy and withdrawn, reluctant to offer information or consider any of the therapist's suggestions. He seldom spoke, and when he did, the pace was slow and the thoughts confused. The difference in participation quality was reflected in the couple's differences in appearance: Caryn was elegantly and meticulously dressed; Ronald was disheveled and slovenly.

After three sessions with little progress, the therapist decided to bring up the apparent differences in the couple's participation:

Therapist: Something has struck me ever since we started therapy together a few weeks ago, and now I'd like to mention it to you. Caryn, since the beginning you've been an active participant . . . it seems like that's the way you are naturally . . . Ronald, you've been reticent and reserved . . . I'm not sure if what we're doing here has the same meaning for you as for Caryn. Is there something we could change for you to feel more comfortable?

Caryn: I think he's always like this—in all aspects of his life. Ever since we met, I've seen that . . .

Therapist: [*interrupting*] Sorry to cut you off, Caryn, but I'd like Ronald to express his point of view.

Ronald: There's no problem, she's right . . . she knows me well.

Therapist: I'm sure, but really, I'd like to hear your point of view and how you'd express it.

Ronald: Fine, I think I'm making a big effort, and it's getting me nowhere.

Therapist: Can you explain this? Give me an example of what you consider an effort and tell me what makes you think it's getting you nowhere.

Ronald:	She's like that in my life, she's always been special, she's awe-some . . . she can easily talk to people. If someone calls, she can talk for 10 or 20 minutes. . . In here, she knew right away what to do. It's impossible for you to understand how hard it is for me to talk about problems, how hard it is for me to even be with her when we're with other people.
Therapist:	Yes, I can imagine that it's difficult to live with a person who's so efficient and verbal. How do you feel when you're with her and other people?
Ronald:	I feel like I fall behind, that I'm not going to do well . . . and the thing is that I always want to be with her. I still ask myself why she decided to marry me. Sometimes I try to talk about my prob-lems, but she's so fast that she doesn't realize when I'm making a big effort, and I end up getting blocked, just like what's hap-pening to me right now . . . sorry I'm not doing better . . .
Therapist:	When you used to drink on weekends, did you ever have a simi-lar feeling?
Ronald:	Yes, until the third or fourth drink. We'd go out a lot because she had many social engagements, and I felt a little embarrassed . . . like Beauty and the Beast!

This bit of humor, surprising in Ronald, produced laughter that was shared by the therapist and couple—the first lighthearted moment since therapy began.

Therapist:	Caryn, can you tell Ronald why you chose him as your partner?
Caryn:	I've always loved him very much—he's always been very good to me. Now I realize that maybe I don't listen to him enough.
Therapist:	I'm afraid that in the other sessions we talked a lot about you, Ronald, about what you might be feeling and what you're going through, but we haven't given *you* time so that you could ex-press all this yourself. How can we make this up to you?
Ronald:	There's something that's helped in rehab . . . writing. I can write things, and we could read them and talk about them.
Therapist:	Of course, that's a great idea!

From that moment on, things changed radically. The focus became Ronald's ideas and needs. Caryn discovered many new things about her hus-band, his feelings about getting married and his hopes for their life together. For her, it was difficult but gratifying to hear what Ronald, with great effort, needed to say.

As is common when family members display varying engagement lev-els, the key to success in this case was recognizing the extraordinary effort Ronald was making to get psychological help and to talk about his problems.

Both partners became engaged in the therapeutic process, and it was a balanced involvement in which they jointly considered their life as a couple and made plans for their future together.

CONCLUSION

Engagement in the therapeutic process requires client and therapist to have congruent perspectives on the problem and a sense of working together. Although common to all treatment formats, engagement poses unique challenges when family members are in conflict with each other, have different motivation levels, or have different perspectives on the problem and the path to its solution. Clients can also have difficulty collaborating with treatment when the goals, tasks, and procedures proposed by the therapist clash with their worldview or their characteristic way of understanding problems. Difficulties arise when the therapist's approach is discordant with the family's past or present experiences in solving other problems, or when the family is blocked by some covert conflict that makes change more threatening than the status quo.

Although the family's relationship with the therapist is the product of a professional contract in which the therapist is deemed the expert in evaluating and solving problems, clients are not passive recipients of a process that is simply imposed on them. Very much to the contrary—strong engagement requires clients to understand that the goals and tasks of therapy must be actively discussed and negotiated with the therapist. Although engagement is not straightforward when family members disagree with each other or with the therapist's point of view, cooperation can be elicited by proposing manageable changes and amplifying small successes.

Engagement has another essential feature, a cognitive one. For engagement to be strong, clients need to view improvements as related to the act of working together and with the therapist. When a client recognizes an improvement but does not associate it with the treatment (e.g., seeing it as luck, fate, or chance), engagement in the process is hindered because being in therapy simply does not make sense to the client.

5

EMOTIONAL CONNECTION
WITH THE THERAPIST

When Janyce and Roger Lafitte suddenly began screaming at each other in the middle of the therapy session, the volume high and their faces grimacing intensely, 4-year-old Louis started plucking violently at the skin on his arms. Standing up to forcefully interject herself between the adults, the therapist got them to stop yelling and fall silent. As the therapist sat back down, Louis jumped headlong into her lap and threw his arms and legs around her torso. Surprised and touched, she hugged the little boy. Louis's behavior reflected the gratitude of a child frightened beyond words by his parents' verbal aggression.

This event dramatizes an important mechanism in family therapy: Relief, trust, gratitude, and eventually affection are engendered in hopeless clients when a therapist is able to disrupt their rigid, toxic cycles of interaction. With time, clients' optimism rises ever so cautiously as they begin to see the therapy making a difference. Often family members attribute the differences they witness not to the therapy per se but to the personal charisma and caring concern of the therapist.

Gibney (1998) commented that "[i]n therapy, power and love play a balancing role with each other . . . and both must be kept alive in the therapeutic equation" (p. 91). Our definition of *emotional connection* in the System for Observing Family Therapy Alliances (SOFTA) is consistent with Gibney's sentiment:

> viewing the therapist as an important person in the client's life, almost like a family member; a sense that the relationship is based on affiliation, trust, caring, and concern; that the therapist genuinely cares and "is there" for the client, that he or she is on the same wavelength with the therapist (e.g., similar life perspectives, values), and that the therapist's wisdom and expertise are valuable. (Friedlander, Escudero, Heatherington, Diehl, et al., 2004, p. 5)

Although this definition refers to individuals' relations with the therapist and not to the therapist's bond to the family as a whole, the two are intricately related. Clients notice how other family members talk about the therapist outside the consulting room and watch closely how everyone interacts with the therapist during the session. Pinsof and Catherall (1986) found that the most positive therapeutic outcomes in couple therapy occurred when the wives saw a strong bond between their husbands and the therapist, and indeed this seemed more important than their own feelings toward the therapist.

Typically, the more motivated members of a family are heartened when they observe less motivated family members warm to the therapist and when the therapist reaches out to those who are reluctant, unsure, scared, or defensive. Veronique, for example, worried that her 11-year-old son, Robert, would balk at therapy, but her fears dissipated quickly in Session 1 when the therapist began by asking Robert where he got the "cool cap" he was wearing. When Robert answered, "From karate. I'm a black belt," the therapist responded amiably, "Wow! I'd better watch myself around you!" Robert's easy smile reassured his mother that they were off to a good start.

In many circumstances, an emotional connection is made with little effort. Over time, as the therapist's individual bond with the family group grows, so too does his or her bond with each individual and vice versa. The reverse can occur, too, if family members become disenchanted with the therapist. In one of four cases studied intensively with the SOFTA–o, M. Beck et al. (in press) found that despite a positive connection with the therapist early in treatment, one mother left abruptly after Session 23 when the therapist shifted focus from the son's drug use to the dysfunctional marital relationship. Clients who come as "hostages" of other clients or who are mandated by outside parties like Child Protective Services, Family Court, or the criminal justice system may start out seeing the therapist as an extension of the punitive authority (see chap. 11). In these cases, any small disappointment with the therapist can get magnified until the family (or the therapist) gives up on treatment.

THEORY AND RESEARCH

Studies of the frequency of verbal interactions between family members and expert therapists like Salvador Minuchin, Carl Whitaker, Don Jackson, and Murray Bowen, among others, have repeatedly shown that therapists position themselves in the midst of the therapeutic system (Friedlander, Ellis, Raymond, Siegel, & Milford, 1987; Friedlander et al., 1985; Raymond, Friedlander, Heatherington, Ellis, & Sargent, 1993). In other words, effective family therapists are active, not merely onlookers who direct the family traffic from the sidelines. Because therapists are at the center of the action, they must recognize just how important and powerful they can become for family members.

It took 25 years from the advent of family therapy for theorists and researchers to recognize the therapist's relations with the family as a catalyst for change. With the notable exceptions of Virginia Satir and Carl Whitaker, theorists initially saw the therapist as an external force, a change agent outside the family system. Authors were at once awed by the cybernetic intransigence of family systems and eager to distance themselves from psychoanalysis, a lengthy approach in which the therapeutic relationship takes center stage (Flaskas & Perlesz, 1998). In the first wave of family theorists, Minuchin (1974) emphasized the importance of "joining" with the family to obtain the leverage needed for change, and Haley (1976) advocated strategic posturing to avoid duplicating the identified patient's power struggles with significant others. Bowen (1976) and the Milan systems theorists (Selvini-Palazzoli et al., 1978) adamantly maintained that neutrality was the only way to keep a clear head when they were immersed in "too richly cross-joined" (Hoffman, 1981, p. 74) families, such as those dealing with anorexia and schizophrenia.

In the 1980s the feminist challenge (e.g., Luepnitz, 1988) to the authoritative role and high-powered techniques of the field's founders was echoed by a new wave of theorists who advocated a softer, more collaborative approach with family members. Some researchers described the traditional devaluing of therapists' emotional attachments to clients as "male-stream" thinking—that is, the emphasis of rationality over feeling states (Smith, Osman, & Goding, 1990, p. 143). These authors focused instead on the therapeutic system (i.e., family group + therapist) as the catalyst for second-order change (Flaskas & Perlesz, 1998; Smith et al., 1990), acknowledging that "the therapist cannot be an observer from nowhere" (Hardham, 1998, p. 76). Constructivist and narrative authors (e.g., Goolishian & Anderson, 1992; M. White & Epston, 1990) recommended a not-knowing attitude, which would allow clients the freedom to explore alternate meanings to their life stories and find idiosyncratic solutions to their problems.

Prompted by this theoretical debate, researchers began to take note of the therapeutic relationship as a central ingredient in couples and family therapy. In one study, for example, a panel of expert trainers and supervisors identified aspects of the relationship that account for success in treatment (White, Edwards, & Russell, 1997). Aspects related to the emotional bond included mutual respect, a willingness to work together, a cooperative atmosphere, clearly defined boundaries, perceptions of the therapist as helpful and competent, and rapport with the therapist. Noting that the literature weighs far more heavily on the side of what therapists do to create a successful climate for change than on how clients think and feel about what is taking place in treatment (Friedlander, Wildman, et al., 1994), other researchers turned their attention to family members' perceptions of their experience in therapy. Some studies involved uncovering clients' feelings about the therapist by asking them to describe critical moments in the treatment (e.g., Kuehl et al., 1990). Other studies involved investigating the emotional bond component of the therapeutic alliance in relation to other variables (e.g., L. N. Johnson et al., 2002).

In general, clients value therapists who are warm, active, down-to-earth, informal, trustworthy, optimistic, secure, humorous, caring, and understanding (e.g., Bischoff & McBride, 1996; Kuehl et al., 1990). A study of 83 families seen at a child guidance center (Firestone & O'Connell, 1980), for example, showed that the therapist's reactions to the family after Session 1 predicted which families eventually dropped out of treatment. It is not surprising that showing what family members perceived as indifference or contempt on the therapist's part was predictive of drop out. However, liking the family, trusting the family members, and feeling involved with them were associated with continuation in treatment. In terms of improvement, first impressions were less important, but better outcomes occurred when therapists viewed their relationships with families favorably and when they saw their clients as flexible. It is interesting that larger families were relatively more successful in treatment, a finding Firestone and O'Connell explained as related to either the presence of more allies or greater motivation. Because it is harder to get large numbers of people together, when families manage to do so, it is often because the presenting symptoms are incredibly disruptive.

Studies show that the bond aspect of the therapeutic alliance is particularly important for families (M. Beck et al., in press; L. N. Johnson et al., 2002), possibly more so than for couples; when the bond is strong, clients tend to experience their sessions as smoother and easier (Heatherington & Friedlander, 1990b). Clients in one study said, "I just feel really safe with [therapist], her personality . . . . She just stays on our level and doesn't try to use a bunch of big words and everything to make us feel less adequate" and "[The therapist] just identifies with me and family members as real people, not subjects, not specimens" (Christensen et al., 1998, pp. 183–184). In another study (Kuehl et al., 1990), the qualities described as most helpful in a therapist were caring and understanding. One dissatisfied client remarked, "Sometimes the counselor's question didn't seem to apply to us. Sometimes it was like he was talking about a family different than ours" (p. 313).

Housgaard (1994), distinguishing between the *personal* and the *collaborative* aspects of the therapeutic alliance, has maintained that personal aspects are socio-emotional (p. 70). Furthermore, the behaviors that participants display are reciprocated, such that clients' confidence, friendliness, compliance, and receptivity reinforce and are reinforced by the therapist's authenticity, warmth, acceptance, unconditionality, and empathy. As a consequence, the relationship comes to be characterized by mutual liking and understanding, with a tacit understanding about the acceptable level of intimacy and degree of therapist directiveness.

In a study of therapeutic attachments in individual therapy, Saunders, Howard, and Orlinsky (1989) distinguished the bond aspect of the working alliance from two other aspects: *empathic resonance* and *mutual affirmation* (p. 323). *Empathic resonance* has to do with therapist–client compatability in terms of communication and reflects the client's perception of the therapist as attentive, understanding, and interested. *Mutual affirmation*, however, refers to client and therapist having concerns about the other's welfare and sharing care and respect. Clients perceive their therapists as affirming when they have a person-to-person relationship and the therapist appears warm and friendly, accepting, and agreeable.

In the next two sections, we discuss the circumstances that are favorable and unfavorable to the development of strong emotional connections between therapists and family members.

STRONG BONDS ALL AROUND

As we discuss in chapter 7 ("Shared Sense of Purpose Within the Family"), family members who seek treatment voluntarily and who have similar goals, such as dealing with a problematic third party (particularly an absent one), come without too much defensive armor and are prepared to like their therapist. Solid emotional connections with all family members are relatively easy to achieve when motivation is high and when family members see treatment as a chance to improve relations with one another rather than as a stage on which to fight a battle.

Likewise, clients and therapists connect most easily when they have similar life experiences or backgrounds, shared values and worldviews, or complementary personality styles. In individual therapy these points of connection only need to take place between two people, but in conjoint couples or family therapy, especially when people are at different life stages (parents, young children, teens, grandparents), the forging of bonds is all the more complicated.

If the therapist comes from the same cultural background as the family, there is often an instant recognition and basis for rapport. Indeed, when clients have a choice about whom to see, they often expressly ask to be referred to a therapist from a similar racial, ethnic, or religious group. A young lesbian couple, both Jewish, remarked that because their issues had to do with how badly their families were reacting to their alternative lifestyle, it was more important to them that the therapist be Jewish than that she be a lesbian. Other lesbian or gay couples might only feel comfortable with a therapist who has a similar sexual orientation, however, just as some individuals with alcohol or drug addictions feel more comfortable with therapists who are themselves in recovery. A single adoptive mother wanted to see a therapist who was also an adoptive parent to be sure that her son's depression would be considered in the context of his adoption rather than because of it, a nuance that the client feared would be lost on a therapist who had no personal experience with adoption. (See chap. 10 for a detailed discussion of diversity issues.)

Clients tend to be attracted to therapists who speak from their own personal experiences, especially when those experiences are similar to their own. It is perhaps because the similarity itself is a connection, or because by disclosing something personal the therapist is in effect saying, "I'm just a person here, too." After a tension-filled dialogue with each other, Jason and Olivia looked sheepishly at the therapist, who had intervened throughout the dialogue, trying (without much success) to teach the couple to argue more productively. Recognizing their disappointment with themselves, the therapist remarked:

> Yeah, I know, it's hard! And how we interact with the most important people in our lives is so automatic that what we're doing to each other eventually becomes invisible to us. If you guys were to take a peek at the fights I have with my wife, I'm sure you would see things that *we're* doing wrong that I have no clue about!

At this, Jason and Olivia chuckled and the session moved forward smoothly. Disclosures that are at an appropriate level of intimacy and not too frequent are appreciated in this way.

Self-disclosure is just one way to communicate a shared life experience. Hoffman (1991) wrote about the value of openness, including sharing personal thoughts and "the subjective nature of our understandings" of the family's trials (p. 5, as cited in Flaskas & Perlesz, 1998, p. 128). Having a similar background as one's clients provides a therapist with an empathic window on the family's pain that another therapist might not be able to intuit. To illustrate, the Baptiste family was grieving the loss of the father, Juan Carlos, a patriarch who had managed to endear himself to every member of his family, despite being a harsh taskmaster who used physical punishment freely. Hearing the Baptiste adolescents describe their father in glowing terms, the therapist thought back to her own father's death and her feelings afterward. Consequently, when she saw one teen staring off into the distance, a scowl on his face, the therapist gently remarked that it was normal and acceptable to have mixed feelings when people died.

Another therapist may have made the identical intervention without having personally experienced a difficult death. However, because of her own experience with a father like Juan Carlos, the therapist's eyes teared as she took in the Baptiste family's grief. Rather than try to hide her feelings, she simply said, "As you can see, I'm touched by what you're going through." Although unspoken, her behavior said in effect, "I know what this is. I've been there, too."

Other issues, such as parenting, are trickier. Therapists who are parents themselves can chuckle along with their clients about the foibles of child rearing in ways that might not occur to a therapist who is childless. Adult clients tend to be quite attuned to the age of their therapist and might directly ask whether the therapist is married or, more often, if he or she has children. When they need a therapist to be a nurturant, authoritative figure or a role model, adult clients prefer a therapist who is older than themselves, particularly if they have sensitive problems like loss of sexual desire. Adolescents, too, tend to note the therapist's age right from the start, and young therapists have a definite advantage with teens who see their parents as old-fashioned or "over the hill."

In a similar manner, therapists who share the same values or worldview as their clients can connect easily with them. In the United States there are many Christian counseling centers that, by advertising themselves in this way, inform potential clients that Christian values are an acceptable and desirable feature of therapy. Similarity of values need not be so explicit, however. People judge one another's lifestyle as liberal or conservative on the basis of clothing, hairstyle, neighborhood, even room decor, and bonds can develop when clients and therapists make seemingly off-hand comments about political events or, more generally, about how the world works. One therapist created a connection by an emphatic head nod when the client said, "I'm a stay-at-home mom. I won't trust my kids to strangers." In another case, a therapist asked an elderly client who had just lost his wife, "Do you sometimes talk to Suzanne when you're feeling lonely?" and thereby communicated a spiritual point of connection that did not need to be elaborated to be understood.

Similarity in values or worldview is also communicated through humor, and on a metacommunicative level, light-hearted banter may tell family members that the therapist sees them as people, not as problems (Reynes & Allen, 1987). Laughing at a joke together says in effect, "We are on the same wavelength. I see the world as you do." Humor is a powerful joining mechanism and a mood lightener in any social context. In therapy, humor can reduce tension, increase motivation, facilitate emotional release, reveal incongruities, expose irrational thinking, and help clients develop a more realistic appraisal of the magnitude of their problems (Carroll & Wyatt, 1990). On an emotional level, humor creates bonds between people and levels the playing field between therapist and client. Bruce, who was in marital therapy at his wife's command, was having an especially difficult time with the verbal commerce of therapy. Over the course of a few weeks, a ritual evolved whereby Bruce would start each session with a joke, saying, "Hey, Doc, I got a good one for you this week!" The therapist's obvious enjoyment of Bruce's joke would set an easy tone for the session. More important, however, was the covert understanding that helped Bruce get through the painful ordeal of trying to talk with his wife about how he felt. Seeking to build on this connection, the therapist would occasionally tell Bruce, "I heard a great one [joke] this week, and I'll bet it's one you haven't heard yet!" This simple banter says volumes: "I care about you. Even if therapy is not your cup of tea, you matter to me."

The third circumstance in which emotional connections are easily made is when the therapist and client have complementary personality styles (Horvath & Bedi, 2002), which, by definition, are comfortable for people and not anxiety arousing (Kiesler, 1983). Complementarity can be conceptualized in a variety of ways, in terms of the Myers–Briggs Type Indicator (Myers & McCaulley, 1985; Nelson & Stake, 1994), for example, or as control-defining behaviors that fit together (i.e., dominance and submission; e.g., Friedlander & Heatherington, 1989). It is not surprising that research has shown that friendly interactions that promote clients' autonomy are preferable to those that are hostile or controlling (Horvath & Bedi, 2002). Clients with a need to control are not threatened by therapists who are content to lead by following, and clients who prefer to be led tend to "click" with therapists who take charge. Clients who are highly anxious are more at ease with relaxed therapists, and shy or reluctant clients are more comfortable with extraverted therapists who can draw them out.

A difficulty may arise, however, when only some people in the family have a personality style that complements the therapist's. In these situations, therapists who recognize from the outset that there are strong differences between themselves and various family members will look for ways around problematic personality clashes to establish rapport. In the Brown family, for example, Sheilah was an extraordinarily powerful matriarch, and the therapist quickly recognized that she would be threatened by any intervention that was in the least challenging or confrontational. Sheilah simply had too much to lose, and she would rather forgo the opportunity to get help for her children than be seen by other family members as submitting to an outsider's authority. To circumvent a possible clash, the therapist treated Sheilah as a co-therapist, consulting her in a one-down fashion about the best way to help the others change. Interventions went something like this: "Sheilah, do you suppose that if we asked Stephen to keep track of the days he behaved himself at school, that he'd be able to? . . . or do you think it'd be better for you to monitor it all yourself through the guidance counselor?"

When family members connect on an emotional level with the therapist, a sense of ease pervades the session. On a nonverbal level, clients may have good eye contact with the therapist or may sit in such a way that they mirror the therapist's body language. As mentioned earlier, clients may joke or share gentle teasing with the therapist, ask the therapist personal questions ("Do your kids go to school in this district too?" or "Have you tried the new Italian restaurant up the road?"), or demonstrate caring, trust, or affection in other ways. Examples include bringing small gifts, showing photographs of their home, or saying something personal like, "We wanted to tell you about the little beach we found on our vacation. You'd love it, too!"

Behavioral indicators of a client's poor connection with the therapist include avoiding eye contact, refusing to speak when addressed, responding in a hostile manner, or criticizing the therapist as incompetent or inadequate. In the next section, we discuss various circumstances that can strain or challenge the therapist's ability to establish an emotional bond with family members.

WHEN CONNECTING BECOMES THE PROBLEM

Seeing emotional connections as the beat and therapeutic interventions as the melody, we might not be overly concerned about the quality of our connections with family members if we believe that strong interventions make the music work. In many cases, this is so. Circumstances like those previously described are ones in which emotional connections come easily and naturally, especially with high functioning, voluntary clients. When, however, the family and therapist have different values, cultural backgrounds, and life experiences, or their personality styles and ways of relating clash, difficulties in establishing an emotional connection can quickly take center stage. The problematic tempo overrides the melody, so to speak.

Connecting can be problematic for many reasons; therapists who push their agendas or who are cold or irritable tend to be disliked (Horvath & Bedi, 2002). Complementary styles of relating can be harmonious in some instances, but in others they can perpetuate vicious cycles of negativity, such as when optimistic therapists attempt to work with pessimistic family members or when self-righteous therapists attempt to work with family members who tend to blame each other (Rait, 1995).

Some poor connections have more to do with the systemic qualities of the family or the nature of their problems than with therapist negativity or a lack of common ground. Pseudomutuality (false togetherness that masks conflict and blocks real intimacy) and communication deviance in severely disturbed families often make it incredibly frustrating for therapeutic helpers to find a point of connection (L. Wynne, Ryckoff, Day, & Hersch, 1958). The Sanz family, for example, was seen on an inpatient unit after the first psychotic breakdown of their son, Theodore. Despite Theodore's manic mood, incoherent speech, and flight of ideas, the therapist found it impossible to focus his parents on the need for treatment. Rather, grasping for some sign of normalcy, the parents got excited when Theodore mentioned wanting to travel out west. As the session progressed, the only topic that the three family members could focus on was when and how Theodore could get to California. Every attempt the therapist made to get the conversation back on track was deflected by one or the other family members, who seemingly saw the meeting as a social occasion rather than as a treatment consultation. As the session progressed, the therapist had a sense of unreality about what was taking place, stymied at the parents' apparent disregard for the seriousness of their son's disturbance.

People need not have a psychosis for there to be a sharp breakdown in emotional connection. Many clinical problems can strain a therapist's ability to empathize, such as child molestation, for example, or other kinds of domestic violence. In such situations, the therapist's authority usually takes center stage. When concern and respect are communicated alongside authority, the probability of creating a bond is enhanced.

Some families are able to connect reasonably well with a therapist at the start of therapy but draw back as problems in the relationship develop gradually, reifying over time until the family drops out of treatment. Problems of this sort reflect the nature of the family's struggle. When it's a zero-sum situation (e.g., to divorce or not; see chap. 12) and there seems to be no possibility of win–win outcomes, clients eventually start vying for the therapist's attention and concern. Even if the therapist successfully avoids taking sides in these kinds of triangles, family members may not see it the same way. As one example, when a therapist's countertransferential feelings grew over time to the point that she could only see family members as villains or victims, the family intuited these feelings and acted accordingly. (See chap. 13 for an in-depth discussion of countertransference.)

Therapists make mistakes. Some mistakes can effectively end a family's involvement in therapy, especially if clients sense that the mistake was not due to faulty reasoning but rather to a lack of caring or concern. When the therapeutic relationship is solid, mistakes can be tolerated more easily. Unfortunately, when troubled family members get together, events can occur that even the most skilled therapist cannot forestall.

Consider the Graves family. Nineteen-year-old Nick had become increasingly volatile and hostile as he approached adulthood, to the point that he needed repeated hospitalizations. Getting nowhere in individual therapy with Nick, the therapist requested a family meeting. A crisis developed within the first 15 minutes of the session when Nick began talking about how he just couldn't get over his father's death (which had occurred 4 years earlier).

Furious at his mother's complacency when he talked about missing his father, Nick's temper quickly flared. He accused his mother of having pushed his father to suicide. This confrontation may have been therapeutic for Nick, but his two young sisters were profoundly shocked to learn for the first time that their father had died by suicide and further, that he had shot himself in the head. Seeing his sisters' horror, Nick was overcome with guilt and ran out of the room. Without missing a beat, Anthea Graves unleashed her fury on the therapist, outraged that her youngest children were informed of these facts in such a brutal way. Anthea screamed that the therapist didn't know what he was doing, how could he be so incompetent as to insist that the whole family attend this meeting, how was she going to handle *three* emotionally disturbed children, and so on.

Not everyone can be helped. When clients offer themselves into therapists' hands, however, therapists must try their best to find some way to reach them.

JOINING AND THE EMPATHIC USE OF SELF

In the family therapy literature, authors have traditionally been more concerned with how to engage and retain families in treatment than with how to establish emotional bonds with them. Among early theorists, Salvador Minuchin (1974; Minuchin & Fishman, 1981) had the most to say about specific ways to join a family system prior to restructuring boundaries and alliances between and among family members. In the structural model, the therapist becomes inducted into the family system (Minuchin, Montalvo, Guerney, Rosman, & Schumer, 1967) by adopting the family's customary ways of interacting. Although this process occurs naturally to some extent, the therapist must deliberately track clients' behaviors as they occur and accommodate himself or herself to the family's pace, tempo, and idiosyncratic ways of interacting.

Tracking interactions, the structural therapist observes the ways clients sit, share, or avoid eye contact with each other and also how they describe their presenting concerns. To establish common ground, the therapist adopts the family's language (e.g., do the children say *mommy* and *daddy*, or do they call their parents by their first names?), follows themes as they arise in the conversation, and intuits the family's values from how they describe one another. A gay couple frequently used the word *honest* to describe various supportive family members. At the end of an early session with them, the therapist summed up his perceptions thus, "While you're both hurting a lot over the fights you've been having, honestly, I think you two have a lot going for you as a couple. I want to be open and frank, though, and say that this may be rough going for awhile until you start seeing some concrete changes."

In a process Minuchin (1974) called *memesis*, the therapist deliberately becomes like a family member in manner of speech, body language, and eye contact, and by self-disclosing points of similarity (e.g., "Yeah. I can relate. I'm a terrible procrastinator myself"). Accommodation also involves following the family's typical transaction patterns, respecting the existing hierarchy, and asking permission for change. Only by behaving in a congruent way with existing family transactional patterns can the therapist gain the family's trust. Minuchin likened the accommodation process to the behavior of an anthropologist going into a foreign culture. By inferring and then obeying the culture's rules, the anthropologist demonstrates good faith to the community.

Although structural-strategic therapists have numerous behavioral techniques for joining with a family, these behaviors are seen as strategies or attitudes (Minuchin & Fishman, 1981) rather than as empathy. Furthermore, behavioral strategies have traditionally been of far greater importance in our field than emotional expressions of caring and concern (Flaskas, 1989). Consistent with this observation, descriptive research on the work of early leaders in the field showed that, in contrast to individual therapists, these family therapists tended to use few reflections of feelings or other interventions that are commonly associated with empathic resonance (Friedlander et al., 1985).

Indeed, the word *empathy* appears sparingly in the family therapy literature. Perhaps, as Flaskas (1989) pointed out, the absence of a focus on empathic relating is not due so much to a discounting of emotion as to the difficulty of thinking about feelings from a systemic perspective, "in a milieu which privileges techniques, miraculous interventions, and the absolute virtues of cybernetics" (p. 1). Furthermore, because the term *empathy* implies linearity, Flaskas recommended talking about *emotional interactions*, which refer to an interpersonal process rather than to a personal quality or one-sided communication.

To some extent, empathy is communicated by tracking and accommodating behaviors, but the basic point is to act from *within* the system rather than as a force acting from outside the system (Real, 1990). From within the system, there are numerous ways to connect with families on an emotional level. For instance, therapists comment on how difficult it is to change, tell stories that communicate understanding metaphorically, or simply remember important facts about the family from Session 1 to the next. Indeed, accurate recall of things clients have said in previous sessions makes a powerful statement: "You are unique" and "I've been thinking about you." Examples include remembering the names and ages of family members the therapist hasn't met or that a grandparent was due to go in for surgery or that the 17-year-old was supposed to get his driver's license last week. Therapists can also enhance clients' connections with them by expressing concern for what they're going through as a family ("It's just so hard to see your parents get old and frail—it's actually scary, I think") and asking questions about them as people apart from the problems that brought them to treatment. Friendly, personal small talk communicates a liking for the client regardless of how rough going the session may be (e.g., "I was just admiring your funky shoes. Are they new?"). Other ways of connecting include commenting on shared values and perspectives or asking about a family's culture, traditions, or lifestyle. Of course, a genuine expression of pleasure at seeing the family or in working with them goes a long way, such as, "It's been awhile since you two were here! Good to see you!"

Beyond the initial joining and empathizing with family members, emotional bonds need to be strong enough to weather the ups and downs of therapeutic change, particularly when people are challenged to take emotional risks with one another. One of the most important considerations in this regard is the need to avoid shaming or humiliating clients when challenging or confronting their behavior. This means not asking too much of people when assigning a homework task and not criticizing or blaming them for not completing the assignment. Direct confrontations are far riskier than indirect ones, and, in fact, research on the behavior of expert family therapists has shown that indirect communications, those we would never do in polite company, are commonplace in family therapy (Friedlander et al., 1987).

CASE ILLUSTRATION: VICARIOUS INTROSPECTION

As an example, consider how a therapist handled the following situation. Ten-year-old Amy was in the hospital with a high fever of unknown origin. Her mother, Carla, had been keeping a vigil at her bedside for days while her father, Frank, was out of town on business. On his return, Frank went directly to his office, not stopping at the hospital to see his daughter. Carla arrived at the next couple session still furious with Frank, and the battle lines were drawn. Frank's use of work to avoid intimacy was an old fight between them, one that had been discussed in therapy many times. Self-righteously indignant, Carla looked the therapist in the eye and challenged, "Well, who's right about this?"

The therapist, on the spot, saw from Frank's sheepish look that he regretted his actions. Consider how Frank would feel if the therapist were to confront him directly in front of his wife like this: "You're jeopardizing your relationship with both your wife and your daughter by this kind of withholding behavior." Indirectly, though, the therapist could turn to Carla and say, "I suspect that Frank knows that keeping his distance from you and your daughter at a time like this is risky business, and I don't think he's happy about it either. Maybe he even worries that in the long run it can jeopardize what you've both worked so hard for." This indirect message challenges Frank but in an empathic way that he's more likely to hear than if he had been confronted directly.

Here, then, is a hypothetical conversation with Carla and Frank:

Carla: [to therapist] Well, who's right about this? I just can't go on like this anymore. Would he have stayed away even if . . .

Therapist: I can see you're boiling mad about this.

Carla: Yeah!

The therapist needs to acknowledge Carla's feelings before intervening because the therapist has no intention of directly answering Carla's question about who's right and who's wrong in this situation. Empathy at a deep level is shown by the therapist's words *boiling mad*, which reveal her understanding that Carla is beyond anger. Indeed, she feels rage.

Therapist: [to Carla] Let me ask you this. I suspect that Frank knows that keeping his distance from you and your daughter at a time like this is risky business, and I don't think he's happy about it either. Maybe he even worries that in the long run it can jeopardize what you've both worked so hard for. Let's see if we can figure out what kept him away.

Carla: [angry] Well, he should know . . .

At this point, the therapist needs to cut Carla off from further hostile attacks. Carla needs prompting, though, to move from such an intense feeling state so that the therapist's intervention can have an impact on her as well as on Frank.

Therapist: [interrupting] Sorry. Let me stop you a moment here. Hold on! Can you think for a moment about what I just asked you?

Carla: [pause] You mean about Frank being worried? [calmer]

Therapist: Yes.

[silence]

Carla: [softer] I don't know. [turns to look at Frank]

Therapist: Frank?

Frank: [painfully, to therapist] Well, I . . . you said "ruin my relationship," and I . . .

Therapist: I think I said "jeopardize," but what's your thinking about this?

Frank is clearly intuiting the potential disastrous consequences of his behavior in this circumstance, as evident in his substituting the word *ruin* for the therapist's milder word, *jeopardize*. The therapist corrects him, not to point out that he made an error but to imply that things aren't quite that serious.

Frank: [silence] I don't know really.

> Carla: [*angrily, to Frank*] What do you mean, you "don't know"?!

Needing to curb Carla's anger before it boils again, the therapist interrupts, deciding to rescue Frank by speaking for him. Frank's shame and guilt are readily visible on his face, and the therapist realizes that Frank needs help in expressing himself. If Carla were to continue in the same vein, infuriated by Frank's bumbling about, she might say something irretrievably harsh.

> Therapist: Carla, I sense that Frank's having a hard time with this. Look at him. [*Carla turns to face Frank*] I may be wrong, of course, but I think there's an apology trying to get out. [*pause, then softly*] Frank?
>
> Frank: Yeah. [*louder*] I blew it!
>
> Carla: You certainly did!
>
> Therapist: Carla, I know you're still hurt by this, but let's see how Frank feels about it all. I'm going to help him talk with you about it.
>
> Carla: Okay.

At this moment, the therapist needed to forestall Carla from letting loose on Frank again. The previously described message was simultaneously an empathic statement to Carla as well as a strong indirect message to Frank, telling him that now he has to speak up. Note that the therapist implies that Carla is hurt, not that she's angry, even though until this point Carla has not expressed hurt. By bringing "hurt" into the picture, the therapist gives Frank a nudge toward Carla, something Frank would not be inclined to do if he only saw her as furious.

> Frank: Well, I am . . . I *am* sorry. I don't know what I was thinking. I was just so worried about Amy.
>
> Carla: Then why . . .
>
> Therapist: Let him finish, please. Frank . . .
>
> Frank: I don't know why! I was scared, I guess.
>
> Carla: Well, so was I!

The therapist is beginning to feel annoyed with Carla because she's keeping up the self-righteous blame, without recognizing or appreciating the extraordinary effort Frank is making to accept responsibility for his poor performance. Realizing that she now feels more in tune with Frank than with Carla, the therapist decides to talk with them as a couple.

> Therapist: Carla, Frank, wait! This is just so tough. I know you're both suffering, and you're both worried to death about Amy, but you're not hearing each other. You're both feeling bad, *bad*, BAD about this! Let's take a step back and see just how much each of you

understands about how the other is feeling, okay? [*pause*] Frank, what's going on with Carla right now, right this minute?

The decision to ask Frank to demonstrate an empathic understanding for Carla is deliberate. The therapist begins with Frank rather than with Carla to re-balance the emotional scale, having recognized that in the previous sequence she (the therapist) was feeling too much on Frank's side, seeing him as the underdog. By asking the couple to talk to her directly rather than to each other, the therapist gives each partner the space to listen, think, and calm down.

This time Frank takes the hint and describes the level of anger, hurt, fear, and abandonment he imagined Carla felt when he wasn't there for her at the hospital. In listening to him, Carla is shocked to hear the words *afraid* and *abandoned,* words she was feeling but that she had kept hidden from Frank and even from herself. Recognizing Frank's implicit apology and request for forgiveness, Carla begins crying. At this, the therapist sees that the emotional breakthrough she'd been hoping for has come about. Nudging Frank to offer Carla a hug, the therapist remains silent. When Frank moves toward Carla, Carla lets loose with her pain. She relaxes into his arms, holding on tight, finally allowing herself to be comforted.

Spontaneously, then, Frank begins talking from the heart about his own self-doubt and insecurity, his feeling that he would be "in the way" at the hospital, that in fact he *always* feels "in the way." He thought he couldn't do anything for Amy or for Carla, and he now sees that he rationalized his staying away to avoid his own overwhelming fears for his daughter and his sense of impotence in the situation. These were thoughts and feelings that Carla had no clue about, and hearing Frank express them is, for her, profoundly healing.

In this situation, the therapist was able to avoid alienating either spouse by running through the following process in her mind as Carla heatedly expostulated her blaming point of view. The therapist's first reaction was horror that a father could be so "cold-hearted" as to "abandon" his wife and child under life-threatening circumstances. Then, the therapist remembered that she liked Frank and had always seen him as a good person who tried his best and genuinely cared for his family. Seeing his miserable countenance as his wife railed at him, the therapist wondered why Frank had behaved so badly. Yes, he was a "workaholic," but that epithet did not explain his behavior in this circumstance. A mother herself, it would have been easy for the therapist to take Carla's side, and, in fact, she'd thought, "If I were in her shoes, I'd be incredibly mad at him, too. I wouldn't tolerate this kind of a thing in a husband."

The therapist's next thought was, "But if it *were* me, I'd be sad and scared, too, that maybe this means my husband is not the guy I thought he was. I'd think that I can't back down now, and maybe it'll wind up that I'll just have to leave him. Maybe it's inevitable." With this vicarious introspection, the therapist recognizes just how scared Carla must be under her angry bravado. Having this understanding, the therapist realized that how she chose to respond to Carla's challenge would have powerful, potentially irreversible consequences for this couple, especially if to save face Carla needed to push the issue beyond the point of no return. If the therapist could find a way to allow Frank to explain himself, maybe even to apologize, then Carla might just be able to back down enough for some kind of mutual understanding to take place.

Empathy is not about sympathy; nor is it about simply showing concern. Fundamentally, empathy is about understanding (Nichols, 1987) or creating shared meanings through which people come to know one another (Weingarten, 1992). In this illustration, the therapist observed the pain in Frank's face and intuited that he felt bad about his behavior. She could also put herself in Carla's shoes, and she realized that Carla could hardly back down after she had described Frank's behavior as inexcusable.

This vignette illustrates the therapist's strategic use of "felt reality," as described by Hardham (1998):

> Our emotions or felt realities can only be understood in relation. That is, I can only make sense of my felt reality in the context of [a] particular therapeutic relationship. . . . My felt reality is the most immediate way in which I am embedded within the relationship. Our felt realities (or emotions) may also be the most significant way in which we are embodied. . . . [U]nderstanding our felt reality is understanding the link between our embeddedness and our embodiedness. To make a systemic sense of our felt reality in relationships we need to address the way in which relational, cultural, and theoretical constructions shape our individual experience, and the ways in which our felt reality shapes our relationships and our practice. Our felt reality, as shaped by our pre-reflective reactions and our rational (even if "forgotten") theoretical reflections, is what is enacted in the process of therapy. The expression of our felt reality is use of self in relationship. (p. 80)

Any time a therapist uses the self, whether consciously or unconsciously, he or she is experiencing a felt reality in a specific therapeutic context (Hardham, 1998). Detached from an awareness of their own values, reactions, and embodied feelings, therapists risk becoming "technocratic and impersonal" (p. 82). When the therapist is unresponsive on an emotional level, the therapy is devoid of the humanness that is a necessary prerequisite for change.

BEING THERE

It is not enough to join with a family at the outset of treatment or express empathy whenever people are hurting. A sustained emotional con-

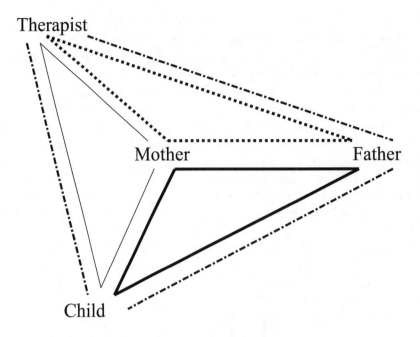

Figure 5.1. Interlocking triangles in a four-person therapeutic system.

nection is the analgesic to dull the pain of potentially tumultuous change in the treatment process. After all, therapists ask clients to take enormous risks with the people closest to them, and the consequences of taking those risks can be disastrous or liberating. To take risks, clients need to be assured that the therapist believes in them, applauds their efforts, and takes pleasure if they succeed or feels badly if they fail.

When a therapist joins a couple, the system changes from a dyad to a triad. When there are three members in a family, the therapeutic system is therapist + family group as well as the therapist as one leg of four interlocking emotional triangles (see Figure 5.1). With four family members, there are 4 within-family triangles and 10 additional triangles when a therapist enters the system. In other words, the exponentially increasing number of triadic subsystems reflects the complexity of developing and sustaining positive emotional relationships within a conflict-ridden family system.

Triangular subsystems are interdependent, and flexibility is the essential approach for keeping the system as free as possible from growth-inhibiting tensions (Bowen, 1976). As the newest member in the group, the therapist has the most flexibility to influence the affective tensions between and among family members. To do so, he or she must constantly shift emotional positions, moving close in and far away as the process demands (Minuchin & Fishman, 1981).

The following case illustrates the use of triangles in regulating the therapy's emotional process. The Lopez parents, Jenri and Angelina, were struggling to adjust to a rapidly changing adolescent, Milvia (14 years old), while they were still grieving the loss of their older daughter, Ana, who had died of cancer 2 years earlier. When Milvia refused to attend the first therapy session, Jenri and Angelina came alone. Thus, the initial therapeutic connection was with the couple, who, as parents, were at once outraged with and hurting for their child. They described Milvia as "mouthy" at home, failing in school, and an outcast with her peers.

With great reluctance and fanfare, Milvia arrived at Session 2. Her silence spoke volumes, as she sat slumped in her seat, arms crossed across her chest, a baseball cap shading her downcast eyes. Unable to engage Milvia in small talk, the therapist redirected the session. He asked Milvia to help him construct a genogram of the family history. All she had to do was draw the circles, squares, and lines with the therapist's guidance. The therapist made it clear that there was no need for Milvia to comment on anything that was being discussed.

Developing the genogram, the therapist engaged each parent in a lighthearted discussion of the background and relationships of all extended family members. As the session progressed, Milvia began commenting on what was being said, correcting her parents' mistakes. Eventually she made eye contact with them as they joked good-naturedly about this or that member of the family.

When the session was coming to a close, the therapist thanked Milvia for her help. Because she nodded in response, smiling, the therapist decided to try connecting with her in a personal way. "Milvia," he said, "you seem to have a better memory for the facts about your family than your Mom and Dad do. This makes me think that you might have a lot to say about what concerns them. But, probably . . . no [pause], I don't think you're quite ready to let me in on what you're feeling just yet." At this, Milvia began talking rapidly and with feeling about how far off base her parents were about her: She *had* no problems. *They* had all the problems. *Who* did they think she was, anyway? and "I'm not their 'perfect little Ana!'" Hearing this, the therapist moved his seat so as to be in front of Milvia and block her view of her parents. Speaking slowly and deliberately, he said, "No, of course you aren't Ana. And you *shouldn't* be. We don't have the time to get into this today, but eventually, if you let me, I want to help you explain that to your parents, because maybe they don't get it. And if they don't, they need to." Milvia sniffed back a tear in response, and without letting her answer, the therapist quickly brought the session to an end.

This vignette illustrates the therapist's use of emotional triangles to connect first with the parents and then with a reluctant adolescent. The bond with the parents began in Session 1: three adults putting their heads together to try and figure out how to reach a troubled child. When Milvia joined her parents in Session 2, she made it abundantly clear that she would have nothing to do with an emotional process in which she was labeled the problem. Modeling flexibility, the therapist redirected the session, enlisting Milvia's aid in an easy, nonemotional task that allowed her to be a part of things but stay on the periphery.

At first, Milvia watched the therapist's easy, playful manner with her parents as they discussed their relationships with her grandparents, aunts, uncles, and cousins. Then, as Milvia loosened up enough to banter with her parents about various family members' foibles, the mother–father–daughter triangle reasserted itself, this time with the therapist in the background. Sensing the positive energy in the system, the therapist took the risk to speak directly and personally with Milvia, first complimenting her on her memory and then suggesting a perspective on the family that empowered her. When Milvia responded with anger and finally gave a clue about where the hurt really was for her ("I'm not their 'perfect little Ana!'"), the therapist aligned with her, offering assistance in the battle *she* wanted to fight, that is, to stop competing with her deceased sister.

By ending the session abruptly after Milvia's tearful disclosure, the therapist gave her space and privacy, modeling sensitivity. Another aspect of the therapist's work in this session is noteworthy. He delivered his thoughts about Milvia in a personal, tentative, and transparent manner. Transparency builds connections where concealment threatens them.

As the therapy progressed from this point on, the therapist moved closer to and further from each dyad in the family as the content demanded. For example, the therapist encouraged mother and daughter to talk about "girl stuff," joking with Jenri about how they two (Jenri and the therapist) really didn't "get it." Later, the therapist helped Angelina sit on the sidelines while father and daughter argued about Jenri's involvement in Milvia's soccer team. Eventually, two sessions later, Milvia was finally ready to tell her mother how she felt second-best to her deceased older sister. The therapist first supported Milvia in her right to express herself and then supported Angelina in how hard this was for her to hear. When Jenri tried to jump in to rescue his wife, the therapist told him, "We men need to sit back and watch them work it out. I know they can!" After a time, Angelina tearfully apologized to Milvia for having set her up in a competition she couldn't win. When Milvia, crying now too, went to hug her mother, the therapist motioned for Jenri to reach out and join them in their emotional release.

CONCLUSION

When couples and families get to the point where they need professional help because their lives together have become unmanageable, they are understandably tense about what will be said in therapy. How will the problem be framed? Will someone be blamed? Is there any hope? Although at the outset of treatment family members are concerned about what the therapist will be like and how astute he or she will be, establishing an emotional bond with the therapist is unlikely to be of prime concern. What is more likely to be on the minds of each family member is what the *other* family members will say.

Eventually, however, the therapist comes to take on more importance in the emotional life of the family. Like a nurturant grandparent, the effective therapist uses both affection and influence to move around the emotional energy in a conflict-ridden system. The therapist's use of self is the most powerful tool for effecting change.

6

SAFETY WITHIN THE
THERAPEUTIC SYSTEM

Risk taking in the presence of a therapist can bring people to a new level of intimacy, trust, and optimism, a new beginning for a shattered family. When all seems hopeless, many clients (with the support of a therapist) get the courage to say something risky to other family members, only to discover that their long-held, private fears were groundless. A wife finally tells her husband that she'd been raped as a child, and he responds with loving reassurance. A child tells his father that he can't possibly measure up to expectations, and the father shows gentleness, understanding, and humor.

Arguably, couples and family members need to feel vulnerable at some point during treatment to reap the full benefits of therapy. Indeed, vulnerability is so closely associated with therapeutic change that many therapists consider it a necessary part of the process. A founding father in the field, Carl Whitaker, made it his business to raise a family's anxiety to an uncomfortable level. According to Whitaker, heightened anxiety is necessary to crack the homeostatic barrier to true intimacy (Whitaker & Keith, 1981).

Long-standing relationships naturally make family members vulnerable to each other. When difficulties arise it is common for people to feel vulnerable or fearful. Fear arises not only from uncertainty about how significant others will react to frank disclosure but also from concerns about what those others might reveal to a therapist. For this reason, the decision to expose a close relationship to a professional can be frightening.

In many cases, a couple or members of a family seek therapy together when they see their relationships as damaged or affected by some other problem. Often before even seeing the therapist's reaction, family members are so acutely aware of their difficulties that they believe negative consequences are inevitable. For example, a few minutes into Session 1, a husband described this feeling to his wife: "You see, we're in this together, the two of us in a cage with the beast we most fear—our arguments." Hearing this, the therapist pictured himself as a lion tamer, striking the whip.

In the System for Observing Family Therapy Alliances (SOFTA), we define *safety* as

> the client viewing therapy as a place to take risks, be open, vulnerable, flexible; a sense of comfort and an expectation that new experiences and learning will take place, that good can come from being in therapy, that conflict within the family can be handled without harm, that one need not be defensive. (Friedlander, Escudero, Heatherington, Diehl, et al., 2004, p. 5)

Therapists cannot take for granted that therapy is a safe place for all clients. On the contrary, it is vitally important to consider, at the outset as well as throughout therapy, whether the context that clients are experiencing is safe enough for them to risk change. To create a safe therapeutic system, therapists must consider not only their implicit contracts with clients (and with other professionals involved in the case) but also how the clients perceive the treatment context and procedures. Note that the nature of the family's problems and the historical intrafamilial relations play a major role in the safety clients feel in a conjoint treatment format.

THEORY AND RESEARCH

How can a therapeutic system (i.e., therapist + family) reach an optimal level of safety? To date, little has been written about ensuring safety in couple and family therapy. However, in one qualitative study (Christensen et al., 1998), safety was found to be an important precondition for change in couple therapy. As the authors explained, "A safe context means that clients feel that they have a trusting connection with the therapist and do not fear repercussions from their partner for what is said or done in therapy" (p. 183).

In a study of time-limited therapy with low-income families (Friedlander, Escudero, Horvath, et al., in press), we found that safety-related behaviors (showing vulnerability, expressing painful emotions, family members asking each other for feedback, etc.) in the middle of treatment (Session 6) were positively associated with clients' possession ratings of the depth or value of the session. By Session 9, safety behavior was strongly associated with therapists' evaluations of the session as well.

In M. Beck et al.'s (in press) case studies, safety behaviors varied widely, depending on who in the family attended the session. It is important to note that the only families to show negative indicators of safety (SOFTA–o) in early sessions had the poorest outcomes. In private interviews with the researchers, some clients explained that they distrusted professionals or felt unsafe because of historical mistrust between family members, blame, self-blame, and fears about privacy violations.

Although writers have had little to say about strategies for ensuring safety in couple and family therapy, therapeutic handling of intrafamilial hostility is undoubtedly the most important factor in creating safety. The therapist's ability to control and channel expressions of blame, contempt, and hostility depend on the nature of his or her training and therapeutic orientation. Regardless of approach, however, effective therapists do not ignore their clients' feelings of vulnerability (e.g., signs of fear or defensiveness, excessive anxiety, or tearful outbursts). It is not uncommon for family members to need protection from others' harassments and accusations or from intrusiveness into their personal lives. Obviously, therapy is not therapeutic when family conflict escalates to the point of verbal and physical threats or intimidations.

Studying therapists' responses to family blaming, Friedlander, Heatherington, and Marrs (2000) analyzed seven therapy sessions conducted by constructivist theorists Harlene Anderson, Carlos Sluzki, Bill Lax, Steve de Shazer, Michael White, and others. Of the 17 strategies that these experts used in response to intrafamilial blaming, ignoring–directing kinds of responses (e.g., focusing on the positive and highlighting neutral information) were most common, but the therapists also challenged all-or-none thinking, questioned the blamer about the other person's perspective, and reframed the family's conflict when blame was displayed.

In a recent study of blaming events in emotion-focused couples therapy (Bradley & Furrow, 2004), therapists were successful when they "facilitated clients' emotional experiencing and promoted their disclosure of fears around attachment needs" (p. 243). Asking clients to forgo blame and imagine new ways of interacting with each other, the therapists explicitly modeled vulnerability and risk taking. One therapist in the study said the following to a blaming wife:

> If you said to him, "Phil, right now, some part of me wants to connect with you but a lot of me is afraid and tells me to stay back and defend myself, and don't trust, and I feel scared. . . . I feel cornered. I feel scared. . . . I have waited for you all this time and now when you say you want to be here, the ironic thing is, I can't come out and meet you." If you were

to say that to him and he said (therapist gets soft) "It's okay Julie. Come here and let me give you a hug. I understand you're scared." Could you let him? Could you let him comfort you? (p. 239)

SAFETY: A CONTEXT FOR RISK TAKING AND CHANGE

An obvious clue to the client's comfort is relaxed nonverbal behavior, even if he or she is not feeling well. However, anxious nonverbal behavior does not necessarily signal a lack of safety. Anxiety often accompanies significant risk taking. When, despite anxiety, clients show flexibility—not only accepting the need but also actively trying out something different—clients are affirming therapy as a safe place.

Marta Everley, the 35-year-old mother of a 7-year-old daughter, came to therapy with her 36-year-old husband, Peter, because she was dissatisfied with everything about their family life. Marta complained about a lack of energy and motivation to care for her daughter. She also felt an inexplicable indifference in her relationship with Peter and scorn for everything related to the family that only 6 months earlier had been her life's project. For his part, Peter tried to avoid therapy (which had been recommended by the family physician); at first, he assigned little importance to Marta's problems, and later, he attempted "home remedies," such as a weekend ski-trip and dinner with friends. Finally Peter and Marta took the plunge.

In Session 1, Peter compulsively listed his virtues to the therapist, relating all he had done for the family, what a great father he was, and so on. Marta, however, was tremendously nervous, her anxiety evident not only in her speech but also in her rigid posture. When the therapist said, warmly and empathically, "Making the decision to come to therapy demonstrates your interest in one another and in your relationship, and also shows your *bravery* in the difficult situation you're going through," both spouses responded emotionally. Peter began crying, timidly and discreetly. Later, he confessed his fear that Marta would use therapy to tell him she was no longer in love with him. Marta, also holding back tears, disclosed her fear that the therapist's interpretation of her depression would hurt her husband or her daughter.

Taking a meaningful risk (as did both Peter and Marta) is the clearest evidence of safety within the therapeutic system. Another indicator of safety occurs when one family member asks another for feedback or for an honest impression of himself. When, for example, a man asks his wife, "Do you think I'm a good father?" or "Do you think I 'lose it' with our daughter too often?," he has taken a risk, exposing himself to possible responses that could very well hurt. Obviously, the tone of such questions needs to be sincere and genuine. When a wife tearfully asks her husband if he still sees her as attractive, the question—seen as a bid for intimacy—can stimulate a caring response. When asked in a reproachful tone of voice, the same question communicates blame and defensiveness.

Indeed, how members of a couple or a family communicate with each other in front of a therapist is a fundamental source of information about feelings of safety or lack thereof. What is important to note is the *relational* or interpersonal level of communication (Heatherington & Friedlander, 2004), that is, not the content of what family members say to each other but the manner and tone of these interchanges. Thus, for example, a family member's reluctance to answer a question or respond to another's comment could be a clear sign that she or he is feeling threatened if, in the tone of voice, the relational meaning is, "I don't want to talk about this here" or "It's not something I could or would share with you." Nonverbal behavior can suggest whether silence in response to a question is simply the result of not knowing how to respond or a sign of reluctance or a refusal to engage.

The act of diverting the communication toward a third person, either the therapist or another family member, can signal a lack of felt safety. In response to a question of the type, "Why won't you let my son succeed in your company?", a stepfather shows his discomfort by turning away from his wife and commenting to the therapist, "Do you have any idea of the responsibility a person has in a business like mine? Can you explain this to my wife?"

A lack of safety in therapy can also prompt competitive symmetry, that is, sequences of interaction in which two members of the family struggle for dominance. Such a struggle is evident when, for example, a husband says, "We haven't come here to talk about what I do or not do at home, but about our son's problems at school" and the wife answers, "We've come here to talk about *everything* that's important for our son to get a good education!" or "Why should *you* be the one to decide what we are going to talk about?!" Although competitive interactions between family members can signal problems other than a lack of safety (see chap. 7, "Shared Sense of Purpose Within the Family"), defensive exchanges between family members are common indicators of threat.

When family members are on the defensive, it is common for one person to criticize or demand an explanation, prompting a laundry list of complaints from the recipient. This cross-complaining pattern of communication (Gottman, 1994) occurs when one family member complains about another's behavior, asking for an explanation, and the other responds by complaining about the first person without providing any justification for the original complaint. Being on the defensive is not necessarily a result of hostility or guilt, but it may be a way of not facing responsibility. In a session with a couple and their adolescent daughter, the mother (speaking in the plural to include her daughter) said to her husband, "You have to tell us what's making you so aggressive in the last few months. You never used to shout at Julia or me over such unimportant issues." Raising his voice defensively, the husband replied, "I don't know why you're asking *me* this! *You* were the one who yelled at everyone last summer when we accidentally left the water running!"

It is relatively easy to recognize threats generated within the family itself and threats that are by-products of difficulties between individual family members and the therapist. Other threats to safety, often overlooked, arise from within the therapist system, that is, from strains or conflicts between the therapist and important members of her or his professional system—supervisor, team, or other professionals involved in the case (see chap. 14). On occasion, these others get involved in the treatment as members of a reflecting team, cotherapists, or supervisors who intervene periodically. Consider the exponentially increasing complexity as more individuals are added to (a) the *direct system of the patient* (family members who attend therapy conjointly), (b) the *indirect system of the patient* (members of the patient's family not involved directly in the therapy), (c) the *direct system of the therapist* (members of the professional team directly involved in a given session at a particular moment in time), or (d) the *indirect system of the therapist* (team members not directly involved in the therapy; Pinsof, 1994). Because the sources of potential threat, both intrasystems and intersystems, are multiple, having a broad "systemic map" of the treatment process offers us many potential resources for creating and consolidating safe therapeutic contexts for our clients.

A lack of safety can be pronounced and dramatic when clients are mandated for treatment by Family Court or Child Protective Services, when clients are pressured into therapy by family members, or when outside institutions, without legal mandate, have direct or indirect power over them. Chapter 11 deals specifically with mandated clients and the many ways people can wind up feeling like "therapy hostages." We cannot make the point strongly enough that attempts at treatment are futile if the therapist does not ensure a minimum level of safety.

Juana and Ramón, a young couple, successfully completed a family reunification program. Both were recovering from alcoholism when their son, Raúl, was born. Everything was fine until the boy began school at age 6, when both parents had been unemployed for quite awhile. Ramón started drinking heavily, arguments at home escalated, and Juana became overprotective of Raúl, keeping him out of school—for even minor ailments and colds. The boy's school absences, the increasing marital conflicts, and the husband's alcoholic relapse alerted social services. The legal measures were severe. Raúl was placed in a residential facility while his parents were mandated for treatment.

In situations like this one, Session 1 offers clients the opportunity to complain bitterly, sometimes with hostility, about everything that has happened to them. When the circumstances feel punitive, it is not unusual for the therapist to be seen as an enemy, even if he or she is working independently of the mandating referral source. How can therapy feel safe under these circumstances? Sometimes it's not even safe for the therapist.

For Juana and Ramón, despite the rocky start, important changes did take place, resulting in a joyful reunion with their son. In a follow-up session, the therapist asked Juana to reflect on how treatment began. She said,

> When I had already come here 6 or 7 times and was feeling calm and helped, I kept thinking that your explanation for using a video camera to work in a team was a lie. I know I signed a document or something like that, but I always thought that later you'd show the videos to Child Protective or that they'd be used as evidence to show the judge. Later, and I don't know why, I trusted you . . . and I felt good.

The therapist used a video camera to tape the sessions to analyze the case and design interventions with a team. Although this procedure was explained to the clients (and they signed an informed consent document), they nonetheless believed the video would be used as "evidence" by Child Protective Services. This example, as so many others, reminds us not to undervalue our clients' feelings of vulnerability and, in some cases, justifiable mistrust.

SECRETS, INTIMACY, AND INTENSE EMOTIONS

Family secrets have a particularly negative effect on safety. A secret that produces shame, causes symptoms (Imber-Black, 1993), and interferes with or muddles family relationships (and relations with the therapist) can have an unknown influence on the therapeutic process. Clues that secrets are in the air include excessive anxiety and defensive or avoidant maneuvering when specific topics are brought up or alluded to.

The Martínez family is a case in point. Manuel Martínez and his wife, Rosa, came to therapy with their two sons, 16-year-old David and 20-year-old Roberto. The initial motivation was the younger son's drug use (hashish and pills), which had led to problems at school, heated arguments at home, and aggression directed at Roberto. After several sessions, the therapist was worried and confused about the parents' passivity and heightened anxiety when talking about what was or was not "normal" drug use. As expected, the younger son had an extremely tolerant and unrealistic view of drugs (e.g., "Everybody takes them nowadays," "They help you when you want to have fun, also to work"). David's older brother, well aware of drug usage among high school youth, was openly worried about the risks his brother was taking. The parents, however, aside from emphatically rejecting all kinds of drugs in their lives, were reluctant to discuss how David's substance abuse related to his circle of friends, the school environment, or his extracurricular activities.

After four sessions, Rosa requested a session alone with her husband. The therapist acceded, with the children's knowledge. During the couple session, the family secret came out: Manuel had been addicted to both drugs and alcohol during his youth and in his early relationship with Rosa. The boys had no knowledge of their father's history. In the family sessions, the parents' tension arose from fear that this shameful information would have to come out. Rosa and Manuel not only were unsure of their sons' reaction but also feared a loss of parental authority and respect. After revealing the secret to the therapist, the parents had the courage to talk with their sons about Manuel's drug involvement in a way that added to their credibility and enhanced feelings of closeness in the family.

Sometimes, without prompting, a client deliberately reveals a secret or sensitive information that had not been widely known. Doing so is a significant indicator of just how valued and safe the therapy is for the individual. As one example, adolescents may make "revelations" to their parents in therapy that would never take place elsewhere. When therapy is seen as neutral territory and the adolescent feels protected by the therapist, it is not uncommon for his parents to learn important information that the teen had tenaciously kept private. Leah, a 13-year-old who was referred for therapy by the school for behavioral problems and truancy, revealed to her parents not only how often and how she would escape from school, but also how she felt doing it: "Actually, it was boring, sitting there outside on a bench for so many hours, even when it was cold out, but I wanted my friends to know that I was the one who cut class the most. I broke the record!" This revelation, spoken with sincerity, relieved the parents of their worst fears about their daughter's behavior. After this session, the entire family's motivation for therapy increased noticeably. Everyone understood that both conflict and fear could be handled safely and constructively.

Safety is essential when clients express painful feelings or other communications that may be difficult for one reason or another. Particularly when there is a high level of conflict or distrust, it can be painfully difficult for a husband to ask for forgiveness, for a father to tell his son that he lost control, for an elderly parent to speak openly about her terminal illness, for a mother to admit being depressed, for a daughter to ask if her father loves her, for a woman to ask her partner if he's planning to abandon her. Ideally, the therapeutic context should encourage people to open up, share painful feelings, and express difficult emotions to the important people in their lives. It is not necessary, however, for every painful feeling to be scrutinized for therapy to be successful. The importance of doing so varies with the nature of the problem, the therapist's approach, the clients' personal and interpersonal characteristics, and so on. Nonetheless, the inability to be even a bit vulnerable in front of one's family members can be a serious barrier to effective treatment.

Sometimes in-session family interactions, spontaneous or stimulated by the therapist, can enhance safety dramatically. To illustrate, Lindsay brought her adolescent son, Tim, to therapy. Worried that he may be using drugs, she adopted a kind and loving tone of voice, telling her son not to be afraid of telling the truth: "We won't be alarmed or angry if we know that you've used drugs. We can only help you if you are open with us; we need to know the situation you are in so we can help each other." This kind of message is more effective coming from a parent than from the therapist when the tone and nonverbal expression clearly communicate that it is safe to be open in therapy. Even if the child refuses to disclose his problems on demand, the context for safety is made explicit. When a family member's tone is critical, blaming, or tense, the opposite result may ensue, damaging the safety zone for all involved.

SAFETY ON THE THERAPIST'S TURF

Therapists try to create a pleasant setting for their clients and adapt the physical environment to meet their needs. Nevertheless, when coming to therapy for the first time, many clients feel uncomfortable in their therapist's office, which is unfamiliar territory. The lack of familiarity and degree of discomfort clients feel at the outset of treatment varies from setting to setting and from one individual to the next. Therapy sessions conducted in a hospital or health center, with typical medical furniture, colors, smells, and health care personnel, can intimidate some clients, but others may feel more comfortable in this sanitized context than they would in a therapist's private home, for example. Without devaluing therapeutic work carried out in clients' homes, we recommend conducting therapy sessions in a professional setting, one that is neutral for the family. When the context is unfamiliar, it is easier for someone outside the family system to control the situation and set the ground rules for appropriate behavior.

Clients must be able to view the therapeutic environment as safe. Obviously, safety does not depend on the physical conditions per se, but on the impression they make on the client. Some clients refuse to take a comfortable chair or relax on a sofa, preferring to sit rigidly. Some clients keep their coats on even when the room temperature is comfortable. Holding objects in their hand—an umbrella or purse, for example—is yet another clue that a client feels unsafe. We generally interpret these types of behavior as the client's uncertainty about staying and participating, as if he or she is "just passing through." Although such nonverbal displays can be a sign of covert, unspoken tensions among family members, a client's discomfort, especially during the initial therapy contact, may simply be due to the unfamiliar professional setting.

Unfortunately, some aspects of our work detract from our clients' safety, as when we use cameras or one-way mirrors to permit a supervisor or team to participate unobserved. Working with an invisible team (i.e., one that is not introduced to the family) can be inhibiting and even intimidating. All of the clinical information, process notes as well as recordings, can also generate threat, especially if the problems under discussion have potential legal ramifications, as when couples are separating or divorcing, or when Child Protective Services is involved in the case.

In Session 9 of couple therapy, a wife commented, "I've decided to speak clearly about some things, although I'm never sure which people will make up the 'team of spies' each day." She was referring to the observing supervisor and team (students in training) who typically met with the therapist halfway through the session to plan a strategic intervention. The therapist and team members were quite surprised at the "spies" metaphor, inasmuch as the client had come to treatment voluntarily and consented to the team format. Nevertheless, one should not underestimate the threat clients can feel in contexts that we strive to make comfortable for them. In another case, this time with an adolescent, the boy's comment was also telling. When the therapist received an intercom call from the supervisor who was observing the session on closed circuit television, the boy remarked, "So they called you . . . I thought that for the past two or three weeks we weren't doing it right . . . I think it's my fault . . . it's just that there are things that I would rather just tell you."

Although we have been focusing on threats to safety, therapists should also recognize when family members feel "right at home" (or even much better than at home!), appreciating the therapy setting as the only safe place in their lives where they are free to discuss significant concerns. One indication that therapy feels safe is a comment like, "We were about to fight about this yesterday but then decided to wait till we came here to talk it over civilly" or "In the midst of the argument, when we were both upset and angry, I thought to myself, 'What would [therapist's name] say right now?' and so I decided to . . ." Indicators of safety can also be metaphorical. One parent blurted out, just as the therapy session was beginning, "Can we make a suggestion about this plant of yours? We've been thinking about it for several weeks." She was referring to a large houseplant that the therapist had in his office that did not look very healthy. The family kindly offered to resuscitate the plant. They offered not only to show the therapist some gardening tips but also to take the plant home with them. A few weeks later, the plant returned in perfect shape and in a new flower pot.

CREATING SAFETY

Therapy-related changes generally require people to accept and try out new patterns of behavior and different cognitive perspectives on their problems. Indeed, being flexible and willing to consider alternate points of view are fundamental prerequisites for change. However, these attitudes are not always easily elicited when feelings of frustration, psychological fatigue, impotence, and abandonment—all commonly experienced by clients starting therapy—are the motivators for seeking help. Therefore, when therapy has begun, the first change to look for is a shift from an atmosphere of frustration, fatigue, and impotence to one of flexibility, positive expectation, and hope.

Because conflict, whether overt or covert, heightens vulnerability, managing conflict is necessary before problems can be analyzed and solutions found. Therapists working with relationships that are contaminated with accusations and hostility must first create a safety zone where conflict can be approached without harm. Indeed, the level of safety can improve radically when the therapist is able to contain and control the conflict, converting it into something constructive. As one step along the way, the therapist should give family members a clear explanation for all aspects of the treatment context that relate to confidentiality (i.e., content of the sessions, use of tape recordings, reports for third parties, inclusion of a therapeutic team or supervision, use of data for research). As part and parcel of this process, the therapist should encourage family members to talk about aspects in the therapy that may intimidate them or produce mistrust. Particularly when clients seem hesitant or reluctant to speak their mind, it behooves the therapist to directly or indirectly address the source of discomfort.

Other factors that can influence safety within therapy have to do with characteristics of the clients' culture, traditions, lifestyle, or religion (also see chap. 10). When, for example, therapy touches on aspects of the clients' sex life, or conflicts between subsystems (parents–children or grandparents–grandchildren), or decisions about terminal illnesses, or about the education of the children, or a child's use of alcohol or drugs, the therapist's ability to understand and accommodate the therapy to the family's sociocultural or religious values is critically important.

Working with a poor Romani (Gypsy) family in Spain, a therapist was confronted with a conflict over the family decision that it was time for the daughter to marry her boyfriend. It is interesting to note that although this young woman, her parents, and grandparents all liked the boyfriend, and although she loved him and wanted to marry him, the young couple disagreed with the rest of the family about the timing of their marriage (they wanted to wait 2 years) and about whether to have the traditional Romani ceremony. Quickly realizing that the therapist had no knowledge of their traditions, the parents doubted that he could help them through this conflict.

Actually, what had prompted the family to request help initially was the daughter's depression and somatization, expressed as headaches and gastrointestinal problems. The parents not only had voluntarily sought out a therapist for their daughter but also had eagerly played an active role in the treatment process. However, at the point when the daughter's wedding became the focus of discussion, the family's cooperation was severely threatened. Simply put, they mistrusted the therapist's ability to understand the Romani point of view.

In response, the therapist organized a special session in which the oldest, most influential person in the extended family, the mother's cousin, explained to him in detail the family and community wedding traditions. The cousin took on an authoritative role in the session, educating the therapist, while the rest of the family looked on passively. This "teacher" was revered by the parents and the daughter because of her influential role in the community and her knowledge and respect for Romani traditions. She had an open mind and was flexible about the young couple's demands for change. Therapy after the conjoint session was not easy, but the family recognized and appreciated the therapist's willingness to learn about the family's culture and his promise to respect and consider their traditions.

In working with conflict-ridden families in which violence is a real risk, the creation of safety becomes especially important. The therapist must not only deflect blame and hostility, protecting clients from each other, but also stay allied with all members involved in the conflict. The threat may not always be perceptible, however. A client may keep quiet, not trusting that what he says won't be used against him later. Consider Suzanne, an 11-year-old who sat stiffly silent through a meeting with her abusive mother, her social worker, and foster parents. Despite her youth, Suzanne knew that whatever she chose to say about her situation could have major, irreversible consequences. Cases of abuse and neglect, where the need to assess safety is essential, are discussed in more detail in chapter 11 (mandated clients).

In individual therapy, clients have control over what to reveal about themselves. There is no worry that their private concerns will be revealed by another person. In conjoint treatment, however, it is common for secrets or unspoken thoughts and feelings to arise. Whereas such revelations are normal, even routine, for the family therapist, this is not the case for family members. For this reason, effective therapists explain to clients that therapy, by its very nature, involves taking risks and feeling vulnerable at times. Such explanations can also function as "reframes" when the going gets rough. In fact, normalizing fear and vulnerability can go a long way toward restoring safety.

The creation of safety also depends in large measure on the therapist's comfort level. It is essential for the therapist to feel secure as the therapy unfolds, but this is not always possible. The therapist's sense of security may be compromised for any number of reasons—poor training or a lack of experience with difficult cases, personal characteristics or biases, or the interference of a personal crisis. Providing effective couple therapy when having major difficulties in one's own marriage can be particularly challenging. Professional influences can also compromise security; these include such things as fears of criticism from a supervisor or other professionals involved in the case, for example (see chap. 14). When the therapist's sense of safety is jeopardized, he or she may be able to hide the source of his distress from the clients, but a nonverbal expression of anxiety or discomfort may be visible, and it can jeopardize family members' sense of comfort. Effective training and supervision can help a therapist become aware of these problems before they harm clients; a supportive supervisor and staff are the therapist's best safeguards. Simply put, projecting personal fears on a family is a risk that therapists should not underestimate, especially with highly conflict-ridden couples or families and whenever there is a risk of violence or suicide.

CASE ILLUSTRATION: LOVE AND NEED

Charlie and Carmen were married when he was 54 and she was 49. Widowed 6 years earlier, Carmen described her first marriage as a "complete disaster." When she married Charlie, Carmen's finances were in complete disarray, but Charlie's economic situation was sound. Never having lived with a partner before Carmen, Charlie felt vulnerable on that account. Moreover, he was hard of hearing, and consequently his articulation was poor, and he had never learned an alternate form of communication. Both spouses described themselves as "loners" before finding each other, and they had few, generally poor relations with relatives.

After 2 years of marriage, Carmen requested professional help. Although she thought it would be beneficial for Charlie to take part in the sessions, she was unsure how it would go, given her husband's communication difficulties.

In Session 1, the level of tension between Carmen and Charlie was extremely high. They argued loudly, expressing hostility over even the slightest disagreement. The therapist took control and was able to regulate the interaction by asking for Carmen's help to understand Charlie. The therapist insisted that the couple take turns speaking so that she could fully understand their concerns. However, the couple's anxiety was quite evident, along with many verbal and nonverbal indicators of a lack of safety (reluctance to speak directly to each other, defensive responding, demonstrable tension and physical distancing, etc.). The following occurred at a point during the Session 3.

> *Therapist:* Perhaps we should be clear on how therapy can help each one of you. What would you like to accomplish by coming here?
>
> *Carmen:* To make a decision. I want to know if I can live with him or if I have to be brave and get a separation.
>
> *Charlie:* [*very nervous, speaking loudly and noticeably upset*] If we're going to talk about separation, then I'll leave. [*to the therapist*] She tricked me. She said we were coming here to fix things!
>
> *Therapist:* Charlie, she just said how therapy can help her. What could you get out of coming here?
>
> *Charlie:* [*very nervous*] I'm not going to say anything if you are recording the session!

Therapist:	Fine, that won't be a problem. We can stop recording right now. [*turns off recorder*] The important thing is that you feel comfortable enough so that we can work and get the most out of this therapy.
Carmen:	He doesn't want me to say what I am thinking . . . that I married him because it was "practical" for both of us and I thought I'd be able to love him and that he'd be kind . . . but it's impossible.
Charlie:	[*standing up, finding it very difficult to speak*] It's hard for me to express myself, but I don't want to talk about separating. She tricked me . . . she knows that if we talk about a separation, I'm leaving.
Carmen:	[*holding back a lot of emotion*] I can't talk, I don't want him to go . . . I don't know what to do.

The therapist recognized the volatility of the situation at that moment. Charlie, terrified, was about to walk out. Carmen had made it clear that she didn't want him to leave and felt threatened by the possibility that this could happen. Seeing this impasse, the therapist requested time alone with Charlie.

Therapist:	Fine, please keep calm and understand that I'd like you both to collaborate on solving this problem that affects both of you. I also need all of us to agree on what we can do in therapy and what to talk about. We have to find a good way to work, not only one that you both agree on but also one where you *won't* feel cheated or frightened. Carmen, is it okay with you if I talk for a few minutes with Charlie alone, since he finds himself in a difficult situation and you don't want him to leave?

Carmen agreed to leave the room. During the next 20 minutes, the therapist forcefully entreated Charlie to be brave and try to work on the problems with his wife, insisting that the collaboration of both parties was essential. Note that the tone of this dialogue was, for the first time, pleasant and comfortable for Charlie. This new atmosphere, one that seemed to enhance Charlie's connection with the therapist, revealed the following:

Charlie:	The truth is that I love her very much and I'm scared that therapy will be what makes her decide that she doesn't want to live with me anymore. I'm afraid she might not feel for me what I feel for her. I wouldn't be able to live alone now, and I know I haven't been good to her.
Therapist:	What do you mean "you haven't been good to her"?
Charlie:	Well, she's is a very good person and I've pressured her.
Therapist:	Do you mean you've pressured her not to talk in therapy about all the things she's feeling?

Charlie:	Between you and me, although the tape recorder is running again, can I say something?
Therapist:	Of course, and if you want, we can turn it off again. We just use it to help us in our work. [*shuts off the recorder*] You can trust me, but take all the time and precautions you need.
Charlie:	[*highly emotional*] I threatened to commit suicide if she asked for a separation. I agreed to come here to solve our problems, but she knows I'll kill myself if she decides to leave. I made it clear to her that I'd do it. I had a very hard life when I was alone because of the problems with my hearing loss, I can't speak clearly, I don't know how to act with people. She gave meaning to my life.
Therapist:	You're being very honest with me in telling me this, Charlie. How do you feel now?
Charlie:	Better. Deep down, I know I can't do this to her.
Therapist:	Do you think the three of us should talk and try to find a way of continuing our meetings without anybody feeling intimidated? I don't think it will be that difficult to reach an agreement so that we can make progress without one of you hurting the other. I have a feeling that she also appreciates you very much.
Charlie:	Yes, I'm sure she does, and also I know that I can't do this to her. I feel very bad.
Therapist:	And probably your threat makes it even harder for her to fix things.

At this difficult moment in the therapy and with little progress so far, the therapist put the issue of safety squarely on the table, assuring the most vulnerable client that he would not allow a destructive process to take place. Building an atmosphere of safety was key to unblocking the therapy.

Although ensuring an optimal level of safety does not guarantee therapeutic success, when safety is highly threatened, as it was for Charlie and Carmen, the probability of failure is greatly increased (M. Beck et al., in press). Safety is paramount for couples and families who live every day with intense conflict and drama.

CONCLUSION

Effective therapy with couples and families involves two seemingly contradictory adaptations. On the one hand, clients need to feel safe on the therapist's territory, which is at first unfamiliar. On the other hand, clients need to see this context as one that can neutralize their anxiety or fear about the reactions of other members of the family. Optimally, therapy promotes flexibility and the risk to try something new, or at least the risk to speak honestly about problems in order to resolve them. Therefore, therapy needs to be a place where clients can safely open doors that were closed or find doors that were previously unknown to them. Whether clients take risks to change their situation depends on the characteristics of each case. Doing so is eased considerably when the therapeutic context is safe and the therapist is seen as an invested but neutral party who has everyone's best interests at heart.

The major threats to safety come from conflicts, tensions, and intimidation within the family system itself. Problems can also arise from the therapist's style, threats to confidentiality, or conditions that are not adapted to the needs of the family. In this chapter, we defined and illustrated the sources and behavioral manifestations of safety (and lack thereof) within the therapeutic system. In our conceptualization of the alliance, creating a safe environment is of prime importance. Therapists' explanations of various procedures, confidentiality, the reasons for using recording devices, keeping files, and so on cannot be underestimated. Other important aspects of safety have to do with controlling and handling conflict, threats, or intimidations (open or covert) among family members. The potential clash between therapeutic procedures and client characteristics—cultural, religious, or simply lifestyle— can also influence the development and maintenance of safety within the therapeutic system.

In a safe therapeutic context, clients find that conflict within the family can be handled without harm or destruction. In fact, they often discover how easy it is to come up with solutions when they lower their defenses and risk trying something new.

7

SHARED SENSE OF PURPOSE
WITHIN THE FAMILY

Consider the Alfred family: mother (Ruth), stepfather (Jim), and two adolescent daughters, 13-year-old Tina and 8-year-old Alyse, who come for help because "everything is out of control" (Ruth's words). Ruth complains that Jim's behavior toward Tina is "almost incestuous": He frequently comments on Tina's body parts and behaves seductively, pushing her onto his lap or tickling her when she walks by him. Jim counters that Ruth's permissiveness and lack of limits has caused Tina's challenging and obnoxious behavior at home, and Alyse is starting to imitate her older sister. In Session 1, the parents blame each other ("he's behaving like a dirty old man"; "she's a slob") and the girls blame their parents ("they care more about fighting than about us!"). If the therapist is not able to frame the treatment in such a way that validates these disparate perspectives—not a simple task when the specter of incest arises—the risk of a split alliance is great. Even if all family members start out engaged in the process and liking the therapist, it is inevitable that each subsystem will pull the therapist to support its position. In the extreme, the family may drop out of treatment, with Tina especially at risk.

When we conceptualize the therapeutic system as interlocking subsystems, the most prominent of these is the family itself, that is, the family

125

without the therapist. Thus far, we have focused on dyadic subsystems—the therapist with each individual family member—or, in the case of chapter 6 ("Safety Within the Therapeutic System"), how each individual client interacts with the rest of the therapeutic system. Arguably, however, the couple or family group is the most influential unit in terms of motivation for change, setting change in motion (Pinsof, 1994), and influencing the final therapeutic outcome (Knobloch-Fedders et al., in press; Shields et al., 1991; Symonds & Horvath, 2004).

The degree to which family members are cohesively invested in therapy is the *Shared Sense of Purpose Within the Family*, which is defined in the system for observing family therapy alliances (SOFTA) as follows:

> family members seeing themselves as working collaboratively in therapy to improve family relations and achieve common family goals; a sense of solidarity in relation to the therapy ("we're in this together") and valuing their time with each other in therapy; essentially, a felt unity within the family in relation to the therapy. (Friedlander, Escudero, Heatherington, Deihl, et al., 2004, p. 5)

First conceptualized by Pinsof (1994) as a *within-family alliance*, the Shared Sense of Purpose reflects not only family members' agreement on the goals and tasks of therapy but also their cohesiveness as a unit and the value they place on therapy as an avenue for addressing family problems.

We view family members' alliances with one another as qualitatively different from each client's individual alliance with the therapist. Nevertheless, the degree to which a sense of purpose is shared within the family is powerfully influenced by the therapist's attitude and behavior toward each individual family member and toward the group as a whole. Split alliances (Heatherington & Friedlander, 1990b; Knobloch-Fedders et al., 2004, in press; Pinsof, 1994; Pinsof & Catherall, 1986; see chap. 9), in which family members are unevenly allied with the therapist, can be causes or manifestations of a poor sense of purpose within the family (M. Beck et al., in press).

In many instances, families come to therapy ready and eager to work on common goals. Little is needed from the therapist to move the treatment along a mutually agreed on path. In the following section, these kinds of situations are described, along with examples of client behaviors that signal a strong shared sense of purpose throughout the treatment process.

THEORY AND RESEARCH

In this section, we summarize the literature on therapeutic strategies that, at both a macro and a micro level, can enhance a couple's or family's sense of shared purpose. In four intensively analyzed case studies (M. Beck et al., in press), only one family began treatment with a strong shared sense of purpose. Although the son saw himself as a "visitor" who was there only to support his mother, both clients had the same perspective on the problem. They came ready to engage with each other and the therapist to overcome the difficulties that were causing them anguish. Of the four cases, only this one ended with a successful outcome. In the other three, family members came either with directly opposing motives for seeking help or as "plaintiffs," blaming each other for the family's misfortunes. In M. Beck et al.'s interviews with individual family members, clients in these families had less to say about alliances with their therapists and far more to say about differences they had with their other family members' perspectives and goals. Consistent with the interview data, Shared Sense of Purpose (and Safety) ratings on the SOFTA–o fluctuated widely, depending on which family members were present in a given session. In one family, mother and daughter had a strong alliance with each other when the father was absent. In another case, mother and father shared a common sense of purpose in their son's absence. In both cases, it became clear after two family sessions that conjoint therapy was unworkable, and the treatments were divided to provide viable contexts for therapeutic work with each subsystem. Although the outcomes in both cases were not clearly successful, neither were they failures.

A family's sense of purpose can wane at any point in treatment. When it is clear that family members' needs and perspectives are at odds, the therapist must step in to redirect the process. If this is done skillfully, clients come to see that therapy can help the entire family, that defining therapy in win–lose terms makes everyone lose in the end, and that compromise does not signal humiliating defeat.

Such a transformation involves eliciting each client's view of the difficulties (Sluzki, 1992) and offering a new, unifying perspective on the problem, one to which every person can relate. The process of moving from individual to family goals can be done directly or indirectly (Rait, 1998). In the direct approach, reframing or creating a new working reality (Minuchin, 1974) is a powerful intervention, particularly when blame is evident (Friedlander, Heatherington, & Marrs, 2000), when family members see limited options for solutions (deShazer, 1985), or when one or more family members are reluctant clients. The task is particularly difficult when family members are in conflict and they express opposing needs. With adolescents, for example, the therapist must find a way to support their personal goals (G. S. Diamond & Liddle, 1996) in a way that does not undercut the parents' authority or goals. In Liddle and Schwartz's (2002) approach to treating depressed adolescents, the objective is to help the teen tell her parents where they let her down or why she is angry and hurt about their behavior or choices (e.g., to divorce). An individual session with the parents is held prior to the adolescent's disclosures to prepare them for listening empathically and nondefensively. This process cannot work, however, unless the parents are convinced that an openness to being faulted furthers their own aims as well as their child's.

To some extent, the ways therapists go about enhancing the family's shared sense of purpose is theory specific. Taking an indirect approach (Rait, 1998), experiential therapists like Whitaker and Keith (1981) or Satir (1964), for example, use play, fantasy, humor, self-disclosure, and confrontation to nudge family members together. Indeed, in a "battle for structure," Whitaker deliberately makes himself the family's common enemy, forcing family members to experience themselves as a cohesive unit (p. 334). When blamers are encouraged to show their hidden pain and those who are blamed respond with kindness and empathy (Greenberg & Johnson, 1988), everyone sees that therapy can change people's feelings, that heartache can be replaced with new and stronger emotional connections.

Constructionists such as Tomm (1987), Sluzki (1992), and M. White and Epston (1990) work toward offering families a new experience by targeting their cognitions. Tomm provided couples with a new experience by having each partner, in turn, talk at length about the problems between them from the perspective of the other. This process, in which each partner is asked to listen and not interrupt, dramatizes the couple's common experiences of being hurt and feeling misunderstood, victimized, or needy. Like Tomm, Sluzki uses circular, reflexive, and transformative questions ("How will your mother react when your father stops being depressed?") to move clients from the "old story" to a new one in which everyone in the family plays a vital part. Research on Sluzki's model (Coulehan et al., 1998) suggests that clients become hopeful when therapists explore shared family values and point out how individual problems are related to family history or structure (e.g., single parent, remarried, cross-cultural). In one case, the grandson's attitude problem was attributed to the difficulty of growing up as an only child living with elderly grandparents (Coulehan et al., 1998).

Reflecting teams (e.g., Andersen, 1991; Lax, 1991), a hallmark of the constructionist approach, are effective when they model for the family how a group can achieve a shared sense of purpose. In this process, the team observes a family session and then, midway, switches places with the family to compare perceptions of what has been said. Typically, each member of the team begins by voicing or empathizing with one family member's perspective, but by the end of their conversation, the team has reached a consensus about the nature of the problem and the most helpful way to proceed. Although not an explicit aim of this approach, the reflecting process itself demonstrates how unity can emerge from disunity.

Therapists who take a multigenerational (Bowen, 1976; Framo, 1992; Kerr & Bowen, 1988) or psychodynamic (e.g., Scharff & Scharff, 1987) approach use reframing or interpretation to achieve this end. By offering family members a novel perspective on the problem, the therapist facilitates new insights about their relationships. Seeing things in a different light underscores the value of therapy. For example, when adult siblings come together with their parents in conflict about something going on in their present lives, Framo would help them see the connection between the present quarrel and the old dynamics, unresolved hurts, and resentments. As family members begin to recall and then to work through the long-standing, deeply entrenched sources of misunderstanding and pain, they see the importance of the therapeutic work—to put "new wine in old bottles," so to speak.

Arguably, strategic and structural therapists like Haley (1976), Minuchin (1974), and Fishman (1988; Minuchin & Fishman, 1981) have had the most to say about getting families "on board" in therapy by actively challenging the status quo. At the outset of treatment, structural therapists make explicit the purpose of the sessions and the ground rules, and they clarify their own and the family's expectations. Throughout treatment, they direct the family's interactions or create enactments that involve everyone (Piercy, Laird, & Mohammed, 1983). When necessary, they block clients' attempts to align with them at the expense of other family members, and they work toward forging within-subsystem alliances, such as "executive" (parental) subsystem (Minuchin & Fishman, 1981, p. 21) and sibling subsystem, to empower individuals and avoid scapegoating or "detouring" (p. 147). Structural therapists forcefully put a stop to unproductive blaming and chaotic interchanges between family members (Piercy et al., 1983). When a child refuses to open up, Minuchin might deliberately ignore him (Heatherington & Friedlander, 1990a), instead asking other family members about him in a provocative way ("How do you contribute to your son's misbehavior?") until he fights his way into the conversation. Inducting himself into the family system, Minuchin et al. (1967) forged alliances between family members by rearranging the seating (e.g., so that the siblings are closer together) or by reframing an individual problem in interpersonal ways ("He's not a delinquent. He's just dumb and young, and *you* [mother] keep him young!"; Heatherington & Friedlander, 1990a). Structural and Milan systemic therapists use circular questioning (Selvini-Palazzoli, Boscolo, Cecchin, & Prata, 1978) and indirect messages (Friedlander et al., 1987) to help clients view their problems less personally and more *inter*personally. From that vantage point, clients soon recognize that everyone needs to contribute to a family solution.

In research on how structural–strategic therapists get reluctant clients to move from disengagement to engagement with one another (Friedlander, Heatherington, Johnson, & Skowron, 1994; Heatherington & Friedlander, 1990a), the more effective therapists redirected their efforts after unsuccessfully asking family members to engage in conversation with one another. When engagement was not forthcoming, these therapists moved from content to process, focusing clients on the nature of their interpersonal impasse and the thoughts and feelings sustaining it. Throughout these episodes, the therapists explored, cajoled, and challenged family members to see the need for working together. In one case, for example, the therapist pointed out that if the parents could not cooperate to control their out-of-control daughter, she was at great risk of being placed in residential care. In another case, the therapist encouraged an estranged couple to keep talking with each other long after they preferred to quit. Finally, the man reached out to his ex-wife, exclaiming, "They're *our* kids! We gotta raise 'em!"

One way to get clients to engage with one another in problem solving involves focusing on family members' reluctance to work toward a common goal (Friedlander, Heatherington, et al., 1994). In one family, the mother tearfully explained that underlying her anger over her son's behavior was her profound hurt that he was growing apart from her. Hearing her pain, the teen softened his angry stance, reassuring his mother that their relationship was as strong as ever, only different. From that point on, it was relatively easy for the therapist to propose a therapeutic objective that would suit them both: to forge a new, respectful, and caring relationship with each other.

In the Friedlander, Heatherington, et al. (1994) study, successful "sustaining engagement events" were contrasted with unsuccessful ones in which the session ended without a productive family discussion (p. 438). The most striking difference between the two was the therapist's failure in the unsuccessful events to direct the conversation to the underlying impasse. In one case, a couple was directed to create a plan for their children's chores. The husband met each of his wife's suggestions with reasons why it wouldn't work, how the kids were unmanageable, and so on. Finally, getting increasingly agitated, he turned to the therapist and said something like, "*Nothing* will work," to which she countered by asking why he was in therapy. The husband replied boldly, "I'm only here because my wife said she'd leave me if I didn't come!"

Strategies to increase a family's shared sense of purpose, although congruent with various theories, are not entirely theory-specific, however. Indeed, family therapists from widely different orientations behave similarly in many ways (Friedlander et al., 1985, 1987). Examples of specific behaviors to accomplish this aim include eliciting family dialogue, using enactments (Butler & Wampler, 1999), deliberately drawing in the quieter members with questions or empathy, encouraging clients to compromise or to ask each other for their perspective, and praising family members for respecting each other's point of view even when they disagree. To help clients see themselves as a unit, effective therapists draw attention to family members' shared values, experiences, needs, and feelings to offer them a unifying perspective on their situation.

However, therapists often unwittingly contribute to weakening a family's sense of shared purpose. This unfortunate outcome can occur all too easily when therapists who only have experience with individuals start seeing couples and families without theoretical and practical knowledge of family systems and without supervision. It is neither possible nor desirable to do individual therapy with one client when other family members are silently present in the session. The process can lead to labeling, scapegoating, and blame when the therapist ignores, or is blissfully unaware of, important systemic dynamics that sustain the problem.

Even with a family systems perspective, therapists can unknowingly compromise the within-family alliance. This occurs most often when, right from the outset of treatment, the therapist accepts one client's definition of the problem, a definition that faults another client (Symonds & Horvath, 2004). Indeed, at any point in treatment a therapist can compromise the family alliance by not challenging a family member who consistently behaves as if he or she is the cotherapist or by tacitly accepting one perspective on the situation without eliciting alternative views. Typically, a parent complains about a child's misbehavior and the therapist launches into a treatment plan to correct the misbehavior without considering the child's perspective. The child, seeing the therapist as another interfering authority figure, is likely to balk at any suggestion. Only when the therapist reframes the goals and tasks of therapy in such a way that the child sees the value in cooperating are parent and child able to sustain a strong sense of purpose in the therapeutic process.

More subtle threats to the family alliance occur when the therapist goes along with one client's agenda for the session without asking others if they are willing to follow suit, or when the therapist does not intervene when family members argue with each other about the value or purpose of therapy. Therapists who, smiling or laughing, join in on the teasing of one family member by another can also unwittingly compromise the family alliance.

FELT UNITY WITHIN THE FAMILY SYSTEM

Couples and families have a history together and an "allegiance" to one another (Symonds & Horvath, 2004) that precedes the development of the alliance with the therapist. When they present for therapy, three situations easily lend themselves to a strong shared sense of purpose within the family: common enemies, stumbling blocks, and threats to family integrity.

Common enemies refers to situations in which family members request help in dealing with the "indirect patient system" (Pinsof, 1994, p. 174), that is, when some *other* person, or side of the family, is viewed as problematic. All those who present as clients are, from the outset, in agreement that they must follow a certain course to deal with the problematic individual or individuals, whose behavior jeopardizes their comfort or safety. A common situation is an in-law problem, either in the family of origin of one of the parents or with a soon-to-be daughter- or son-in-law. Another common concern is how to cope with a troubled family member, such as someone with a serious alcohol or drug problem. To illustrate, Alice and Brad Harrison sought help when 22-year-old Jason, who had a bipolar disorder, began repeatedly bouncing between hospital inpatient units and jail cells, oblivious to treatment recommendations and seemingly determined to kill himself with alcohol or other dangerous behavior. The Harrisons struggled not only with Jason but also with third parties—doctors, probation officers, lawyers, extended family members—who were insisting on mutually exclusive courses of action.

Presentations in which the offending person is described as a common enemy should be dealt with cautiously. One client may simply be paying lip service to another in condemning the third party without feeling personally threatened or outraged in the same way or to the same degree. "Going along for the ride" may be seen as the lesser evil. If the therapist is not sensitive to the likelihood of nonuninformity within the family, a split alliance may evolve, derailing the process or resulting in the family's dropping out of treatment.

Some families present with stumbling blocks along their developmental life path. These often involve issues of parenting, particularly when new situations arise. Kaiesha Collins, for example, sought help when 7-year-old DeJohn began regressing and throwing tantrums after the birth of his brother. She and DeJohn agreed that they needed help because, as DeJohn put it, "Our family is different now, and I don't like it!" A divorced couple sought consultation when their formerly sweet, cooperative 13-year-old daughter began mouthing off, demanding autonomy and privileges that her parents were not comfortable with. Figuring that their daughter was using the divorce as an excuse for inexcusable behavior, the parents came together to seek help, even though they had not lived together in many years.

Other kinds of stumbling blocks bring families to treatment when the choices they face can have a dramatic effect on the quality of life for one or more family members. Examples include making decisions about adoption in the face of infertility, conflicts over career changes (relocation, retirement, or changing status from worker to stay-at-home parent or vice versa), or differing opinions about whether to invite an ailing parent to move in. Most families find ways to resolve these issues without treatment, but sometimes the problem can take on a life of its own. When that happens, it is not uncommon for one family member to develop symptoms, and these symptoms prompt the family to seek help.

Another developmental stumbling block is family separation. The Douglas family, Lily and her three children, sought therapy after the father left home to live with another woman. Because he was verbally and physically abusive, the family had been more traumatized living with him than without him. The purpose of therapy was not only to allow the children to voice their hurt and anger but also to provide an opportunity for the mother and children to come together into a harmonious family unit. As presented by Lily, "we need to figure out how to be a single parent family."

Yet another presenting situation that lends itself to a strong shared sense of purpose occurs when there is a threat to the family's integrity. The most common circumstances involve grief and trauma. One family sought help 6 months after their 22-year-old son had a diving accident that left him a quadraplegic. Both parents were profoundly greiving their son's condition, and neither had the inner resources to support the other in the face of this tragedy. As another example, a family came for help after a fire destroyed their home; the children were suffering nightmares, flashbacks, and behavior problems, and both parents were depressed and irritable, finding it hard to keep their restaurant business going.

In all of these cases, a change had occurred or was going to occur, and there was a clear recognition by all involved that professional help was needed. In such situations, minimal work is required on the therapist's part to create a mutually agreed on goal or set of goals, and the family members who come for treatment usually do so voluntarily and express a desire for change or resolution. Behaviorally, family members who share a strong sense of purpose are willing to compromise, ask each other for their perspective, and explicitly validate each other's point of view, even when they disagree ("I understand where you're coming from, although I still think that . . ."). In session, all are engaged or attentive, or, if not, the more active family members try to draw out the quieter ones. Nonverbally, family members express their shared sense of purpose by sitting close together or by mirroring each other's body language; they exchange eye contact frequently and are careful to share the floor so that everyone can be heard. Joking, sharing a lighthearted moment, leaning forward, or touching each other during difficult discussions also signal a sense of unity or an appreciation of the time spent together in therapy.

In the next section, we present common scenarios in which the family's shared sense of purpose is weak, either from the beginning of treatment or when it dissolves over time as the therapy unfolds.

DISUNITY WITHIN THE FAMILY ALLIANCE

Ed and Marianne Wilson sought help for a specific problem, which they described as figuring out how to help Ed's younger brother, Todd, get launched on his own. Two years earlier, they had invited 17-year-old Todd to live with them after he'd run away from his irresponsible, alcoholic parents. Marianne, feeling sorry for Todd, had originally embraced the idea. Now, however, Todd was disrupting their tight family unit, coming in drunk late at night, teasing their children mercilessly, and contributing in no way to the collective. In session, Ed agreed with Marianne that Todd had to leave, but secretly he was filled with guilt when he compared Todd's situation with his own; he had "a beautiful wife, good job, great kids" and Todd had "nothing but horrible memories." Not wholly in Marianne's camp, Ed indirectly sabotaged her efforts to set limits with Todd and made excuses for not inviting his brother to join them in therapy. After several weeks in which Ed's ambivalence was neither addressed nor recognized, the marital relationship showed signs of strain.

The Wilsons had initially presented with a clear-cut, seemingly manageable problem. Both clients were "on the same page," so to speak, about the purpose and importance of seeking professional help. In the early sessions, they sat together on the couch, smiled frequently at each other, and completed each other's sentences. There was an eagerness and genuine sense of commonality about their therapeutic goal and what they wanted from the therapist. Over time, however, it became clear that Marianne could not handle Todd without Ed's support, and Ed was not up to the task of confronting his brother. Coming for sessions became burdensome, as each client feared what the other would say. Their young children began to feel the strain, and life at home became increasingly tense. To avoid facing their disagreement over Todd and their disappointment with each other, the Wilsons began spending the therapy sessions arguing about how to discipline their children.

Unfortunately, the Wilsons' experience in therapy is all too common. In the language of SOFTA, their early sessions were characterized by high energy and engagement; strong emotional connections with the therapist; a sense of safety; and a clear, cohesive purpose. Three months later, Marianne felt as hopeless about the therapy as she did about her family situation, Ed feared that Marianne would use the therapy sessions to present him with an ultimatum, and their sense of purpose waned in a process of collusive avoidance.

A diminishing sense of purpose is likely in other situations. One common scenario is when the family's problems are numerous and the family structure chaotic. We call this situation *crisis as the norm*. Families that are crisis prone may present with a strong shared sense of purpose at the outset of treatment, and the goals they identify often seem reasonable and manageable. Over time, however, it becomes clear that the family's life is perpetually colored with drama, and their initial presenting concern is drowned out by waves of other serious problems.

As an example, after Carlos Ortíz had a serious work injury, he and Teresa (with their three adolescents) came for help at the urging of their parish priest. The family defined the problem in behavioral terms: to figure out how to care for Carlos, to decide whether Teresa should go back to work, and generally to learn how to live in these changed circumstances. During the first month of treatment, the 16-year-old daughter, Miriam, was raped. Her older brother Jorge, seeking revenge, was hospitalized after a vicious fight at school, and the younger boy, David, was arrested for stealing hub caps. Each therapy session had a new, crisis-oriented topic, and within the chaos none of the family members could articulate a coherent purpose for the therapy.

A family's shared sense of purpose can also diminish over time when there is an unwelcome revelation. In these instances, treatment begins with a strong within-family alliance, but something is said in therapy that shifts the focus and draws boundaries around family loyalties. Typical of this dynamic is an expressed attitude or event that changes the focus from the children to the couple. Terrell and Josie Hubbard began therapy to help 10-year-old Duane, who was having academic problems and fighting with peers. The therapist's suspicion that all was not well with the couple was confirmed when, in Session 6, Josie revealed that Terrell's driver's license had been suspended. Josie's insistence that Terrell's problem drinking be addressed in therapy was too uncomfortable for him, and the couple's disagreement over this issue resulted in their discontinuing treatment shortly thereafter.

A diminishing sense of purpose within the family can also occur when the therapeutic work starts having positive effects but unanticipated changes threaten the status quo. A typical situation occurs when the symptomatic family member's improvement forces changes that are unwelcome for other family members. In systems terms, the homeostasis is disrupted and second-order change is set in motion (Hoffman, 1981). As an example, Adrian's extreme obsessive–compulsive behavior had been so debilitating for many years that when treatment began he could not work or do much of anything around the house. Although Robin, his wife, complained about the excessive burden his problems placed on her, when Adrian began to improve, her power in the family was shaken. When Adrian started asserting some authority and making demands, dormant marital issues began surfacing. Robin blamed the therapy for these unexpected, unwanted problems.

The situations previously discussed are examples of a solid sense of purpose disintegrating over time. It is all too common, however, for treatment to begin without a strong within-family alliance. Clients who are mandated for treatment or who are therapy "hostages" (see chap. 11) tend to have little investment in the treatment process right from the outset. Other clients, although voluntarily seeking professional help, do not formulate a shared sense of purpose because each person is unwilling or incapable of seeing the situation from any perspective other than his or her own. Unfortunately, the prognosis for families like these is poor unless the therapist is able to forge alliances so that everyone feels personally invested.

In these situations, polarization is evident from the beginning of treatment, with one person (or subsystem) blaming the other and no one listening in a way that invites compromise or promotes respect. Behaviorally, clients may be hostile and sarcastic with one another, devaluing each other's opinions and perspectives, and arguing about the purpose or value of therapy or about who should or should not attend the sessions. A telling behavior is a client attempting to align with the therapist against other family members by, for example, asking the therapist to choose sides, to decide who is right, or to intervene in a specific way. More subtle examples include accentuating a controversy (e.g, "Can you tell my daughter again what you told her last week?" or "My father needs to be told that he has to see a heart doctor") or joking with the therapist at another family member's expense.

Nonverbally, family members can show a lack of shared purpose by avoiding eye contact with one another, tuning out, monopolizing the conversation, or sitting in a defensive posture whenever other family members are speaking. In the extreme, no family members feel safe in the therapeutic context because finding a shared sense of purpose requires taking personal responsibility. It takes maturity and courage to look critically at one's own behavior and attitudes.

CASE ILLUSTRATION: THE HOUSE THAT FEAR BUILT

Michael and Tiffany Rosen, a middle-class couple, were married for 8 years with a baby son, Philip, who was 5 months old. Michael was employed by the government, and Tiffany was a computer programmer who worked part-time from home.

Until 9 months previous, Tiffany had no idea that her marriage was in trouble. Although she didn't like the fact that Michael spent most of his free time after work with male friends, usually drinking beer, she spent most of her own time with her mother. Tiffany described herself as a "clone" of her mother—they looked alike, had the same values and beliefs, and in many ways were like one person. They had been extremely close since Tiffany's father deserted the family when Tiffany was 10 years old. Because of her father's desertion, Tiffany felt it important to be "in control" of her life. Michael was passive, just like Tiffany's stepfather. Actually, Tiffany's marriage mirrored her mother's second marriage. Although Tiffany complained about Michael's passivity, at least he didn't try to control her.

When Tiffany announced to Michael that she wanted to start a family, she told him that she had discussed the issue at length with her mother before coming to that decision. (The couple, married 7 years, had never seriously discussed having children.) It did not occur to Tiffany to talk her decision over with Michael because he always did what she wanted. One month before their son was born, Michael told Tiffany that he was unhappy in the marriage and would leave her after the baby was born. He staunchly refused to discuss his reasons despite Tiffany's pleas, anger, and tears.

When the baby was 1 month old, Michael moved in with some friends. He continued to see Tiffany and Philip a few times a week and supported them financially. Three months later, Michael announced that he wanted to return home. He did not explain why, however, and Tiffany insisted that they go for marital therapy before she would allow him to return.

In Session 1, Tiffany expressed her tremendous hurt, anger, and confusion at what Michael had done. He was passively uncomfortable during her speech. When asked for his point of view, Michael only said that he'd been unhappy in the marriage because Tiffany and her mother were such a close team that he felt excluded. Being away for a few months, however, Michael was lonely and wanted to come home to his wife and baby son.

At first, the Rosens had a strong sense of purpose: to decide whether the marriage could be saved. It was a clear-cut goal, and they began working with the therapist toward that end. The therapist, believing that catharsis, forgiveness, and sharing of pain and hurt would be helpful, oriented the treatment toward the expression of feelings.

After a few weeks, however, Tiffany expressed hopelessness about the situation. She began each session by asking her husband what he wanted to talk about, but Michael would merely shrug and hang his head. Then Tiffany would tearfully exclaim that she couldn't trust him, he'd hurt her deeply, she felt helpless. Michael would sit quietly, visibly anxious and fearful of speaking to avoid annoying her further. It became clear that Tiffany was looking for an emotional response that Michael hadn't a clue how to offer. Although Tiffany was seemingly more engaged in the therapeutic process and felt safe enough to express herself fully, she came to resent Michael's passivity, feeling that it signaled a lack of investment in saving their marriage. She expressed her dissatisfaction with how therapy was going, musing about whether she should continue to come for sessions, "only to cry and still feel invisible."

At this point, the therapist, recognizing that the verbal "currency" of therapy was not working for Michael, suggested an alternate path. Asked what he would be willing to do to help the situation, Michael hesitatingly suggested that he and Tiffany "go out on a date." Hearing this, the therapist proposed a new goal, to which both partners readily agreed: to try to function more like a couple without discussing the past or demanding a commitment from each other. Tiffany was eager to try anything that Michael suggested. The therapist cautioned her not to bring up her mistrust, fear, or hurt during their dates, and Michael was challenged to do whatever he could to show Tiffany he cared.

Two weeks later, the couple came to the session lighthearted and joking. They had suspended all discussion of what had driven them apart and whether they would ever live together again, and something had clearly clicked. When asked, Tiffany praised Michael's efforts to be romantic (bringing her flowers, dressing up for their dates, complimenting her appearance). Heartened, the therapist suggested that rather than Michael continuing to take out his baby son as a divorced father would do, the couple should plan a special family outing as a threesome. Without missing a beat, Michael suggested a trip to the zoo, and Tiffany was only too happy to oblige.

The first turning point in the treatment was this shift from emotional to behavioral interventions. The second one was fortuitous, and it was this second turning point that solidified the couple's mutual goal to reestablish the family unit. It came about like this. In session, Tiffany remarked offhandedly that she loved watching Michael and baby Philip making playful grimaces at each other. The therapist, seeing a flicker of a smile on Michael's usually impassive countenance, asked Tiffany to tell Michael what she thought of him as a father. Without hesitation, she looked at Michael and said, "You're a *wonderful* father!" Then, at the therapist's urging, she described in detail how he behaved with Philip that led her to this conclusion. Seeing that she was about to follow up with renewed complaints about Michael's abandonment (". . . and that's why it hurt . . ."), the therapist cut her off and turned to Michael, asking for his reaction. Suddenly, with great, heaving sobs, Michael poured out his heart. He had left his wife and son out of tremendous fear that he would be a terrible dad like his own unavailable, emotionally neglectful father had been. When Philip was born, Michael convinced himself that the boy would be better off without him. Completely blindsided by these heartfelt disclosures, Tiffany was silent.

Now the therapist's opportunity to provide a curative reframing was at hand. Praising Michael for overcoming his fear enough for this emotional breakthrough to happen, the therapist pointed out that both spouses had "skeletons in their closet" from the past that had clouded their marriage and their ability to coparent. As Michael said, he feared duplicating his parents' loveless marriage and worried that he would be an ineffective, distant father like his own. As Tiffany had said many times, she never got over her own father's abandonment. Thus, she too feared duplicating her family of origin. Reassuring the couple that they were not the people their parents were, that they were not doomed to recreate the past, and that their coming for help was a sign of their goodwill and motivation to change, the therapist commented on the "spark" he had seen between them, even throughout this difficult period. He, for one, had faith that this spark that would ignite and move the couple past all the pain and hurt.

Over the next few sessions, Michael was able to tell Tiffany how threatened he felt by her strong connection with her mother, a relationship that excluded him. Startled, Tiffany responded quickly that he, Michael, was her "top priority," not her mother; she had only turned to her mother for comfort when Michael avoided her. This time, however, Tiffany was able to explain herself without blaming Michael. She did not excuse her own feelings, but the strident righteousness that had colored her previous expostulations was gone.

Michael and Tiffany reconciled, Michael moved back home, and they eventually had two more children. Their marriage was not without its problems, but it was a solid one, and they and the children thrived.

In the language of SOFTA, whereas both spouses liked the therapist (Emotional Connection), at first Tiffany was far more engaged and felt safer in the therapeutic process than did Michael. When the couple's sense of purpose wavered and then was on track again by a redirection of the therapy, Michael's sense of safety and his engagement were enhanced. The partners' alliance with each other had faltered because the early sessions were simply too threatening for Michael and, getting nowhere, the couple began doubting the hoped for reconciliation. When an intermediate goal (to behave as if they were dating) was offered, one that Michael felt he could accomplish successfully, his participation and resolve strengthened. The couple's desire to mend their relationship became the basis for a new and stronger sense of purpose in therapy—to rekindle their love for each other.

The second turning point in this treatment, when Michael showed his vulnerability and finally explained his fear, was fortuitous. If this emotional breakthrough had not occurred, this couple might have remained stalemated, in therapy and in life. In the next section we describe a clinical tool that we believe can help move along a stagnant therapeutic process like this one with the Rosens.

USING QUESTIONNAIRES TO ENHANCE A SHARED SENSE OF PURPOSE

The Constructions of Problems Scale (CPS; Heatherington et al., 1998), a clinical measure, was developed to provide a different perspective on individuals' reasons for seeking professional help. Unlike other questionnaires, which focus on clients' desired treatment outcomes, the CPS (see Appendix C) provides therapists with information about how individuals construe the nature and causes of the difficulties that bring them to treatment. In the first section of the questionnaire, clients are asked to write a statement about the "family problems" for which they want help. Following is a series of 27 questions targeting clients' attributions for the problem or problems they described. These items reflect important dimensions of causal attributions, such as internal (e.g., genetics, personality, behavior, mental illness) versus external (e.g., fate, luck, circumstances, other people, divine will) and global versus specific causes. Development of the items was also influenced by family systems thinking, that is, linear versus circular causality and the influence of multiple generations.

As described more fully in Heatherington, Friedlander, et al. (1998), the CPS is appropriate for adults and adolescents. Responses to the various items are not summed, but rather a profile can be developed (also in Appendix C) that provides a pictorial view of the degree to which family members ascribe similar causes to the same presenting problem.

Each family member may describe the problem differently in the first written section of the questionnaire, and this information is instructive in and of itself. Consider the Rosen couple, for example, who might have initially described the problem as "my mother-in-law's interference" (Michael's view) versus "a lack of trust or intimacy, and poor communication" (Tiffany's view). The CPS can also be administered at midtreatment. At this point, Tiffany might have written "not being able to forgive what Michael did to me," whereas Michael might have written "finding common ground between us" or, if he felt safe enough with the therapist, "wondering whether I can be a good father to my son." On the second section of the CPS, changes in causal attributions for the marital problem might be observed over time. At midtreatment Tiffany, who originally blamed Michael for all the problems, might now indicate seeing herself as partially responsible or might recognize, for the first time, the contribution of "other family members" (i.e., her mother) to the problem. Michael, for his part, might now endorse the multigenerational item, suggesting his new understanding of the marital difficulties.

The measure can be administered before treatment begins or at any point along the way. In our clinical work, we have found that most children aged 12 years and older are able to complete the measure, though some verbal explanation may be needed. (The same is true for adults with lower reading levels.) With younger children, the therapist (or a member of the observing team, if available) can take each child aside individually and ask in a more informal way what she or he thinks about the causes of the problem.

Because the CFS asks family members about each other, it is essential that therapists respect the confidentiality of these responses by not sharing the written information with other family members. Doing so would seriously compromise the clients' feelings of safety in therapy as well as their trust in the therapist. However, family members may be moved to share what they wrote with each other. If this sharing is initiated in the session by the clients and agreed to by all present, such discussion can be highly productive.

When the questionnaire is used as an intervention tool, family members should be aware before they are asked to complete the measure that the therapist intends to share the responses with others. Such sharing needs to be done delicately, however, and with the recognition that the responses may not be veridical. Although discussing responses with the family has the potential to open dialogue in productive ways (*mother to daughter*: "Why did you say this has anything to do with how we interact?"), clients might be tremendously hurt by the knowledge that others see them as blameworthy or "mentally ill."

There is, unfortunately, no ready formula for therapists to adopt a treatment plan after reading clients' responses to these self-report questionnaires. Rather, these tools are just that: tools. When clients are fully open and nondefensive in session, the data obtained from the questionnaires may not deviate much from what they have publicly declared. Discovering this consistency would be reassuring for the therapist, if not terribly informative. However, seeing in writing exactly how clients express their problems may be enlightening. On the CPS, Michael Rosen might have described his problem as either "to go home to my family" or, more boldly, "to make my wife see that I love her." These two goals, although congruent, suggest rather different treatment strategies.

CONCLUSION

It has been argued that in contrast with individual treatment, in couple and family work the within-family alliance is the most important consideration at the start and conclusion of treatment (Pinsof, 1994). In other words, "in systemic therapy, the therapeutic relationship is 'de-centered' in favor of the client's current relationships with significant others" (Flaskas, 1989, p. 37).

A strong or weak sense of shared purpose with respect to the goals and tasks of therapy influences the degree to which individual family members feel safe, are engaged, and (to a lesser extent) create an emotional bond with the therapist. Indeed, our research with the SOFTA–o has repeatedly shown greater variability in this dimension of the alliance than in the other three, regardless of the point in treatment when it is observed. Although it remains to be demonstrated whether the degree of dysfunction is reflected in a family's ability to share a sense of purpose (cf. Dore & Alexander, 1996), clinical experience suggests that when clients are absolutely incapable of finding common ground, the prognosis for improvement is poor.

The therapist is not negligible in this process. Speaking of couples, Haley (1976) pointed out that "whatever partners do in relation to each other is also in relation to the therapist" (p. 160). From a systemic perspective, the family in treatment is simultaneously a product of and a contributor to the therapist–family bond (Rait, 1998). Thus, the family's shared sense of purpose does not depend only on what the family brings to therapy; rather, it evolves as family members interact with the therapist, each client observing the others' behavior as the therapeutic process unfolds.

Ruptures or "tears" (Pinsof, 1995, p. 62) in the shared family alliance, like those in any other form of treatment, are at times unavoidable. However, repairs to the alliance, as illustrated in the Rosen case, can move the process along and teach clients how to approach future problems between them more constructively. Consider, for example, a family in which people have never before been able to listen respectfully to and validate one another's point of view. Having such a novel experience in therapy has a powerful impact when clients realize that they can be attached and involved with each other while still maintaining their individual freedom of expression.

Essentially, therapy is an encounter in which family members learn to see one another as resources. Whereas the individual therapist's empathy and unconditional acceptance are all too often discounted as being "unreal" or "artificial," the healing experiences that family members share together in therapy cannot be so easily dismissed or forgotten.

8

BUILDING BLOCKS OF THE ALLIANCE

When a therapeutic alliance is strong and intact, even neophyte therapists can identify it. Why, then, is it necessary to define, describe, and discuss the various elements of the System for Observing Family Therapy Alliances (SOFTA) model? Granted, when all four dimensions of the alliance are at their peak with every client in the room, there is little need to distinguish them or to consider how to enhance them. In our experience, however, alliances must be carefully nurtured throughout treatment; they do not develop at a steady pace for all family members, and ruptures can happen even with the most motivated families in the most private of therapy settings.

In this chapter, we discuss interrelationships of the SOFTA dimensions—the building blocks of the alliance—as they develop naturally and change over time, when outside events or circumstances interfere, or when therapists' errors threaten their stability. In our view, the multiple factors affecting therapist–family relations and intrafamilial alliances are so dynamically complex that a vigilant assessment of engagement, emotional connection, safety, and shared purpose is needed with each and every turn in the treatment process.

To facilitate this discussion, we introduce a visual representation of the SOFTA in the form of graphic displays. In these displays, each of the four dimensions is conceptualized on a low (–3 = *extremely problematic*) to high

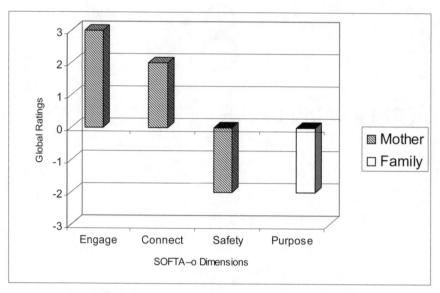

Figure 8.1. One family member's experience of the alliance in Session 1. SOFTA–o = System for Observing Family Therapy Alliances—observational.

(+3 = *extremely strong*) continuum, where 0 refers to *unremarkable–neutral engagement, emotional connection, safety,* or *shared purpose.* (As described in detail in chap. 3, these anchor points are used to rate clients' and therapists' behaviors on the SOFTA–o for purposes of training, supervision, and research.)

Figure 8.1 shows one family member's experience of the alliance in Session 1. In this example, the mother is strongly engaged and well-connected with the therapist. She does not, however, feel safe with the other family members in the room, who have a different attitude about the value, need, or purpose of therapy and who blame her for airing the family's "dirty laundry" to a professional stranger.

A different kind of display compares all family members on a single SOFTA dimension. In Figure 8.2, for example, the Safety dimension is displayed. The adolescent son, in contrast to his parents and sister, feels anxious and defensive—in other words, not at all safe—in this session.

A more detailed graph is used to profile fluctuations in the four alliance dimensions across individuals and over time. Figure 8.3 depicts one family's experience in therapy throughout the course of their treatment. This family (a mother, father, and 18-year-old son) was in such conflict during the first two interviews that subsequent sessions were held with no more than two family members at a time. The graph shows unremarkable Engagement and Emotional Connection in Session 1, but notably low Safety and Shared Sense of Purpose. After the therapist began seeing only two family members at a time (beginning with Session 3), all dimensions of the alliance improved. The display shows that Safety was optimal when mother and son were seen together in the father's absence. When father and son were seen together

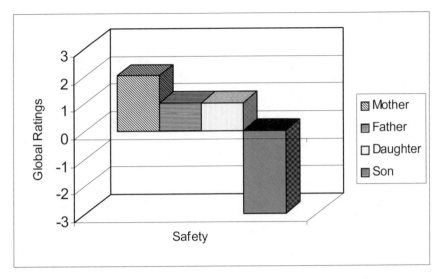

Figure 8.2. All family members on a single SOFTA–o dimension. SOFTA–o = System for Observing Family Therapy Alliances—observational.

(Session 6), both Safety and Shared Purpose plummeted. Indeed, the son shut down whenever his father was in the room. The mother's connection with the therapist was consistently positive after Session 3, whereas the father had a lukewarm attachment to the therapist throughout. Notably, connections to the therapist changed little for either father or son, whereas their sense of safety was highly volatile. Not surprisingly given his SOFTA profile, the father dropped out after Session 6.

Figure 8.4 depicts a therapist's contribution to the alliance across three early sessions. In Sessions 1 and 2, the therapist focused primarily on Engagement and Shared Purpose, but in Session 3, the interventions were geared toward enhancing Emotional Connection and Safety.

In the sections that follow, we use graphic displays to illustrate interrelations of the SOFTA dimensions within families and over time. We discuss influences on the developing alliance and how therapists can deliberately enhance the Safety dimension to affect the others. The chapter concludes with a discussion of circumstances that place the alliance in jeopardy and how skillful behavior on the part of the therapist can avert treatment disruptions.

NURTURING ALLIANCES: THE EARLY PHASE OF TREATMENT

Even when everyone in the family agrees that therapy is needed and desirable, and even when the therapist comes highly recommended, the first appointment can trigger intense anxiety. Sometimes the fear is not so much about what the therapist will say, but about what other family members will

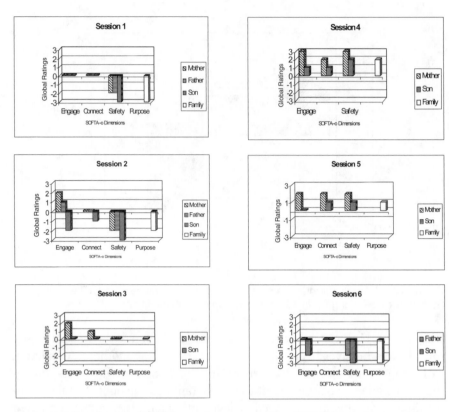

Figure 8.3. One family's SOFTA–o ratings across time. SOFTA–o = System for Observing Family Therapy Alliances—observational.

disclose. For some clients, the real-life consequences for what is revealed in a therapist's office can be extreme. A mother finds out that her teen son has been molested for years by his grandfather. A husband finds out that his wife is having an affair and plans to leave him. A 9-year-old "tells all" and afterward is beaten at home for her honesty.

When, however, the therapist controls the intensity and pace at which emotionally difficult material is brought up and discussed, the first few interviews can energize family members and fill them with hope. Take Andrew and Lois, for example. Married only 8 months, they were constantly at each other's throats. Each privately feared the marriage was over, but they sought professional help to try everything before calling it quits. After some angry words were exchanged on the hottest topic (Andrew's "workaholism" and Lois's feelings of abandonment), the therapist gently steered the conversation away, judging that the alliance was not strong enough to withstand a heated argument in session. Wrapping up Session 1, the therapist explained that if their attachment to each other were indeed dead, they would likely feel indifference toward one another, but the "fireworks" in their relationship suggested that there were "still some positive but very, very hurt feel-

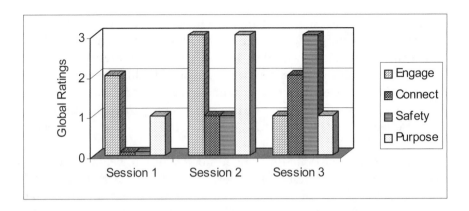

Figure 8.4. A therapist's contribution to the alliance on the four SOFTA–o dimensions. SOFTA–o = System for Observing Family Therapy Alliances—observational.

ings" on both sides. Reframing the couple's problem as "learning to fight fairly," the therapist offered hope. His encouragement and normalization of the problem ("You're two young people just trying to be a couple") was balm to their souls.

Influence of Theory

Depending on the therapist's theoretical approach, he or she is likely to attend to different aspects of the alliance. Structural, strategic, solution-focused, and constructivist models emphasize engagement and, by extension, a shared sense of purpose within the family. The Milan systemic therapists (Selvini-Palazzoli et al., 1978) and others who use reflecting teams (Andersen, 1991; Lax, 1991) or work in other ways to transform clients' constructions (Goolishian & Anderson, 1992; Sluzki, 1992; M. White & Epston, 1990) begin by eliciting the problem story from each family member in turn. Doing so enhances everyone's engagement and gives the therapist enough information to craft a therapeutic goal or set of goals that take into account all points of view, in other words, a shared sense of purpose. Arguably, structural theorists (Fishman, 1988; Minuchin, 1974; Minuchin & Fishman, 1981) have had the most to say about how therapists should enter a family and strengthen within-family bonds before exiting the system. See chapter 10 for an illustration of Charles Fishman's work with two remarried parents who were at war over their suicidal daughter.

Therapists working within the multisystemic (Henggeler & Borduin, 1990), multidimensional (Liddle, Dakof, & Diamond, 1991), brief strategic (Szapocznik & Kurtines, 1989), and functional family therapy (J. Alexander & Parsons, 1982; Sexton & Alexander, 2003) models recognize the importance of engaging delinquent and substance-abusing adolescents in a process that, by definition, labels them "the problem." Proponents of these models recommend reframing parental blame and encouraging adolescents to specify personally meaningful goals, two interventions that help therapists avoid being seen by the child as siding with the parents. Indeed, recent research on functional family therapy underscores the need to avoid split alliances (Robbins et al., 2003). Therapeutic outcomes tended to be least favorable when the alliance was "unbalanced," that is, when the parent (particularly the father) had a stronger alliance with the therapist than did the adolescent (Robbins et al., 2003, p. 540).

Theoretical approaches focusing less on cognition, behavior, and goal setting and more on emotional experiencing (e.g., G. S. Diamond & Siqueland, 1995, 1998; Greenberg & Johnson, 1988) direct our attention to another aspect of the alliance: safety. Although this term is not prominent in the writings of experiential theorists, these authors do emphasize behavioral manifestations of safety (showing vulnerability, honest disclosures, the expression of painful feelings) and a lack of safety (observable anxiety, suspicion, defensiveness). In emotionally-focused therapy (Greenberg & Johnson, 1988), for example, couples are encouraged to air their most difficult struggles, with the therapist focusing the blamer on the hurt, pain, and longing underneath the anger. When the process is successful, the recipient of the blame observes this emotional transformation (called *softening*) and is moved to express caring and attachment. Closeness and reconciliation is also the goal of attachment-based family therapy (G. S. Diamond & Siqueland, 1995, 1998), where a safe space is created for the depressed adolescent to explain to the parents how they have failed him or her and the extent to which their care and support are needed. Even therapist-facilitated confrontations are risky, however, and much anxiety and defensiveness may be displayed before clients feel secure enough to be vulnerable with the people who have hurt them the most.

In our review of theory, we found little on the topic of emotional connections between clients and therapists. Presumably, couple and family theorists take for granted their rapport with clients, a necessary condition for change but one that seemingly does not warrant much discussion. Theory and case illustrations in clinical texts, however, suggest that expert therapists do foster trust and caring through their timing, choice of words, attention and balancing of family members' needs. In contrast to the paucity of theory on the topic, empirical investigations underscore the need to make strong emotional connections with couples and families. As discussed in chapter 5, several qualitative studies show just how important therapists' personal characteristics are to their clients (e.g., Bischoff & McBride, 1996; L. N. Johnson et al., 2002; Kuehl et al., 1990; White et al., 1997).

Influence of Family Differences and Therapist Style

One way to use the SOFTA is to contrast the two dimensions that are related to what the family brings to therapy (i.e., Safety and Shared Purpose)

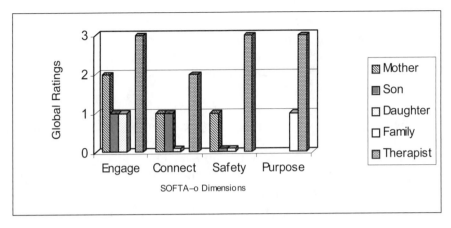

Figure 8.5. A therapist's contribution to the alliance in an initial session with a mistrustful family. SOFTA–o = System for Observing Family Therapy Alliances—observational.

with the two that have more to do with how clients experience the therapist and the therapeutic process (Emotional Connection and Engagement). Even when family members agree on the need for and goals of therapy and are not embroiled in conflict with each other, a poor match with the therapist can put a damper on their engagement in the therapeutic process. Consider, for example, a couple who came to Session 1 determined to work out a specific conflict between them but was turned off by the therapist's insistence on taking a detailed history, which lasted the entire session. In this case, Safety and Shared Purpose were notably higher than Engagement and Connection to the Therapist.

In a different case, a skillful therapist enhanced all four SOFTA dimensions and made a strong connection with the family by speaking with everyone in turn, asking each person, "What's your view on the family's problems?" and then "What about the family's strengths?" During this go-round, the therapist prevented interruptions, short-circuited blame and hostility, and found something personal to say to each individual. (This is by no means the only way to enhance engagement and connection, but the strategy worked in this case.) Although family members had come to the first appointment with great trepidation and sharply opposing views on the problem (i.e., low Safety and Shared Purpose), by the end of the session everyone was engaged and felt at least neutral toward the therapist (see Figure 8.5).

As discussed in chapter 7, some family problems easily lend themselves to a strong shared sense of purpose right from the start, as when there is a common threat or when everyone in the family agrees on the nature of the problem. Even when one person is singled out, this person may agree that the therapy should focus on her or him, seeing other family members as supporters or consultants.

Safety is a bit trickier to achieve, however, particularly when family members differ in their ability to trust and engage with a therapist. Joanna and Elaine, a middle-aged lesbian couple, decided that their relationship was far too "intense" and that they urgently needed to address the violence in the air. Despite the couple's strong shared sense of purpose, Joanna was far more comfortable expressing herself to a professional. Elaine had been in numerous physically abusive relationships and feared being blamed for the couple's fights. Her fear was unfortunately reinforced when the therapist inquired about each woman's background. Joanna, who'd been in a stable but unloving marriage for 9 years, saw herself reflected in the therapist's eyes as the innocent victim of Elaine's emotional volatility. The therapist, unaware of the growing imbalance in safety, unwittingly compounded the problem with recommendations that both clients viewed as "protecting Joanna from Elaine." By Session 3, Joanna felt far more engaged, connected, and safe in therapy than did Elaine, and the couple's sense of purpose about the therapy had begun to waiver (see Figure 8.6).

Either by nature or by training and experience, some therapists are more attuned than others to the feeling side of the therapy equation. Two SOFTA dimensions, Safety and Emotional Connection, emphasize affective responsiveness, whereas Engagement and Shared Purpose highlight cognition and behavior. When there is a match between the clients' preferred mode—affective or cognitive–behavioral—and the therapist's, the corresponding aspects of the alliance are likely to develop with greater ease. A husband and wife, for example, had positive feelings about their therapist right from the beginning but strong disagreements with each other about the value of therapy for solving their problems. Nonetheless, they "hung in there" because they saw therapy as the only safe place for them to argue. Another family, seeing all professionals as vastly different from themselves in background and culture, was predisposed to dislike any therapist and fiercely protective of their privacy. Yet over the course of a few sessions, as the therapist succeeded in engaging everyone in the process, family members warmed up and, little by little, felt safe enough to let down their guard.

SAFETY FIRST

On the same day two families come to the same therapist for their first appointment. At 3:00 p.m. the Belzers sit in stiff silence in the waiting room. In the office, the mother leans forward anxiously, the children (aged 10 and 12) slump in their seats, baseball caps pulled down low over their brows. The father marches in last, a stiff half-smile on his lips. Tension abounds. The DeMartino family, at 5:00 p.m., is playful, almost boisterous. As they enter the office, the two preteens poke and jab at each other, giggling, and the parents confer about who should sit where. Although nervous, everyone smiles when the therapist goes around the room to ask for names.

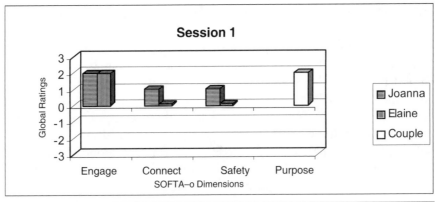

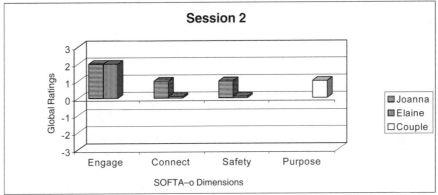

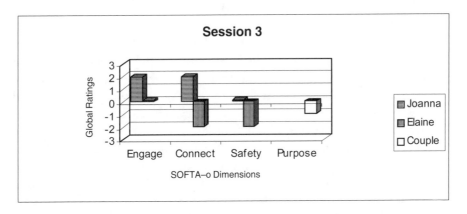

Figure 8.6. A couple's experience of the alliance over three sessions. SOFTA–o = System for Observing Family Therapy Alliances—observational.

Because of the obviously different comfort levels in these families, the therapist approached the two initial visits differently. Because the DeMartinos seemed at ease with each other, it was reasonable to expect their comfort level to increase as the session progressed. With the Belzers, however, the therapist engaged in small talk at first ("Did you have trouble finding the office? Has it stopped raining yet?"), showing the children the tropical fish tank in the corner of the room, and so forth. To ease the tension further, the therapist began the session by suggesting that therapy is a voluntary process: "We have about an hour to get to know one another. Then you can see if you think I have something worthwhile to offer you and if you'd like to come back another time." He went on to ask if anyone in the family had ever consulted a therapist. When they said "no," the therapist explained confidentiality and its limits. As the session continued and only the mother seemed willing to speak, the therapist decided to see the parents alone and then each child separately for a few minutes. Bringing the Belzers together toward the end of the session, the therapist summarized the family's concerns, taking care to mention everyone's point of view (without revealing any secrets). Then he concluded:

> I can see that coming here was difficult, something new for all of you, but I'm glad you did. I sense a lot of worry on your part, Mom and Dad, but also I see your family as one that has much going for it. Connor and Lucas, you help your parents out in your own way, and you know how much your parents love you and want the best for you. I'd like to help you all get back on track as a family so there's not so much arguing and fighting that none of you like. It seems to make everyone unhappy. And I think we can work on that together here, if you decide you'd like to come back.

Everything this therapist did with the Belzers was intended to raise the family's level of safety. It is interesting that the DeMartinos' presenting problem—children fighting, parents screaming at them and at each other—was identical to the Belzers'. It was not the problem per se that occasioned different safety levels in the two families. Because the Belzers were ashamed of what they were experiencing, unaccustomed to speaking frankly without yelling at each other, and generally wary of professionals, their anxiety stalled the therapeutic process before it began. Furthermore, the family had been referred to therapy by the school counselor, who was concerned for the children's well-being, whereas the DeMartinos were seeking help on their own. Recognizing that they were going through a difficult period adjusting to preadolescence, the DeMartino parents saw the problem as serious but neither shameful nor threatening to the stability of their marriage. They had no fears that their children were into drugs or that the juvenile justice system would need to be called in. The Belzers, however, worried that Child Protective Services would be contacted and their children removed from their care. The father's drug problem was a secret everyone in the family wanted to hide from the authorities, including the therapist. The point of this comparison is that when a family feels threatened (from within or without), safety must be attended to before any progress can be made in therapy. In the case of the Belzers, everyone was afraid. They were afraid of the therapist's power and felt unsafe with each other.

In other families, a single individual may feel unsafe. When this person has the power to keep the family from continuing in treatment, the situation is urgent. As a precautionary measure, the therapist may need to see that client alone, possibly even for a few sessions, to ease the way. In extreme situations, the family may never be able to come together in the therapist's office. Rather, the therapist might need to work with subsystems—parents one week, siblings the next, or father–child and then mother–child, mediating the conflict to prevent harmful escalations.

Although some anxiety is needed to motivate change, it can cripple the therapeutic process when there is long-standing mistrust in the family, distrust of professionals, and repeated treatment failures. In M. Beck et al.'s (in press) four case studies of the alliance, the two families who experienced the therapeutic context as unsafe early on had minimal success in treatment.

In our view, ensuring safety should be the therapist's primary objective when treatment begins. Safety first.

SUSTAINING ALLIANCES

In any personal relationship, bonds develop naturally over time. When people are not unduly threatened and they see some gain from their interactions, emotional connections are made and the relationship increases in perceived value. So, too, in therapy. In most cases, clients naturally become attached to their therapists and more engaged in the process with the passage of time. Early on, clients wait to see what the therapist expects and how the "game" is played. As the sessions take on a predictable rhythm, clients tend to become more involved. They bring up new problems without being asked, they talk about their experience of the therapeutic process, they report on their progress at home, and so on.

In other words, when there are no roadblocks and people come prepared to speak truthfully and to work with each other toward a common goal, the between-systems and within-family alliances strengthen naturally. Particularly as people begin to notice their family members changing in positive ways, their own engagement and sense of purpose about the therapy grow. When they can relax in therapy, family members start looking forward to their sessions and feel an even stronger bond with their therapist.

The alliance-building process is not always a smooth one, however. When a client comes to treatment as a "hostage" because someone else is mandating it (see chap. 11), the client's safety and shared purpose with other family members can stay fragile for quite awhile. Here is where the SOFTA constructs can be useful. To enhance the family's sense of safety and shared sense of purpose, therapists can focus on increasing engagement and emotional connection. To engage reluctant family members, therapists can define a shared sense of purpose by repeatedly pointing out commonalities in people's perspectives, values, and experiences, encouraging family members to ask each other for feedback or for their perspective on the problems discussed, praising clients for respecting each other's point of view, and so on. As reluctant clients come to see that their opinions and feelings are respected, they tend to feel more comfortable and willing to get involved.

Sustaining the alliance on all fronts simultaneously can be challenging when events in the family's life or within the treatment process are disruptive. As described in chapter 9 ("Repairing Split Alliances"), when the therapist makes an error in judgment or is perceived as playing favorites, emotional connections become strained. Disruptions also occur when a powerful third party interferes. One client, for example, was trying hard to do what was needed to have her three children returned to her. After a meeting with the Child Protective Services worker went sour, she criticized the therapist for siding with the social worker against her. At the therapist's suggestion, another single mother took out a Person In Need of Supervision petition on her uncontrollable 14-year-old son. Six months later, when the Probation Office threatened to remove the boy from their home, the mother blamed the therapist, claiming the therapist should have known what could transpire.

In complex cases, the comings and goings of family members in treatment can make navigating the alliance particularly challenging. When a group of clients has developed a comfortable rapport with the therapist and a unique style of working in therapy, allowing a new family member to attend the sessions is likely to be disruptive. At best, the disruption is minimal; at worst, it is counterproductive.

Estela Jiménez, a 64-year-old grandmother, had been taking care of two grandchildren, a girl and a boy, while her daughter was in prison for selling illicit drugs. Two months prior to Ruby's release, Estela sought help to prepare the family for Ruby's return. The therapeutic alliance was solid all around until Ruby came for her first session. Resentful of her mother's influence, Ruby had threatened to leave home, with or without her children. In session, the children clammed up, Estela sat stiffly with pursed lips, and Ruby stared defiantly at the therapist. Eventually, after meeting alone with Ruby for two sessions (Sessions 1 and 2 in Figure 8.7), then with both women for one session (Session 3), the therapist was able to bring the four family members together for a productive new beginning (Session 4).

It was not merely the separation of family members that saved the day in this case. The therapist diligently focused first on Ruby's sense of safety with him and then on the shared sense of purpose between Ruby and her mother. To raise Ruby's comfort level, the therapist made a connection with her on a personal level, saying,

> Ruby, of course I know your mother and children much better than I know you. And I hope to get to know you well, too, if you'd like to work

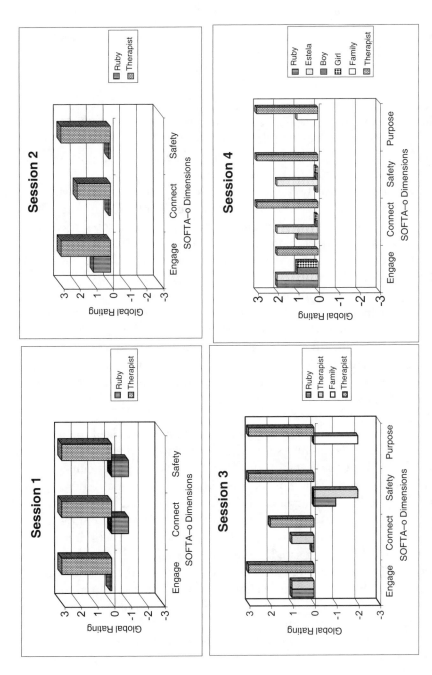

Figure 8.7. Therapist repairs to a split alliance with Ruby and Estela Jiménez. SOFTA–o = System for Observing Family Therapy Alliances—observational.

with me. As you know, your Mom contacted me to help all of you learn to be a family again. With anyone being away for 5 years, that'd be hard!

As Ruby's body posture relaxed, the therapist put all the cards on the table: "Here's what I know about you and your situation. Let me know if it's right." He went on to summarize his knowledge of Ruby—how she "got in with the wrong band of friends" and was "set up," how she maintained contact with her children regularly from prison, that she has "some real talent as a singer," was an "awesome track and field star in high school," and is a "good friend whenever anyone else is in trouble." Doing so, the therapist let Ruby know that what was said in her absence had not been focused on her mistakes and that, in fact, the therapist had a positive impression of her.

Session 2 alone with Ruby went much smoother and dealt with the issues Ruby wanted to negotiate with her mother. Implicitly and explicitly, the therapist explained his role as mediator; he had no personal agenda to keep Ruby away from her children. When Estela joined Ruby in the following session, the therapist focused on challenging their zero-sum (i.e., win–lose) perspective. Reminding Estela of the many times she'd said that her main concern was the children's welfare, the therapist reframed the situation as one in which everyone could gain from "being together as a family again, whether or not you decide to share a household." By the end of Session 2 with Estela and Ruby, the goals were clear and acceptable to both mother and daughter. In the therapist's words, they were going to "find a way to be a family—to parent the kids together and hopefully support each other without competing for the children's affection or putting them in the middle of a custody battle in the courts."

In this illustration, the therapist had originally misjudged the family's ability to tolerate a conjoint session when Ruby entered the scene. By working with Ruby alone, the therapist aimed to remove the threat of being "ganged up on" by her mother, children, and an unknown professional. Then, by engaging Ruby and making a personal connection with her, the therapist increased the client's sense of safety. Focusing on Ruby's goals, he showed her that therapy could be for her as well as for her mother and children. After Ruby acknowledged her gratitude to Estela for parenting the children in her absence, the final step could be accomplished, redefining the treatment goals. Together with the therapist, Estela and Ruby were able to sidestep the win–lose definition of their circumstance. By the time the children were brought back into treatment, it was clear that everyone could be a winner.

Some ruptures in the alliance actually occur because of the progress being made in therapy. As family members come to trust the therapist and feel more and more secure in the therapeutic context, they may take far greater risks than anticipated. In their Session 7, Olivia told her husband, Ted, that because their sex life had come to a "virtual standstill," there were moments when she considered leaving him. She simply could not imagine "giving up that part of life at age 35." Ted, asked by the therapist for his reaction, commented that Olivia was being "much more direct about it" than she ever was at home. Crying quietly, Olivia quickly interjected, "I feel braver here." The situation was especially delicate because Ted saw their female therapist as Olivia's ally. Humiliated and defensive, Ted refused to explain his lack of sexual interest in his wife. Olivia's high level of safety had prompted a process that split the alliance and damaged her husband's safety and involvement.

In a more dramatic instance, a startling disclosure shattered a family's growing sense of safety and shared purpose. Kate Arnold brought her children for help after it was discovered that Tony, age 13, had been molesting his younger sister in the afternoons while Kate was working. After six productive sessions with frank discussions about boundaries, guilt, and self-control, Kate asked her daughter if she could ever forgive her brother. In the long pause that ensued, Tony blurted out that *he* could never forgive his uncle (Kate's brother) for molesting *him* for the past 5 years. Furiously unbelieving, Kate turned on Tony, accusing him of lying. In an instant, everyone was screaming.

Dramatic reversals like these need not bring the treatment to a halt, however. They do call for prompt, active attention on the therapist's part. Just like the therapist who worked with Ruby and Elena, the Arnolds' therapist focused on the family's motivation to face its problems honestly. He praised their courage and supported Kate in her shock and grief. Using their personal connection to help her assimilate the terrible news she had just heard, the therapist was gradually able to effect a change. By the end of the session, Kate could reach out to her son and comfort him in his pain.

CONCLUSION

One of the most frustrating aspects of nurturing and navigating alliances in couple and family therapy is differences in family members' starting points. Some family members are more able than others to observe a process and redirect their behavior accordingly. Some people are more trusting, open, and flexible than others. Some people have more at stake and thus more to lose. Some just have more goodwill toward others.

Not all of these factors can be discerned in Session 1 or even in the first few sessions. When a client makes even a small attempt to understand how his or her behavior is affecting others, however, there is hope for therapeutic progress. "Hostages" to the therapeutic process can become "clients." Indeed, the mere act of letting a therapist into the family's most intimate space can be transformative. Process is progress.

In this section of the book, our aim was to show how focusing on the four SOFTA dimensions—Engagement in the Therapeutic Process, Emotional Connection With the Therapist, Safety Within the Therapeutic System, and Shared Sense of Purpose Within the Family—can help therapists initiate and sustain alliances with multiple clients in all kinds of circumstances. In the chapters that follow, we offer a more nuanced discussion of *mis*alliances, challenges to the alliance arising from within the family, between the family and therapist, and from external influences.

III

ALLIANCE CHALLENGES
AND OPPORTUNITIES

9

REPAIRING SPLIT ALLIANCES

When people decide—or are compelled—to bring their most intimate problems to a stranger, the anxious anticipation can be almost too much to bear. Sometimes everyone in the family is at the desperation point, thinking, "We can't go on like this anymore; something *has* to be done!" However, family members may have different views on the problem or different tolerance levels for stress. When this is the case, one or more people think, "Things aren't so bad. We've managed before, we can manage now."

When the decision is eventually made to seek help, the ambivalence within the system can evolve into polarization in various family members. Suggesting the need for therapy, Bill Lee was adamant that the family was in deep trouble, but wife Marlena and son James were not so sure. Maybe therapy was a good idea, but then again maybe Dad was blowing the problem all out of proportion. Bill dug in his heels, made the appointment, and Marlena and James agreed to go along for the ride. By Session 1, however, their ambivalence had turned into stubborn negativity. Indeed, if mother and son had been open to the idea originally, by Session 1 they had no memory of feeling that way.

This, then, is the family that begins treatment with a weak sense of purpose. Two things can happen. The ambivalence in the system can result in the therapy never getting off the ground. The family either decides to

161

leave treatment or just cancels appointments with one excuse or another until the therapist gives up. Alternatively, the resistant or defiant members settle down after a few sessions and, if they do not exactly enjoy the process, neither do they actively resist it. Over time, though, as problems are faced head on, it becomes clear to everyone involved that the system cannot return to its original state. Anxiety mounts. This is when a split alliance may occur. That is, the family's ambivalence about being in treatment shifts from a polarization about the need for help to a polarization about the person of the therapist. Bill might like her, think that what she is doing is helpful, but Marlena and James might see her as intrusive, ridiculous, overbearing, cold, or just off the mark.

We do not mean to suggest that split alliances and a poor shared sense of purpose are mutually exclusive. It is, however, typical for a family's resistance to manifest itself more strongly in one process than in the other. As discussed in chapter 7, when a sense of purpose about the therapy is not shared, family members disagree about the value of coming to therapy, about who in the family does or does not need to come to sessions, about the nature of the problem, the goals they should be striving for, and, needless to say, how they should go about resolving their difficulties. With a split alliance, these issues are not contentious, or at least not overtly contentious. Rather, family members disagree about the therapist—how good he or she is, whether she or he really cares, whether he or she knows what to do, whether he or she is helping or harming the situation.

Negative feelings toward the therapist can come about even when the family is not in the least ambivalent about getting professional help. Some therapists are simply less skilled, some therapists have difficulty relating to children, some therapists are culturally insensitive, some therapists always see parents as bullies, some therapists play favorites, some are burned out. In other words, a split alliance with the therapist can mirror the family's own split, or it can arise over time as the family interacts with the therapist.

In this chapter, we define the split alliance in couples and family treatment and discuss possible causes for its occurrence and strategies for avoiding and repairing it.

SPLIT ALLIANCE DEFINED

As originally introduced in the literature by Pinsof and Catherall (1986), the term *split alliance* referred to significant differences in family members' attitudes toward the therapy or the therapist, specifically the goals or tasks of the therapy or the emotional bond with the therapist. In the System for Observing Family Therapy Alliances (SOFTA), we define a split alliance more narrowly, as notable differences in individual family members' emotional connections with the therapist, which may or may not stem from disagreements about the appropriate goals and tasks of treatment. Differences among family members about the value or direction of therapy are reflected in a poor shared sense of purpose, which Pinsof (1994) called a poor *within-family alliance*.

As previously discussed, however, the two processes overlap. When family members start out polarized about being in therapy or about what should be addressed in treatment (i.e., when they have a weak sense of purpose), some members are more emotionally available to the therapist than others. Conversely, when all family members begin "on the same page," so to speak, different perceptions can emerge over time about the therapist's skill, impartiality, or personality, resulting in disagreements about the direction therapy is taking or about the value of therapy itself. People who feel less comfortable with the therapist are not likely to value the sessions as highly. Moreover, people who believe that the therapist has not paid enough attention to them or their concerns can feel disenfranchised, becoming less and less invested in working toward common goals.

In other words, although split alliances and a weak sense of purpose may be inseparable processes in clinical practice, for conceptual clarity we treat them as different phenomena. In chapter 5 we discussed ways in which therapists can develop and enhance their emotional bonds with family members. In the following section, we focus on sources of variability in emotional connections with the therapist, that is, the causes of a split alliance.

Before doing so, however, let us consider how split alliances have been operationalized in the literature. Pinsof and Catherall (1986) recommended comparing family members' self-reported scores on the Couple Therapy Alliance Scale or the Family Therapy Alliance Scale. Following this recommendation, Heatherington and Friedlander (1990b) found that after Session 3, a sizable proportion of the couples and families in their outpatient sample could be characterized as having a split alliance; this finding was recently replicated (Mamodhoussen, Wright, Tremblay, & Poitras-Wright, 2005). In both studies, a considerable percentage of family members tended to have differing views on how the therapist was conducting the therapy and about the quality of their relationship with the therapist.

Split alliances in couple therapy were the focus of two recent studies. In one investigation (Knobloch-Fedders et al., 2004) of integrative problem-centered therapy (Pinsof, 1995), couples' split alliances with the therapist in Session 1 were significantly related to a history of distressed family-of-origin relationships. In Session 8, split alliances were most frequent when the wives continued to view the marriage as distressed. However, outcomes were better when husbands' alliances with the therapist were stronger than those with their wives' (Knobloch-Fedders et al., 2004). In the other investigation (Mamodhoussen et al., 2005), split alliances were more frequent in younger, recently married couples. It is interesting that divergent perspectives on the alliance were likely when men were highly distressed about the marriage and their wives had few mental health symptoms.

A split alliance can be identified in other ways. Bennun (1989) compared clients' perceptions of the therapist's postive regard–interest, competency–experience, and activity–direct guidance at the beginning of the second family session. Results showed that the greater the difference between mother's and father's scores, the poorer the eventual clinical outcome. Notably, split alliances were predictive of outcome, whereas no differences in outcome stemmed from the therapist's approach.

Difference scores in family members' alliance-related behaviors were used to operationalize *unbalanced alliances* in functional family therapy (Robbins et al., 2003). Although family members' individual scores did not predict retention in treatment beyond Session 1, dropout was more likely the greater the discrepancy between parents' and adolescents' alliance scores.

In another recent study, Symonds and Horvath (2004) calculated a correspondence index from couples' scores on the Working Alliance Inventory—Couples. Agreement between the partners about the strength of the alliance played an important role in treatment success, regardless of whether the alliance was rated favorably or unfavorably. Moreover, correspondence between the clients about the alliance was more influential than either partner's correspondence with the therapist.

In a qualitative study M. Beck et al. (in press) conducted semistructured interviews with individual family members in four Spanish families immediately after they completed the revised Family Therapy Alliance Scale (Pinsof, 1999), and they compared these results with observer ratings on the SOFTA–o. As in Heatherington and Friedlander (1990b), self-reported alliances with the therapist as measured by the scale were positively skewed, but signs of mildly split alliances were present (i.e., where one family member reported somewhat less positive feelings than did others in the family). These findings were consistent with the SOFTA observational ratings, which showed moderately positive emotional connections with the therapist across the board and little within-family variation.

In postsession interviews with each family member, it became clear that some clients came as "visitors" and others came as "plaintiffs" (M. Beck et al., in press). Overall, these clients said little about their feelings, positive or negative, toward the therapist. When they did remark negatively about the therapist, they tended to mention a general mistrust of professionals or disagreements with the therapist about the goals for treatment. Indeed, the clients in M. Beck et al.'s sample had much more to say about the positive and negative aspects of being in therapy with other members of their family (e.g., feeling blamed, having a loss of privacy). M. Beck et al. concluded that split alliances may have less to do with perceptions of the therapist and more to do with differing (and conflicting) motives within the family for seeking help.

Indeed, it would be too facile to lay the blame for a split alliance only at the feet of the therapist. Even experienced, well-meaning therapists can lack the skill to create a bond and negotiate therapeutic goals and tasks that engage everyone and help them feel safe in the process. In other words, it is not only the talents, skills, experience, and attitudes of the therapist that contribute to an intact or a split alliance—but also the characteristics, motivation, clinical problems, and structure of the family, as well as the interaction of the therapist's qualities with the qualities of individual family members.

Being in Connection

The literature has little on the theory of split alliances and few studies have been conducted to explore this area, although there is some relevant work on therapist qualities that contribute to a strong alliance. In individual therapy, the qualities that promote a strong alliance can be categorized as follows (Horvath & Bedi, 2002): interpersonal skills (e.g., responsiveness, ability to generate hope), communication style (e.g., clear communication, conveying understanding), empathy, openness, exploration, and experience, although results are mixed with respect to experience. In family therapy it is logical to expect that the absence or negative dimensions of these qualities can result in a split alliance (e.g., lack of responsiveness, unclear communication, etc.), and in fact several theorists (e.g., Flaskas, 1989) and researchers have highlighted the special importance of empathy (Bischoff & McBride, 1996; Helmeke & Sprenkle, 2000; Kuehl et al., 1990).

Direct extrapolation from individual to family therapy should be made cautiously, however. Research on individual therapy, for example, suggests that assuming a "take charge attitude" early on in treatment can result in a poor alliance (Horvath & Bedi, 2002), but clients in couple and family therapy tend to view the alliance less favorably when the therapist does not take charge (Friedlander & Heatherington, 1989). A strong power differential between family and therapist is necessary for managing conflicts when clients have varying perspectives and competing agendas (Bischoff & McBride, 1996).

Aside from empathy, optimism, and skill, one can argue that the most important quality in a family therapist is the ability to understand and relate to the family as a system (Andolfi & Angelo, 1988). Having a systemic perspective, the therapist is less likely to make errors such as viewing only one person in the family as hurting or colluding with one partner to keep an affair secret from the other partner.

Results from several empirical studies underscore this point. In one study (Sigal, Barrs, & Doubliet, 1976), clients who terminated treatment prematurely were more likely to comment that the therapist did not understand the family's problems. In an analogue study (Dozier et al., 1998), family members perceived the therapeutic alliance as stronger when the therapist used circular questioning (e.g., asking one person to comment on the relations of others, as in "How do you avoid getting in the middle when Dad and Mom argue?") than lineal questioning (e.g., "Whom do you argue with the most?"). Interviews with couples in another study (Christensen et al., 1998) suggested that an important preventative measure against a split alliance is the clients' perception of fairness. This point was underscored by Kuehl et al. (1990), who concluded that family members found it difficult to watch other family members be "picked on" or "torn apart" by the therapist (p. 315).

When the family *relationship* is seen as the client and the "problem" is seen as a relational impasse, rather than a person, the therapist's lens shifts from pathology to competence (Madsen, 1999). When this attitude is visible to family members, the therapist's interventions are likely to be experienced as evenhanded, impartial, and hopeful. Thus, for example, the systemic therapist avoids identifying the therapeutic goal as "helping Sabina leave home," choosing instead to frame it as "helping the family transition to a new stage" or better still, "helping Sabina leave home in a way that all of you feel positive about her ventures and still connected to each other, but in a new and different way." In other words, identifying therapeutic goals as system change ("to get the family back on track after the hurricane" or "to restore intimacy and trust in your marriage") is the *sine qua non* of promoting a sense of fairness and thereby avoiding a split alliance.

Although it is crucial to view the family as a system of people with interlocking agendas, each person struggling to balance autonomy with connection, even systems-oriented therapists can make tactical errors. One of these is not appreciating the hierarchical power structure in the family (Pinsof, 1994). In five studies of the alliance (Bennun, 1990; Bourgeois et al., 1990; L. N. Johnson et al., 2002; Knobloch-Fedders et al., in press; Quinn et al., 1997), there were differences in family members' self-reported perceptions; in most cases, the father's or husband's alliance score was more closely associated with treatment success than was the mother's or wife's score. The most powerful person in the family is not always the male or even the head of household, and indeed this person may be the quietest individual in the therapy session, the one most easily overlooked (Stevenson, 1993). Simply put, if the therapist does not connect with the person who can keep the family from "coming to the table," a split alliance can destroy the therapy for everyone (Pinsof, 1994).

This is not to say that therapists should pander to powerful family members by, for example, excessively empathizing with them or accepting their perspectives on the family's situation as gospel. To the contrary, various authors (e.g., Haley, 1976; Keith, Connell, & Connell, 2001; Pinsof, 1994) have pointed out the importance of the therapist's hierarchical position within the therapeutic system. Family members are the authorities on their own lives and responsible for their own choices, but the expert on the therapy is the therapist (Keith et al., 2001).

Taking charge does not imply authoritarianism but rather a nurturant authoritativeness. Like Haley (1976), who advocated using *metacomplemen-*

tarity, that is, taking charge passively by "going one down," Keith et al. (2001) recommended the strategic use of "impotence" in working with resistant families (p. 80). Therapists cannot make family members change, and rather than risk a split alliance by going head to head with a defiant or hostile client, the therapist can stimulate change through playful passivity, as illustrated in the following example:

> The G's were a family of five: mother, father, an older brother, and two sisters. Bob, age 17, talked about being a witch. He dressed in a dark, Gothic manner and painted his fingernails black. His parents were stiff and tight, and assumed everyone thought of their son as an idiot. With the help of the school and their pastor, they came to view Bob's role playing as a mental illness. Halfway into a very tense first interview in which the parents could only talk about Bob and elaborate on what they feared and disliked in him, the therapist said, "You know, I think Bob is a creative kid, but what worries me is that he has turned into such an isolate." And turning to Bob, "Had you thought of trying to cultivate some of your pals into a coven, so that you can have some disciples? You know you can't be a messiah without disciples." Mother, a very humorless 6th grade teacher, lips pursed in permanent disgust, went after the 60-year-old therapist as though he were 11 years old: "That's ridiculous. We didn't come here for more silliness." She paused, then challenging the therapist, "Why are we here anyway?" Smiling, and without pause, the therapist answered, "I'll tell you something. I have been ridiculous for a long time, and I'm good at it. I suppose you're here to learn a different way to be ridiculous." The content of this absurd message had abrasive and rude elements, but simultaneously and nonverbally, it was nondefensive, playful, and inviting. But most importantly, it was oddly self-deprecating—a social non sequitur. Continuing, the therapist asked mother how she arranged to upset her parents when she was in high school. Within the next 10 minutes, jaw loosened and smiling broadly, mother laughed at some of her own exploits as a high school senior, while her husband and son looked amused. She had stepped aside from her dominant mother/teacher role. In her amused, nonanxious remembering, the family and therapist had access to her personhood. (Keith et al., 2001, pp. 81–82)

In this example, the mother was ready to do battle with the therapist for not regarding her son's behavior as disturbed. If the boy appreciated the therapist's supportive remarks but the therapist was not able to win the mother over, a split alliance could have derailed the treatment before it began.

It is easy to speculate about why some family members may be more disconnected from the therapist than others. When family members feel ashamed, have something to hide, or worry that they will be blamed, it is natural to transform their resistance to treatment into a devaluing of the therapist. In one of M. Beck et al.'s (in press) case studies, a mother left treatment abruptly after the therapist began focusing on the dysfunctional marital relationship rather than on the son's drug addiction. Or consider Louann Johnson, a single parent who was mandated for therapy with her two oldest children. The adolescents hoped that the therapist would help their mother overcome her drug habit. Louann, however, was predisposed to hate the therapist. After a social services worker had removed her youngest children from her home, Louann saw all professionals as enemies.

Even when resistance is low, the therapist's personality may not complement the preferred interactional style of every member of the family. Moreover, even when the therapist thinks systemically and is comfortable with people at different life stages, her or his ability to make connections can be challenged by the structural features of the family and by the problems embedded in those structures. In the next section, we discuss how therapists can avoid split alliances with couples, families with adolescents, and three-generational families.

Working With Difficult Family Constellations

Sometimes a therapist's problem relating impartially with family members has more to do with the structure of the family system than with anyone's personal qualities. When a therapist joins any client system, new triangles are formed (Andolfi & Angelo, 1988). If the system is a couple, the therapist's entry turns a dyad into a triad. As Bowen (1976) eloquently described, triangles can either stabilize highly anxious dyadic systems or can lead to destructive coalitions.

As discussed in chapter 10 ("Diversity Within the Alliance"), the gender of the therapist (as well as other demographic characteristics) in and of itself creates alignments through perceptions of similarity and dissimilarity. A therapist of either gender working with a heterosexual couple will be the same gender as one client and the opposite gender of the other. In cross-gender relationships there may be not only dissimilarities in life experience and outlook but also covert sexual tensions.

With couples, the "therapy triangle" can become pernicious if the therapist is reactive to the couple's emotional process (Guerin, Fogarty, Fay, & Kautto, 1996). Even when the couple's problem is a lack of intimacy rather than overt conflict, there is invariably a polarized disagreement, either about the nature of the difficulty or about how to rectify it. Thus, the emotional pull for the therapist can quickly become, "Whose side are you on?" Even when trying to avoid taking sides, the therapist often senses a split alliance when the couple does not see his or her behavior as neutral. Unless the couple's relationship is unworkable, it is counterproductive for the therapist to see members of the couple individually on a regular basis or to work with the couple after having seen the partners in individual therapy for more than a session or two. More often than not, complaints about one's partner made in private discussions with a therapist compromise the couple's trust in each other.

Even when the therapist only sees the couple conjointly and is equally allied with both partners, the very nature of their problem can invite a split alliance. Rob and Heather Michelson, for example, came to therapy to decide about whether to move their autistic, retarded 23-year-old daughter from their home, where she'd always lived, into a group home. After a few sessions describing their history and heartache, therapy gradually took on the quality of a debate, with pros and cons, arguments and rebuttals. Over time, as Rob and Heather became polarized in their views, the therapist recognized that his covertly assigned role was as judge. When the couple argued, each client looked more to him than to the other, weighing the effect of the words on the judge's opinion. Because the "judge" tried mightily to refrain from making judgments, wanting only to monitor the debate and clarify the issues, the hidden challenge moved from "Who's right?" to "Whom do you like more?"

The solution to this conundrum is easily seen but not easily implemented. The therapist needs to define his "client" not as two individual members of a couple but rather as a relationship in trouble. Empathic interventions at the relational level are key, as in, "You two are having a hard time with this today, I can see. I really feel your struggle," or

> I'm impressed with how much thought you've both given to this problem. When you go home this week, how can you celebrate the progress you're making? Because *I* see it, and I see that even though you're not yet where you want to be, you're getting there.

In a therapist + couple triangle, the risk is creating two positive alliances against one negative one. When, however, the family is a single parent and adolescent in conflict, the hierarchical structure of the therapeutic system adds to the complexity of the emotional balancing act. That is, even though there is a three-person system similar to therapist + couple, the nature of this triangle is different by virtue of the power differential, that is, two adults versus one child. The emotional question is not so much, "Who's right?" but "How will you use your power?" Naturally, a mistrustful adolescent will expect the adult therapist to join with the parent in an alliance. The parent expects (or at least hopes) to be supported and not blamed or criticized by the therapist in front of the child. Indeed, either it does not occur to the parent to wonder whose side the therapist will be on, assuming that adults stick together, or the parent may worry that the therapist will undermine his or her authority in an effort to form a relationship with the defiant adolescent.

Parents in a two-parent family can have similar worries about the therapist's alliance with their child. However, when there are two parents, a therapist, and at least one adolescent, interlocking triangles are formed (Bowen, 1976). With an increased number of potential allies, the therapist's coalitionary moves, or side taking (Sluzki, 1975), can be a mechanism for change rather than a threat to the alliance. In attachment-based family therapy, for example, G. S. Diamond and Siqueland (1995, 1998) work with the parents and child separately at first, empathizing with each in turn before attempting to see them together. In most cases, according to these authors, the teen's depression is related to some absence of attachment with the parents. In multiproblem families, the teens are often reactive to family problems like marital conflict or divorce, parental drug dependence, or abusive stepparenting. A reattachment intervention is planned to air the child's complaints and help the parents listen to, comfort, and accept the child's perspective without becoming judgmental or defensive. If, however, the therapist has not made an empathic connection with both teen and parents prior to the reattachment intervention, the potential for a split alliance is great. After all, consider what is being asked in this situation: A therapist is encouraging a child to tell her parents how they failed her. Only if the parents know that they are liked and respected by the therapist, and that the therapist believes that they have been trying their best in a difficult situation, can they listen nondefensively to their daughter and respond with empathy to her pain.

Working with acting out adolescents in multidimensional family therapy, G. S. Diamond and Liddle (1999) emphasized the importance of joining with the teen by supporting his or her life goals. This can be challenging if the teen's only goal is to make the parents pay for his or her misery! Diamond and Liddle found that when acrimonious parent–teen impasses were successfully worked through, the therapists directly addressed their alliance with the parents, even if only minimally. Indeed, these researchers recommend addressing the potential rift in the alliance before it occurs, as did one of the therapists in their study.

> Ms. Roberts, I'm not blaming you for your son's problems. Do you feel I am? . . . Would you tell me if I did? . . . Good! Because I am suggesting that your son has some things on his mind, big things, that are fueling his anger and lack of cooperation. If we could hear him out, it may diffuse some of his resistance and mistrust. Don't feel like you have to defend yourself now. Let's just hear what he has to say. (p. 17)

The typical goal of a rebellious adolescent is to have more independence or control over his life. For the therapist to suggest that the parents are overprotective or overcontrolling would not only damage the alliance with the parents but would not be helpful in the long run for the adolescent. Another strategy would be to direct an empathic but challenging intervention at both subsystems simultaneously.

> Tim, you're mad, I know, and you say you need more freedom, and your parents are worried and say that you can't be trusted. I don't live with you folks, and I'm in no position to make a judgment about the "truth" of

this situation. But I *do* know that what you're asking for is a typical request for teens your age, and I know also that it's incredibly hard for parents to figure out how much freedom their son or daughter can handle, just because kids grow and change so fast. It's tough for parents to keep up and figure out where the limits should be to keep you safe but also give you freedom, at the same time, to grow up. How about this for a deal? I'd like to help you talk with your parents about what kinds of freedoms you need and want, but talk in such a way that they will listen to you and not dismiss you out of hand. But I'll also need from you a deal that you'll keep your cool in this conversation and hear *their* concerns. Then, if we can all do that, maybe we can propose some new things to help you start getting what you want, but also make you accountable in case you blow it. How's that for a start?

The empathy in this message is to both sides of the conflict: Parents are concerned, worried, and want to do the right thing, and the teen is determined and outraged but also wants to stay attached to his parents without appearing to need to. To the family as a whole, the message is, "I hear your growing pains. I'll help you through this."

Another challenging family constellation is the three-generational family, especially when family members literally share a household. Because the emotional system in such family constellations varies, depending on the family's ethnicity, socioeconomic class, and values, the therapist needs to know how common or unusual this living situation is for the people involved. Apart from the meaning of this arrangement in the family's culture, the power in three-generational systems depends on who is being seen as living with whom. That is, have the married children always lived with their parents, and for what period of time do they expect to do so? Did the widowed grandmother move in with her daughter's family because she couldn't continue to live alone? Or did the divorced daughter move into her mother's home for financial and emotional support? Systems like these are triangular by definition, with the middle person often the most vulnerable because she is simultaneously living two roles, as child and as parent.

When therapists join a three-sided system, the challenge is twofold. First, the therapist needs to connect emotionally with individuals who are at very different life stages, which is especially difficult when the clients do not understand or appreciate the challenges facing each person in this complex system. In the Cohen family, the grandfather did not recognize either his daughter Joan's difficulty in bridging two generations or his grandchildren's vulnerability at the bottom of the hierarchy. Joan did not understand either her father's struggle to retain some authority and respect when he became frail and ailing or the divided loyalties felt by her children. The young children, of course, had little understanding of what either their mother or grandfather was feeling or coping with.

The second challenge for the therapist is to figure out the emotional system, which may or may not reflect the hierarchy, and join with the existing power structure without alienating the less powerful individuals. An especially difficult three-generational system is one in which the parent is peripheral and the strongest bond is between grandparent and child. The risk is that the therapist's support for this dyad may alienate the mother who, if personally vulnerable, could well respond by leaving the family.

The point we are making here is that in addition to making an empathic connection with each individual client, the family therapist must understand the structural and dynamic forces within the system that can result in a split alliance. Even under the best circumstances, however, splits can occur.

ADDRESSING ALLIANCE RUPTURES

In Pinsof and Catherall's (1986) Family Therapy Alliance Scale, family members are asked to report on the therapist's bond with them as a group. When scores on this subscale did not predict treatment success in L. N. Johnson et al.'s (2002) low-income sample, the authors surmised that their clients had little awareness of how other members felt toward the therapist. Indeed, when filling out the measure, some clients in M. Beck et al.'s (in press) study said something to this effect: "How would I know what my husband thinks? I'm not a mind reader."

When there is an overt rupture, such as when a client curses at the therapist, the split alliance is there for all to see. The first consideration in repairing a split alliance is determining its intensity; is it "extremely pernicious" or "merely bothersome" (Pinsof, 1994, pp. 180–181)? Recall the case of Bill Lee and his family. Despite a rocky start to therapy, all was going reasonably well until Bill accused Marlena of hiding her alcoholism. When the confrontation unfolded, the therapist, taken off guard, asked Marlena how much and how often she drinks. Furious, she directed her anger at the therapist and stomped out of the room.

Here is a case in which one client's mistrust of the therapeutic process and of the therapist's ability to ensure safety resulted in a disastrously split alliance. Events like these may not be irreversible, however, if steps are taken to repair the alliance with the client who is hurt or who feels persecuted. Marlena suspected that her drinking would come up at some point in the therapy, but she was not prepared for how vulnerable she would feel when it did. She could not forgive the therapist for asking about her drinking ("just assuming I'm guilty!") in front of her 13-year-old son. Although Marlena also blamed Bill for introducing the topic, it was safer to feel and express anger toward the therapist, and it gave her an excuse to drop out of treatment.

When Marlena left the room, the therapist was taken aback and at a loss of how to proceed. Until that point, the therapy had focused on keeping the adolescent son out of gangs and away from drugs. With instant hindsight clarity, the therapist realized that the focus on James's health and safety had been a covert metaphor for Bill's concern about his wife. To cover her confusion, the therapist continued the session, asking both Bill and James for the details on Marlena's not-so-secret dependence on alcohol.

As the questioning progressed, however, the therapist noticed her own growing discomfort, which she was unable to label until the session ended. She realized that continuing the session without Marlena was an error. Furthermore, questioning the other family members about Marlena's drinking only reified the split alliance, making it more difficult to reconnect with Marlena in the future, even if Bill did not tell his wife what took place after she had left.

The split alliance in this case is particularly delicate because a parent was embarrassed in front of her child. To draw her back in would require a sensitive handling of the family dynamics, and it was essential to do so before the next scheduled session. There are any number of ways the therapist could try to reconnect with Marlena—by calling her, writing her a letter, or asking to see her individually. Regardless of the means, the break in the therapeutic process needs to be addressed before any concerns about Marlena's drinking are mentioned. If Marlena is at all responsive, the therapist could begin like this:

> Marlena, I need to apologize to you for how things got out of hand on Wednesday. We had agreed that therapy would focus on your and Bill's concerns about James, and so I should not have asked you the questions I did about your drinking. We got off track, and I want to say I'm sorry for how that happened.

If Marlena is able to accept the apology, even tacitly, the therapist could then inquire about her experience of what took place. The repair to the alliance would proceed in a way similar to that suggested by Safran and Muran (1996, 2000), that is, with the encouragement of Marlena's assertive expression of anger and the therapist's appreciation for Marlena's frankness and the therapist's acknowledgement of her own role in the rupture. The point of this process is to model for the client how to resolve an interpersonal conflict reasonably and without destroying the relationship.

At some point, the therapist must inform Marlena about what took place after she left and apologize for talking about her in her absence. There is no knowing how this will go, because Marlena's willingness to repair the therapeutic alliance depends on many factors, not only the therapist's sincere attempt to reconnect. If the repair process is successful, it may be because after the session Bill had reassured Marlena of his unconditional love, or because at some level Marlena wants to face her alcoholism, or because the therapeutic relationship had been a strong and positive force in her life up to this point. If the repair is unsuccessful, it may be because Marlena has already gone too far in condemning the therapist to others or because she fears that therapy will unravel her tenuous hold on reality. In other words, the success of the therapist's efforts to reconnect in the case of a split alliance depends not only on how skillfully she approaches the disaffected client but also on the quality of their prior relationship, on the family system configuration, and on the client's personal motivation and strength to face her "demons."

Ideally, the repair to the alliance with Marlena should take place in the presence of Bill, and possibly James. If Marlena decides to continue in treatment, the therapist must nonetheless bring up Marlena's excessive drinking. Because, invariably, all parties will see the therapeutic process in terms of *before* and *after* the difficult session, therapy cannot proceed without a discussion of how the focus changed and of what should be the focus in the future. Again, what is decided at this point depends on many factors: the severity of Marlena's problems, the strength of the marriage, and the degree of concern about James's behavior, among others. Marlena's drinking may be addressed now, later in the treatment, or not at all. If it is not addressed immediately, Bill may decide to follow the therapist's lead in backing off, or he may refuse to continue in therapy if the problem is not a part of the therapeutic contract.

Handling a split alliance in this case is especially tricky not only because of the denial and mistrust that accompany addiction but also because the alliance rupture involved a parent who felt humiliated in front of her child. This example reflects three important variables affecting the severity of split alliances: (a) the client's interpersonal qualities, (b) the family member's roles, and (c) the point in treatment when the split occurred.

Not all split alliances are signaled by clients becoming hostile or running out of the room and refusing to return to treatment. Less obvious behavioral indicators of a poor or merely neutral emotional connection (see chap. 5) with one or more family members, in the context of a strong connection with others, can signal an alliance split (Pinsof, 1994). Although some therapists may be skilled enough to bring the split to everyone's attention and work it through directly, more subtle interventions can be used. These include humor, varying the therapeutic context, and the strategic use of indirectness.

Humor is at once a powerful joining mechanism and a mood lightener in any social context. As illustrated in the earlier example with the G family (Keith et al., 2001), humor can create connections by reducing tension, highlighting absurdities, and giving clients a more realistic appreciation of their problems (Carroll & Wyatt, 1990). On an emotional level, humor restores bonds and levels the playing field. On a metacommunicative level, humor tells the disaffected client that the therapist sees her or him as a person, not as a problem (Reynes & Allen, 1987).

Rait (1998) described how playfulness was used to coax a reluctant adolescent into the therapeutic process. Noting that 13-year-old Joseph behaved with other family members as if he were royalty and they were his subjects, the therapist asked the boy's family to make him a crown. Then the therapist engaged in a lively discussion with Joseph about "the prerogatives of royalty": ordering others around, speaking with authority, and so on (p. 66). Getting into the role, which allowed him to behave as he wished without admitting the need for help, Joseph found a way to enjoy the therapy. Later on, the therapist met alone with Joseph to talk "man to man" about ways he might feel more powerful with his peers.

Naturally, when a client is angry and feels betrayed by the therapist, a playful, humorous response is likely to be seen as patronizing or hostile. In some cases, the alliance can be rebalanced simply by meeting alone with the client who is out of reach. In a one-on-one session, the therapist can devote all of her or his attention to communicating empathy and understanding— inquiring how the client sees the therapy going, how he thinks other family members need to change, what needs to happen next, and so forth. This intervention can be doubly powerful if the therapist or the client begins to feel more emotionally connected or a renewal of connection.

Yet other variations in context can be useful, such as inviting a peripheral or nonfamily member to the session to support the client who feels alienated. After three sessions in which 16-year-old Shanquia refused all attempts at rapport, the therapist suggested that for the next session, her father and stepmother stay home and Shanquia come to the session with her best friend. Shanquia did so, and watched at first while the therapist bantered with her friend about what the two girls did for fun. Gradually, the lighthearted topic and the friend's nonanxious presence helped ease Shanquia out of her emotional corner. By complying with the therapist's request to bring a friend, Shanquia had tacitly lowered her resistance and also found a face-saving way out of her defiance.

Strategic indirectness, unique to family therapy, allows the therapist to make a point without directly confronting or embarrassing a family member in front of others (Friedlander, Wildman, et al., 1994). Toward the end of the session, when Shanquia had warmed up, even laughing a bit, the therapist turned to her friend and said, "You know, I'm concerned about Shanquia, just as her father is, but I don't think she trusts adults much. Of course, with what she's been through in the past few years, that's understandable." This remark, neither a question nor a directive, left the door open for anything to happen next. Because Shanquia was not directly addressed, she had the emotional space to consider the empathy in the therapist's message without being on the spot to reply.

Uncertain, the friend said, "I don't know what to say about that." After a moment the therapist, offering patience and understanding, commented, "Well, I don't know either. I just wanted to say that so Shanquia would know I want to help her." Then he thanked the friend for coming and ended the session, putting no pressure on Shanquia to respond one way or the other.

This intervention was risky, but the therapist was reasonably certain that a best friend would know about Shanquia's problems at home. Because some easing of tension had taken place prior to this point, this brief exchange affected Shanquia more deeply than she could admit in the moment.

During the ensuing week, Shanquia asked her father if she could see the therapist alone. Three individual sessions were held and, then, feeling understood and supported by the therapist, Shanquia wanted to try working things out with her parents.

Indirectness can also be used when the only responsible course of action is bound to alienate one or more family members. Nineteen-year-old Barbara Shawcross lived with her 10-month-old baby in a one-room apartment after her boyfriend had deserted them. Incredibly stressed and trying to put her life together on her own, on one occasion Barbara left the baby alone for an hour. A neighbor called the police. Although Barbara was mandated for therapy by Child Protective Services, over the course of 2 months she came to trust the therapist and enjoy her individual sessions with him.

Then, because of intense conflict with her mother, who wanted Barbara to move back home, the therapist suggested inviting Barbara's mother into the treatment. Barely 10 minutes into the first family session, the mother angrily described Barbara's negligence toward the baby in such detail that the therapist realized that the child was not safe in Barbara's care. Watching the therapist's concerned reaction, Barbara scowled and crossed her arms defensively across her chest. Knowing his obligation to keep the child safe, the therapist wanted to strengthen his connection with Barbara before notifying the authorities. Taking a risk, he asked Barbara if she would agree to let her mother take the baby overnight and come back with her mother for another session in the morning. At first Barbara was angrily resistant, but the therapist told her that this had to happen or he would be obliged to call Child Protective Services immediately.

The therapist needed time to reconnect with Barbara after these events, and a precipitous loss of her child would undoubtedly have driven her out of treatment. Although the therapist could have seen Barbara alone the following day, he suspected that the only way for Barbara to retain custody of her baby would be for her to move back in with her mother. To make this happen, a strong family intervention was needed.

The next morning, knowing that his alliance with Barbara was in danger, the therapist quickly cut the mother off when she began to fault Barbara: "Mrs. Shawcross, I know how upset you are about all this, and I appreciate your willingness to come tell me about it. But even more, I appreciate Barbara's willingness to let me hear all this, because she must've known you'd speak up before you even came here yesterday." At this, the mother calmed down and listened, and Barbara let a tear slip down her cheek. Continuing, the therapist directed his comments only to Barbara's mother:

> I'm concerned as you are, and as I know Barbara is, about the baby. We have a chance here today to see how we can make this right. As you know, Barbara came to me to help her juggle all her responsibilities, and now you've told me it's not working. Barbara wants to keep Sandy safe, just as you do—she loves him to pieces—but she's tired, overwhelmed, and scared. We three need to figure out how to help everyone, and we can only do it by helping Barbara first. She has some hard choices ahead.

Barbara began to weep silently during this exchange. Then, when the therapist asked Mrs. Shawcross to look directly at her daughter, she too began to cry: "You're *my* child, honey! Let me help you, please!" Grabbing onto her mother, Barbara sobbed. After a while, a plan was made for Barbara to call the authorities herself, tell them what had happened, and state her motivation to do whatever was necessary to avoid losing her son.

Not all ruptured allliances can be repaired. In this case, Barbara's motivation to help herself and her son, and her strong prior connection with the therapist, gave her the courage to follow his directives and stay in treatment. When the initial confrontation with her mother unfolded and Barbara had too much anxiety, humiliation, and defeat to bear, she directed her anger toward the therapist, whom she saw as aligning with her mother against her. Because the therapist's mandate to inform the authorities risked driving Barbara further away, he skillfully reached out to her through her mother. In the end, the family was reunited and Barbara continued in treatment, finished high school, and felt empowered to parent her child alone.

CONCLUSION

Although little has been published on split allliances, all the evidence points in the same direction: Alliance splits are common, they are often unavoidable, and they challenge therapists' ability to connect emotionally, take charge, think systemically, and find clarity through murky emotional waters. If not repaired skillfully, with attention to family members' hidden agendas, secrets, and personal areas of vulnerability, a split alliance can bring the treatment to an abrupt halt. When this happens, some families seek help elsewhere; others just muddle along. The risk, however, is that what begins as a split alliance in therapy can end as a family split apart.

10

DIVERSITY WITHIN THE ALLIANCE

In recent years, race, ethnicity, sexual orientation, and other sources of "difference" between therapists and clients have attracted increased attention among couple and family therapists. Because the within-family alliance is as important as the therapist–family alliance, it also behooves us to consider how diversity among family members can influence the therapeutic alliance. In this chapter, we discuss several diversity topics and offer strategies for thinking about differences and figuring out how to work with them rather than around them.

CULTURAL DIFFERENCES, BROADLY DEFINED

When working with families with strong racial, ethnic, or religious identities, building a good alliance depends on having some understanding of the clients' culture and considering the "So what?" question: "So what does this cultural characteristic mean for family members' engagement in the therapeutic process, emotional connections with me, feelings of safety in this context, and shared sense of purpose about the therapy?" Answers to this question can help therapists select good alliance-building interventions.

Race and Ethnicity

Eve, a young family therapist, listened carefully as her new clients described their troubles against the backdrop of their strong Italian American identity, working-class consciousness, and boisterous family interactions. Eve could not help but reflect on the differences between their stories and her own upbringing as the only child of Eastern European Jewish parents, survivors of the Holocaust. In families like hers, fathers (in this case, a physician) spoke to their children only to educate them, never about frivolous or personal matters, and ethnic pride signaled danger, whereas assimilation signaled safety.

Eve had thick jet black hair and olive skin. Unbeknownst to her, her clients assumed she was Italian, like them. The therapy progressed well. Toward the end, a family member mentioned off-handedly, "Your being Italian of course helped us feel really comfortable with you." The family was as surprised to discover that Eve was not Italian as she was to learn of their assumption about her and how much it mattered to them.

In this case, family and therapist had a close bond despite their (real) differences in background and family-of-origin experiences. As discussed in chapter 5, effective therapists are able to build emotional connections with their clients above and beyond whatever individual differences may exist between them. Over time, by disclosing sensitive personal information, taking risks, and making progress on difficult issues, family members come to feel closer to their therapist, paralleling their improved relations with each other. As in any social relationship, shared experiences over a sustained period of time, especially emotionally charged ones, build bonds. However, clients can do this only if they are successfully engaged in therapy in the first place.

All too often, ethnic and racial differences between clients and therapists make it more difficult to progress past the "getting to know you" stage (Coleman, Wampold, & Casali, 1995; Knobloch-Fedders et al., 2004). The literature has a fair amount to say on engagement with diverse families. One successful and long-standing clinical research program (Szapocznik & Kurtines, 1989; Szapocznik & Williams, 2000) focuses on involving Hispanic (and, more recently, African American) delinquent youth and their families in treatment. Reasoning that resistance to treatment (and to therapeutic change) needs to be understood in interactional terms, Szapocznik and colleagues devised a specific engagement intervention in which the family member requesting therapy (typically a parent) helps "restructure the maladaptive family interactions that are maintaining the symptom of resistance" (Szapocznik & Williams, 2000, p. 124). Research has demonstrated the success of this approach in difficult-to-engage populations, in large part because the family-based interventions reflect community values.

Therapists who are knowledgeable about cultural norms and expectations are best prepared to connect with diverse families. Cultural groups differ in the preferred nature of their interpersonal relationships (e.g., hierarchical vs. collaborative or democratic, collectivist vs. individualistic). In Hispanic–Latino and other ethnic groups, there is a tendency to prefer hierarchical relationships, where open disagreement between children and parents is considered disrespectful (Santiago-Rivera, Arredondo, & Gallardo-Cooper, 2002). As Muir, Schwartz, and Szapocznik (2004) suggested, a therapist who opens Session 1 democratically ("Let's go around and have each of you speak your mind about what's wrong here") risks losing credibility. Family relations may worsen if the children comply by criticizing their parents and an open argument ensues. Rather, the therapist should acknowledge the hierarchy by asking the father, "In your family, do your children have permission to disagree or challenge you?" This question respects the father's authority to decide whether to allow his children to speak their minds (Muir et al., 2004). Moreover, the question does not threaten the father's engagement in the therapeutic process or connection with the therapist; it may also enhance the children's feelings of safety, assured that the therapist is unlikely to ask them to do something that might harm them or their parents.

Some values are common to many cultures; others are culture specific. Szapocznik and Williams (2000) noted that values of family, respect, and leadership are shared by Hispanic and African American clients, but there are important differences in family structure and the people of influence. In working with African American families, it may at times be wise to work with blood relatives and others (e.g., ministers, neighborhood elders) who are considered family and have influence inside and outside the family's home (Muir et al., 2004). In Korean families, respect for elders and family status determines basic features of social interaction, including how individuals should be addressed and how to bow in greeting. It is not enough just to "get it right" with one person. Because family members observe all interactions with the therapist, the latter's credibility may be earned (or lost) indirectly. In one case, an experienced and culturally knowledgeable therapist made certain to use a highly honorific title and to bow low when he greeted a Korean grandfather who was attending one of the nuclear family's sessions. Shaking the grandfather's hand with both of his hands—a humble stance that conveys honor—and citing the Korean saying "Even a tiger will appear if you talk about him" quickly earned the therapist credibility with all family members, who observed his approach to the oldest generation (Kim, Bean, & Harper, 2004, p. 363).

In addition to influencing the understanding (and potential misunderstanding) of therapists and clients, culture also influences the ongoing process of therapy through the preferred interpersonal styles of the therapist and clients. *Achieving styles* (Lipman-Blumen, Handley-Isaksen, & Leavitt, 1983, p. 158)—characteristic ways in which people interact with others to accomplish goals—are shaped by culture and are thus highly relevant to therapeutic collaboration, especially early in the treatment while negotiating goals and building emotional connections. In an interesting cross-cultural study of the achieving styles of more than 1,000 clinicians (Lu, Lum, & Chen, 2001), differences were found between minority and dominant group clinicians, as well as among the various minority group clinicians. Non-Latino White clinicians scored higher than all other groups on the "power direct style;" Asian Americans scored higher on "vicarious relational" (i.e., "pleasure through relating to the goal accomplishments of others"); African Americans scored higher on "competitive direct style;" and Native Americans were distinguished by high scores on the "collaborative relational" and "contributory relational" styles (p. 151). These results have many clinical implications, and here we cite two: that personal questioning and intrusive interventions may be uncomfortable for Native American clients and that greater expressed emotion among African American family members may be misunderstood as hostility and threat by White therapists.

The importance of attending to culture-based norms was a lesson learned the hard way by a novice, White therapist, who was working with a Puerto Rican family: 25-year-old Maria Arroyo; her 9-year-old daughter, Linda; and her grandmother, Marcela, who lived alone in the apartment above Maria and Linda. The family was referred to therapy by school personnel who were concerned about the child's repeated tardiness and truancy. In Session 1, it was revealed that the grandmother routinely set her alarm clock to wake Linda in time for school. Maria greatly resented this "interference" and was angry with Marcela for this and other undisclosed reasons. The therapist, assessing the problem as enmeshment and poor parenting, quickly decided to focus on the mother–child relationship, strengthen Maria's independent parenting, and delineate clear boundaries between mother and grandmother. This approach ultimately was unsuccessful, and the family dropped out of therapy. Only later did the therapist learn that (as in many Latino families) Maria depended on her mother greatly, and both women valued their close relationship. Maria, however, was a heavy cocaine user. Because she stayed up late and slept well into the afternoon, Marcela's "interference" was the only thing keeping Linda in school.

Knowledge of cultural influences is one thing, and working with them in therapy is another. How does one communicate respect and empathy, convincingly and effectively, across the divides of race, ethnicity, religion, and other differences? One way to strengthen the alliance is to admit to ignorance and ask the family's help, but enough knowledge of the culture is needed to know how to ask for help in a culturally respectful way. As illustrated in our case example in chapter 6 of a Romani (Gypsy) family in Spain, a respected elder in the community was invited to the session to educate the therapist about Romani wedding traditions, a point of disagreement between the parents and daughter. Although interventions like this one can work well, they must be used judiciously. Ideally, bringing in a community expert should be used only when the therapist cannot reasonably be expected to know a family's cultural traditions. Clients should not be expected to educate their therapists about cultures that are substantially represented in the therapist's own community.

In addition to these more didactic solutions, therapists should be aware that racial and ethnic differences can influence transference and countertransference as well as the alliance. When a client (or therapist) identifies as a member of a minority group, the transference (or countertransference) can be affected if one party treats the other as a symbol of that group. It has been convincingly argued (Gelso & Mohr, 2001) that alliance and transference are reciprocal phenomena. Strains in the transference inevitably strain the alliance and vice versa.

Acculturation: A Special Consideration

Cultural differences can present a unique dilemma for family therapists. In immigrant and first-generation families, split alliances across generational lines can be problematic when the therapist is of the majority culture and the children are more acculturated than their parents and grandparents. It is easier for therapists to make quicker or stronger connections with family members with whom they can share jokes, references to popular culture, and assumptions about values and family role expectations than with those to whom they cannot relate in these ways.

When older family members are uncomfortable speaking English (or do not speak English at all), there is an immediate challenge to the therapeutic alliance (Muir et al., 2004). Language brokering with children—using children as translators, literally or figuratively—is to be avoided (Santiago-Rivera et al., 2002) because it disenfranchises and disempowers the parents and parentifies the children. At a minimum, therapists should be sensitive to behaviors that wittingly or unwittingly foster split alliances and search for other ways to make emotional connections with less well-acculturated family members, such as joining over the rewards and worries of being a parent. Because it takes a high level of fluency to navigate the emotionally charged, multiperson conversations that characterize family therapy, ideal therapists are native speakers or fluent in their clients' primary language. If not, a referral should be made early in treatment. In many communities, however, there are few bilingual therapists.

The same sort of challenge affects therapeutic work with deaf clients (C. Crane, personal communication, May 6, 2005) because of the distinct language and culture in the deaf community. Indeed, the challenges with deaf clients are probably even greater because few therapists are fluent in American Sign Language. Although interpreters are an option, many communities lack qualified interpreters. Moreover, having an interpreter may add to the cost of therapy, making it unfeasible for many families. Beyond this consideration, the introduction of a third party into intimate therapeutic conversations creates other challenges, such as diminished privacy and decreased therapist credibility and rapport, all central features of the alliance.

Other within-family differences in acculturation, such as divergence in personal goals and assumptions about family responsibilities, can negatively influence the family's shared sense of purpose. Therapists should consider these questions: What do family members really want out of therapy, as a group and as individuals? What does each person express as a hoped-for outcome, and what else might each family member privately wish to have happen in therapy? In families with first- or second-generation teens and young adults, there may be very different expectations about autonomy and connection to the family. Consider this anecdote. A psychologist, who was teaching a course in abnormal psychology at a community college in a multiethnic town, was asked for two therapy referrals in a single week. Both requests came from the parents through their offspring, students in the course. One student from a close-knit, first-generation Greek family asked,

> My parents want you to recommend a psychiatrist or a special school for my sister. She's 20 years old and wants to move out of the house and live on her own. She's not married, and this is a huge blow to my parents. They think there's something wrong with her, and they want it fixed.

The second referral request, from a highly assimilated Irish family, was for a therapist or a postsecondary boarding school for the student's 19-year-old brother, who was refusing to move out of the family home or get a job. The parents were highly concerned about his "retarded social development" and lack of ambition.

A Caveat About Social Class

Therapists from middle-class backgrounds often have little awareness of their own privilege and even less awareness of how social class influences the goals and tasks of therapy they plan for their clients. In an early session with the large McCarthy family, the conversation turned to the need (identified by the therapist) for communal evening meals. Typically, the five McCarthy children, aged 10 to 17, would just find something in the refrigerator to eat, running out the door to be with friends. Unaware of why the McCarthys seemed reluctant to embrace her many suggestions about family meal times, the therapist pressed on, ever more eagerly. Finally, Bruce McCarthy blurted out, "We just don't have enough chairs for that!" The therapist was shocked into silence.

Because much of the literature on working with families of color has focused on low-income families, and because for certain groups (e.g., African American, Native American, Mexican American) minority group status and poverty are sizably confounded, racial-ethnic identification and socioeconomic status are often treated as one and the same. In the United States, poverty has an independent set of implications for engagement in therapy, the most immediate being an entry barrier: lack of health insurance. The barrier is particularly high for the "working poor," who often have neither insurance, nor the ability to pay out of pocket, nor Medicaid benefits for mental health services. Indeed, utilization of mental health services tends to be greatest among very low-income and very high-income youth (Cohen & Hesselbart, 1993; Koot & Verhulst, 1992). Among African American youth, this curvilinear trend is particularly extreme.

Whereas people who are well-off financially tend to be referred to therapy by family and friends (i.e., trusted others), poor people are more likely to be referred by social service agencies (Cauce et al., 2002). Indeed, indigent families who are coerced into therapy by school officials, Child Protective Services, or juvenile justice workers tend to have numerous disempowering interactions with these authorities before they even see a therapist. Thus, as discussed in chapters 11 and 14, the therapist may represent yet another threat. Negotiating goals that are important to the family, and cooperating with other agencies while delineating clear boundaries are essential to foster clients' feelings of safety within the total therapeutic system. Although being aware of the politics of power is important in all cross-cultural therapeutic encounters, it is particularly important when working with socioeconomically disadvantaged clients. As therapists, we must be aware of our own power, use this leverage to empower our clients and help them find their voices, and acknowledge and challenge any of our own behaviors that could lead to a misuse of power (Hardy & Laszloffy, 2002).

When treatment is underway, social class considerations continue to be threaded throughout the process, with implications for sustaining a favorable therapeutic alliance. In an early research study (Cline, Mejia, Coles, Klein, & Cline, 1984), clients from low socioeconomic groups responded more favorably to a therapist's directiveness than did their middle-class counterparts. Moreover, directiveness was associated with the low socioeconomic status couples' expression of positive behaviors in therapy (e.g., agreement, taking responsibility), but the opposite was true for the middle socioeconomic status couples. It is interesting that these differences were far more pronounced for husbands than for wives.

Because poor families tend to be involved with several social service agencies simultaneously, they are likely to be influenced by others' views on the value of therapy for solving their problems. Moreover, these families' extra-therapy burdens (health and safety concerns, finding transportation, work, and a place to live) may mean that mental health goals, even those that are reasonable, practical, and meaningful, are often superseded by the need to cope with an immediate crisis. When therapists provide help and support on these other tasks while not losing focus on the mental health issues, clients' trust and cooperation are strengthened.

Religion: The Last Taboo

The Marchionne family (Betty, Jimmy, and three children) sought help after a devastating hurricane destroyed their trailer park home. In a matter of hours, their lives were reduced to a frantic search for food, water, and a roof over their heads. They found their way to a shelter and, a month later, to a community mental health center. Aside from the youngest child's extreme anxiety, the family had few mental health concerns. Rather, Betty and Jimmy felt an urgent need to answer the question, "Why us?" The therapist's willingness to talk openly and at length with the family about their crisis of faith had a greater impact on the therapeutic alliance than any other intervention.

It is well documented that, at least in the United States, clients tend to be far more religious than their therapists (Hall, 2001). Many therapists are unwilling to disclose their personal beliefs on religious and spiritual topics, despite evidence that clients tend to prefer therapists from similar religious backgrounds (Hall, 2001).

Religious differences between therapists and clients can cause problems, even when they are not a focus or topic of discussion. Hal and Louise Emerson, a childless Roman Catholic couple, had been in therapy for 2 months when Hal opened the session by telling Louise he wanted a divorce. Furious at her husband but afraid to voice her anger, Louise turned on the therapist, demanding that she "do something." When the therapist did not challenge Hal's decision, Louise accused her of "standing idly by," saying, "I know you're a Jew, and so of course you don't value the sanctity of marriage like we do."

In recent years, many therapists have begun to incorporate spirituality into therapy discussions. There is, in fact, a burgeoning literature on spirituality in psychotherapy (e.g., Hathaway, Scott, & Garver, 2004; Rose, Westefeld, & Ansely, 2001). According to some authors (e.g., Hall, 2001), religion and spirituality tend to be especially important for many families of color, and ignoring these issues may compromise the effectiveness of therapy.

Because religious involvement may have great effect on some clients' day-to-day functioning, effective therapists take this into account in their work. Therapists should also be aware that religion as practiced in middle-class White families can differ widely from such practices in minority cultures. Religion tends to be an integral part of African American family and communal life, particularly in low-income neighborhoods where churches offer economic, educational, and social support (Hall, 2001). Religious and cultural values of collectivity, connection, and loyalty to family (including cherished ancestors), unfamiliar to most White Americans, guide everyday rituals and decisions in traditional Asian families. Native American and other healing rituals (cf. Fadiman, 1997) are an important part of some families' belief system, and they can and should be respected as a complement to traditional psychotherapy. In any case, awareness of how religious belief systems influence clients' constructions of their problems ("Why is this happening?") and constructions of solutions ("What will be helpful?") can enhance the therapist's credibility and promote emotional bonds.

GENDER AND SEXUAL ORIENTATION

Gender intersects with culture in myriad ways that may be relevant for the therapeutic alliance. The concepts of *machismo* and stereotypes of the "Jewish mother" or "Greek father," for example, may be particularly salient in a given family's worldview. Knowledge of these stereotypes, a respectful curiosity, and sensitive discussion about them can enhance the therapist's credibility and further the treatment goals.

It is well-known that gender is an especially significant factor in help-seeking, with women being far more likely to seek outpatient therapy than men. Indeed, the first contact for marital therapy is likely to be made by the wife. In the case of family therapy, it is typically the mother who first recognizes a mental health problem and then seeks and chooses services (Cauce et al., 2002), bringing (or in some cases coercing) the family into treatment. Thus, even before the couple or family arrives at the therapist's door, there may be a gendered dynamic in which the wife or mother feels more positive about the therapy and more willing to collaborate, connect with the therapist, and experience the context as a safe one.

Whereas some therapist characteristics are invisible to clients (religion, marital status, socioeconomic status), gender is not. Working with a heterosexual couple, a therapist is inevitably the same sex as only one partner. Consider the threats to safety when a male therapist and dissatisfied wife happen to "click." In the extreme, a split alliance could ensue (see chap. 9). However, same-sex participants—wife and female therapist, for example—might share gender-based values and worldview, prompting a greater understanding between them than between the therapist and the opposite-sex family members.

Even when there are no obvious causes for split alliances, problems can stem from gender-related interactions of which the therapist is blissfully unaware. Gender role stereotypes, socialization within families of origin, and popular books like Gray's (1992) *Men Are From Mars, Women Are From Venus* shape expectations about how people will behave in social relationships, including therapy. A cartoon entitled "Exasperated? Try to think of your mate as a cross-cultural experience!" shows a dog and a cat in bed, each reading a book like Gray's. The cat says, "I am *not* trying to be aloof—I'm a *goddamned cat*, okay?"

Indeed, a number of authors (e.g., Luepnitz, 1988; Shields & McDaniel, 1992) have argued that family therapists unwittingly reinforce damaging gender role stereotypes. Werner-Wilson, Price, Zimmerman, and Murphy (1997) found, for example, that the therapists in their study tended to interrupt women more frequently than men. Postner, Guttman, Sigal, Epstein, and Rakoff (1971) reported that addressing fathers more often than mothers had a more powerful impact on treatment outcome. In yet another study (M. D. Brown-Standridge & Piercy, 1988), therapists responded differently to husbands and wives who seemed defensive. Yet when asked about their intentions, 80% of the therapists in the study denied any awareness of behaving differently toward their male and female clients.

In creating alliances, therapists should pay close attention to ways in which gender role expectations and gender stereotyped behavior influence family members' interactions. Do the women in the family do all the talking about feelings? Is the couple resigned, or do they resist a Mars–Venus interpretation of their relationship problems? Is the division of household labor an issue on which one or the other partner is hoping to "test" the therapist's values and, by extension, his or her willingness to trust the therapist? Gender-based expectations and dynamics extend to the youth in the family as well. Evidence suggests that female adolescents are more likely than males to have positive attitudes toward seeking help and are more willing and able to use emotion-focused coping and social support (Cauce et al., 2002). In a family with two parents, the children and teens may take their cues from same-sex parents or siblings with whom they are allied, and effective therapists recognize these gender-based influences when establishing rapport and choosing interventions.

A therapist's awareness of and careful attention to gender dynamics can enhance the alliance. Some early research suggested that in heterosexual couple therapy, the woman's alliance with the therapist may be less important than the man's, at least in her eyes (Pinsof & Catherall, 1986). In a study of 47 couples in brief couple therapy, the relationship between alliance and outcome was significant only when the male partner's alliance score was higher than the female partner's (Symonds & Horvath, 2004). These findings are provocative and require further exploration. However, split alliances in family therapy have been shown to be more detrimental to outcomes when the father–child alliance is unbalanced as compared with mother–child (Robbins et al., 2003). Indeed, it has repeatedly been found that husbands' or fathers' self-reported alliance scores are more predictive of outcome than those of their female counterparts (Bennun, 1989; Bourgeois et al., 1990; Cline et al., 1984; L. N. Johnson et al., 2002; Knobloch-Fedders et al., 2004; Quinn et al., 1997).

For the gay or lesbian couple, the therapist's sexual preference or orientation is likely to be of more importance than his or her gender. In many communities, therapists (regardless of orientation) who work well with gay, lesbian, bisexual, and transgendered (GLBT) clients tend to be widely known, so that potential clients are well aware of the therapist's sexual orientation before making an initial appointment (L. S. Brown, 1996). Clients who are seen in agencies or clinics typically do not have the option of requesting a specific therapist, and in these cases the therapist's sexual orientation may be unknown.

Many gay and lesbian clients consider working only with a therapist of the same orientation, fearing that a straight therapist might subscribe to dated and inaccurate notions of homosexuality as a mental disorder (Ritter & Teardrop, 2002), a view that continues today in the minds of many (L. S. Brown, 1996). Some clients just want the comfort of knowing that the therapist has firsthand experience with their lifestyle and its difficulties. Others, however, are content with a "straight" therapist who is knowledgeable, nonjudgmental, and empathic.

Depending on the presenting problem, the therapist's sexual orientation or competence in this arena may be of less concern to the couple than other cultural factors. Alec, who is White, and Clayton, who is African American, were more concerned about the therapist's sensitivity to the problems of interracial couples than his expertise with gay men. Jessie and Belinda, a middle-aged couple, preferred a female therapist with a strong family systems perspective regardless of her knowledge of lesbian issues. Being "out" in the community and having a stable, long-term relationship, they wanted help to deal with Belinda's aging mother, who needed Belinda's care on a daily basis but was antagonistic to and rejecting of Jessie.

Arguably, the most salient aspects of the alliance in therapy with lesbian or gay couples are emotional connection and safety. Many authors (e.g., Morrow, 2000) have argued that to make a strong connection, the therapist should explicitly disclose his or her sexual orientation. Some clients do not ask about the therapist's orientation directly, but GLBT individuals tend to be acutely aware of the sexual orientation of others, not only by nonverbal cues but also by verbal innuendo, which reveals a person's comfort level with these issues as well as knowledge of GLBT culture. Sharing a joke or a light-hearted moment about some aspect of the lifestyle can go a long way in forging an emotional connection with these clients. Doing so communicates, simply and directly, "I appreciate you."

Safety is important, of course, with all couples when intimacy problems are part of the clinical picture. Gay or straight, many clients who are comfortable discussing all sorts of other problems can become highly avoidant or defensive when the topic of sex is brought up. In a gay–straight therapeutic situation, this topic is naturally all the more sensitive. To put the couple at ease, the straight therapist's best strategy is frankness, as in this example with Leslie and Shari:

> *Leslie:* Well, we have another issue, but [*looking at Shari*] I don't know how comfortable you are about getting into it here.

Shari:	[*eyes downcast*] Go ahead.
Leslie:	[*to the therapist*] Our love life is all screwed up.
Therapist:	Leslie, it's hard for most couples to talk about sexual matters with a third party. So I can appreciate Shari's hesitancy, and the fact of you both being women may make it all the more difficult to bring this up with me. I want to let you know that I'm comfortable talking about sex with the two of you, at whatever level you want to do that.

As challenging as it is for straight therapists to work with GLBT clients, having the same sexual orientation as gay or lesbian couples can pose unique difficulties. Take the case of Jay and Richard, a young couple who sought a gay therapist to deal with escalating violence in their relationship. Richard, 7 years older, had initiated Jay into the gay lifestyle. Now, 2 years later, Richard became increasingly hostile and depressed as Jay began to distance himself from him. Jay, for his part, had a secret. He had become infatuated with Jennifer, a young woman who worked in his office. Wanting out of the gay world, Jay began to see Jennifer as his ticket to "normality." The therapist, however, was closer to Richard's age and a well-known figure in the gay community. Jay, guilty over his betrayal of Richard and lacking the courage to tell him the truth, was convinced that the therapist would take his rejection of the gay lifestyle personally and align with Richard against him. Rather than take that risk, Jay provoked Richard's anger until he threw him out, at which point Richard attempted suicide.

When the family includes children, other issues become salient in establishing a good alliance, especially with regard to safety. For example, lesbian couples with children from previous marriages struggle with the questions of if, when, and how to tell the children of the reasons for the divorce and the nature of their relationship (Ariel & McPherson, 2000). As discussed in chapter 6, secrets create their own tensions outside of the therapy, as well as fear of unwanted or inept disclosure during therapy, potentially impairing the full investment of clients in the therapeutic work.

Finally, therapists should also be aware of special challenges in intimacy and sexual relationships in both heterosexual and homosexual couples in which there is HIV/AIDS, and especially for couples in HIV serodiscordant relationships (Palmer & Bor, 2001). The changing physical health status of the clients, disclosure decisions, concerns about the future, and other relationship issues may result in shifting goals over the course of therapy, calling for attunement to the couple's shared sense of purpose as well as the relationship between the therapist and each partner. Given that heterosexual women are the fastest growing group at risk for HIV, these considerations pertain not only to gay male clients but also to heterosexual couples and families in therapy (Serovich & Mosack, 2000).

There is an important and growing literature on working with GLBT clients in family therapy (cf. Laird, 2000, and related articles in the 2000 volume of the *Journal of Marital and Family Therapy*), as well as literature on educating and training therapists in GLBT issues (e.g., Long & Serovich, 2003). Recently, to provide practitioners with general information related to psychosocial development, assessment, intervention, and ethical practice in working with gay, lesbian, and bisexual clients, the American Psychological Association's Council of Representatives adopted 16 *Guidelines for Psychotherapy With Gay, Lesbian, and Bisexual Clients* (American Psychological Association, Division 44/Committee on Lesbian, Gay, and Bisexual Concerns Joint Task Force, 2000), four of which specifically refer to the relationships and families of gay, lesbian, and bisexual clients.

DIVERSE FAMILY STRUCTURES

Family structure is not typically considered to be an individual difference variable in the same way as race, ethnicity, socioeconomic class, religion, gender, or sexual orientation is. When clients and therapists differ on these variables, the differences may be apparent and, in many cases, a topic for discussion. Differences between the clients' and the therapist's personal family situation tend not to be discussed, however. Yet these differences are not irrelevant in establishing and maintaining a strong therapeutic alliance.

Consider, for example, the therapist who has never had children. Until one is a parent, the ability to empathize with parents' struggles is clouded by only having personally experienced a parent–child relationship from the child's perspective. Annabelle Carlson, coming to therapy after her husband Bryan disclosed an extramarital affair, asked early in Session 1 whether the therapist had children. Annabelle worried that if the therapist was not also a parent, she would be judged harshly for wanting to hold onto a philandering husband for the sake of her children. Although this concern may be a projection of Annabelle's own ambivalence about her marriage, interpreting that her question is a projection could damage the therapeutic relationship before it gets off the ground.

Clients going through divorce, struggling with infertility, caring full time for aging parents, raising grandchildren, or coping with widowhood at a young age can feel greatly out of step with their peers. Even if the family situation is hidden from others, there is often a sense of shame or stigma associated with living a life that is not the norm. Moreover, even when the therapist is not directly questioned about his or her own family or asked for an opinion about the family's situation, clients can feel inferior if they assume the therapist is leading a more "normal" lifestyle.

Suzanne and Bob Miranda, married for 8 years, had two young children by adoption. A month earlier, Bob found out to his amazement that he had fathered a son by a woman he had known prior to meeting Suzanne. This woman showed up unexpectedly, demanding help with the child, Alexander, who was now 6 years old. The financial issue was not a sticking point for Suzanne, nor was the fact that Bob had fathered a child before they met. Nonetheless, she had a strong reaction to the situation.

Bringing Suzanne to therapy to mend the ever widening gulf between them, Bob was stymied at the depth of Suzanne's anger and depression, because she had warmly greeted the boy when they met. Although Suzanne had no problem with either the therapist or the need for marital therapy, she was nonetheless unwilling to divulge her true feelings about the situation.

Then, when the therapist mentioned that he also had two children by adoption, Suzanne felt empowered to face Bob with her deepest fears. She had felt humiliated because now it was apparent to everyone in their social circle that she was the infertile one in the couple. Moreover, although she could understand Bob's happiness at meeting Alexander, she was saddened to see her husband's physical appearance reflected so clearly in the boy's face and physique. All the insecurity she had previously felt about their marriage, pushed out of her mind since their children's adoption, had come flooding back. Feeling tremendously vulnerable, Suzanne now had to ask Bob the question she'd been carrying for so many years: Did he feel he had missed out on an important part of his life by staying with her?

Bob reassured Suzanne that he had never considered leaving her. Now the couple was over the hump. From there, the therapy was an easy, fluid process as the Mirandas focused on how to explain Alexander's presence to their children, how to integrate the boy into the family's life, and so on.

It was fortuitous that the therapist's own children had also been adopted, because his self-disclosure gave Suzanne the strength to divulge her deep feelings of shame. How might a therapist proceed in the absence of this particular bond with the Miranda family? Whether or not the therapist intuits Suzanne's feelings, he could address himself to Bob.

> Therapist: Bob, I see a big question mark on your face. You seem confused when we talk about Suzanne's reaction to meeting Alexander.
>
> Bob: Yes, that's it, exactly! I don't get what's going on!
>
> Therapist: What ideas do you have about what she might be feeling?
>
> Bob: Well, like I said, I keep asking her if she's upset that Alex is my kid, or that I was with someone else before her, but she says it's not that, she's not jealous because it happened before we met. I don't get it!
>
> Therapist: Tell me a little about Alex.
>
> Bob: He's just a great kid! [looks at Suzanne, who's trying not to cry]
>
> Therapist: I know she's hurting, Bob. I think she's wanting to tell you something but is not quite ready yet. Tell me more about Alex.

Bob: Well, he's blond, like I am, but he has his mother's eyes. [*sees Suzanne, crying freely now*] Geez, honey!

Therapist: [*softly*] Bob, Alex looks like you. He's your biological son. I think Suzanne has some feelings about that, maybe more about that than about how you knew Alex's mother. Can you help her tell you what she's going through?

Bob, consumed with his own thoughts and feelings since he learned about Alex, could not step outside himself long enough to consider the impact on his wife. In Bob's mind, the couple's infertility was in the past, and until this point he had no clue that his biological link to Alex could be the source of Suzanne's pain.

In this example, the therapist addressed the client who was most comfortable in the therapy, taking the pressure off the person who felt unsafe. By deftly guiding Bob to understand his wife, and then to reassure and comfort her, the therapist relied on the couple's own resources to break through the barrier that separated them.

Like infertility, divorce is an issue that brings up feelings of shame and a sense of failure. The divorced family challenges the therapeutic alliance in special ways. The first issue to arise is, Who is the client? Often the custodial parent brings her children for help. The single mother may ask for help for the family but be so needy that the treatment process comes to resemble individual therapy for her, with the children as onlookers. Alternatively, the mother may only want the children to be "fixed," refusing to engage in any discussion in which she is more than just an onlooker. In joint custody situations, matters are complicated if the therapist is required by state law to get consent from both parents before seeing the children.

When it seems to be in the children's interest to involve the absentee parent in treatment, only the most secure and stable custodial parents can consider doing so. When her husband left the family to start another one with a younger woman, Caroline managed to put aside her grief and outrage long enough to bring her 11-year-old son, Ricky, for therapy. Although Caroline knew Ricky was confused and hurting over his father's abandonment, she wanted Ricky to get help managing his feelings, not to reconnect with his father. Although Caroline knew better, even imagining Ricky getting closer to his father threatened her fragile sense of security.

When Caroline balked at the therapist's suggestion that Ricky have a session alone with his father, the therapist knew that his alliance with Caroline was in trouble. Without strong measures, Caroline was likely to pull out of treatment altogether. To re-establish their bond and give Caroline the privacy to vent her anger and explore her fears, the therapist suggested they have a few individual sessions together. In the third meeting, feeling more certain of the therapist's understanding and empathy for her plight, Caroline was able to consider Ricky's needs apart from her own.

Yet another challenging family structure is the remarried family, where the children (and the therapist) can be caught between two worlds at war. Some stepparents come as disinterested "visitors," seeing the therapy (and the children) as their spouse's problem, whereas others come to therapy as "plaintiffs" (M. Beck et al., in press), wanting a platform from which to criticize their spouse's "ex" for poor parenting or (in more dysfunctional cases) for making their own lives miserable. When there are two remarried families battling over the children, the four parents' conflicting agendas can easily derail the treatment, with each side vying to win the therapist over. Keeping a focus on the child's welfare, often very difficult, is the only route to treatment success in such cases. Connecting with and engaging all the parents in the therapy is the first step. The second step involves crafting a shared sense of purpose around coparenting: respecting boundaries, compromising on rules, zero tolerance for anyone's manipulation of one side against the other, and so forth.

The following excerpts from Charles Fishman's (1988) *Treating Troubled Adolescents: A Family Therapy Approach* illustrate Fishman's unrelenting demand that four divorced, remarried parents put their needs aside to help Faith, a suicidal adolescent. While Faith was in the room, Fishman made several attempts to create a shared sense of purpose.

> It seems to me the difficult part is that the adults aren't exactly clear on the way to approach Faith on what's best for Faith. . . . What Faith needs so she won't feel criticized is that all of you agree . . . (p. 172) We're here for one very simple reason. . . . If you parents can bury some hatchets, she won't be doing things like this—she won't have to. If you can't bury hatchets and speak to her with one voice, if you can't agree on what all four of you are doing, she is going to grow up very confused. She is in a very dangerous position. Whatever has happened is water over the dam. Everybody is equally at fault, even though nobody believes it. The only reason we're spending our time here—we're not doing marriage therapy, or divorce therapy or anything like that—the only reason is for Faith. Is everyone agreed that that's why we're here? . . . The way to help Faith— it's not easy, but it's very simple. All four adults must be clear on what they want from her and what the consequences are. . . . (p. 174) If you're going to call each other names and cast aspersions we're going to get noplace . . . The reason for this meeting is because she did something and she could have died. (p. 175)

After Faith had left the room, Fishman continued trying to forge a bond among the parents.

> I can tell you on the basis of experience and the basis of research, if your daughter is not to do things like she has done, if she is to grow up so that she is not conflicted, the four of you have to speak to her with one voice . . . . (p. 177) The question is how to get this girl out of the middle . . . (p. 185) We're talking about both parts of Faith's life being there for her.

. . . Assuming that the four of you are grown-up (p. 186). . . . The question is, can you be decent and distant to each other? (p. 187). . . . The four of you know the situation, the challenge—and I mean it as a challenge—how can you find a way of working together? That's what Faith needs . . . I don't think we're really here to clear the air [*between them*]. We can't clear the air. You guys are going to have animosity for the rest of your lives. Are there concrete, specific ways in which you can present a united front to Faith? . . . (p. 191) I think everybody feels the same way. Everybody wants to protect Faith . . . (p. 192) How can all of you separate some of your egos and say, 'Wait a minute!' (p. 194).

This example illustrates Fishman's deliberate and forceful crafting of a shared purpose around effective coparenting. His comments empowered the parents while insisting that they could and must behave as adults.

At the end of this session with the family, a milestone was achieved: The parents not only came to an agreement about how to handle one aspect of Faith's life but also communicated their expectations to her in one voice, supportive of each other. More poignant still, after Faith had left the room, her father reached out his hand to his ex-wife, who responded by pulling him toward her. Then the following exchange took place:

Mother: I don't hate you, you know.

Father: I don't hate you either. I want us to stop fighting. We're going to burn these bridges. That's the way I want it.

Mother: I've been afraid of you. It took me a long time to be able to talk to you.

Father: It took me a lot of guts just to shake your hand. (Fishman, 1988, p. 199)

In the case of blended families with several children, it is helpful to build an alliance with at least one child from each of the parent–child and stepparent–child subsystems. Given the sheer number of people involved, this can be difficult in conjoint sessions. One strategy is to assess, early in therapy, each person's construction of the problem, either publicly in the conjoint sessions or privately ("Write me a letter about what you think is going on in your family") or with self-report questions like the Constructions of Family Problems Scale (Heatherington et al., 1998; see chap. 7 and Appendix C).

In the emotionally close but highly volatile O'Brien family, composed of "his" (stepfather and three teen girls) and "hers" (stepmother and two teen boys) subsystems, it was clear in Session 1 that each individual had a different perspective on the family troubles. At the beginning of Session 2, family members were asked to write individual narratives or accounts of the family problems, to be read only by the therapist. This intervention yielded some surprises: The stepfather was less blaming of the oldest daughter than expected, the older boy took much more responsibility for his acting out than he appeared to do, and the younger boy revealed many wise, systemic attributions and a longing for a closer relationship with his older brother. These revelations proved highly useful for the therapist. More important, writing the narratives jump-started the alliance; each person, knowing that the therapist knew his or her innermost thoughts, felt safer and more emotionally connected. Throughout therapy, family members made indirect references to what they had written, everyone assuming that they and the therapist had a special, private understanding and bond. In fact, they did.

CONCLUSION

Although professional guidelines for cultural and other competencies can be helpful, therapists should be careful not to act on the uniformity myth (Kiesler, 1966). Middle-class African American families, for example, tend to experience different kinds of power and value conflicts than low-income African American families, and the nature of these conflicts is likely to influence the families' therapy goals and willingness to cooperate with a therapist. As another example, our earlier recommendation to approach Latino fathers as family authority figures, for example, may be especially or only true with recent immigrant or low-income families (which have been the focus of attention by researchers and theorists), which, if followed blindly, would make the therapist seem foolish with highly acculturated Latino families (Bean, Perry, & Bedell, 2001).

Indeed, most couples' and families' identities are multifaceted. For this reason, the varying intersections of culture, ethnicity, race, religion, social class, and other factors render inexact a systematic "science" for building alliances across lines of difference. That is, it is simply not possible to prescribe a method for building alliances with clients from every possible combination of social identities. Rather, alliance building with clients whose life experiences or identifications are different from the therapist's (and differ within the family itself) is better conceived of as a *science-informed art*. This art, when well-practiced, blends an understanding of the relevant literature on culture (broadly defined) with respectful curiosity and sensitive attention to clients' in-session behaviors as expressive of their multiple identities, the use of personal experiences as bridges, and attention to the well-known therapist characteristics that build trust and emotional bonds: warmth, empathy, acceptance, and positive regard.

Family members reveal their sense of safety, shared purpose, emotional connection, and engagement in the therapeutic process in myriad ways. Therapists who keep diversity issues in mind as they try to "read" and then enhance these elements of the alliance will maximize the potential for successful collaborations, in the early stages of treatment and as the therapy relationships mature.

11

THERAPY WITH UNWILLING
AND MANDATED CLIENTS

How can we create good therapeutic relationships with people who do not voluntarily seek our help? Obviously, it is not easy. How can we develop a solid alliance with people who are angry about being forced to see a therapist? Generally therapy is voluntary and is defined as such, but it is also common for one member of a couple or family to attend sessions unwillingly or to refuse to come altogether. People who come to treatment under pressure may accept the need to show up, or even the need to change something in their lives, but the choice to seek professional help was not their own. A 15-year-old client, for example, was aware that the events at school leading to her expulsion were her own doing. Privately she admitted having personal, social, and family problems. She knew she needed help, but the obligatory therapy dampened her desire to help herself.

In other cases, clients refuse to admit to having a problem. An adolescent who is having the same antisocial difficulties at school as at home believes that he is simply defending himself from unjust treatment by others. For him, being forced into therapy is another example of adult oppression. Feeling oppressed by an authority figure is not limited to adolescents, however. When a Family Court judge prescribes therapy as a condition for parents' visits with their children, who are in foster care because of abuse or neglect, the therapy referral is seen as just more government interference and punishment.

Sometimes therapy is an obligation but not a mandate. Often pressure comes from outside the family, as when Child Protective Services "suggests" therapy to parents who are under investigation, or when a school principal "advises" therapy to avoid expulsion, or when social services "recommends" therapy to a client on disability. Sometimes the pressure comes from within the family itself. An adolescent's parents told her that therapy was her choice but that if she did not agree, she would forfeit the camping trip she was planning with friends. A husband did not "believe in therapy," but his wife let him know that she saw his attitude as yet another indication of his indifference toward her. She also hinted that her husband's refusal to accompany her to therapy confirmed her suspicions about his infidelity.

When the obligation is explicit and recognized as such by everyone involved, the therapist can plan appropriate strategies to nurture the alliance. In Session 1, the therapist should talk with family members about the pressure or mandate to negotiate the goals and terms of therapy as well as the kind of relationship they are to have. The therapist should be clear and transparent about his or her commitments to the referral source, detailing any limiting conditions imposed by the third party. By encouraging an open discussion of thoughts and feelings on the topic, the therapist demonstrates the intent to create an atmosphere of trust and freedom within the bounds set by the referring body.

When the pressure is covert, however (i.e., when therapy appears to be voluntary but is not), the therapist can detect hidden pressures by considering different dimensions of the alliance. It is unlikely that therapy "hostages" will "click" with the therapist early on (i.e., Emotional Connection) or that they will readily cooperate in the tasks and procedures of the therapy (Engagement in the Therapeutic Process). Probably the most recognizable signs of resistance will occur in the System for Observing Family Therapy Alliances (SOFTA) dimensions of Safety Within the Therapeutic System and Shared Sense of Purpose Within the Family, as discussed in the next section.

CUSTOMERS, PLAINTIFFS, VISITORS, HOSTAGES

In the early phase of treatment, brief strategic (Fisch, Weakland, & Segal, 1982; Watzlawick, Weakland, & Fish, 1974) and solution-focused therapists (de Shazer, 1984, 1985) focus on the type of relationship family members initiate with the therapist. Although not explicit about the therapeutic alliance, solution-focused theorists define three types of therapeutic relationships that characterize the start of treatment: the customer, the complainant, and the visitor (Berg & Miller, 1992; DeJong & Berg, 1998; de Shazer, 1988).

The customer relationship is optimal for the therapeutic alliance: Client and therapist define the problem together and negotiate how to address it. The client recognizes her or his part in the problem and collaborates in planning what is needed to improve the situation. When a customer relationship is established in individual therapy, difficulties in facilitating a strong alliance are rare. In conjoint therapy, however, it is common for a customer relationship with one family member to complement a visitor or plaintiff relationship with another family member.

In a complainant or plaintiff (M. Beck et al., in press) relationship, client and therapist agree on the nature of the problem, but the client does not see himself or herself as part of the solution. The client may even be highly motivated to solve the problem but believes that others—family members, agencies, or outsiders who are complaining about the client—must change for the situation to improve. For example, Celia Stokes began treatment with her husband and son at the suggestion of a school social worker. Although Celia readily saw the conflicts and the risk of violence in the family, she was adamant that only her husband needed to change. In this case, Celia's husband was a customer. He saw himself as responsible for the marital fights and wanted help because he knew his behavior was affecting his children's welfare. Therapy could well have stalled, however, if he thought that Celia was the one who had to change, or if both members of the couple thought the social worker was meddling in their private affairs.

Finally, the client who is a visitor to therapy does not recognize a problem to work on. In these kinds of relationships, it is impossible to negotiate treatment objectives. In many cases the client believes that others are mistaken ("there is no problem") or that other people are the ones with problems. The visitor relationship is common when clients are pressured into therapy. In these circumstances the therapist risks responding to the client's lack of motivation with frustration. Making negative attributions about the client's poor motivation can hinder the creation of an alliance with someone who may well need and benefit from treatment.

We propose a fourth type of therapeutic relationship, one that is unfortunately common in mandated cases, the *hostage relationship*. This relationship occurs when the client not only does not perceive a problem to be addressed but also views the therapy referral as unjust. Consequently, the client is resentful or hostile toward the therapist. This is a highly delicate situation that requires careful handling so as to avoid counterproductive or harmful outcomes.

In conjoint couple and family therapy, the co-occurrence of different types of therapeutic relationships (consumer, plaintiff, visitor, hostage) is not only possible but in fact highly probable. In addressing relational problems between parents and adolescents, for example, it is stereotypical to find a parent who sees the teen's problem clearly and insists on change through therapy. Immersed in the culture of adolescence and blissfully free of worries about his future, the adolescent does not see anything in his life that should worry his or her parents.

Brief strategic therapists (e.g., Coyne & Pepper, 1998) recommend specific maneuvers to establish working relationships with visitors and plaintiffs. Adopting a one-down attitude can often avoid rivalry and coercion. In doing so, the therapist communicates that the clients are responsible for making the therapy work and trust in their ability to do so. When a client views other members of the family as responsible for the problem, the therapist can avoid challenging this point of view by suggesting that the client change whatever he or she is doing that is maintaining the other person's problem or help out by trying a new and different solution. With mandated clients, the therapist can point out that only they can demonstrate the injustice of the referral or, if they wish, they can take advantage of what is being offered to discuss something interesting or practical. Generally speaking, the objective is to generate an atmosphere of collaboration and avoid contaminating the therapeutic relationship with coercion. Strategic therapists do not, however, refer to these maneuvers as building a therapeutic alliance but rather as techniques to draw in reluctant clients who do not view themselves as part of the problem or the process (Coyne & Pepper, 1998).

In the remainder of this chapter, we offer a number of recommendations for working with involuntary clients, followed by two case examples.

ALLYING WITH CLIENTS UNDER PRESSURE

One question haunts therapists who are routinely confronted with clients who reject treatment or who trudge along with ill will: What is the point of initiating therapy with involuntary clients? Undoubtedly, finding an answer to this question is essential for facilitating alliances and making progress.

Bad Therapeutic Relationships as Symptoms of Family Conflict

When a plaintiff accompanies a family member who feels like a hostage, it is likely that the clients' presentation in session mirrors the conflict-ridden relationships in the family. Typically, the hostage feels blamed by the plaintiff or by other members of the family, who in turn feel guilty or ashamed of the hostage's behavior and their inability to control it. To work under these conditions, the therapist must create a safe space for everyone, possibly by seeing family members individually at first. Whether seen separately or conjointly, family members need to be assured that their perspectives and feelings are understood and respected. At the same time, they need to be made aware that continued cross-blaming can negatively affect their progress in therapy.

Rather, to achieve a minimally workable shared sense of purpose, family members must make a commitment to respect each other's point of view and work together to improve their situation. The therapist needs to resist the impulse to impose goals or tasks on the family without a collaborative commitment. When hostages see that the therapist not only understands their positions and the pressure they are under but will not force them to do anything against their will, they often become amenable to treatment. Not to underestimate the power of the hostage, the therapist needs to negotiate each small commitment carefully, all the while taking advantage of the plaintiff's motivation to find a workable solution. It goes without saying that the best solution sidesteps attributions of guilt and blame.

Bad Therapeutic Relationships Due to Mistrust of Professionals

When a couple or a family is forced into treatment by an external agency or institution (e.g., Child Protective Services or Family Court), the clients typically come as visitors, plaintiffs, or hostages. The therapist needs to recognize the coercive context and, difficult as it may be, avoid seeing the family's resentment or hostility as a commentary on his or her own adequacy or skill. Collaboration is hindered if the therapist immediately and exclusively focuses on the problems for which the family was referred, particularly in cases of child neglect or abuse. In a vicious cycle of mistrust, the family's lack of collaboration can be seen by the therapist as proof of dysfunction or pathology. Progress will be painfully slow at best, if the family stays in therapy at all.

However, when the therapist makes a genuine effort to understand the family's deep mistrust of professional "helpers," the therapist's empathy with the clients' sense of invasion or betrayal may nurture the alliance. This understanding is crucial when children have been removed from the home or when this threat hangs over the family.

When client mistrust is high, it is difficult to create a safe space and make emotional connections, and therapists often question the merit of trying to engage a resistant family. Before declaring the case hopeless, however, the therapist must consider whether the situation is truly unworkable or whether his or her personal response to the family is contributing to the barrier (see chap. 13 on countertransference). It is helpful to recall that people who are sent to therapy have often been victims as well as perpetrators of abuse or neglect. A lifetime of interference by social service agencies naturally colors people's views of well-meaning professionals. Moreover, when the referring agency has a tense relationship with the family and the family feels mistreated or betrayed, the logical conclusion is to see the therapist as an extension of the coercive referral source. The natural fear of revealing family dysfunction is compounded when family members know that the therapist is writing (and receiving) reports on their attitude and behavior. The mistrust can be even more extreme when the family is aware that the therapist's fee is paid by the referring agency.

Unfortunately, mothers and grandmothers of children who have suffered abuse from fathers or other men often have a sense of guilt, not only for the children's suffering but also for the measures taken by social services. MacKinnon's (1998) qualitative research suggests that child abuse is not simply the result of family pathology but rather "the inevitable outcome of an individual's position within gender and class contexts, as well as a particular genealogy of relationships" (p. 233). According to MacKinnon, therapists who pay attention to the influence of gender and social class are better equipped to provide help that is not tainted by power relationships between professionals and clients. This point is crucial for creating alliances with clients who consider themselves therapy hostages. Indeed, MacKinnon found that most clients referred to therapy by Child Protective Services are low-income women, even when they themselves are not the victims of abuse. The referral itself often makes these women feel inferior in relation to the professional, just as they do in the patriarchal relationships in which they have been raised.

To create a strong alliance with clients who are reluctant to collaborate with any professionals, the therapist must make his or her first priority to understand the clients' point of view and prior experience in helping contexts, be they institutional or therapeutic. With understanding comes patience and greater motivation to help mandated clients. In our experience, when a therapist adopts an understanding attitude about a client's reasons for mistrust, the client usually responds positively. Consider the irony in this client's comment: "This therapist is different. She seems to want to *help* us!"

Children: The Tender Visitors

Typically, children and adolescents are taken to a therapist by parents or guardians, who are well aware that their children see therapy as foreign, something that belongs to the adult world. Indeed, it's hard to imagine a 10-year-old boy telling his parents, "I just want you to know that I need a therapist, and I think you should go, too, because my problem affects all of us."

Often parents have mixed feelings about treatment for their children, even when they know that professional help is warranted. To avoid admitting failure or feeling self-blame, parents often seek consultation with a therapist when all other avenues for solving the child's problem have been exhausted.

Creating therapeutic alliances with children involves adapting the process to their developmental and cognitive levels. To offer safety, make a strong emotional connection, and engage the children in a process that fosters a within-family alliance, therapists need to adjust their language as well as the rhythm, content, and duration of the conversation to the children's level.

When a therapist assigns tasks for homework, the assignments should be appropriate to the children's age and motivation level. It is all too easy for the therapist and the adult plaintiffs to impose tasks that reduce rather than facilitate a child's engagement in the therapy process.

Many therapist behaviors that contribute to the SOFTA–o dimensions with adults also pertain to children (see Appendix A), such as sharing a joke or lighthearted moment with the client or disclosing some fact about one's personal life. To help children define personal goals for therapy, the therapist needs to use appropriate language and explain how therapy works. Drawings, stories, and metaphors can be helpful, as can toys, sand trays, noncompetitive games, or the incentive of having fun, "alone time" with a parent.

Safety is indispensable. For children to trust the therapist, they must see that their parents also trust him or her. Indeed, the first sign of a therapeutic misalliance may be a child's reluctance to participate. When the parents are merely paying lip service to the treatment, young children have no such ability to dissemble.

With adolescents and preadolescents, trust in the therapist is facilitated by confidentiality and respect for their point of view. Teens are especially impressed when the therapist does not immediately favor the adults' perspective on the problem. Adolescents who live in highly conflicted or unstable family situations (e.g., with parental violence or alcoholism) tend to mistrust all adults. In these cases, the therapist's patience, genuine interest, and personal disclosures (especially about difficult or ridiculous situations the therapist had to endure at the same age) go a long way, as do commitment and follow through on confidential conversations or agreements made in the parents' absence. Indeed, emotional connections are helped along through reciprocity: A teen is more likely to try something new after the therapist follows through on a pact, such as mediating with the parents for some concession that furthers the teen's personal goals.

A strategy likely to facilitate engagement and connection with rebellious adolescents involves challenging the parents' position as visitor or plaintiff in the therapy. Jessica, a 14-year-old who was privately terrified of the lengths she was going to in order to get her parents' attention, was resentful about being forced into therapy and outraged when her mother denied all personal problems and stresses. However, when the therapist reframed the problem in a way that put Jessica's mother squarely "in the mess" with her, Jessica was elated. Of course, this strategy can backfire if the parent feels misunderstood or blamed by the therapist for a problem that he or she views as solely the child's.

Offering "Treatment" or "Mediation" Rather Than Therapy

Simply put, working with mandated clients is challenging because the therapeutic goals tend to be predetermined by a third party. Sometimes the referring agency or individual also decides who the consumers of the therapy are to be as well as the frequency and duration of the treatment.

When therapeutic goals are defined by self-referred clients, therapists tend to respect the family's wishes. When child abuse is suspected, however, "therapy" can be differentiated from "treatment" in its objectives and procedures (Turnell & Edwards, 1999). Typically, the treatment goals tend to be set by the referring agency on the basis of social norms about appropriate and safe family environments for minors. In many cases, the process can be reframed as *mediation,* which allows the mandated clients to accept the therapist's help to show that they have changed or that the referring agency's accusations are inaccurate. When this is the only way for families to follow through, the therapist can negotiate with the agency about conditions the family must meet to ensure minimal safety requirements for children. Sometimes the goodwill that is generated can turn the process from mediation or treatment into therapy. Accepting a redefinition of the therapist's function does not necessarily depreciate the alliance. Although the intervention may not, strictly speaking, be therapy, the alliance must be strong for any progress to be made.

Social service workers frequently complain that it is frustrating, inappropriate, or unproductive to work with mandated clients who refuse to comply with goals that have been set for them. Some workers are surprised when families do not understand that the changes they are being asked to make are reasonable and necessary to ensure their children's safety. In a training workshop, one social worker blurted out, "When the objectives and conditions we set for these families are carried out, it's obvious they work! So why do they refuse to cooperate?!" This comment reveals the worker's ignorance of how people experience a mandate or coercion to change.

When the clients' guilt, shame, or prior experience with therapy generates mistrust, a defensive response toward any imposition of help is a natural response. As we have discussed, a frank discussion of the obligations and limits imposed by the referring institution is essential for developing an alliance, whether the intervention is defined as treatment or mediation. In the absence of collaboration, it is a mistake to introduce elements that may well be therapeutic but are incompatible with the mandate.

Sometimes, despite our best efforts, there are cases in which the level of mistrust or antagonism toward the referring party (or the therapist) makes it impossible for the family to collaborate in therapy, treatment, or even mediation. In such circumstances it is wise not to insist on a course of action that becomes a punitive extension of social control.

CASE ILLUSTRATION: THE COTHERAPIST NEIGHBOR

Julia Phelps and her husband, Richard, began family therapy as one of several conditions imposed by a Family Court judge. Their 6-year-old son,

Christopher, was in residential care as a result of parental fights that had been reported to the authorities by neighbors. The judge's decision was also influenced by Richard's lengthy absences from home (several days at a stretch, sometimes a week), which left Julia and the boy in precarious economic straits. Julia was unemployed but received some help from her 18-year-old son (by a previous marriage), who worked and lived with the family. Although there was no evidence that Christopher had been physically abused, whenever his parents fought the older brother or a neighbor would remove the young boy for several hours, sometimes for the entire day.

The first therapy interview could not have been more discouraging. Julia was upset and hostile, accusing the therapist of separating the couple from their son and damaging the boy, who was terrified of being separated from his mother. Richard, however, was distant and contemptuous of the therapy and the therapist.

The therapist, focused on building an alliance, began by saying that he understood what the mandated removal of their son meant for the couple, not only from a professional point of view but also from a human point of view. He explained the referral mandate and the obligations imposed on him as the professional in their case. The more meaningful communication, however, was that the therapy could be instrumental in helping the couple, if they wanted to take advantage of it.

Despite the therapist's empathy, the mother's anxiety and anger increased until she wound up crying disconsolately. At this point, the therapist reassured the couple that therapy was an appropriate context to allow sad and angry feelings to surface and that these emotions would not hinder his or their efforts to reunite the family. This climate of welcome and gentle understanding comforted both parents. Haltingly, they began describing the circumstances surrounding their fights, the accusations of others, and their severe financial problems. Despite their openness, however, Julia and Richard rigidly maintained that their treatment by social services was unjust and that going to therapy was "proof of guilt." They intended to take legal measures to overturn the judge's decision, and they had enlisted the help of a neighbor, whose testimony would support their contention that they had not been fairly evaluated by the court-appointed psychologist. This neighbor was an older woman, respectable and friendly. She was practically a member of the family, and she treated Christopher like a grandson.

The therapist's intervention in the initial session had three objectives. First, he showed understanding and empathy with the couple's feelings of loss, reframing their anger and hostility as motivation to fight for their right to care for and raise their child. Second, the therapist explained that therapy was not in itself a legal tool and that complying with the mandated treatment was not incompatible with the couple's intent to initiate legal action; in fact, they could use the time in therapy to discuss the conflicts in their relationship that had led to this terrible situation. Finally, the therapist asked the couple to consider making a second therapy appointment with the friendly neighbor who had witnessed their relationship with Christopher for many years.

In other words, the interview was one of acceptance rather than a battle of wills, which the embarrassed couple had been anticipating. After the therapist gave Julia permission to show her vulnerability, the couple trusted his pledge not to impose any restrictions on what was discussed in treatment. Then, when the therapist offered to invite the person whom they trusted most to speak on their behalf, the couple began to see the therapist as a resource rather than as an arm of the court.

When Edna, the trustworthy neighbor who was a mother figure for Julia, spoke reasonably about the family's problems, in just two sessions the couple accepted that their son could be harmed by witnessing their fights. In fact, some of the arguments presented to the judge by Child Protective Services made sense to the couple when Edna explained them. Over time, Julia and Richard became more invested in treatment. Through exploration of their differences, the couple decided to separate. Eventually Christopher was returned to Julia and had supervised visits with his father.

Building Julia's trust in the therapist was key in this case. After she accepted the therapist as her ally, Julia revealed her fear that social services would terminate her parental rights if she and Richard separated. (In fact, this fear was what had kept her in the destructive relationship with her husband.) Until Edna and the therapist convinced her otherwise, Julia's mistrust of social services, her sense of being watched at every turn, and her fear of losing her son made it impossible for her to separate from Richard and find work that would alleviate the family's financial burden.

This example illustrates the importance of not giving up on an alliance that was threatened from the start. The therapist's success in this case was due to his calm acceptance of the couple's resentment and mistrust in a hostage-like therapy situation, his focus on safety, and his decision not to impose treatment goals beyond those that were mandated. By inviting a trusted neighbor, whom the couple saw as an ally, to the sessions, the therapist demonstrated goodwill and a desire to ease the way for the angry and mistrustful couple. Moreover, by not imposing his authority but rather respecting the couple's own pace in facing their problems, the therapist was able to effect a safe return home for a frightened child.

CASE ILLUSTRATION: THE SILENT HOSTAGE

Seventeen-year-old Frank Osita was suspended from school for repeated misconduct. After he was accused of trashing a house during a party, the school counselor attributed Frank's antisocial behavior to long-standing conflicts with his parents. On the counselor's recommendation, the parents found a family therapist.

In Session 1, the therapist noted that both parents attributed all Frank's problems to his character; they saw no reason for their son's rebellious attitude toward them. For his part, Frank was morose and refused to speak up for himself, even when invited to do so. He volunteered a comment only once, when his parents mentioned having had marital problems that led to a temporary separation. According to the parents, Frank's aggressive misconduct had intensified when his father returned home after the separation. Encouraged to express his view of his parents' situation, Frank said that his mother had promised not to let his father come home, but she had not kept that promise. When the mother began justifying her decision, Frank remained closed, defensive, and walled off from any further discussion.

In view of their son's attitude, the school pressure, and accusations made by the owner of the vandalized home, Frank's parents demanded that the therapist see the boy individually. Frank's school was one of the most prestigious and expensive prep schools in the area, and his suspension did not reflect well on the family's social position. Acceding to the parents' request, the therapist agreed to see Frank privately if the parents would attend sessions as needed.

In his first individual session, Frank warned the therapist that he had "nothing to say." He answered every question with a monosyllable or gesture of indifference. The only forceful and direct answer came when the therapist asked, "Can you see any advantage or benefit, no matter how small, in coming to see me each week?" Frank replied, "My parents have calmed down a lot, and they don't make life miserable for me at home anymore." The therapist then asked, "If they've calmed down because you're coming here and they don't make life impossible anymore, does this calm *you* down, too, and make *you* feel better?" Surprised, Frank answered thoughtfully, "Could be . . . I think so." The therapist then gave Frank an appointment for the following week, offering this deal:

> You see that the simple act of coming here has a positive effect on the whole family, and it gives you some space to face your problems better. It's an easy way to help you, so I'm expecting you to show up next week. Please bring something to read or do for the 45 minutes of the session. I'll also take advantage of that time to read something. I'm not saying we can't talk, but it's just in case, like today, that you don't feel like talking or answering my questions.

Frank was clearly surprised, but as the therapist's tone was not in the least sarcastic, this practical solution to their dilemma appealed to him.

Frank arrived for the next session with his mother, who came along to "make sure Frank wouldn't miss his appointment." She announced that she would be in the waiting room until the end of the session. Obviously, Frank felt pressured and was humiliated by his mother's patronizing behavior. He'd brought along a textbook, but as soon as he sat down, he took out a motorcycle magazine that was hidden in the pages of the book. Understanding that Frank had complied with his part of the deal—to come but not to engage—the therapist began perusing some papers on his desk, without paying much attention to his client.

After about 10 minutes of silence, Frank casually started a conversation about motorcycles and his interest in racing. A half hour later, the conversation turned from Frank's hobbies to a description of his friends, Frank remarking that he did not have time to do what he wanted because of the punishments he had received at school and at home. He clearly expressed his distaste at being "watched" every minute of every day.

The therapist ended the session abruptly a little early, telling Frank that he'd bring his mother in briefly to ask "how things were going." When the therapist added, "I won't say anything that can hurt you, but I must be honest," Frank cringed, no doubt expecting another betrayal by an adult. However, the therapist simply told Frank's mother that they had been "very comfortable together" and that the session had been "extremely useful" for him (the therapist). Not giving her time to question what had gone on, the therapist added that the next session would be in 3 days and that Frank should come alone by public transportation. When the mother agreed, not pressing the issue, Frank smiled to himself.

In the next session, the therapist did not inquire whether Frank's coming alone had been freeing or relieving for him. In fact, the therapist did not ask anything about Frank's life. He simply began by inquiring, "What would you like us to do today?" Frank had a short list of things to talk about; he railed against the "unfair" and "hypocritical" educational system.

The fourth individual session began with the same question, but this time Frank informed the therapist that he had had a "big fight" with his father. He went on to explain that he had "proof" that his father had "another woman, a lover."

This disclosure signaled Frank's growing trust in the therapist and the start of a satisfying therapeutic relationship. Although Frank did best in individual therapy, his parents participated on occasion, and progress was made in making Frank's home life more tolerable for him. This outcome reflected the school counselor's assessment in making the referral; she saw Frank's antisocial behavior as a response to conflict at home. The boy's engagement in therapy and his strong connection with the therapist facilitated the parents' participation in treatment, paving the way for changes in their relationship with each other and with Frank.

In terms of the therapeutic alliance, this case is a good example of how to work with a therapy hostage who has burned his bridges with everyone else in his life. In the language of SOFTA, when the family could not agree on a shared purpose (Frank blamed his parents, his parents blamed him), the therapist used safety and an emotional connection to nurture the client's engagement. With greater engagement came a closer bond and an increased sense of security. With patience, confidentiality, and a clear understanding of the client's significant relationships with others, the therapist built an alliance that gradually promoted change. If instead the therapist had pushed Frank by confronting or interpreting his silence as a symptom of emotional or social difficulties, effective therapy would no doubt have been impossible.

CONCLUSION

For many therapists, working with a highly motivated couple or family is a pleasant exception to the rule. For therapists who work in social services or child protective agencies, having all family members start out with a similar view of the problem is a "gift from heaven."

Working with several family members conjointly requires paying attention to the clients' relational difficulties with each other. When there is conflict and some family members feel pressured or prejudged, attributions of responsibility and blame abound. It is common for the clients on the receiving end of the pejorative attributions to engage reluctantly in the therapy process. Indeed, their resentment of feeling exposed and blamed by other family members can easily extend to dislike for the therapist.

In other cases, clients are obliged by judicial or social service institutions to seek treatment. When mistrust of the system translates into mistrust of all helping professionals, the therapeutic alliance will invariably have a rough start. In contrast to families divided by blame and accusations, mandated families often come to treatment with a shared purpose: to defeat the therapy!

In both situations, the therapist's primary objective at the start of treatment should be to create a balanced alliance with all family members. No problem- or solution-related discussions are possible when even one person feels like a hostage. In SOFTA language, without ensuring minimal levels of safety and shared sense of purpose (including any conditions imposed by the referral source), it is difficult to prompt enough client engagement to effect a meaningful change.

To create a strong alliance with pressured or mandated clients, we recommend that therapists refrain from (a) attributing the clients' indifference or rejection of treatment to personal ill will, or (b) telling clients that their problem or behavior reflects dysfunction or pathology. Rather, the therapist should identify the specific family dynamics that are prompting the clients' defensiveness and thoroughly analyze the entire social context experienced by the family to understand their mistrust of professional helpers. In doing so, it is especially important to consider how differences in gender and inequalities in social class prompt feelings of mistrust and betrayal (MacKinnon, 1998).

With clients who see themselves as visitors, plaintiffs, or hostages, the therapist has two options: focusing on problems and treatment goals without the clients' collaboration or renegotiating the context and meaning of treatment to enhance all aspects of the alliance. Although it is complicated and requires time and energy to navigate multiple alliances with mandated clients, the imposition of treatment against their will has little chance of success.

12

ZERO-SUM PROBLEMS

Will we relocate for your job? Have a baby? Let our son go to college or make him work in the family business? Get a divorce? Some disagreements just do not lend themselves to an easy compromise.

Unlike other problem definitions, zero-sum conflicts can wreak havoc in the lives of couples and families. For this reason, when people bring these kinds of problems to a professional, the alliance is in jeopardy right from the start. Typically, clients are just as anxious about the therapist's "take" on the situation as they are about what their family members say on the topic.

Andrea Jasper, for example, suspects that her husband, Thomas, is waiting until their first therapy appointment to tell her that their marriage is over no matter what she does. Andrea thinks—or hopes—she can convince her husband otherwise, but what if the therapist says that in the face of Thomas's decision, there is nothing to be done? If that happens, Andrea thinks, Thomas's resolve will be strengthened, and then there will be no turning back.

When clients view their situation in black and white terms, they usually have exhausted all avenues for compromise and mutual understanding. What is framed as a polarized decision point is likely to be a complex issue with ambivalent feelings on both sides. As soon as the conflict is framed in zero-sum terms, however, only the outcome matters; all the former ambivalence is pushed aside.

Now focused only on holding onto her husband, Andrea has all but forgotten her misgivings about him, about how badly he treats her, and about the sacrifices she is making to keep their marriage together. For Andrea, at this moment the only thing that matters is, Will he leave me? Thomas, for his part, is only able to see Andrea's needy clinging, which alienates him. He has forgotten the joys and comforts they shared in the past, the spiritual feeling he had at their wedding, the sense of security he used to have in her arms. For him, the only thing that matters now is, How can I get out of this?

As another example, take the Carters. Having struggled for 6 years with infertility, Eric and Lindsay decided that "enough is enough"—no more humiliating medical intervention. Although they had both been indecisive about adoption before, Lindsay is now ready to adopt. Eric, however, has serious reservations. After a year of considering the possibility from all angles, Eric concludes that he wants no part of adoption. What began as a problem in the life of a couple is now a battle of wills. If asked, Lindsay might deny ever having been ambivalent about adoption, just as Eric might deny the intense need he'd felt to become a father. At this point in the Carters' relationship, there is a dangerous undercurrent: Will we split up over this?

Zero-sum conflicts like these can be the primary reason for seeking help or a struggle over whether therapy is needed; it can arise when a choice becomes essential in the family's life, or it can surface unexpectedly in the course of therapy. It is easy to see how treacherous the therapist's path is in these kinds of circumstances. Although many factors affect the resolution of zero-sum conflicts, delicate handling is essential to avoid escalation and prevent unfortunate outcomes.

In this chapter we consider therapeutic interventions pertaining to engagement, connection, safety, and family collaboration (i.e., the four System for Observing Family Therapy Alliances [SOFTA] alliance dimensions) when clients define their problems in terms of winning or losing.

"WE (DON'T) NEED THERAPY"

Sometimes when a problem is too hot to handle, it is recast into a struggle about whether therapy is needed. A therapist's willingness to work on family problems without everyone's cooperation is to some extent a matter of personal preference, theoretical orientation, and the nature of the therapist's practice. Some experts recommend treating only the most motivated family member, arguing that fundamental change in one person will invariably touch all family members (Bowen, 1976). Other experts insist on having as many family members present as possible, viewing an individual's resistance to treatment as reflecting a systemwide ambivalence about change (Whitaker & Keith, 1981).

Typically, the family's controversy about whether therapy is necessary covers up a disagreement about whether something is amiss in the system or in the life of one family member. A wife thinks her husband's marijuana use is an addiction, but he sees it as only an enjoyable pastime. A father insists that his son should move out and find a job, but his wife thinks the young adult just needs more time and support. A woman wants her partner to commit to marriage, but the partner does not see the need. A daughter wants her elderly mother to move into an assisted living situation, but the older woman will not consider leaving the home she has lived in for 50 years.

If these people do make it to an initial appointment, the discrepancy in engagement levels is likely to be quite noticeable in the first few minutes of the session. The person who wants therapy is eager to tell his or her side of the story. The client sits forward, makes eye contact with the therapist, and may try to engage the reluctant family member in various ways: "Is that when it started, honey?" "Why don't you just tell your side of it?" The person who is resisting therapy (the therapy "hostage"; see chap. 11) may be angry or look defeated, thinking that he or she has lost the first round just by showing up for the session. The person may adopt rigid or defensive body posture, avoid eye contact with everyone, tune out, or show indifference in various ways.

In circumstances like these, the therapist's initial concern is to reduce anxiety and engage the reluctant individual. However, pushing a resolution to the win–lose struggle over therapy can quickly backfire. Consider what happened with the Hoffmans. Daniel was adamantly opposed to therapy, knowing that his wife, Nadine, wanted to talk about their sexual incompatibility. At the beginning of Session 1, Nadine laid out the couple's differences of opinion about seeking therapy. In response, the therapist asked the Hoffmans to decide whether to commit to treatment before anything could be discussed. His back against the wall, Daniel relented. Ten minutes later, however, when Nadine brought up her dissatisfaction with Daniel's sexual performance, he burst out, "That's it! I'm not doing this," and left the room.

In retrospect, the therapist thought he should have spent more time discussing the couple's disagreement about the need for professional help. Doing so may have been more effective than forcing a commitment and then pushing forward as he did. However, Daniel was unlikely to have said what he truly felt about treatment to a therapist he had just met.

What was going on for Daniel is typical of zero-sum conflicts about engaging in therapy. The problem is lack of safety. How can Daniel, already distressed by his perceived sexual failure, feel comfortable discussing such an intimate problem with a stranger? It is not that Daniel denied or was unaware of the problems in his marriage or that he was opposed (in principle) to couple therapy. It was, however, far more face saving for him to refuse treatment than to endure the humiliation of admitting sexual defeat.

In this situation, the preferred therapeutic strategy would have been to enhance Daniel's sense of safety by establishing rapport (i.e., emotional connection), engaging him in a nonthreatening discussion, and working toward defining a shared sense of purpose for the couple. The following hypothetical scenario picks up early in the session, just after Nadine mentions the couple's disagreement over coming to the session:

> *Nadine:* I know Daniel didn't want me to bring this up, but we're having some problems with sex.
>
> *Therapist:* Nadine, I can certainly appreciate your wish to get to the more important issues right away, but I'd like to first hear a bit more about you two as people. Then we can talk about what couples therapy would look like and if you and Daniel want to come back and try it. You two weren't in agreement about coming today, and so I'm reluctant to just forge ahead right now. So, what I'm proposing is that, since you're here, we talk about you as individuals and as a couple. Then, if I can offer you something worthwhile, you can go home and decide about whether to make another appointment. Would that be all right? Nadine? [*she nods*] Daniel? [*nods*] Let me also just say that couple therapy is not everyone's cup of tea, and many marriages do just fine without it. Now that you're here, though, let's spend the rest of the hour getting some idea of what might be helpful to you.
>
> *Nadine:* Fine with me.
>
> *Daniel:* [*simultaneously*] Okay.

The therapist's mention of therapy as "not everyone's cup of tea" is an indirect message to Daniel that says, in effect, "I won't force you to do this or humiliate you if you choose not to."

With Daniel on board at least for this session, the therapist engages him in some relaxed questioning about his age, job, education, and family of origin (where he grew up, number of siblings, parents' occupations, and so forth). As they talk, Daniel loosens up a bit, even enough to make a joke when the therapist notes things they have in common, growing up on a farm and serving in the military. With Daniel talking a bit more freely, Nadine sits back to listen, occasionally chiming in. However, only when her comment is positive does the therapist respond to her. When she interrupts to bring up a problem, the therapist ignores her, continuing with his own agenda:

> *Daniel:* So, being a country bumpkin, I had a hard time fitting in with some of the city-smart boys I met in the Army.
>
> *Nadine:* [*to Daniel*] You have the same problem around *my* family.

Therapist: [*to Daniel, ignoring Nadine*] Hmm, did it get any better after you'd been in the service for awhile?

After 15 or 20 minutes focusing on Daniel, the therapist turns to Nadine, repeating some of the same background questions. Understanding that the therapist wants to avoid focusing on problem areas, Nadine answers the questions easily, brightening up when Daniel interrupts to clarify a point:

Nadine: I'm closest to my youngest sister. I was . . . am . . . like a mother to her.

Daniel: [*to Nadine*] She *needed* you to be that for her.

Nadine: Yes! Exactly!

With 15 minutes left in the session, the therapist offers some general but positive comments about what each spouse seems to have brought to the marriage, normalizing their difficulties (as yet undefined), and offering his help.

Therapist: You know, as I listen to you, I see two people from very different backgrounds who've come together, wanting to make something work. And, as you've told me, you found each other when you, Nadine, had dated quite a bit, but you, Daniel, were young and just back from the military, and you had little experience with women. Just that difference there can make it tough on a couple. While there are some other important differences in your background [*describes the other differences*], you've made a home together for 10 years, started a family, and woven your lives together. You both agree that your kids are doing well, and when you talk about them, your eyes light up and I can see the real caring both of you have for your family life, and you see each other as a good parent and are happy with this family piece of your life. [*Daniel and Nadine nod*] Although we haven't talked about the specific problems you're having, I can see where some conflict might be due to the different backgrounds and the stresses in the *individual* lives you're leading. Nadine, you're running your own business from home, and Daniel, you're needing to respond to so many people and stakeholders in your position as an administrator. Life is complicated these days, trying to do it all—kids, marriage, two careers!

Gradually, from here, Daniel's engagement picks up. So as not to back Daniel into a corner, the therapist ends the session by asking the couple to go home, talk over whether they want to have another "getting-to-know-you session," and call him with a decision within the week. By not forcing the issue, the therapist not only respects Daniel's privacy and trepidation but also models thoughtful decision making. Essentially, asking the couple to decide about a second session is a "homework assignment," one that requires

Nadine and Daniel to problem solve together on one small, specific, manageable issue. Defining their immediate decision as simply "whether to come back for a second session" redefines the struggle about the need for therapy.

If Daniel agrees to another session, he won't feel that he totally capitulated to Nadine, and Nadine will have some sense of achieving her goal. Then, at the end of Session 2, if Daniel continues to show comfort and engagement, the therapist could comment, "So, here is how I'd propose working with you, if you decide you want to come back." He might then suggest that the goal of therapy would be "to get the marriage back on track," "to soften the differences" between Daniel and Nadine to "use what's already wonderful and satisfying" in their marriage "to reach a new level of intimacy." Defining the goal of therapy in this way, rather than in terms of sexual difficulties, is the road toward forging a shared sense of purpose about treatment. As in previous sessions, the therapist requires the couple to decide at home about working toward this goal. Regardless of their decision, Daniel and Nadine will have made some progress toward learning to problem solve.

"MY WAY OR THE HIGHWAY"

Power runs a close second to attachment as the most salient factor in the health and well-being of the relationship of couples and families. That is, families that function well have strong, cohesive attachments between people, healthy connections to significant others in the extended family and the community, and shared power and influence. The parents are clearly in charge of the children, make joint decisions in major areas of the family's functioning, balance power and influence between them, and give the children a developmentally appropriate measure of control over their own lives. Georgia Blake, for example, has the final word on the health and education of the children, the running of the household, and all decisions about vacations and social engagements; her husband, Al, handles all repairs to the home, maintains the cars and the lawn, and takes care of the bills and financial investments. Although the Blakes' division of labor and influence reflects traditional middle-class gender roles, this family "works" not because the responsibilities are defined by gender but because each spouse has a sphere of power and influence that is respected by the other.

Problems can arise, however, when one partner has far more responsibility and control than the other (a pernicious overfunctioning–underfunctioning dynamic), when the family is under acute stress (e.g., from a substantial loss of income), or when the children rebel against parental authority. If all of these conditions are present simultaneously, the family can find itself in a precarious state. When family members exhaust all options to resolve their problems, they may seek therapy voluntarily. In extreme cases, therapy may be mandated by outside authorities, such as Family Court or Child Protective Services.

If the problems are multiple and complex and the anxiety in the system is dangerously high, the presenting issue may be defined in zero-sum terms. Each family member is stretched beyond her or his limits. To regain a feeling of control, one person or the other poses an ultimatum: Do it my way or else! When the recipient of this message resists this power play, the problem may get thrust in the therapist's lap. Taking sides is a sure way to split the alliance and threaten the success of therapy.

Carole and Steve Kemp had been married for 3 years, the second marriage for each. Having had no children in her first marriage and approaching menopause, Carole eagerly looked forward to coparenting Steve's twin 13-year-old daughters. The girls, however, would have none of it; as far as they were concerned, Carole was not their mother and therefore had no right to tell them what to do. Repeatedly thwarted in her attempts to be close to the twins, Carole began pushing the power button: "As long as you live under my roof, you'll do what I say." It is not surprising that the girls refused to comply, and screaming matches became commonplace. Steve, for his part, distanced himself more and more until the marriage began to dissolve. After 3 years, life was unbearable.

Referred for treatment by the school counselor who was concerned about the girls, Steve reluctantly made an appointment at a local clinic. By the time the family came for the first appointment, Carole had given Steve an ultimatum: "The girls go back to their mother, or I leave you."

To manage her overwhelming anxiety, Carole had developed tunnel vision. In her mind, the only solution was to oust the girls. Naturally, such an extreme measure had to be opposed by someone in the system. Even if Steve had considered the possibility of sending the girls to their mother, capitulating to Carole without a struggle not only would have been "unmanly" but also would have given his daughters the message that by not fighting for them, he did not want them or love them. Ironically, the girls had privately talked over the idea of going to live with their mother, but they were adamantly opposed to giving Carole her way without a fight, and Dad might think they did not care about him.

When treatment began, none of these private thoughts were expressed. As unpleasant as it was, it was easier for everyone to blame, attack, and confront everyone else than to express painful longings and hurt feelings. Session 1 was loud and chaotic, and the therapist was drowned out when she attempted to intervene. In SOFTA terms, although everyone was engaged in the therapy process, there was a heightened feeling of risk (i.e., lack of safety) and no shared sense about the value or purpose of therapy. With Carole framing the problem as "my way or the highway," all family members only saw a need to make a choice. How could therapy be helpful when either Carole would win and the girls would lose or vice versa? This being a win–lose situation, what does it matter that the therapist is a nice, caring person?

As explained in the following section, this case highlights the importance of using emotional connections and defining a shared purpose to enhance safety. Safety is of prime concern in situations like these, because something said in anger in the consulting room can have disastrous consequences. When families fight at home, they usually have tried and true methods for de-escalation: Someone storms out, slamming the door; someone else tunes out or finds a solitary activity; or the argument occurs early in the morning before school or work, when it cannot boil over. When a fight happens in a therapist's office, however, people tend to feel trapped, and they may wind up saying something so contemptuous or mean-spirited that it simply cannot be forgotten or forgiven.

To enhance safety in this situation, the therapist needs to redefine the problem in non-zero-sum terms. In other words, by framing the goal of therapy in a way that does not threaten family attachments, the therapist may be able to lower the family members' private fears about rejection and abandonment. The tricky part is the power of an ultimatum. If the therapist implies that Carole's ultimatum is wrong, inappropriate, or harmful, Carole's natural response will be to flee. She might well flee the family as well as the therapy.

The other tricky piece is that something dramatic needs to happen in Session 1, or the family will drop out. Recall that Carole and Steve did not see the need for treatment on their own; the referral came from the school counselor. The 13-year-old twins had no notion of how therapy could help them get Carole off their back, and Steve and Carole came out of guilt. To them, the girls were in trouble in school and they were to blame.

In Session 1, the mistrust and hostility in this family were palpable. Yet some measure of anger needed to be expressed so that everyone could feel heard. The therapist knew, however, that letting mutual blame continue unchecked would be counterproductive, if not harmful.

Forcefully getting their attention, the therapist told the family that although she saw their anger and hurt, she was not going to provide them with a platform to hurt each other further. This intervention put the power squarely in her hands and had a calming influence. Although still too anxious to think clearly, all four family members felt relieved that their hostility would not get out of hand in front of a stranger.

Then, to enhance her credibility further, the therapist took a brief history of the problem, cutting off all attempts by family members to interrupt, blame, or attack each other. Next, she asked Steve and Carole to talk about what had brought them together as a couple. As they spoke about falling in love and their strong early attraction for each other, Carole began to cry silently. Shocked at the vulnerability of this powerful authority figure, the girls simply stared.

Showing compassion and empathy, the therapist (with deliberate vagueness) commented briefly on how hurt Carole seemed to be at the situation.

Then, quickly the therapist turned to question the girls about their lives. This two-step intervention accomplished several things simultaneously. First, the therapist made a connection with Carole, who felt understood and accepted. Second, by focusing only briefly on Carole's pain and then turning rapidly to the girls, the therapist gave Carole some space to recover. Third, when the therapist engaged the twins in a lighthearted conversation about music, boys, and the trials of middle school, the girls took notice of her. By focusing on what they liked to do and talk about, the therapist implied that she did not see them as "The Problem," that she *did* see them as worthwhile, would take them seriously, and that their views mattered.

Slowly, the tension in the room decreased, and as the session was winding down, the therapist said,

> You have spirit, you four! And despite all the angry feelings, I see that you sometimes have fun together, you can laugh together. Stepfamilies are hard, very hard, and although you've been in this situation for 3 years now, you haven't figured out yet how to do it as well as you could. I'd like to help you with that because, whether or not the girls do go live with their mother, you're still a stepfamily. That won't change.

By reframing the problem as "figuring out how to be a stepfamily," the therapist avoided taking sides, redefined the problem in non-zero-sum terms, and put herself in the picture ("I'd like to help you with that"). Noticing the family's nonverbal responses to her comments—the girls were leaning forward, the parents were exchanging eye contact—the therapist saw that she had gotten their attention and that they felt safer. Now she could be more direct:

> But I'm not going to accept an ultimatum, Carole, and if you all decide to work with me, there are two conditions. First, there will be no screaming, name calling, or swearing in my office. [*Pauses to look for agreement. The girls nod.*] Second, there will be no discussion of the four of you breaking apart as a family for at least 12 weeks, while we work together. No discussion here *and* no discussion at home. It took 3 years for you to get to this point, and I'm asking you for 12 weekly therapy sessions to work with me without considering the pros and cons of the girls leaving. Carole, you're not to threaten leaving either, and Steve, girls, you neither. People can't feel comfortable and safe enough to talk about wanting to be a family if they think the other person is going to walk out the door at any moment. After 12 weeks, we'll see where we're at, and at that point you can reconsider the decision about staying together, if you like. Hopefully, though, by then it will be a nonissue. In other words, what I'm proposing to do is help you become a family in a way that everyone feels comfortable and accepted. And I have every reason to think you can do that. [*The therapist goes on to mention their strengths and attachments to each other.*]

This was a bold intervention, setting clear limits, yet offering hope and a focus on strengths as well as problems. The intervention could be attempted only because the therapist had gained control of the session, stopped the escalating blame and hostility, and made a personal connection with each family member.

The rest of the session was spent clarifying the treatment contract and the therapist's two conditions: no hostility in the sessions and no threats to break up the family. In doing so, the therapist normalized the family's struggles, pointed out that everyone was hurting, and made it clear that for everyone's good, no decision about their future should be made hastily or in anger.

As in the preceding example with Daniel and Nadine, this therapist asked the family to consider her proposal for a week. Steve and Carole were to discuss it together as a couple and with each girl separately before recontacting the therapist. The therapist allowed the family to return only when everyone had agreed to her terms.

This case illustrates using a personal connection with each family member to reframe the problem from a win–lose situation to a common goal, "figuring out how to be a stepfamily." Over the next 3 months, Carole and Steve came together a few times without the girls, the girls came together with either Steve or Carole, and the family came as a foursome. In these sessions, Steve and Carole explored their marriage and renewed their commitments to each other. As they discussed coparenting in a stepfamily, Steve came to see how deeply hurt Carole was not only by the girls' rejection but also by his rejection of her, and Carole came to understand that her ultimatum had put Steve in a hopeless, helpless position. Carole and the girls found that they could be friends and have fun together, that Carole didn't (and couldn't) replace their mother in their affections, but that her place in the girls' lives could nonetheless be special and meaningful. To get to this point, voices were raised and many tears were shed in the consulting room, but these emotional outbursts felt safe because the therapist was clearly in charge and no one was going to move out of the house in a burst of anger. In other words, the therapist deftly used the alliance between herself and each family member to affect the power imbalance and build attachments in this fragile stepfamily.

CHANGING HORSES MIDSTREAM

Families often come for help with a "ticket of admission," a presenting problem that the most powerful family members can discuss with some degree of comfort in front of a stranger. Even though the person defined as having the problem may be upset or embarrassed, often that person has little power to resist the label of Identified Patient. It is not that the family deliberately chooses someone to focus on or conceals a more disturbing problem (although that scenario is certainly possible), it is just that the second problem stays hidden in the background until at least one family member feels safe enough to allow it to surface. This is not always a deliberate decision, and the family may indeed be unaware of how the hidden problem relates to the publicly declared concern.

When the more fundamental problem is named, the treatment can be derailed quickly if family members take sides about whether to address it. The Houghtons, for example, came to treatment with 20-year-old Tara and her three younger siblings at the insistence of Tara's individual therapist. Tara was the problem child, having been in therapy since age 16 for her anorexia. Now facing hospitalization, the Houghtons agreed to outpatient family therapy as a last resort. Tara was amenable; after all, her problem was serious, she could admit that, and her parents were worried. Tara and her parents, Curt and Stephanie, did not realize, however, that family therapy meanders into many byways. Although Tara's problem was life threatening and everyone was worried about her chronically precarious state, the more dangerous topic was Dad's gambling. After 3 months of family therapy, just as Tara began to make some major strides toward recovery, this other problem was named and brought to the table. Tara's mother, Stephanie, had come to understand the relation of her husband's addiction to Tara's anorexia, but Curt Houghton clearly did not, nor would he admit publicly that his behavior had anything to do with anyone but himself. This was his own private demon, not something to "interfere with my daughter's therapy," and certainly not something the three younger children should know about.

The dilemma for the therapist was that this choice point—to discuss Curt's gambling problem or not—framed the continuation of treatment in zero-sum terms. Curt would not "play" if his problem were addressed, and Stephanie would not play otherwise. Tara, caught in the middle, seemed poised to deteriorate. In the week since Curt's gambling was first mentioned, she had lost 4 more pounds, putting herself in dangerous territory.

This, then, is a family whose hidden problem turns the therapy into a struggle over winning and losing. If the therapist is skillful enough, if the person under pressure is hurting enough, and if the alliance is strong enough, there is hope for salvaging the situation. To do so involves redefining the treatment to encompass the newly identified problem, but delicately enough that its discussion will not be a vast departure from the previous therapeutic contract.

In SOFTA terms, when an event that cannot be ignored occurs in the family's life, or a problem that was hidden is named, the family's shared sense of purpose can abruptly evaporate. Whereas before the revelation of the secret concern everyone was in agreement about the need for treatment, the therapy goals, and the value of working together for a common purpose, now all those cards have been thrown into the air. Anxiety is high, and to manage it one (or more) family member frames the problem in stark, black-and-white terms: We address this problem NOW or I quit.

Here is where knowledge of systems functioning is crucial. Whereas families tend to see their problems as different and distinct, the therapist needs to look beyond the content to the relational function of the problems. Stephanie and Curt had a covert pact, never actually discussed, to ignore the severity of Curt's gambling. Over the years, the tension between the couple focused on Curt's absence (he spent most of his nonworking hours at off-track betting parlors) and on Stephanie's nagging him to be part of the family. Overt conflict was avoided, and Stephanie turned more and more often to Tara for comfort and closeness. At first, Tara coped by focusing on weight loss and exercise, trying not to think about her parents' failing marriage. Eventually, though, when her anorexia became apparent, concern about Tara's health united Curt and Stephanie. Four years later, the family was in a stable detouring pattern (Minuchin, Rosman, & Baker, 1978). To Curt, Tara's anorexia was one problem, his own out-of-control gambling something else altogether. Stephanie, however, had begun to see the connection between the two problems. She decided to break the silence when she understood that her marriage and Tara's very life depended on bringing Curt's problem under control and into the open.

Seeing it the same way, the therapist privately agreed. Without deft handling, however, she would be viewed by the family (and particularly by Curt) as taking sides. Various in-session behaviors signaled an alliance in trouble. Family members blamed each other for both problems; Stephanie made repeated, overt attempts for the therapist to side with her; hostility was in the air; and Tara began to voice doubts about continuing in therapy. Indeed, she went so far as to offer to hospitalize herself, something she had vigorously opposed in the past.

The therapist recognized that in the 1 week since Stephanie had named Curt's problem, the Houghtons had gone from seeing therapy as a haven of safety to considering it as a threat to the integrity of the family and to the well-being of everyone, not only Tara. Fortunately, the therapist had made strong connections with each person, and Tara's earlier weight stabilization had relieved and comforted her parents and siblings. Here, then, is how the therapist used her bond with Stephanie and Curt to de-escalate the situation and reframe the continuation of therapy in non-zero-sum terms:

> Everyone, stop! This argument is going nowhere now but toward more and more hurt and misunderstanding! I know, Curt, that you see the gambling as unrelated to what we're doing here for Tara, but you, Stephanie, have a different view on it. I want to slow this down and help us get back on track.

Hearing this, family members turned expectantly to the therapist. Stephanie leaned forward but was anxiously wringing her hands. Curt, more wary, nonetheless relaxed his posture. After a pause, the therapist continued:

> We started together 3 months ago to help Tara feel comfortable enough to gain some weight and start doing normal 20-year-old things, working and going out with friends, right? [*Stephanie nods*] But now we see that

you, Stephanie, and you, Curt, hovering over her at every meal, focusing only on her problems and not on her life outside those problems, were keeping the anorexia alive. You love her and worry about her, but your way of worrying was getting in the way. So, as we went on, we began talking more about how to have a positive family life for everyone, while letting Tara take charge of her personal eating problem with her individual therapist. And now I'm concerned that we don't go down the same road with Curt, focusing on and worrying about his problems in a way that's not helpful. [*Curt nods emphatically*] I'm not suggesting that we ignore your concerns, Stephanie, or that we cover them up and forget about them. Tara and the other kids have been worried about Curt, too, and I think finally naming this family concern is a good thing, something that had to come out of the closet. But I'm not willing to make it a choice between discussing Tara's life or Curt's gambling. What we're doing here is figuring out how to help everyone in this family in a way that's supportive and empowering, *not* harsh or blaming, forcing people into a corner. Only when people feel supported can they face their problems and have the courage to overcome them.

With the family listening attentively, the tension in the air slowly began to dissipate. The therapist continued. She asked to see Curt and Stephanie alone the next day to discuss "the problems you're having about money," remarking that this is "an adult concern that needs to be dealt with apart from the children." The family sessions were to continue, focusing on "how to help the family as a whole work together to solve problems, enjoy your time together more, feel closer to each other, and trust each other enough to ask for and give help in a way that is respectful and supportive." The point was "learning to help each other handle problems without anyone hovering, blaming, or making verbal threats."

Thus, the goals and values of the family therapy were framed in relational terms, not in terms of this or the other disabling problem. Reframing was necessary to defeat the pernicious ultimatum that would either make Curt the identified patient or force the family to quit therapy altogether. Just as it would have been a mistake to ignore Curt's out-of-control gambling, it would have been equally problematic to completely redirect the family treatment in that direction. Curt's addiction affected the children, but the struggle was primarily between him and Stephanie. Labeling him "an addict" and focusing on his failures in front of the children would have been intolerable for Curt. Undoubtedly, he would have refused to continue treatment under those circumstances. Moreover, it was clear, at least to the therapist, that pursuing the issue in the family sessions had the potential to distress Tara beyond her ability to cope, endangering her welfare and perhaps even her life.

Because Curt had come to trust the therapist, having witnessed positive changes in Tara's life since the family sessions began, he was willing to consider discussing his problem as long as the children were not present. When, in the couple session, Stephanie gave Curt her second ultimatum, "get help or get out," Curt was willing to face his demon. He began going regularly to Gamblers Anonymous meetings, he and Stephanie saw the therapist weekly for 2 months to work on their marriage, and the family sessions continued less frequently.

Although Curt never understood the connection between his behavior and Tara's anorexia, he knew that he had to stop gambling not only to help himself but to keep the family intact. This motivation, coupled with his trust and liking for the therapist, gave him the push he needed to overcome his addiction. Six months later, Tara was happily working and studying part time, Stephanie and Curt were rediscovering their love for each other, and the younger children were flourishing as well.

NAVIGATING DANGEROUS WATERS

Essentially, zero-sum conflicts are within-family disagreements that either inhibit the formation of a shared sense of purpose about treatment or destabilize an already solid family alliance about therapy. In previous sections, we discussed three types of zero-sum dilemmas: whether therapy is necessary, ultimatums that threaten abandonment, and conflicts over what should be discussed in treatment. Common to the solutions we presented was the therapist's refusal to define the outcome as one in which there would be winners and losers.

The therapist's refusal to "play the game" is a challenge to the family member (or members) who frame the issue in all-or-none terms. By refusing, the therapist takes control of the process, reminding the family who is in charge. Clients have the right to lead their lives as they wish, but if they want a therapist's help to sort out a mess, at the very least they need to consider the therapist's recommendations.

Simply refusing to play the game without offering an alternative perspective is rarely effective, however, and can make people feel even more helpless. After getting the family's attention, the therapist needs to suggest a process solution that is empowering and respectful of differences. In the case of Nadine and Daniel, for example, the therapist converted the couple's disagreement over the need for therapy to a small, manageable decision: whether to come for a second session. Then, by engaging a reluctant, fearful husband in a nonthreatening discussion, the therapist worked to make a connection with him that would enhance his feeling of safety. When Daniel responded positively to the therapist's attempts to establish rapport, the therapist reframed the goal of treatment. It was not, as Nadine had named it, about fixing their inadequate sex life. It was rather about achieving a new level of intimacy in an already strong marriage.

In the second illustration, the Kemps had come for help when relations between Carole and the rest of the family were deteriorating. Rather than agreeing to deliberate Carole's ultimatum (that either the girls move back with their mother or that she and Steve separate), the therapist removed the threat of break up and abandonment by insisting on 12 weeks of therapy with no discussion about this possible outcome. The reframed therapy goal (figuring out how to be a stepfamily) put blame, counterblame, and threats of abandonment out of bounds.

Finally, in the third case example, Stephanie Houghton insisted that the therapeutic contract be changed midtreatment to focus on her husband's gambling addiction. Just as adamantly, Curt resisted. The therapist refused to bow to Stephanie's demands, but neither did she sweep aside this serious problem. Rather, by recommending that the couple come alone to "discuss your differences of opinion about money issues," the therapist respected Curt's need to save face in front of his children as well as Stephanie's need to address what she saw as an unmanageable problem.

When a family views its situation in stark, zero-sum terms, the task of the therapist is to sidestep the implicit request to decide who is right and then model effective problem resolution. To do so, the therapist either deliberately teaches clients how to compromise or indirectly models it through actions: that is, by taking a step back, delaying the decision, examining alternatives, reducing the anxiety surrounding the ultimatum, or proposing a solution to accommodate everyone's needs.

SPECIAL CONSIDERATIONS

In some circumstances, no compromise is possible. Either the couple will have a baby or they will not. Either the father-in-law moves in or he does not. It is not uncommon for a client to bring his spouse or partner to therapy to announce a divorce or separation. In this situation, the therapist can do little but offer support to the rejected individual.

In other circumstances, what is framed in zero-sum terms can eventually be turned around. Black–white decisions can result in compromise when clients are encouraged to weigh the two outcomes in light of other aspects of their life and consider the implications of each possible outcome for the person who "loses."

To illustrate, Sandra Jackson wanted a child, but Nat did not. Nat agreed to a baby if Sandra would agree to accept the limits of his tolerance and not make specific demands on him (e.g., for diapering or for giving up his weekend golf games). Sandra and Nat came to this compromise when the therapist asked them to spend a week separately considering the strength of their love for each other and the value each of them placed on staying married. Although they were afraid that, in the end, Nat's reluctance to become a father would result in divorce, they decided to take the risk. Because Nat felt that he had not capitulated entirely to Sandra, he was more relaxed about the prospect of fatherhood than he had anticipated. When the baby arrived, he fell in love with his daughter at first sight.

In this situation, it was relatively easy for the therapist to avoid taking sides. Such avoidance is not always possible, however, especially when issues of health and safety are in the picture. Eliza, age 72, was a heavy chain smoker who had resisted all attempts by her grown children to get her to quit smoking. Fearful of doctors (her husband had died abruptly of a misdiagnosed illness), Eliza refused to seek medical attention when her bronchitis turned into pneumonia. Somehow, Eliza recovered. When the family returned to therapy, Eliza's obstinence about her health was the only topic that Jayne and her brother, Nick, were willing to discuss. Relying on his strong connection with Eliza, the therapist joined the chorus. However, he did so in a way that allowed Eliza to save face and retain her authority as the parent in the family. That is, the therapist urged Eliza to make an appointment with his own personal physician, telling Eliza, "I'm *sure* you'll like her. *I* do, and I'm not easy to please when it comes to doctors, either." Trusting the therapist, Eliza agreed to go for a physical, but she set her own condition: Her son, Nick, needed to make an appointment for himself, too. He was only too happy to oblige.

Eliza was not in imminent danger, but her stubbornness and fear could have put her in serious jeopardy. There are other, even more serious health and safety circumstances in which therapists must risk their clients' disapproval, or even the premature end of treatment. When a child's welfare is compromised through neglect or abuse, for example, the only course of action is to insist on protection and safety. The same is true when suicidal or homicidal intent is in the air. Although the therapist may need to side with the family member who is demanding action, supportive and empathic attunement to the person at fault may keep the alliance intact (see the case example of Barbara Shawcross in chap. 9).

CONCLUSION

In the life of a family, positive change can be slow to occur and thus destabilizing. Sometimes it comes about only when one family member pushes an issue to the extreme. Unless the ultimatum requires immediate, protective action, the therapist's best course of action is to reduce anxiety and defensiveness, build connections, and reframe the process and goal of treatment to emphasize common values and mutual collaboration. Sensing the therapist's strength, wisdom, and support, the family will (more often than not) appreciate working toward a solution that avoids declaring winners and losers.

13

THERAPIST COUNTERTRANSFERENCE

Francine Noonan, a therapist in training, was in over her head, and she knew it. The Ellison family stymied her, so much so that she had begun ruminating about her work with them day and night. Her supervisor commented that Francine seemed to have been "sucked into" the Ellisons' dynamics, but what that meant in practical terms was obscure. All Francine knew was that she needed to redirect this family's treatment if at all possible. She was not at all sure the family would come back for another session.

The Ellison family—father, mother, son David—had sought therapy at David's request. An attractive, intelligent, socially skilled, artistic, and psychologically minded 13-year-old, David had become increasingly depressed, angry, and irritable over the past year. At present, he was isolating himself from both parents and friends, saying he hated himself and his life. David explained that he had been "treated like royalty" by his parents until "everything changed" a year ago when his father fell in love with a man and decided to live with him. Never having considered that his parents' marriage might be in trouble, David was devastated. His parents rarely argued, and feeling close to his father, David thought he had "the perfect life" until this happened.

When the family came for therapy, David was living part time in each household. Although he hated being with his father and lover, he was even more uncomfortable with his mother. In Session 1, David expressed anger at both parents for what they had done to him. Moreover, he called his father's affair "immoral"; his father should feel guilty for "breaking his marriage vows." David was also angry because for the past year he had been taking care of his mother emotionally, when neither parent was taking care of *his* emotional needs. These issues were, in fact, more important to David than the knowledge that his father's lover was a man. David did admit that it was upsetting to think of his father as gay, although for him, this was "really not the point."

Both parents denied being angry with each other, having discussed the father's interest in men for a number of years before the breakup of their marriage. By this time, both had "moved on" in their lives; they were only coming to treatment for David, not for themselves. The father complained about David's dark moods and what he described as David's "self-centeredness" (e.g., calling him on the phone several times a day). The father was sorry that David and his mother were hurting, but he had made this decision for his own happiness. He could not see why he should spend the rest of his life in an unhappy marriage.

During Sessions 1 and 2, Francine found herself drawn to David, never having met a young boy so insightful and sensitive. She could intuit his feelings and felt that she understood perfectly where he was coming from. David's parents, however, were another story. Francine was only slightly less peeved with David's mother than with his father. In supervision, Francine described both parents as "narcissistic" and "emotionally unavailable" to David. In session, she felt compelled to speak for David, repeatedly pointing out to his parents why and how much he was hurting. When David cried and said that he hated himself, both parents sat stiffly through this emotional display, eyes downcast. Francine felt like shaking them.

Francine's reactions to the Ellisons were strong but understandable. She saw David's plight clearly and had little appreciation for his parents' pain. Because they had come to therapy at David's request, neither parent was personally invested in the process. In essence, they behaved like guests; in their minds, it was Francine's job to help David with his turmoil.

THE MANY FACES OF COUNTERTRANSFERENCE

How, then, had Francine been "sucked into" the family's emotional system? In Bowenian terms (Bowen, 1976), by seeing herself as David's champion, she found herself in an emotional triangle with him against his parents. In the Ellisons' emotional system, drawing in a third party (i.e., triangulation) was the preferred method to diffuse tension among family members. Before David's father had found a lover, his mother had had one, and before that David's paternal uncle had lived with them, mediating the Ellisons' deteriorating marriage. From a systemic perspective, Francine had abandoned neutrality. Judgmental, she imposed her own meaning on the family's story and directed the process toward her own ends (Nichols, 1987): to make David's parents apologize for the pain they had caused him. Alternatively, from a structural therapy perspective (Minuchin & Fishman, 1981), Francine was sucked into the family system when she stopped focusing on family members' interactions with one another and aligned herself with a child against his parents.

In their first book on structural family therapy, *Families of the Slums*, Minuchin and colleagues (1967) distinguished *suction* from *induction* (i.e., the natural, perhaps inevitable process by which the therapist adopts the typical transactional patterns of a family) and from *accommodation* (i.e., the deliberate use of induction for therapeutic benefit). According to Minuchin et al., *suction* is unplanned induction, occurring when the therapist feels pushed by the family to behave in ways contrary to her choosing. They explained that multiproblem families have "extremely inflexible and stereotyped patterns of disordered interactions [that] place the new member, the therapist, under considerable pressure to respond only along lines that are in harmony with the family's prevailing organization" (p. 285).

Terms like *suction* and *loss of neutrality* (Boscolo, Cecchin, Hoffman, & Penn, 1987) are as close as many traditional systems theorists have come to acknowledging countertransferential processes in family therapy. One exception is Carl Whitaker (Neill & Kniskern, 1982), who embraced his countertransference, using it to bring to light dangerous undercurrents in his clients' lives, such as incestuous impulses and homicidal rage.

In contrast to psychoanalytic explanations in which countertransference is said to arise from the therapist's own unresolved emotional entanglements, in systemic thinking problematic reactions tend to be attributed to dysfunctional entanglements within the family. In the preceding case, for example, it was the Ellisons' inflexibility, lack of differentiation and high level of anxiety, their tendency to triangulate, and the parents' failure to nurture their son that contributed to Francine's difficulty in working with them.

Several recent theorists (e.g., Flaskas, 1989; Flaskas & Perlesz, 1998; Luepnitz, 1988; Nichols, 1987; Pinsof, 1994) have challenged the traditional emphasis in family therapy on strategy and technique, arguing that understanding the therapist's personal contribution to the process deserves as much attention in conjoint treatment as it does in individual therapy. In this chapter, we focus on therapist countertransference for better or worse, that is, as a window into covert emotional processes in the family and as an obstruction to effective treatment. The following sections present (a) classic and contemporary views on countertransference and (b) applications of the construct to work with couples and families.

Classic and Contemporary Views on Countertransference

First described by Freud (1910/1959) as the mirror image of transference, countertransference has been said to be evident when the analyst acts out his or her unconscious conflicts and defenses in the therapeutic relationship. As an example, a patient repeatedly cuts herself in a desperate attempt to win the analyst's attention, yet the analyst stays aloof, unconsciously distancing himself from this needy patient, who makes him feel helpless. In the classic view, countertransference is an impediment because, as this example shows, the analyst's personal issues and problematic reactions can damage the therapeutic process by contaminating the transference (Hedges, 1992).

This early definition of countertransference has repeatedly been challenged within the psychoanalytic community, beginning in the mid-20th century when theorists (e.g., Little, 1951; Winnicott, 1949) pointed out the value of considering all of the analyst's emotional reactions, regardless of origin, for understanding the patient's core conflicts. From this perspective, defensive reactions on the analyst's part, conscious as well as unconscious, could arise either from unresolved emotional attachments or simply from provocation by the patient.

A middle ground in the debate has evolved over the past 30 to 40 years (Hayes et al., 1998). Rejecting the broad view of countertransference as any emotional reaction to the client, Greenson (1967) distinguished countertransference from the working alliance and from what he called the analyst's *real relationship* with the client. According to Greenson, countertransference is neither the realistic, genuine bond that develops naturally over time between people (i.e., the real relationship) nor the important emotional component of good collaborative therapeutic work (i.e., the alliance). In line with this thinking, interpersonal theorists define *countertransference* as any conflict-based emotional reaction on the therapist's part triggered by the relational demands of the client (e.g., Epstein & Feiner, 1979). Thus, countertransference is not uniquely a product of unconscious reactions but can also arise from difficulties in the therapist's personal history, particularly his or her early familial relationships (Blanck & Blanck, 1979; Gelso & Carter, 1985, 1994). With the Ellisons, for example, Francine Noonan's intense reactions could reflect unresolved issues in her past, such as having neglectful parents or simply a troubled adolescence, stirred up by David's distress and his parents' apparent emotional withholding.

According to object relations theorists (e.g., M. Klein, 1946; Searles, 1963), one form of transference, projective identification, occurs when people disavow threatening emotions by projecting them on others. By behaving consistently with his or her projections, a client can actually induce the therapist to experience warded off feelings, perhaps even to act on them. This is explained succinctly in the following:

> The theory goes like this: Within therapy (and not just within therapy) the person or family is likely to have feelings which are unmanageable, unacceptable, or just too painful to bear. These feelings are split off and handed over in the context of the relationship with the therapist. The

therapist in turn takes these feelings on board and experiences them, at least initially, as if they were her own. (Flaskas, 1989, p. 3)

Failure to contain and resolve the client's projective identification can result in a "therapeutic misalliance" (Slipp, 1984, p. 74). Therapists should consider the possibility of projective identification when they experience uncharacteristic or extreme feelings toward a client that have no clear origin. With the Ellisons, projective identification could be suspected if Francine had no personal conflicts surrounding divorce, homosexuality, emotional neglect, or abandonment. Her extreme reactions, however, could be understood as an unconscious identification with disavowed anger on the part of David's parents.

Contemporary researchers (e.g., Hayes et al., 1998; Rosenberger & Hayes, 2002) have sought to define countertransference by identifying its potential origins (unresolved conflicts), triggers (therapy events that tap into those conflicts), manifestations (cognitive, emotional, or behavioral), and consequences. In-depth interviews with experienced clinicians suggested that in individual therapy, countertransference reactions are particularly likely when therapists view their clients in a pejorative light or when family conflicts are discussed (Hayes et al., 1998). Although not all manifestations of countertransference hinder the therapeutic process, treatment is facilitated when therapists are able to recognize and manage their emotional reactions constructively (Gelso & Hayes, 2002).

It's All in the Family

Even among experienced therapists, countertransference is a frequent occurrence, and because this phenomenon cannot be reported on reliably, its prevalence may be even greater than suspected (Hayes et al., 1998). Indeed, the phenomenon is likely to be just as common in the couple and family arena as it is in individual therapy. One might well argue that countertransference is more common in conjoint treatment, where the family drama is played out *in vivo*, than in individual therapy, where the client merely reports on family experiences (Nichols, 1987).

Although there is no empirical literature on countertransference in a family context, some research suggests that premature termination or unsatisfactory outcomes are more likely when therapists are defensive or have negative feelings toward family members (Firestone & O'Connell, 1980; Shapiro, 1974; Waldron, Turner, Barton, Alexander, & Cline, 1997). In a qualitative study (Sells et al., 1996), clients readily identified and described unhelpful therapy events, but their therapists had little to say on the topic, suggesting that clinicians may have difficulty seeing what is not working in therapy. From the clients' perspective, therapists were ineffective when they failed to understand or address the problem, had unclear goals, did not give equal floor time to everyone, or followed an agenda that was at odds with the family's needs.

Logically speaking, if countertransference arises from conflicts experienced in one's earliest family relationships (e.g., Blanck & Blanck, 1979), then focusing explicitly on family ties is likely to trigger the therapist's own conscious or unconscious childhood conflicts or conflicts about the therapist's current roles as parent and spouse. For this reason, Bowen (1976) insisted that therapists work vigorously to "de-triangle" themselves from toxic emotional processes in their families of origin. If Francine, for example, had felt emotionally abandoned by her own parents (whether or not they had divorced), observing David Ellison's predicament in the face of his parents' nonresponsiveness could well account for her sense of outrage. What if Francine were going through a divorce herself? Comparing her attitude toward her own children with the Ellisons' behavior toward David could also account for Francine's self-righteous indignation.

It is important to note that psychoanalytic family therapists have written less about countertransference than about the power of transference within the family itself, using various terms to describe this phenomenon, such as *scapegoating* (Vogel & Bell, 1960), *trading of dissociations* (L. C. Wynne, 1965), and *irrational role assignments* (Framo, 1970). A wife, for example, experiences her husband's controlling behavior as she experienced her father's domineering attitude while she was growing up. When she faults her husband for stifling her, she is unconsciously blaming her father. Even more complicated transferences and projective identifications can occur, as when the wife behaves in a controlling manner toward her husband, projecting on him the helplessness she had felt on the receiving end of her father's tyranny.

Although writings on countertransference by analytically oriented family therapists are limited, they are instructive. Scharff (1989) defined *countertransference* as "the totality of the affective responses that occur when the family creates an impact that penetrates beyond the therapist's conscious and relatively reasonable capacity to understand," explaining that "[t]he family's object relations system reaches an area of the therapist's unconscious where it resonates with the therapist's own internal object relations" (p. 424). To illustrate this process, Nichols and Schwartz (2004) described the case of Gwen and Andrew, whose "virulent reactions" to each other about money triggered excessive peacemaking efforts in their therapist (p. 244). Acting on his own needs and projections, the therapist was overly anxious to promote the couple's marital harmony. In session he short-circuited what could have been an important therapeutic exploration of Gwen and Andrew's long-held anger and resentments toward one another.

Addressing countertransferential induction into the family system, Nichols (1987) explained that therapists are commonly drawn into "playing out a missing role" in the family (p. 276). Nichols noted, however, that the concept of induction is mechanistic and overlooks the human side of the drama. To breathe life into the concept, Nichols distinguished between *concordant* identification with family members and *complementary* identification, both of which can arise from the therapist's personal needs, conflicts, and defenses in relation to those of the family. In concordant identification, the therapist is in sync with the family's needs, playing a parental role, for example, when the parents are ineffectual and helpless. In complementary identification, the therapist acts in opposition to the family's needs, typically as a result of the clients' projective identifications. As an example, a court-mandated single father passively avoids engaging in treatment by canceling or failing appointments, to which the therapist responds with hostile confrontation (i.e., acting out the father's warded off rage toward authority figures).

Although object relations family theorists (e.g., Scharff & Scharff, 1987; Slipp, 1984) have minimally addressed countertransference in their writings, they make the point that "being sucked into" (Slipp, 1984, p. 74) the family's emotional dance is a threat to treatment. As Slipp explained, a powerful misalliance can result from a familywide projective identification process that uses the therapist to maintain an unhealthy status quo. That is, caught on all sides by the family's "pooled transferences" (Scharff, 1989, p. 423), the therapist unwittingly colludes with the family's dysfunction by, for example, minimizing the harm done to one spouse by the other or by allowing the family bully to go unchallenged.

In contrast to object relations theorists, systems theorists tend to focus less on the hazards of countertransference and more on the positive use of self in therapy (e.g., Ackerman, 1966; Minuchin & Fishman, 1981; Satir, 1964; Whitaker & Keith, 1981), entering the system in a way that is compatible with the family's culture, linguistic style, or energy level. With the exception of Whitaker, who saw countertransference as inevitable if the therapist wanted to get close enough to the family to produce change (Neill & Kniskern, 1982), most early theorists were reluctant to use the intrapsychic term *countertransference*. Nevertheless, they did acknowledge problematic reactions on the part of the therapist. Bowen (1976), uninterested in the content of the therapist's personal conflicts or the family's, for that matter, argued that "the automatic emotional responsiveness that operates covertly in all relationships is the same in the therapeutic relationship. As soon as a vulnerable outside person comes into viable emotional contact with the family, he or she becomes a part of it, no matter how much he protests the opposite" (p. 348). Minuchin (1974) described how a young therapist may not fully appreciate the perspective of parents:

> The therapist, a young single person, feels that the parents, particularly the
> father, are not allowing the children the autonomy that is necessary or
> appropriate for adolescents. She sees the children as fighting for freedom
> from overly rigid parents, and she becomes strongly affiliated to the sibling
> subgroup. As a result, the father increases his controlling demands and
> becomes proportionately more ineffective. The wife finds herself caught

between her husband, now ever more demanding and powerless, and the children, who now have the strong support of the therapist. (p. 108)

COUNTERTRANSFERENCE FOR BETTER OR WORSE

Some family problems are just worse than others. Summarizing clinical wisdom about working with incestuous families, McElroy and McElroy (1991) noted that in these cases countertransference can be reflected in extreme anger at and distancing from the offending parent, a close alliance with the nonprotective parent, and a strong desire to rescue the child victim. In its most harmful form, countertransference can lead a therapist to collude with the offender in denying the extent of the abuse.

Child abuse of any sort is likely to trigger strong reactions in therapists. Although it is natural for clinicians to want to protect a victim and punish an offender, one way to determine whether countertransference is operative in these (or other) clinical situations is to consider the degree to which the therapist's reactions hinder his or her work. Protecting the offender is an extreme response, but there are more subtle manifestations of countertransference. Overidentifying with the victim, the therapist might wind up competing with the ineffectual, nonabusive parent (McElroy & McElroy, 1991) by, for example, showing extreme care and concern for the child.

It is not a distant leap from recognizing the manifestations of countertransference in family work to predicting its effects on the alliance. When family members are viewed strictly as either victims or villains with no appreciation for the systemic, contextual, and personal factors contributing to these roles, the therapist's ability to engage and connect emotionally with everyone is sorely compromised. If the family does not actually flee treatment, the therapeutic process may simply limp along with a split alliance (see chap. 9).

Alternatively, the alliance may be compromised by the therapist's failure to ensure safety. Stacy had moved into a shelter with her children after her boyfriend, Luke, burned her youngest child's arms with a cigarette. Having an intense reaction to this story, the therapist dramatically applauded Stacy's actions and formed a close emotional bond with her, spending much of the family sessions discussing Stacy's emotional pain over what had happened. Unfortunately, the therapist failed to elicit the full story. In fact, Stacy was also abusive, and the cigarette incident had occurred during an alcoholic brawl, one of many between her and Luke. Stacy was only too willing to lay all the blame at Luke's feet, and the therapist unwittingly reinforced this perspective. The children, age 6 and 8, were too frightened to speak the truth, especially now that the only adult they could rely on was the one who had hurt them the most.

As described in chapter 7, crafting a shared sense of purpose is challenging when family members are in conflict and blaming one another. The

Ellison family is a case in point. Francine's overidentification with David prompted her to become his mouthpiece, in response to which his parents became less and less engaged in treatment as time went on. After Session 3, the parents were experiencing the therapy as a trial to be endured. It was only a matter of time until they decided they had had enough. Had Francine been less "triggered" by David's neediness, she might have been able to create a safe place for family members to explore ways to preserve and enhance their relationships with one another.

In supervision, Francine recognized that in working with the Ellisons, her countertransference had more to do with parenting issues than with either the divorce or the father's choice of a gay lifestyle. It was not, however, as simple as that. Yes, she did fault David's parents for their emotional nonresponsiveness, but her identification with David and her feelings of anger toward his parents were also fueled by a strong need to rescue the boy and her belief that, in families, children's needs always come first.

When therapists are able to acknowledge that their reactions to family members are extreme and that the alliance is suffering accordingly, they have an opportunity to turn it around and learn something about themselves in the process. They must first consider the basis for their countertransference and the therapy events that may have set off their extreme reactions. Here is where the research on countertransference in individual therapy can be instructive. In Hayes et al.'s (1998) interviews with expert therapists, personal issues related to parenting, being a partner, and family of origin were the most frequent sources of countertransferential reactions. Therapists also identified their own grandiosity, narcissism, and devaluing of dependency as contributing factors. Countertransference tended to be prompted by clinical material related to death and family of origin issues; emotional arousal; negative perceptions of clients (particularly dependent and noncompliant ones); and feelings about the therapeutic relationship, about how treatment was progressing, and about termination.

The idea that therapists can use their awareness of countertransference to therapeutic advantage is not a new one, but doing so is notably trickier in a couple or family context. Take, for example, the female therapist who finds herself attracted to a man whose wife is critical and emotionally disengaged. In session, when the spouses begin discussing problems in their sex life, the therapist becomes aware of her attraction to the husband, whom she sees as unusually open and genuine. If this were individual therapy, the therapist need only be concerned about the client's awareness of her feelings. With his wife present, however, the transparency of the therapist's attraction could have a detrimental impact on the alliance and on the couple's marriage.

Consider the therapist who worked with Stacy, the single mother previously described. Several weeks after treatment began, Stacy came to a session upset because recent bruises on the children, noticed by the school nurse, were being investigated by Child Protective Services. This information startled the therapist, leading him to consider for the first time that Stacy might be abusing the children herself. Reflecting on his zeal to support and comfort Stacy, the therapist recognized his mistake and its origin in his personal history. Having been battered repeatedly by his own father, he had distanced himself from Stacy's children so as not to be touched by their pain. Instead, he had focused on Stacy's courage to remove the children, something he had always faulted his own mother for not doing.

Considering the possibility that his countertransference had endangered the children's lives, the therapist was consumed with guilt and shame. With peer consultation, however, he was able to redirect the therapy. When he became aware of his misguided behavior, he managed to put aside his personal feelings and focus on what could be done for the family. With his colleague's help, the therapist saw that his strong alliance with Stacy could help her face what she had done and motivate her to work with him in a different way. Eventually, Stacy took responsibility for her behavior and was eager to overcome her problem and preserve her family.

The self-aware therapist who is not afraid to consider the full range of his or her feelings toward clients can use this knowledge therapeutically. In the following case, a therapist describes how countertransference and projective identification helped her understand a family in crisis:

> My stomach always turns in reaction to abuse, and I found the story of . . . parents seeing a five year old child as possessed, stripping her off and forcing her into the shower, triggering a particular reaction. Quite simply, I don't like to look at abuse, I find it difficult and painful. I distance myself from feeling that, and it doesn't surprise me that for a time I felt unable to stay in touch with the mother or father, that I found myself looking at them but not really seeing them. In fact, when the mother said her child's eyes were pure evil, I thought "your eyes are pure evil." Now I could just censor this thought, tell myself that it's a dreadful thing for a therapist to think, not to mention linear, and most unhelpful in maintaining engagement. But it seems to me that I wasn't the only person involved in that kind of emotional response. The mother clearly found something unbearable in the level of her daughter's anger and fear, and handled it by not seeing her as a five year old child but as possessed by an evil spirit. The child in turn probably threw that back at the mother in the same way I did—you're evil; no you are; no, you are—and so it became passed around the family like an emotional hot potato. As the therapist, I had taken up a place in the family and my reaction was to want to follow the same sequence. During the time I was out of touch with the parents, I was intensely aware of the child in the room, and right at that point I think I had taken the place of the child and felt something of what she felt. It was a rugged interaction to be involved in, and it may well have been that I wasn't the only person who felt sick and fearful. (Flaskas, 1989, pp. 3–4)

When, as in this case, family entanglements are projective identifications gone wild, therapists can reflect on their experience, compare it with their own history and areas of vulnerability, and intervene accordingly.

Therapists who do not shy away from a genuine expression of feeling can, in appropriate circumstances, have a powerful impact on their clients' experience. As an example, consider Alicia's work with the Boyds, Jack (father) and 14-year-old Ashley, who were mandated for treatment by the county probation officer after Ashley had run away from home. Despite many false starts in which Jack cancelled or did not show up for appointments, Alicia was gradually able to engage him and Ashley in a light dialogue about "growing up today" versus when Jack was a boy. Alicia knew that Ashley's mother had deserted the family 4 years earlier and then died of a drug overdose hundreds of miles away. Since she left, Jack had made it a rule never to speak of his wife, and he was particularly averse to doing so in therapy.

Over several sessions with the family, Alicia worked hard to contain her anger toward Jack, who had shown little of himself other than sarcasm, blame, and criticism. Recognizing a profound sense of sadness in herself while sitting with these clients, Alicia suspected that she was containing a reservoir of grief that was too great for the family to bear. Along with her anger and sadness, Alicia found herself wanting to nurture and comfort Ashley, who seemed in desperate need of tenderness despite her angry defiance.

Understanding the pool of transferences and disavowed emotions that she was personally experiencing, Alicia knew that to play a mothering role with Ashley would let Jack off the hook and do little to bring father and daughter closer together. Moreover, Alicia could not really be Ashley's mother, and to step into that role would, in the long run, be damaging.

Alicia appealed to Jack to talk with Ashley about her mother, a suggestion he angrily resisted. Jack cancelled the next appointment. Although Alicia worried that her strategy was a serious mistake, the family came back. Beaming, Ashley explained that for her birthday Jack had given her an album filled with photos of her and her mother in all kinds of funny and loving poses. As Ashley showed the therapist the album, a tear slipped down the therapist's cheek. At first, Ashley and Jack stared in amazement. Smiling, Alicia grabbed a tissue to wipe her eyes and, voice quivering, said, "As you can see, Jack, your doing this for Ashley really touches me." At that, father and daughter looked at each other, slowly began to cry, and then embraced each other tightly.

INDIVIDUAL AND SYSTEMIC MANIFESTATIONS

On reflection, the therapists who were interviewed in Hayes et al.'s (1998) study believed that their countertransference reactions had led them to approach or avoid their clients differently than they might have done otherwise. Thoughts and feelings prompting approach behaviors included compassion, nurturance, and identification with the client, whereas thoughts and feelings related to avoidance behaviors included boredom, fatigue, distancing, disappointment, and a sense of blocked understanding. Universally, countertransference reactions were accompanied by negative emotions—anger, frustration, sadness, inadequacy, anxiety, pressure, or a sense of being burdened or overly responsible for the client. Worrying about where the therapy was heading, some therapists chose to be more active or directive, others less active or directive.

Hayes et al.'s (1998) participants described *conscious* thoughts and feelings about their clients., although by definition, countertransference includes reactions that are out of a therapist's awareness. Supervisors can suspect the presence of countertransference when their supervisees behave uncharacteristically or have extreme or inconsistent reactions to their clients. Furthermore, projective counteridentification should be suspected when a supervisor begins to have strong reactions to the supervisee's presentation or description of a client (Ladany, Friedlander, & Nelson, 2005). This "parallel process" phenomenon occurs when the supervisee experiences the client's disavowed feelings (typically, dependence, rage, or confusion) and unconsciously projects them on the supervisor, who then experiences the supervisee in much the same way as the supervisee experienced the client (Doehrman, 1976). Sorting out the origins of feelings in this three-person relationship is challenging, but untangling the projections is possible because neither the supervisee nor the supervisor has a personal history with the client, nor do they live with the client. They can go home, reflect on what has occurred, and come back refreshed and ready to work the problem from a different angle.

No such reprieve exists for family members caught in an emotional web of transferences and projective identifications, and the therapist who enters a dysfunctional family system is a potential recipient for everyone's unconscious projections. Because the family dance is played out overtly as well as with covert communications and innuendo—shoulder shrugs, rolling eyes, and the like—the therapist can experience countertransference not only in response to one client but to each individual in relation to everyone else in the room. Working with the Ellisons, for example, Francine was triggered by David's sensitivity and distress in the face of his parents' nonresponsiveness. Francine's overidentification and protective behavior toward David was thus a manifestation of her reactions to him as an individual and to his role within the family, to his treatment by his parents, and to the covert demands being placed on her by the whole system. Moreover, by acting on David's wish to make his parents appreciate his pain, Francine was seen as a critical judge by the parents; it is not surprising that they responded defensively. Observing their defensiveness, David felt even more hopeless and isolated, prompting still more nurturance and caring concern on Francine's part.

In other words, the manifestations of countertransference in conjoint therapy defy straightforward explication. Because the therapist's attitudes and behavior toward each family member are observed and responded to by all the others, problematic reactions on the therapist's part can prompt all sorts of reactive maneuvering by family members. The more there is at stake, the more dramatic the consequences. Take, for example, the obnoxious, defiant preteen who bullies his parents but is secretly desperate for the therapist to make his parents protect him from himself. Caught up in her own feelings, the therapist focuses solely on the boy's defiance, failing to address the parents' passivity. Only too willing to let the therapist take charge, the parents become even more passive. Seeing their defeat, the increasingly hopeless boy escalates his acting out behavior. In short order, he is removed from his parents' care.

Surely one can debate the etiology of the therapist's problematic reactions to this (or any) family: Was it due to projective identification? Was it conscious or unconscious? Was it related to the therapist's own personal history or merely a response to the family's presentation? Whether a given display of behavior is due to unresolved emotional conflicts (i.e., countertransference) or to lack of experience or skill, burnout, or some other factor is a matter for the therapist's personal consideration. Regardless of one's take on the source of the problematic behavior, the presence of the behavior has the potential to compromise the alliance in predictable ways, as discussed in the following sections.

Engagement in the Therapeutic Process

When therapists experience great difficulty understanding a client, they tend to stay outside the system, almost as onlookers (Weingarten, 1992), avoiding engagement (Hayes et al., 1998). In a conjoint treatment context, the therapist's persistent avoidance of one or more family members, throughout a session or over several sessions, can signal a problematic reaction to that client or indeed to another client. That is, when a therapist neglects or overlooks a family member, especially one who displays indifference or boredom, she or he is likely to be overly focused on another. When the family is large, it is common to focus on a single subsystem at a time, but a persistent lack of interaction with one member of the family may signal countertransference. An observer of the Ellisons' therapy, for example, would see David as highly engaged with Francine, who was expending a great deal of effort to draw him out, paraphrasing his comments, exploring his deepest feelings, and so forth. Asked about her behavior, Francine might acknowledge that her relative lack of interaction with David's parents was a reflection of her irritation with them.

Francine's conscious objective was to help a depressed child express his feelings. Doing so, Francine essentially acted on her "premature understanding" of the problem (Weingarten, 1992, p. 53), defining the direction of therapy without consulting the family. By imposing meaning, tasks, or goals on family members in the absence of negotiation and consensus, a therapist risks a decline in engagement by one or more family members (Friedlander, Heatherington, et al., 1994; Weingarten, 1992). Sometimes a client may protest by denigrating the value or purpose of treatment. The therapist who is highly reactive to that individual or to the anxiety within the system as a whole may begin to chastise or argue with the client about the need for therapy.

Emotional Connection With the Therapist

According to alliance theorist William Pinsof (1994), countertransference is the emotional bond from the therapist's perspective. When a therapist feels emotionally connected with a couple or family, there is a visible interest in and appreciation for each individual. In Pinsof's view, countertransference is a "normal process in which the therapist attributes meaning and psychologically cathects key members of the patient system" (p. 184). As an active process of valuing the family, the absence of countertransference "bodes poorly for the future of a therapy system" (p. 184).

When the therapist has a negative response to one client, however, it is often because she or he is overly identified with another. Just as the therapist's overengagement with one family member or subsystem can be a manifestation of countertransference, so can an imbalance in emotional responsiveness. This imbalance may, in the extreme, lead the therapist to moralize or patronize the disliked family member, to respond defensively, or to exchange hostile or sarcastic comments when the client does not "go along with the program." In a milder form, the therapist who dislikes a client might simply avoid eye contact or fail to respond to bids for attention. Clients who complain that the therapist does not understand or listen to them may well be picking up on the therapist's lack of emotional engagement with them.

Family members tend to be highly sensitive to the therapist's personal connections with each one of them and to how much the therapist seems to care for them as a group. Therapists who are stiff or humorless are likely to be perceived by family members as disapproving or pessimistic. When clients sense that they are the focus of the therapist's disapproval, they tend to withdraw emotionally or discontinue coming for sessions with the rest of their family. When the Ellisons' therapy seemed to be faltering, Francine made the error of agreeing to David's request to meet alone with his father. David used the time to tell his father how upset he was about having to live with his mother. Although unaware of what was discussed, the mother knew that David felt closer to his father than to her. Viewing Francine as complicit in her exclusion, the mother felt even more alienated from the therapist, who was now seen as a rival for her son's affection.

Safety Within the Therapeutic System

Making therapy a safe place for everyone can be a challenge, but when the therapist is feeling personally threatened, there is little hope of cultivating the family's sense of safety. Even when the therapist is not afraid, she or he can compromise family members' feelings of safety through displays of anxious behavior (e.g., leg tapping or shaking, sitting rigidly) or by failing to attend to clients' expressions of vulnerability. Weingarten (1992) described a case in which the therapist's silence about marital abuse so shamed the client that the topic was not mentioned again until 2 years later, when the woman decided to divorce her husband. In the case of Gwen and Andrew (Nichols & Schwartz, 2004), described earlier, the therapist anxiously smoothed over the couple's expressions of anger because of his own discomfort. In the same situation, another therapist, more fearful, might allow the couple's blame, shouting, threats or intimidation to escalate unchecked.

Keeping secrets is also problematic and may reflect the therapist's countertransference. Caught off guard when a client in couple therapy telephoned between sessions to confess a prior extramarital affair, the therapist agreed to keep silent. Continuing the therapy for 3 months with this secret in the background was increasingly stressful for the therapist, who came to see her silence as related to feelings about her own husband's philandering. By this point, the client could not divulge the secret to her husband without revealing the therapist's complicity, and the safety of therapy was compromised for everyone.

Shared Sense of Purpose Within the Family

To craft a goal or set of goals that is meaningful for the whole family, the therapist must have a vision of the system's problems that accounts for each individual's contribution. When one family member comes to therapy as a plaintiff (M. Beck et al., in press), complaining that another needs to be "fixed" or "set right," it is only too easy for the therapist to accept that definition of the problem. Sometimes the plaintiff plays the role of cotherapist, and the therapist who is highly reactive to the presenting problem may go along with this fiction, failing to see that there is more than one story to be told.

In other words, countertransference should be suspected when the therapist is persistently unable to see beyond the perspective of a single individual. Manifestations may include failing to elicit everyone's reasons for seeking help, devaluing the point of view of one family member while reinforcing the perspective of another, repeatedly aligning with one person or subsystem against another, or ignoring one client's stated concerns by uniquely focusing on another's. Francine's excessive identification with David Ellison's plight compromised her ability to help the family identify a common, proactive goal for treatment. Recall that the Ellisons had sought help at David's request. Although the parents expected the therapist to support and encourage David, Francine's repeated lack of attention to their concerns led them to suggest that David continue in treatment alone. Sadly, David had wanted therapy to help him hold onto his family, but the process was unfolding in precisely the opposite direction.

AVOIDING AND REPAIRING ALLIANCE RUPTURES

In the 1960s, when analysts cautiously began inviting parents into treatment rooms with their severely ill, schizophrenic children, the analysts were plagued by reality distortions, communication deviance, and extraordinarily high levels of confusion and anxiety. To gain therapeutic leverage, some family therapists began using cotherapists (Whitaker & Keith, 1981) or a larger team (Selvini-Palazzoli et al., 1978) to deliver interventions. Whitaker trusted the "we-ness" of the cotherapy team to keep him on track, whereas the early Milano group (Selvini-Palazzoli et al., 1978) placed the team in an adversarial role with the family to avoid being pulled into covert, unhealthy games. In yet another variation, reflecting teams (Andersen, 1991) promoted collaboration by asking clients to observe and then respond to the team's frank discussion of the family's problems.

Aside from team work, strategies to avoid suction have also been identified. Some therapists deliberately take sides with one subsystem or the other to maintain impartiality (in the long run) through frankness and honesty (Ackerman, 1966; Sluzki, 1975; Whitaker & Keith, 1981). Structural therapists (Minuchin & Fishman, 1981) join and distance as the situation demands. Adamantly opposed to the therapist's use of self, systemic therapists (Boscolo et al., 1987; Hoffman, 1981) strive to maintain neutrality through circular questioning. Bowenian therapists (Bowen, 1976) also see themselves as once removed—as coaches encouraging clients to discuss rather than experience their emotions and avoiding countertransference at all costs.

Avoidance goes only so far, however. When a family is in crisis, when anxiety is running high, or when the family's relational dynamics are rigid and destructive, some measure of countertransference may be inevitable. As soon as a therapist sees a countertransference-based misalliance unfolding, hasty repair is essential.

Clients can be very forgiving. If Francine were to become aware of her countertransference and its effects on her alliance with the Ellisons, how might she put it right? One possibility would be to self-disclose and accept responsibility for the direction therapy has taken.

> As I've gotten to know you, I've been impressed with how much all three of you are struggling with this difficult situation. Thinking about our work together, I've realized that I have encouraged David to speak his

mind, which—although he clearly felt he needed to—only tells one side of the story. You [*parents*] also have an important say, and I've been remiss in focusing too much on David's feelings. After all, you're the parents, and for David to get through this and feel comfortable again, he can't do it without you. And the therapy can't be successful without you.

For some clients, however, disclosing an error can compromise feelings of safety and trust. An alternate repair strategy would be to focus on the family's shared sense of purpose. If the alliance had not faltered too much, Francine might yet be able to reframe the Ellisons' problem as "a family struggling to redefine itself after a divorce." To help David contain his escalating negativity, Francine could point out that the divorce was not intended to destroy David's life and that in fact both parents are hurting because he is hurting. Then, with gentle authority, Francine could urge David to focus less on what was done in the past and more on what kind of relationship he wants with his father and mother, now and in the future. Encouraging the parents to "help David move on emotionally" could empower them to help him recover the sense of specialness he lost when his father left home.

CONCLUSION

When we are invited into the most intimate parts of people's lives, their stories cannot help but stir us. Some family stories are so troubling that intense emotional responses are unavoidable. Self-aware therapists who have worked on their own issues are in the best position to recognize countertransference and use it to therapeutic advantage.

Prevention trumps remediation. To counteract the tendency to respond countertransferentially, therapists can work in teams, consult with supervisors and colleagues, pursue their own therapy, and stay humble. As mentioned earlier, Bowen (1976) coached his trainees to "de-triangle" themselves from emotional entanglements in their families of origin (p. 349). In Bowen's view, it is only by making changes in our own primary relationships that we can hope to effect similar changes in those of our clients.

14

MISALLIANCES BETWEEN PROFESSIONAL HELPERS

Rose, a young mother, brought her 5-year-old son, Michael, to a family therapist. When the therapist inquired about the problem, the conversation went something like this:

> *Rose:* We moved here just a few weeks ago. Michael started school mid-year, and I'm not sure why, but his teacher is worried he might be having socialization problems. The thing is, she told this to the school psychologist, but she [the psychologist] sees no problems with Michael.

> *Therapist:* So the psychologist thinks there's no problem?

> *Rose:* The teacher talked with the school principal, and she asked the psychologist to make a more complete evaluation and observe Michael's behavior in class. The psychologist did that and told us she didn't see any psychological or behavior problems, but Michael was very restless and sometimes was a little aggressive with other kids, although at other times he's quite agreeable. The thing is that, to our surprise, the psychologist told us that now, in the middle of the school year, integrating him with the

other children in the class is giving the teacher extra work and she's "a little tired."

Therapist: I understand. Maybe the psychologist's observations led you to think your child is having some kind of difficulty?

Rose: No. Frankly we were relieved, and she didn't recommend any kind of counseling, but then I casually mentioned all this to the pediatrician, who's also new for us, of course, during Michael's routine check-up. He said there's a high incidence of children with hyperactivity, and these problems are often misdiagnosed in elementary schools.

Therapist: Ah, I see, it was the pediatrician who recommended seeing a therapist.

Rose: No, actually, it wasn't like that. I told all this to my husband; for him, the move has been somewhat traumatic. It's a job change because of my career. The thing is, he thinks that maybe our son is also experiencing the move in a traumatic way, and this is why he's not behaving in school like he did in the other school he was in. So, I've been paying close attention to Michael's behavior.

Therapist: Good. Have you noticed any changes in his behavior that are worrisome?

Rose: Not particularly. It's difficult to say. We have a new house, new neighborhood, new situations at work. Also my husband and I are having some problems in our relationship. With all this, I decided to talk to the teacher again and tell her what was happening at home, and she gave me your phone number and also convinced me that with all this information I was giving, it's obvious that the school psychologist was negligent. I don't know. My husband was also going to come today, but he had to work late.

Therapist: Well, it's good that you're here, but I'm not sure. . . . Do you think Michael is really having some behavior problems that we should be concerned about, or would you like to talk about how the three of you are handling the move here and all the changes in your professional life?

Rose: Actually, I don't think Michael is having any major problems. I think Tom, my husband, and I can work it out with him, I mean, by ourselves.

Therapist: So?

Rose: I *am* worried about the ongoing disagreements between the teacher, the psychologist, and the school principal. I'm afraid Michael may become a source of contention, and this could affect him. Also their different viewpoints make us worry about every little thing that Michael does.

Therapist: I think I understand the situation, but not to worry, we'll just try to figure this out. You just may be right about the situation.

Rose: Now I think that maybe I shouldn't have said anything to the teacher or the pediatrician. Maybe I shouldn't have doubted our own view of Michael so much. But if I hadn't come here to see you, the teacher would've been upset. Then, on the other hand, by coming here I'm going against the school psychologist, who gave a very positive and encouraging opinion of my son. [*Sighs*]

This story about a mother who seeks therapy so as not to upset a professional who is in a power struggle with other professionals illustrates the effects on clients when professional helpers are misallied. In this case, Rose suspected that differences in the teacher's and school psychologist's points of view were not a simple disagreement. At first she doubted her own observations of her son (an understandable reaction), but then she needed help to figure out how to handle the misalliance between the professionals. It is easy to see how this family could be harmed if the therapist were to confront the teacher, school psychologist, principal, or pediatrician, or if the therapist were to stay out of the fray but coach his client to take an aggressive stance with the other professionals.

When a child is the source of concern, clashes between the family, health providers, the educational system, juvenile justice, and social services are all too common. Misalliances are also common when adults in therapy with a nonmedical professional also receive pharmacological treatment from a physician or psychiatrist. For example, 36-year-old Marla and 43-year-old Will Brewster sought help when they feared their marriage was in danger. Diagnosed with major depression, Marla was being treated with antidepressants. The psychiatrist suggested a therapy consult to assess how seriously Marla's depression was affecting her marriage.

Making a strong connection with the therapist at the first visit, Marla and Will began therapy with enthusiasm. Both spouses saw a link between Marla's depression, problems in their relationship, and Marla's grief over being unable to get pregnant (Will was sterile). Therapy progressed nicely, with rapid improvements in the couple's relationship and in Marla's mental status. A month later, the couple decided to become foster parents in hopes of adopting a child.

In light of these improvements, Marla wanted to discontinue the antidepressant. The therapist thought her decision was reasonable but urged the couple to consult the psychiatrist. However, the psychiatrist did not see a significant change in Marla's depression and insisted that she continue the medication, with only a slight reduction in dose. Unfortunately, the conflicting opinions between professionals rattled Marla and Will, making them doubt what had been achieved in therapy. Marla, in particular, began to feel hopeless about overcoming her depression and fearful about bringing a child into their home.

In situations like these, the risk is great that each professional involved in the case will attribute the clients' setback to an error on the part of the other professional. The professionals' willingness to communicate directly with each other about their disagreement may be hindered by concerns about reputation or politics and not the case at hand. In this case, fortunately, there were no such issues. After noting the couple's backsliding and seeing how strongly Marla felt about overcoming her problems without medication, the two professionals conferred by phone and established a joint plan. Independently, they explained to the couple the compatibility of the two treatments and the need to be prudent before discontinuing psychotropic medication. In speaking with the clients, each professional validated the opinion of the other. Their collaboration was evident to Marla and Will, and the adjustment within the professional "system" allowed the therapy to progress and, ultimately, to succeed.

Marla and Will's case was relatively straightforward, as this upper-middle-class couple had many resources—economic, social, and psychological. However, multi-problem families who have multiple stressors (Madsen, 1999) are usually low-income families receiving services from several different sources, and the potential for conflict and mistrust among professionals is great. What can therapists do in a choppy sea of specialized services to create a strong working alliance with other professional helpers? In this chapter, we discuss the sources and consequences of strains in professional systems and offer recommendations for avoiding or rectifying such misalliances.

SYSTEMS ON OVERLOAD

When the health care, educational, and social service systems in any community are strong and specialized, there is the potential for miscoordination and miscommunication primarily because of great complexity. Whether a family is receiving free public health services, private health care, or counseling from a charitable program, it is challenging to work collaboratively with an array of professionals who likely have different points of view, different responsibilities and interests, and different schedules and procedures. Indeed, coordinating services within an overworked, typically underpaid professional system often wastes time that could be better spent on the families it serves. As a consequence, multistressed families easily become "multitreated" families, with no one provider having a systemic, comprehensive view of how well the family functions and of its ability to change. The result is well summed up by a client who was undergoing family therapy at the recommendation of Child Protective Services. After attending a meeting to plan a reunification with one of her children, who was in foster care, the client commented,

> I met two social workers who I hardly know, with the people in charge of the foster program, who seemed familiar but who I don't know well, with someone who I think is the head of Child Protective Services, and with someone who seemed to be a lawyer. It took awhile to understand the whole process. I hope it works out all right, they were actually nice, but I really missed seeing a familiar face, someone I could call by name!

Only in fiction or in a family therapist's worst nightmare could there be an International Conference for Multistressed Families. If such a conference were actually to take place, a workshop called *Alliances Between Professional Helpers* would no doubt draw much attention. Indeed, most multiproblem families would have had numerous experiences with professionals who disagree or find themselves caught in a power struggle. A typical scenario involves a Child Protective Services worker who accuses a therapist of not working hard enough to engage a resistant family into treatment, whereas the therapist accuses the worker of providing too little information, setting unrealistic goals, or even avoiding responsibility and expecting the therapist to shoulder all the risks. In these situations, it is all too common for a powerless family to take advantage or even encourage the split between professional helpers, particularly if the misalliance confers some sort of advantage.

Turf wars can have many causes, ranging from personality clashes and power struggles to political turmoil within or between agencies. Even when all the professionals involved in a case feel positive about their work and the work of their peers, role conflicts can occur when individuals have unwarranted expectations of each other and act on those expectations without conferring (Ladany et al., 2005). An adolescent's probation officer, for example, expected the family's therapist to notify him whenever the teen skipped school, but the therapist thought the situation could be better handled in therapy. When the boy was caught stealing a car after having missed 4 days of school, the probation officer blamed the therapist for withholding information.

Just as family conflict can escalate out of control, so too can an overstressed system of professional helpers. Theorist Murray Bowen (1976) eloquently described how an individual's lack of differentiation, which leads to symptoms and family dysfunction, is mirrored in larger, social systems. When stress and anxiety are extreme and a system's external resources are few or inadequate, family members often turn on each other. The result is miscommunication, misinformation, misalliances, and mistakes. In the language of the System for Observing Family Therapy Alliances (SOFTA), when a professional system lacks a shared sense of purpose in its work with a client system, the negative fallout can be extreme. In the following section we present a case in which a conflicting system of professionals had a particularly iatrogenic effect on a multi-stressed family.

CASE ILLUSTRATION:
PROFESSIONAL MISALLIANCES THREATEN A FAMILY'S SAFETY

Esther Jackson, a 45-year-old widow, and her 15-year-old daughter Katy started conjoint therapy after 2 years of enormous difficulties. Katy was 13 when her father died in a car accident. After this event, the family experienced a cascade of psychological, social, and economic crises. Esther had never worked, indeed hardly had any social life aside from her husband's family, and these individuals offered little support after he died. Esther felt isolated and began showing signs of depression, which went unaddressed. Katy became highly protective of her mother, trying to care for her and keep up the house. With these added burdens, she began missing school and stopped seeing her friends. Moreover, Katy had a history of academic difficulties and was in many ways quite immature.

When social services intervened at the request of Katy's school, both daughter and mother were defensive. They rejected all attempts by the social worker to "reorganize their home life to make it more functional." Rejections of every recommended intervention increased the conflict between the family and social services. Mother and daughter became even more determined to stick together, unwilling to leave each other even for brief periods of time. Eventually, when Katy abandoned all school responsibilities and was truant for 2 weeks, Child Protective Services placed her in a residential facility in a neighboring town. Esther was inconsolable.

Over the next few weeks, Katy escaped from the facility several times, and her mother's arguments with the many professional helpers escalated. One consequence was Katy being labeled with an antisocial personality disorder and Esther with a narcissistic personality disorder. However, because the family did not cooperate with the social service workers, there was in fact no thorough psychological evaluation of either individual.

At the peak of the conflict, mother and daughter barricaded themselves at home for 3 days, barring all doors and windows and refusing to communicate with authorities. A court order was obtained, and the police accompanied Child Protective Services workers to force Katy's return to the residential facility. This traumatic event was witnessed by countless neighbors, leaving Esther feeling shamed and powerless.

At this point, a worker recommended (at the suggestion of the Family Court judge) that mother and daughter each receive individual therapy. A clinician at the local community mental health center evaluated the Child Protective Services report. In light of both clients' negative reactions to the individual therapy referral, an experienced family therapist was also recommended. However, the Child Protective Services worker opposed any measure that would facilitate contact between mother and daughter, insisting that each client receive "adequate psychological or psychiatric treatment." After the supervisor intervened, the caseworker recommended "without enthusiasm" that Esther and Katy be "seen individually to improve their dysfunctional relationship" (i.e., that conjoint sessions be kept to a minimum).

When the family therapist insisted on seeing both mother and daughter together, the individual therapists agreed, and the residential administrators allowed Katy to accompany her mother to therapy. Despite this agreement, at the last minute Katy's teachers "punished" her for some misdeed, making it impossible for her to attend Session 1 with her mother. Esther's response to this event was predictable: She wanted everyone to see that she had been tricked, and she refused to cooperate further.

The therapist explained that Katy's absence was due to a "lack of coordination" between professionals. Assuring Esther that there was no hidden agenda to block the family therapy, the therapist contacted the Child Protective Services worker, Esther's individual therapist, and Katy's teachers, negotiating another therapy appointment for the family.

Although it was agreed that Esther would come to the session on her own and Katy would be brought by a teacher, Esther in fact showed up an hour early at the residential center to ensure that Katy would indeed be allowed to leave. The mother's presence produced a new round of conflict that, fortunately, was resolved when the facility administrators called the Child Protective Services worker and the therapist. Finally, the professionals reached an agreement, and the first conjoint therapy session took place.

In session, mother and daughter sat very close to one another, practically hugging. When the therapist asked, "What would you see as a good outcome of the work we're starting together today? What do you want to achieve?", the answer was predictable. Almost in unison, mother and daughter replied, "To be together." The therapist then asked, "Do you have any idea why the teachers, social workers, and child psychologists are so afraid of you two being together?" Confused, Esther and Katy had no ready answer. The therapist continued, "If, from tomorrow on, you could live together again, how would you organize your lives?" Surprisingly, Esther replied that if nobody "persecuted" them, she would actually prefer her daughter to finish out the school year where she was, which would mean staying at the residential center. It would be enough for them just to spend weekends together, "but I'd call Katy every day." For her part, Katy had yet another condition: "Someone would have to take care of my mother, someone who *really understands* how my mother feels."

The clients' shared goals were reasonable. Moreover, the therapist's genuine interest in the mother, the daughter, and their relationship, as well as respect for the family's needs and empathy with their suffering, made her a good candidate for the person Katy wanted to take care of her mother. Indeed, by bringing about this long-awaited conjoint session, the therapist achieved a measure of credibility with the family that set the stage for a strong working alliance.

What stalled the Jacksons' therapy? Undoubtedly, the problem was in large part a misalliance within the professional system. What was needed to allow mother and daughter to be treated together and also to address Esther's poor functioning and Katy's safety? We believe that cases like this one require the initial, primary focus to be on the professional system: establishing positive contacts among the various professionals, discussing each professional's objectives and the purpose for every intervention, ensuring everyone's safety by de-escalating the spiral of mistrust and confrontation, establishing norms that respect each professional's niche (education, psychotherapy, social services), and building cohesion and goodwill among all people involved in the case. In other words, we recommend creating a strong within-system alliance (Pinsof, 1994, 1995) in which every professional is engaged and positively connected with every other professional as well as with the family. Paradoxically, in the case of Esther and Katy, the professionals were mis-allied, but the within-family alliance was exceedingly strong.

SHARING RISKS TO ENSURE SAFETY

Therapy involves risks not only for clients but also for the professionals who are involved with them. People under pressure sometimes act out their hostility and aggression, attempt suicide, make disastrous decisions about their marriages, and so on. In the face of such risks, the therapist is vulnerable professionally and personally.

Although working in groups or under supervision benefits therapists in many ways and reduces the risk to clients, people feel exposed when they show their work to others. Trust in the supervisor or in the professional peer group is essential. When trust is strong, it is helpful to share one's work directly, using a one-way mirror, videotape, or closed-circuit television. By doing so, the therapist can explain the work in detail as well as share the decision making with others. Indeed, over the past 20 years team approaches to systemic therapy have become commonplace in training programs as well as in clinical agencies with a family focus.

In chapter 6 we emphasized the need for families to feel comfortable with all elements in the therapeutic context—confidentiality, recording equipment, working with multiple providers, and so on—and we described the kinds of tensions that can threaten a family's sense of safety in therapy. The same conditions apply to the therapist within the professional system. When, for example, a therapist fears that a given course of action will be perceived negatively or challenged by another professional involved in the case, the planned intervention risks being compromised. By insisting on seeing Esther and Katy together, the therapist sided with the family in their conflict with social services. Although the therapist strongly believed that mother and daughter needed to re-establish contact to improve their relationship, a negative outcome would have left the therapist in a highly vulnerable position. There was a very real risk that Katy would escape again, or that both mother and daughter would take off or barricade themselves at home, not to mention even more dramatic outcomes.

When a therapist feels alone and isolated in working with a high-risk family, the problem is exacerbated when the family is also under the care of professionals who disagree with the therapist's course of action. It is, however, at least questionable (and potentially unethical) for a therapist to proceed when his or her interventions contradict the aims of the other services being provided to the family, be they social, educational, medical, or legal.

Some of the same SOFTA–o indicators of a lack of safety for families within the therapeutic system also apply to a lack of safety within the professional system of helpers. When communication channels are closed or there are ambiguous reports that hide compromising information about the client (e.g., HIV status, past criminal acts), the professional system is unsafe. Although we tend not to expect professionals to keep secrets from other professionals treating the same family, it is common to hear complaints about a lack of clarity, misinformation, or even willful obstruction. Only when professionals in different agencies can talk openly about their work, disclosing both positive and negative information about the progress of their treatment, and asking each other's opinion about how to proceed when the going gets rough, can we expect their level of safety to be adequate.

Safety can be assumed when professionals cooperate, ask each other for feedback, openly discuss their fears and insecurity about a case, and so on. Safety within the professional system can also be assumed when a family readily discusses with one professional what is going on in the work with the others. When Esther began to trust the facility where Katy was living, she remarked to the therapist, "Yes, things seem to be improving slowly. Katy's advisor said the same thing you did about her!" When therapists are able to work collaboratively, safety can be contagious.

ENHANCING A SHARED SENSE OF PURPOSE

When a family system simultaneously receives specialized treatments from different sources (e.g., couple therapy, alcohol rehabilitation for the mother, and residential care for the oldest child), the professionals often have different answers to the question, "What is the overall treatment goal for this family?" At a general level, the answer might be "to improve the family's quality of life," but each professional is likely to focus on specific objectives for the individual client or subsystem with whom he or she is working. As we have seen, it is not uncommon for one professional's goals to contradict those of another professional, whose lens is trained on a different individual or subsystem.

With the Jacksons, the Child Protective Services worker and professionals at the residential center were helping Katy learn to live independently of her mother, but Esther's individual therapist was focused on the client's depression, brought on by social and emotional isolation after the traumatic loss of her husband, and the family therapist wanted to work directly with the mother–daughter relationship to make it safe and functional. All of these goals were meaningful, compatible, and essential for Esther and Katy. What is the key to identifying a goal that takes into account the needs of all family members? In this case, the key was to include mother and daughter in defining the goals for the family and for each of them individually. Esther and Katy saw the individual therapy referrals as measures designed to separate them. However, when the family therapist asked the clients how they would optimally organize their lives together, both clients were willing to continue living apart.

When all professionals involved in a case organize their work around a single goal that is acceptable to the family and reach an agreement or compromise ("I'll do this if you do that") so that the interventions complement each other, their shared sense of purpose assuredly benefits the clients. The SOFTA–o Shared Sense of Purpose Within the Family indicators can easily be applied to the within-professional alliance. A strong shared purpose is indicated when the professionals involved in a case ask for each other's perspective on the problem or the solution and validate each other's work, either privately or in front of the family. In contrast, a poor sense of purpose is indicated when the various professionals directly or indirectly blame one another for the family's difficulties or lack of progress; make coalitions to block or disqualify one another's interventions; or criticize one another's values, goals, or procedures. In the Jackson case, the family therapist's efforts to broker a shared sense of purpose with the educational and social service workers greatly improved the family's cooperation, even though intensive and long-term work on the part of every member of the team was needed before the general and specific treatment objectives were attained.

Misalliances among professionals are particularly harmful when the therapy is contaminated by social control measures. This situation is quite common when abuse or neglect is present or when an adult member of the family has come to the attention of legal authorities. Therapy should be a context for obtaining help, not used as the arm of authorities who make therapy contingent on the family's cooperation with legal sanctions or who declare the therapy ineffective whenever clients "slip" (e.g., a marital fight or an alcohol relapse). A shared sense of purpose among professionals requires shared responsibility and respect for the work of one another, ensuring adequate conditions to achieve mutually agreed on treatment goals. Just as police officers should not do therapy and Family Court judges should not arrest felons, therapists should neither judge nor control their clients.

ENGAGING MANY PROFESSIONALS IN A COORDINATED TREATMENT PLAN

When a family receives services from multiple service providers, family therapists are often invited to meetings for purposes of treatment coordination. Examples include meetings with Child Protective Services workers, probation officers, or providers of sex offender treatment programs. In a Spanish agency where one of us worked, several therapists were informed of an upcoming "coordination meeting" to focus on several high-conflict cases. The therapists asked their supervisor, "Who is this coordination meeting against? Who's going to represent us?" It goes without saying that "coordination" did not enjoy a good reputation among this particular group of professionals.

Perhaps this anecdote conveys another meaning: Coordination may be inappropriate in some circumstances. Ideally, professionals from different disciplines who routinely work together in a conjoint program should not be pressured or subjected to "coordination." Rather, they should see some benefit from using common procedures, holding joint meetings, and making personal contacts. Coordination should mean more than exchanging information and making decisions, but rather creating and sustaining a thriving alliance among professionals. When those in charge of team meetings recognize the need for a strong within-professional alliance to facilitate proper treatment, the coordination tasks and procedures should further the professionals' willingness to engage with each other.

A common complaint among therapists who work with multiproblem families is that the workload and consequent stress caused by the need to coordinate professionals and agencies (e.g., writing reports, making phone calls, attending meetings) is at least as extreme as the actual work with the families in their caseload. Some professionals believe that only the "real" work with the family counts, that all the "other" work should disappear or at least become peripheral. However, when working with multistressed families (and generally with any clients mandated into treatment by social services), coordination with other professionals and agencies is essential to ensure a strong therapeutic alliance surrounded by a strong within-professional alliance. In the case of Esther and Katy Jackson, the family therapist saw from the start that the other professionals' reluctance to support conjoint family work was a significant part of the problem. The therapist worked diligently to create an alliance among all the professionals involved in the case, knowing that not doing so would make it impossible to work productively in family therapy.

One factor that contributes to misalliances among professionals is the lack of a common theoretical model. Without a common understanding of the problem and how to overcome it, communication is invariably compromised. Indeed, the lack of a common model can hamper the efforts of couple and family therapists working within the same agency or program. When professionals from different disciplines (social workers, psychologists, psychiatrists, lawyers, educators, nurses) regularly work together in a group, delineating a shared theoretical foundation is ideal. In its absence, having a good working knowledge of each other's perspective and intervention model is indispensable; its importance cannot be overemphasized.

MAKING EMOTIONAL CONNECTIONS:
THE VALUE OF A COFFEE BREAK

At the start of therapy with Esther and Katy Jackson, Esther jeopardized the family work by showing up uninvited at her daughter's residence, angering officials at the center as well as the Child Protective Services workers. In their eyes, Esther's behavior confirmed the belief that she could not or would not cooperate. The therapist was informed of the situation and the "punishment": a delay in the family treatment.

Working diligently to rectify the situation, the therapist had numerous phone conversations with all the other professionals involved in the Jacksons' case. The result was permission for Katy to join her mother in an initial session of conjoint therapy. This important intervention not only allowed the family therapy to begin but also ensured Esther's trust in the therapist. The therapist's effectiveness in this situation was due to a strong personal connection with the center authorities and with the Child Protective Services worker involved in the Jacksons' case. Had the therapist instead chosen to make a written report or request, the resulting delay would no doubt have compromised Esther's trust in the long-awaited family therapy.

In some fields, supervision, group work, and mutual support among professionals are absolutely crucial. When a therapist regularly works with neglected and physically or sexually abused children, or when there is a high risk of suicide or family violence, feeling support and caring from the group or supervisor is as essential as sharing the responsibility for technical decisions. Support from other professionals cannot be overemphasized when facing a difficult decision like recommending child placement or a termination of parental rights.

Indeed, personal acquaintance and good relations with other professionals in the network can go a long way toward avoiding or repairing misalliances of the sort we have been discussing. When working with a group, having some informal time to make bonds can be invaluable. On occasion, when team meetings are stalled because of high stress and opposing view-points, solutions come about because of trust and friendship within the group, not because an ingenious technical analysis of the case is proposed. Coffee break conversations on personal topics of interest (e.g., friends in common, sports, children's schools) do not "waste time." To the contrary, these conversations facilitate closeness and mutual support, furthering professional alliances, and in turn helping clients.

Alliances are also facilitated by the professionals' credibility, recognized expertise, and ability to effect improvement in tough cases. To say that a family has an "institutional alliance" (Pinsof, 1995, p. 76) means that the institution of which the therapist is a part has credibility in the eyes of the family. Family members know when there is trust and credibility, even friend-ship, within the team involved in their case. Noticing how the professionals discuss each other's work, clients feel more allied with their therapist when they also feel connected to the entire system of professionals. When the in-stitutional alliance is strong, initial differences between the family and the therapist are more readily neutralized.

CONCLUSION

The creation of a strong alliance within the therapeutic system is not limited to the therapist's office. The therapeutic system can be thought of as the direct (i.e., family) and indirect (e.g., school, neighborhood) systems of which the client is a part, as well as the direct and indirect systems of the therapist (Pinsof, 1994). Often misalliances within the therapist system are the major source of risk in the entire therapeutic system.

In training family therapists, faculty and supervisors should routinely discuss the complexity of therapeutic systems and the many factors that can contribute to misalliances among professional helpers. Trainees should be aware that misalliances often occur when a family is perceived as highly dys-functional and uncooperative, producing a spiral of mutual accusations and defensiveness among overworked, overstressed professionals. Disagreements over and difficulties in coordinating treatment should be anticipated in com-plex cases, particularly when professionals from different disciplines do not share the same theoretical model. Taking active steps to negotiate common goals and treatment plans with other professionals is not a mere nicety—it is an essential part of the job.

The SOFTA can be useful for understanding the dynamics of the within-professional alliance. As we have discussed, levels of engagement, emotional connection, safety, and a shared sense of purpose are indicated by the posi-tive and negative interactions of professional helpers as well as by the in-session and out-of-session behavior of clients. Success is optimized when the therapist actively works with the family and the other professionals involved in the case to establish a comprehensive treatment plan, coordinate the work of each service provider, and nurture professional contacts on the basis of a common philosophy and mutual respect.

IV

CONCLUSION

15

BUILDING AND MAINTAINING HEALTHY ALLIANCES

In the past 10 years, no controversy about psychotherapy has generated more heat than the debate over common versus model-specific factors in therapeutic change (Goldfried & Eubanks-Carter, 2004; Wampold, 2001; Weston et al., 2004). The debate has been slow to reach the couple and family therapy literature, however, possibly because of the historical distinctiveness of that type of therapy. As a field, we have repeatedly emphasized the differences between systemic change models and traditional (individual) models of treatment, as well as the variability among the many "schools" of couple and family therapy (Sprenkle & Blow, 2004). As the preceding chapters illustrate, however, interest in common factors is now firmly in place in couple and family therapy. Nonetheless, cogent arguments are being advanced that "there's got to be more"—the "more" being clearly articulated, multi-level, empirically grounded models of change that explain links between in-session processes, mini-outcomes, and global family outcomes (e.g., Sexton et al., 2004).

We fully agree with the latter. It is abundantly clear that the therapeutic alliance is a critically important common factor, arguably one that, in addition to specific, systemic change processes, accounts for successful couple and family therapy outcomes. Indeed, across couple and family therapy ap-

261

proaches, empirical evidence supports the alliance as a more important common factor than any other, including client expectancy, hope, or emotional experiencing. It is also abundantly clear that in couple and family therapy, the success of model-specific interventions and processes relies on solid and *balanced* therapeutic relationships with family members. Whereas a strong alliance is the foundation for cognitive–behavioral, experiential, or insight-focused interventions in individual therapy, in couple and family therapy a balanced alliance is also the medium for accomplishing systems-specific therapy tasks, such as "re-attaching" a depressed teen and her mother, or brokering a high-stakes compromise between warring spouses.

It is also abundantly clear, as we discuss and illustrate in chapters 4 through 14, that therapeutic interventions that foster the alliance and the resulting within-family interactions are anything but common across families. Emotional connections with the therapist, engagement in the process, safety within the therapeutic system, and shared sense of purpose within the family—all are influenced by the nature of the presenting problem or problems and other factors that vary considerably by individual and by subsystem. Systemic factors include the couple's or family's emotional and behavioral dynamics (e.g., cohesiveness, flexibility, capacity for compromise) as well as its structure, socioeconomic status, and culture (broadly defined). For individuals, gender, age, health status, and sexual orientation are but a few of the many characteristics that can affect the alliance (see chap. 10). The four System for Observing Family Therapy Alliances (SOFTA) dimensions are also significantly influenced by the attachment styles and psychological needs of all participants, including the therapist (chaps. 5 and 13). Moreover, the circumstances under which a family seeks and enters therapy in the first place (chaps. 4, 7, 11, and 12), as well as the direct and indirect involvement of third parties (chap. 14), play a large role in how the alliance develops and is managed.

The suggestions and caveats offered in this book provide guidelines for fostering and repairing alliances and are based on the couple and family therapy literature, our research, and our own clinical experience. At first glance, given the diversity of families and therapists, and the complexity of therapeutic encounters, it seems presumptuous to offer any guidelines whatsoever. How can our experience of the alliance with any one family possibly be applied to others? But, how can it not? To build anything resembling a "science" of psychotherapy—that is, a set of explanatory constructs and operating principles that can be applied to multiple cases, evaluated, and revised on the basis of empirical experience—we need to make generalizations. This we do with a great deal of humility, acknowledging that in the moment-to-moment process of building alliances there is a large element of intuition, creativity, and instinct. This element is the "art" of psychotherapy.

We began this book with the questions, "What makes a good alliance?" and "How can therapists facilitate it?" In several chapters we addressed these questions in depth, keeping in mind that the diversity of families and thera-pists makes this endeavor an art as well as a science. Throughout the book, we address the related question, "How would we know a good alliance when we see it?" Unlike Supreme Court Justice Potter Stewart (1964), who com-mented, "I can't define 'pornography,' but I know it when I see it" (p. 3), we provide a method for "seeing" the alliance through a conceptual lens derived from theory, research, and clinical practice.

In developing the SOFTA, we began with observable client behaviors (e.g., "Family members validate each other's point of view") and client–thera-pist exchanges (e.g., "Client shares a lighthearted moment or joke with the therapist") because we believe that a good alliance *can* be seen. Experienced therapists see good alliances all the time, and even inexperienced ones see them readily. We see *engagement* when family members bring up problems for discussion, a *shared sense of purpose* when clients propose a compromise, *safety* when they divulge a secret, and *emotional connection* when they express warmth or gratitude to the therapist. We also see weak and faltering alliances: when clients "tune out" or "clam up," when they behave defensively or sit guard-edly, when they forget appointments or openly devalue the process of therapy.

From identifying client behaviors that signal a strong or weak alliance, it was a short step to identifying the contributing therapist behaviors. As shown in Table 2.1, many of the SOFTA–o therapist behaviors parallel those of the clients: for example, "Client encourages another family member to 'open up' or speak honestly" and "Therapist helps client(s) talk truthfully and nondefensively with each other" (Safety). Notably, there are far fewer negative therapist behaviors than positive ones (and fewer negative thera-pist behaviors than negative client behaviors). Although a therapist may repeatedly fail to enhance the alliance, or misread a split or faltering alliance by not acting, only in the most obvious circumstances can we observe a thera-pist actually harming the alliance. This is not to say that the health of the alliance rests solely on the clients' shoulders. Rather, the clearest indicators of a strong or weak alliance are clients' ongoing, behavioral reactions to what is taking place in session. Simply put, therapists' behaviors contribute to the alliance, but clients' behaviors reveal it.

In essence, the SOFTA–o is a method of representing clinical experi-ence, a means of making it transparent and systematic, even quantitative, so that the strength of the alliance can be observed in practice, training, (self-)supervision, and research. Certain assumptions and limitations can be made explicit, however. As we implied earlier, because we assume that thoughts and feelings about the alliance are reflected in overt behavior, we defined the SOFTA dimensions inductively, by clustering a pool of rela-tively low-inference, observable behaviors identified from theory, research, and our own clinical experience. We do not, however, assume that these behaviors represent the universe of alliance-related client or therapist be-haviors. Moreover, some behaviors, such as "Client expresses physical affection or caring for the therapist" (Emotional Connection) and "Client makes an uneasy reference to the camera, observation, supervisor, or research procedures" (Safety), do not occur in all clinical contexts or with clients from all cultures. Rather, the items clustered within each SOFTA dimension are behaviors that reflect the alliance in most couple and family therapy approaches.

A second assumption is that therapeutic alliances are bidirectional. Just as some behaviors signal a strong alliance (e.g., "Client indicates agreement with the therapist's goals" [Engagement]), others signal a weak or faltering one (e.g., "Family members argue with each other about the goals, value, or need for therapy" [Shared Purpose]). Consequently, the SOFTA–o dimensional ratings range from *extremely problematic* (–3) to *extremely strong* (+3). In the middle of the scale, 0 = *unremarkable*, because in the absence of behavioral indicators signaling either a highly positive or a negative Emotional Connection With the Therapist, for example, we assume the connection to be neutral (see chaps. 3 and 8). Moreover, the scale is ordinal in nature; thus, we do not assume that one client's Engagement rating of +2, for example, means that he or she is twice as engaged as the client who receives a rating of +1.

Finally, we do not assume that all behavioral indicators in the SOFTA–o are equally indicative of the strength of the alliance. Having an open body posture, for example, is not as powerful an indicator of Safety as divulging a long-held family secret. Asking for another family member's point of view does not add to Shared Sense of Purpose as much as loudly expressing hostility, blame, sarcasm, or contempt detracts from it. Thus, simply noting frequencies of the behavioral indicators is not sufficient; judgment is needed in using the tallies to make global ratings on each SOFTA–o scale. In other words, observers need to take into account verbal, nonverbal, and interpersonal contexts (Heatherington, 1989). Not only the frequency and timing of the behavioral indicators but also the speaker's tone and volume, his or her nonverbal behavior, and the reactions of other family members collectively provide clues to the strength and relative importance of each observed behavior in the ongoing therapeutic context. Essentially, the SOFTA–o rater is a "human synthesizer," making inferences that are based on the same close listening and observing that therapists do less systematically as a matter of course.

IMPLICATIONS FOR CLINICAL PRACTICE, TRAINING, AND SUPERVISION

In using the SOFTA–o, the first step when going from behavioral tallies to global ratings is to decide which client appears to be the least engaged, connected, and safe in the session. This individual is rated first, followed by the person who seems to be the next most engaged, connected, or safe, and so on. In our research, we have found that raters decide which client to rate first with exceptionally high reliability. This is, we believe, because the behavioral indicators sensitize observers to positive and negative alliance-related behaviors. After watching a session and recording each SOFTA–o behavior as it occurs, it is a simple task to decide who in the family is most and least allied with the therapist.

In a similar fashion, learning the SOFTA–o enhances clinical practice. Indeed, a major impetus to our development of the SOFTA–o was its potential for training and supervision. Whether with paper and pencil or with the e-SOFTA (see http://www.softa-soatif.net), students in graduate classes can use the SOFTA–o as they watch videotapes of "master" therapists. By paying close attention to participants' behaviors on all four dimensions, students become attuned to the specific indicators that combine to form global impressions like, "Wow, that family is working hard!" and "The therapist really brought the husband around!" The software technology allows users to stop the video, record their thoughts about what is occurring, and carefully mark the behavioral indicators as they are observed (see chap. 3 for details). Reviewing the tallied items at the end of the session facilitates answers to the question, "Now how did *that* happen?"

Novice therapists are often puzzled when a family that seemed motivated to seek help suddenly drops out of treatment. Supervisees are also stymied when there is a mismatch between their perceptions and those of their supervisors. A supervisee may report, for example, that "everything went pretty well" with Family X, whereas the supervisor (having observed the session through a one-way mirror or closed-circuit TV) has an altogether different take on what occurred. To prepare for supervision, trainees can review their sessions using the SOFTA–o, either with the paper-and-pencil instrument or the software version. Noting high and low points in the session or an apparent split in family members' alliance-related behaviors can direct supervisory discussions toward strategies for repairing these relationships.

Self-supervision is always encouraged. Questions to ask oneself include, "What were the clients doing (in SOFTA terms) at the point where I was overwhelmed and confused?" or "Which client behaviors contributed to my feeling much more connected with the wife than the husband?" or "What could I have done differently when the teenage daughter pulled back?"

In addition to actually using the SOFTA–o, students in training can be introduced to the SOFTA model to help them think systemically, systematically, and multidimensionally about their work with couples and families. For example, the SOFTA can be used as a point of departure for considering which dimensions are likely to be salient with different kinds of families. With adolescents, emotional connection is vital. In families in which physical abuse is prominent, monitoring safety is most critical. When families define the presenting problem in stark zero-sum terms (see chap. 12), reframing the problem in a way that facilitates a shared sense of purpose is most critical. In other words, SOFTA is a language for treatment planning and evaluation.

IMPLICATIONS FOR RESEARCH

Recently, several exhortations have been made, some quite strong (Anderson, 2003; Pinsof & Wynne, 2000), for a stronger research base in couple and family therapy and for clinicians and researchers to work together to build and test theory, evaluate the effectiveness of systemic interventions, and study in-session and between-session processes of change. This book is written with these exhortations in mind. We believe that the SOFTA–o (Appendix A) and SOFTA–s (Appendix B) are useful tools for accomplishing these goals. Moreover, we endeavored, by their dual-language and software training features, to make the instruments user friendly. We hope researchers will use the measures to address some of the myriad questions about the alliance in couple and family therapy that remain to be answered.

One important question is how the alliance develops and changes in the course of therapy. For most families, are there steady, incremental increases in the alliance, or is it a discontinuous process in which a key event (like the bumblebee story at the beginning of chap. 1) plays a big role? It may well be that the four dimensions of the alliance develop at different rates. In chapter 6, we argued that safety comes first. Perhaps, however, safety builds slowly as clients evaluate each small risk taken within the therapeutic setting. In our heuristic model of the alliance-related therapeutic processes (Exhibit 2.1), emotional connection with the therapist is an essential feature of early sessions in couple and family therapy. However, research may show that building connections is a continuous process throughout treatment, facilitated when therapists self-disclose, use joining interventions, make culturally astute comments, and so forth (chap. 5).

Implicit in this discussion is how the four SOFTA dimensions relate to each other. As discussed in chapters 2 and 8, aside from their moderate statistical association, the dimensions are conceptually interrelated, such that enhancing one dimension has reverberating effects on other dimensions. Note that two dimensions contain many emotional elements (Safety, Emotional Connection), whereas two are more cognitive–behavioral in nature (Engagement, Shared Sense of Purpose). Does building rapport also enhance feelings of safety? Does defining a common therapeutic goal enhance engagement? By definition, one dimension (Shared Purpose) refers to relationships between and among family members, whereas Engagement and Emotional Connection refer to each client's interactions and relations with the therapist; Safety has to do with the entire therapeutic system (therapist + family). What happens to the between-system dimensions (Engagement and Emotional Connection) when Shared Purpose is weak or Safety is compromised?

Couple and family therapy alliances are multidimensional in other ways as well. That is, there are multiple (and interacting) relationships to consider, as clinicians well know. How can therapists ensure that developing a strong bond with a powerful family member—let's say, the father—will not threaten the alliance with another family member, for example, a sullen adolescent? How does the overall family alliance reflect each individual's alliance with the therapist? It is unlikely that the whole is simply the sum of the parts. Is there a reciprocal influence process by which some family members wait and see whether the therapist "clicks" with the most reluctant family member before committing to the process themselves? Lessons learned from another context can be informative. In seeking consent for family therapy research, we found that asking for the cooperation of angry teens first was more successful than asking the parents' permission first (Heatherington, Friedlander, & Johnson, 1989). When the teens consented to the research, the parents' pleasure with their children's prosocial behavior seemed to facilitate their own willingness to participate in the research.

Another important empirical question concerns the convergence (or lack thereof) in clients', therapists', and observers' assessments of the alliance. With the SOFTA–o and SOFTA–s, we have conceptually parallel tools for studying the alliance from these three perspectives (see Table 2.1). Literature on the alliance in individual therapy suggests some divergence, and clients' and observers' perspectives have been more consistently predictive of outcome than therapists' perspectives (Horvath & Symonds, 1991). This is not always the case, however, and more work is needed on this question, especially in couple and family therapy. Indeed, the question is an important one clinically as well. It would be important to know, from the clients' perspective, which alliance dimension was suffering the most when a family decided to leave treatment prematurely. A review of videotapes (or even mailing clients the SOFTA–s questionnaire after they drop out) could illuminate whether the problem was a weak sense of purpose among family members, feelings of threat (i.e., low safety), or simply poor rapport with the therapist.

Questions about therapists' contributions to the alliance are critically important. How can a faltering or ruptured alliance get turned around? Does frequent or especially skillful use of certain therapist behaviors make a difference; if so, which behaviors? The SOFTA measures are an excellent starting point for qualitative and quantitative research with small samples, such as case studies (e.g., M. Beck et al., in press) or task analyses of improving versus deteriorating family alliances (e.g., G. M. Diamond et al., 1999).

The alliance–outcome connection is, naturally, the big question. To what extent is treatment success related to the strength, development, and balance in family members' alliances with the therapist and with each other? A global question like this one is, however, less meaningful than a consideration of the multidimensionality of the alliance in relation to outcome. In M. Beck et al.'s (in press) case studies, for example, negative Safety indicators early in therapy were observed only in the families with the least favorable treatment outcomes. If, as has been found (e.g., Knobloch-Fedders et al., 2004; Robbins et al., 2003; Symonds & Horvath, 2004), unbalanced alliances (chap. 8) are more predictive of outcome than any client's alliance considered in isolation, on which SOFTA dimension is an imbalance most destructive? One might well hypothesize that an imbalance in safety or emotional connection with the therapist is more detrimental than an imbalance in engagement.

Considered from another side, how essential is a strong shared sense of purpose within the family? Elsewhere, we have suggested that this dimension is a step along the way toward a positive treatment outcome (Heatherington, Friedlander, & Greenberg, 2005). As discussed in chapter 7, however, some presenting problems, such as a common threat (e.g., infertility), engender no difficulties related to Shared Purpose, whereas having conflicting motives for therapy (chaps. 4 and 11) or defining the presenting problem in stark win–lose terms (chap. 12) is so problematic that little can be accomplished in the absence of a strong within-family alliance.

FINAL THOUGHTS

The questions posed in this chapter are exactly the kinds that best lend themselves to collaboration between clinicians and researchers. Indeed, we anticipate that the SOFTA model and accompanying instruments will facilitate such collaboration for others, as it already has for us. Above all, we hope readers will use this book to further their understanding of the alliance in their own practice, enhancing treatment benefits for clients.

APPENDIX A:

SOFTA–o (Client and Therapist) and SOATIF–o (Client and Therapist)

SYSTEM FOR OBSERVING FAMILY THERAPY ALLIANCES—OBSERVATIONAL (SOFTA–O)

Client Version

DIRECTIONS: Please read the definition of each of the following four constructs. Then, on the coding pages, identify the family members to be rated in the top row. As you observe the session, mark each behavior that occurs in the appropriate column. At the conclusion of the session, use these marks to make a judgment about each family member's alliance on Engagement, Emotional Connection, and Safety. Rate the entire family system on Shared Sense of Purpose. Use the guidelines in the training manual to go from check marks to ratings. Note that items in italics reflect a *lack* of engagement, *poor* emotional connection, a *lack* of a shared sense of purpose, or a *lack* of safety.

Use the following ordinal scale:
–3 = Extremely problematic
–2 = Moderately problematic
–1 = Somewhat problematic
 0 = Unremarkable or neutral
+1 = Somewhat strong
+2 = Moderately strong
+3 = Extremely strong

Engagement in the Therapeutic Process:	Safety Within the Therapeutic System:
The client viewing treatment as meaningful; a sense of being involved in therapy and working together with the therapist, that therapeutic goals and tasks in therapy can be discussed and negotiated with the therapist, that taking the process seriously is important, that change is possible.	The client viewing therapy as a place to take risks, be open, flexible; a sense of comfort and an expectation that new experiences and learning will take place, that good can come from being in therapy, that conflict within the family can be handled without harm, that one need not be defensive.
Emotional Connection to the Therapist:	**Shared Sense of Purpose Within the Family:**
The client viewing the therapist as an important person in her/his life, almost like a family member; a sense that the relationship is based on affiliation, trust, caring, and concern; that the therapist genuinely cares and "is there" for the client, that he/she is on the same wavelength with the therapist (e.g., similar life perspectives, values), that the therapist's wisdom and expertise are valuable.	Family members seeing themselves as working collaboratively to improve family relations and achieve common family goals; a sense of solidarity in relation to the therapy ("we're in this together"); that they value their time with each other in therapy; essentially, a felt unity within the family in relation to the therapy.

Engagement in the Therapeutic Process:

Family Member

Client indicates agreement with the therapist's goals.	___	___	___	___
Client describes or discusses a plan for improving the situation.	___	___	___	___
Client introduces a problem for discussion.	___	___	___	___
Client agrees to do homework assignments.	___	___	___	___
Client indicates having done homework or seeing it as useful.	___	___	___	___
Client expresses optimism or indicates that positive change has taken place.	___	___	___	___
Client complies with therapist's request for an enactment.	___	___	___	___
Client leans forward.	___	___	___	___
Client mentions the treatment, the therapeutic process, or a specific session.	___	___	___	___
Client expresses feeling "stuck," questions the value of therapy, or states that therapy is not/has not been helpful.	___	___	___	___
Client shows indifference about the tasks or process of therapy (e.g., paying lip service, "I don't know," tuning out).	___	___	___	___

Rate Engagement in the Process for each family member: −3 −2 −1 0 +1 +2 +3

Emotional Connection to the Therapist:

	Family Member			
Client shares a lighthearted moment or joke with the therapist.	__	__	__	__
Client verbalizes trust in the therapist.	__	__	__	__
Client expresses interest in the therapist's personal life.	__	__	__	__
Client indicates feeling understood or accepted by the therapist.	__	__	__	__
Client expresses physical affection or caring for the therapist.	__	__	__	__
Client mirrors the therapist's body posture.	__	__	__	__
Client avoids eye contact with the therapist.	__	__	__	__
Client refuses or is reluctant to respond to the therapist.	__	__	__	__
Client has hostile or sarcastic interactions with the therapist.	__	__	__	__
Client comments on the therapist's incompetence or inadequacy.	__	__	__	__

Rate Emotional Connection to the Therapist for each family member: −3   −2   −1   0   +1   +2   +3

Safety Within the Therapeutic System:

Family Member

Client implies or states that therapy is
a safe place.   ___   ___   ___   ___

Client varies his/her emotional tone
during the session.   ___   ___   ___   ___

Client shows vulnerability (e.g.,
discusses painful feelings, cries).   ___   ___   ___   ___

Client has an open upper body posture.   ___   ___   ___   ___

Client reveals a secret or something
that other family members didn't
know.   ___   ___   ___   ___

Client encourages another family
member to "open up" or to tell the
truth.   ___   ___   ___   ___

Client directly asks other family
members for feedback about his/her
behavior or about herself/himself as a
person.   ___   ___   ___   ___

*Client expresses anxiety nonverbally (e.g.,
taps or shakes).*   ___   ___   ___   ___

*Client protects self in nonverbal manner
(e.g., crosses arms over chest, doesn't
take off jacket or put down purse, sits
far away from group, etc.).*   ___   ___   ___   ___

*Client refuses or is reluctant to respond
when directly addressed by another
family member.*   ___   ___   ___   ___

*Client responds defensively to another
family member.*   ___   ___   ___   ___

*Client makes an uneasy/anxious reference
to the camera, observation, supervisor,
or research procedures.*

**Rate Safety Within the Therapeutic
System for each family member:**   −3   −2   −1   0   +1   +2   +3

Shared Sense of Purpose Within the Family:

Family Member

Family members offer to compromise.	—	—	—	—
Family members share a joke or a lighthearted moment with each other.	—	—	—	—
Family members ask each other for their perspective.	—	—	—	—
Family members validate each other's point of view.	—	—	—	—
Family members mirror each other's body posture.	—	—	—	—
Family members avoid eye contact with each other.	—	—	—	—
Family members blame each other.	—	—	—	—
Family members devalue each other's opinions or perspective.	—	—	—	—
Family members try to align with the therapist against each other.	—	—	—	—
Client makes hostile or sarcastic comments to family members.	—	—	—	—
Family members disagree with each other about the value, purpose, goals, or tasks of therapy or about who should be included in the sessions.	—	—	—	—

Rate Shared Sense of Purpose for the entire family: −3   −2   −1   0   +1   +2   +3

Note. From *SOFTA–o for clients*, by M. L. Friedlander, V. Escudero, and L. Heatherington, 2001, unpublished instrument, pp. 1–5. Copyright 2001 by M. L. Friedlander, V. Escudero, and L. Heatherington. Reproduced with permission of the authors.

Therapist Version

DIRECTIONS: Please read the definition of each of the following four constructs. As you observe the session, mark each behavior as it occurs. At the conclusion of the session, use these marks to make a judgment about the therapist's contribution to Engagement, Emotional Connection, Safety, and the family's Shared Sense of Purpose. Use the guidelines in the training manual to go from check marks to ratings. Note that items in italics reflect *negative contributions to* engagement, emotional connection, a shared sense of purpose, or safety.

Use the following ordinal scale:
-3 = Extremely problematic
-2 = Moderately problematic
-1 = Somewhat problematic
 0 = Unremarkable or neutral
+1 = Somewhat strong
+2 = Moderately strong
+3 = Eextremely strong

Engagement in the Therapeutic Process:	Safety Within the Therapeutic System:
The client viewing treatment as meaningful; a sense of being involved in therapy and working together with the therapist, that therapeutic goals and tasks in therapy can be discussed and negotiated with the therapist, that taking the process seriously is important, that change is possible.	The client viewing therapy as a place to take risks, be open, flexible; a sense of comfort and an expectation that new experiences and learning will take place, that good can come from being in therapy, that conflict within the family can be handled without harm, that one need not be defensive.
Emotional Connection to the Therapist:	Shared Sense of Purpose Within the Family:
The client viewing the therapist as an important person in her/his life, almost like a family member; a sense that the relationship is based on affiliation, trust, caring, and concern; that the therapist genuinely cares and "is there" for the client, that he/she is on the same wavelength with the therapist (e.g., similar life perspectives, values), that the therapist's wisdom and expertise are valuable.	Family members seeing themselves as working collaboratively to improve family relations and achieve common family goals; a sense of solidarity in relation to the therapy ("we're in this together"); that they value their time with each other in therapy; essentially, a felt unity within the family in relation to the therapy.

Therapist's Contributions to Engagement in the Therapeutic Process:

Therapist explains how therapy works. _____

*Therapist ask client(s) what they want to
talk about in the session. _____

*Therapist encourages client(s) to
articulate their goals for therapy. _____

Therapist asks client(s) whether they are
willing to do a specific in-session task
(e.g., enactment). _____

*Therapist asks client(s) whether they are
willing to follow a specific suggestion or
do a specific homework assignment. _____

*Therapist asks client(s) about the impact
or value of a prior homework assignment. _____

*Therapist expresses optimism or notes that
a positive change has taken place or can
take place. _____

Therapist pulls in quiet client(s) (e.g., by
deliberately leaning forward, calling them
by name, addressing them specifically). _____

Therapist asks if the client(s) have any
questions. _____

Therapist praises client motivation for
engagement or change. _____

*Therapist defines therapeutic goals or imposes
tasks or procedures without asking the
client(s) for their collaboration.* _____

*Therapist argues with the client(s) about the
nature, purpose, or value of therapy.* _____

*Therapist shames or criticizes how clients did
(or did not do) a prior homework
assignment.* _____

Rate therapist contribution to
Engagement: –3 –2 –1 0 +1 +2 +3

Indicates a similar item is in the client version.

Therapist's Contributions to Emotional Connection:

*Therapist shares a lighthearted moment or joke with the client(s). _____

*Therapist expresses confidence, trust, or belief in the client(s). _____

Therapist expresses interest in the client(s) apart from the therapeutic discussion at hand. _____

*Therapist expresses caring or touches client(s) affectionately yet appropriately (e.g., handshake, pat on head). _____

Therapist discloses his or her personal reactions or feelings toward the client(s) or the situation. _____

*Therapist discloses some fact about his or her personal life. _____

Therapist remarks on or describes how his or her values or experiences are similar to the clients'. _____

Therapist (verbally or nonverbally) expresses empathy for the clients' struggle (e.g., "I know this is hard," "I feel your pain," crying with client). _____

Therapist reassures or normalizes a client's emotional vulnerability (e.g., crying, hurt feelings). _____

*_Therapist has hostile, sarcastic, or critical interactions with the client(s)._ _____

Therapist does not respond to clients' expressions of personal interest or caring for him or her. _____

Rate therapist contribution to Emotional Connection:

−3 −2 −1 0 +1 +2 +3

*_Indicates a similar item is in the client version._

Therapist's Contributions to Safety Within the Therapeutic System:

*Therapist acknowledges that therapy involves taking risks or discussing private matters. _____

Therapist provides structure and guidelines for safety and confidentiality. _____

*Therapist invites discussion about intimidating elements in the therapeutic context (e.g., recording equipment, reports to third parties, treatment team observation, one-way mirror, research, etc.). _____

Therapist helps clients to talk truthfully and not defensively with each other. _____

Therapist attempts to contain, control, or manage overt hostility between clients. _____

Therapist actively protects one family member from another (e.g., from blame, hostility, or emotional intrusiveness). _____

Therapist changes the topic to something pleasurable or non-anxiety arousing (e.g., small talk about the weather, room decor, TV shows, etc.) when there seems to be tension or anxiety. _____

Therapist asks one client (or a subgroup of clients) to leave the room in order to see one client alone for a portion of the session. _____

Therapist allows family conflict to escalate to verbal abuse, threats, or intimidation. _____

Therapist does not attend to overt expressions of client vulnerability (e.g., crying, defensiveness). _____

Rate therapist contribution to Safety: –3 –2 –1 0 +1 +2 +3

Indicates a similar item is in the client version.

Therapist's Contributions to a Shared Sense of Purpose Within the Family:

*Therapist encourages clients to
compromise with each other.   _____

*Therapist encourages clients to ask each
other for their perspective.   _____

*Therapist praises clients for respecting
each other's point of view.   _____

Therapist emphasizes commonalities among
clients' perspectives on the problem or
solution.   _____

Therapist draws attention to clients' shared
values, experiences, needs, or feelings.   _____

Therapist encourages clients to show caring,
concern, or support for each other.   _____

*Therapist encourages client(s) to ask each
other for feedback.   _____

*Therapist fails to intervene when family
members argue with each other about the
goals, value, or need for therapy.   _____

*Therapist fails to address one client's stated
concerns by only discussing another client's
concerns.   _____

Rate therapist contribution to Shared
Purpose: −3 −2 −1 0 +1 +2 +3

*Indicates a similar item is in the client version.
Note. From SOFTA–o for therapists, by V. Escudero, M. L. Friedlander, and L. Deihl,
2004, Unpublished instrument, pp. 1–5. Copyright 2004 by V. Escudero, M. L.
Friedlander, and L. Deihl. Reproduced with permission of the authors.

SISTEMA DE OBSERVACIÓN DE LA ALIANZA TERAPEÚTICA EN INTERVENCIÓN FAMILIAR (SOATIF–O)

Cliente

INSTRUCCIONES: Lea por favor la definición de cada uno de los cuatro constructos encuadrados más abajo. A continuación, identifique en la parte superior de las columnas de anotación a los miembros de la familia que van a ser observados. Comience a observar la sesión marcando en la columna correspondiente aquellas conductas que ocurran. Al finalizar la sesión ha de realizar una valoración sobre una escala, para cada miembro de la familia, acerca del nivel en que ha percibido Enganche Terapéutico, Conexión Emocional con el Terapeuta, y Seguridad dentro del Sistema Terapéutico. También hará una valoración similar para la dimensión de Sentido de Compartir el Propósito, pero para esta dimensión el juicio se realiza sobre la totalidad del sistema familiar como grupo. Ha de sustentar su estimación para dichas escalas en el registro conductual que ha ido realizando en el proceso de observación, y siguiendo las directices del Manual de Entrenamiento. No olvide que los items que están escritos en *itálica* reflejan *la falta* de Enganche, *pobre* Conexión Emocional, *carencia* de Sentido de compartir el propósito, y *falta* de Seguridad.

Utilice la siguiente escala:

–3 = Muy problemática
–2 = Bastante problemática
–1 = Ligeramente problemática
 0 = No reseñable o neutral
+1 = Ligera
+2 = Bastante fuerte
+3 = Muy fuerte

Enganche en el Proceso Therapéutico:	Seguridad Dentro del Sistema Therapéutico:
El cliente le ve sentido al tratamiento, se transmite la sensación de estar involucrado en la terapia y trabajando coordinadamente con el terapeuta, que los objetivos y las tareas en terapia pueden discutirse y negociarse con el terapeuta, que tomarse en serio el proceso es importante, que el cambio es posible.	El cliente ve la terapia como un lugar en el que puede arriesgarse, estar abierto a nuevas cosas, ser flexible; sensación de confort y expectación hacia las nuevas experiencias y aprendizajes que pueden ocurrir, de que hay cosas buenas que provienen de estar en terapia, que el conflicto dentro de la familia puede manejarse sin hacerse daño, que no es necesario estar a la defensiva.
Conexión Emocional con el Terapeuta:	Sentido de Compartir el Propósito:
El cliente ve al terapeuta como una persona importante en su vida, casi como a un miembro de la familia; sensación de que la relación se basa en la confianza, afecto, interés y sentido de pertenencia; de que al terapeuta le importa de verdad y que "está ahí" para el cliente, de que el cliente y el terapeuta comparten una visión del mundo (por ejemplo, que tienen perspectivas vitales o valores similares), que la sabiduría y experiencia del terapeuta son relevantes.	Los miembros de la familia se ven a sí mismos como trabajando en colaboración para mejorar la relación familiar y conseguir objetivos comunes para la familia; sentido de solidaridad en relación con la terapia ("estamos juntos en esto"), de que valoran el tiempo que comparten en la terapia; esencialmente un sentimiento de unidad dentro de la familia en relación con la terapia.

Enganghe En El Proceso Terapéutico:

Miembro De La Familia

El cliente indica su acuerdo con las
metas propuestas por el terapeuta.   ___   ___   ___   ___

El cliente describe o discute un plan
para mejorar la situación.   ___   ___   ___   ___

El cliente introduce un problema para
discutirlo.   ___   ___   ___   ___

El cliente acepta hacer las tareas para
casa que se le sugieren.   ___   ___   ___   ___

El cliente indica que ha hecho una
tarea o la ha visto como útil.   ___   ___   ___   ___

El cliente expresa optimismo o indica
que ha tenido lugar un cambio
positivo.   ___   ___   ___   ___

El cliente cumple las peticiones del
terapeuta para discutir entre ellos o
representar alguna interacción
delante de él.   ___   ___   ___   ___

El cliente se inclina hacia delante
(postura corporal).   ___   ___   ___   ___

El cliente menciona el tratamiento, el
proceso de terapia, o una sesión en
concreto.   ___   ___   ___   ___

*El cliente expresa sentirse "atascado" o
afirma que la terapia no ha sido o no es
útil.*   ___   ___   ___   ___

*El cliente muestra indiferencia acerca de
las tareas o del proceso de terapia.*   ___   ___   ___   ___

**Puntúe Enganche en el Proceso para
cada miembro de la familia:**   –3   –2   –1   0   +1   +2   +3

Conexión Emocional Con El Terapeuta:

Miembro De La Familia

El cliente comparte un momento
humorístico o una broma con el
terapeuta.

El cliente verbaliza su confianza en el
terapeuta.

El cliente expresa interés en aspectos
de la vida personal del terapeuta.

El cliente indica que se siente
entendido o aceptado por el
terapeuta.

El cliente expresa físicamente o
verbaliza su afecto por el terapeuta.

El cliente imita, reproduce, la postura
corporal del terapeuta.

*El cliente evita el contacto ocular con el
terapeuta.*

*El cliente rechaza o es reticente a
responder al terapeuta.*

*El cliente tiene interacción hostil o
sarcástica con el terapeuta.*

*El cliente hace comentarios sobre la
incompetencia o inadecuación del
terapeuta.*

**Puntúe Conexión Emocional con el
Terapeuta para cada miembro de la
familia:**

-3 -2 -1 0 $+1$ $+2$ $+3$

Seguridad Dentro Del Sistema Terapéutico:

Miembro De La Familia

El cliente indica o afirma que la terapia
es un lugar seguro, un lugar en el que
confía. — — — —

El cliente varía su tono emocional
durante la sesión (por ej., se ríe o
llora). — — — —

El cliente "abre" su intimidad (por ej.,
comenta sentimientos dolorosos,
comparte intimidades, llora, etc.). — — — —

El cliente tiene una postura corporal
abierta (relajada; se ha de observar
fundamentalmente la parte superior
del cuerpo: tronco y brazos). — — — —

El cliente revela un secreto o algo que
ningún miembro de la familia sabe. — — — —

El cliente anima a otro miembro de la
familia a abrirse o decir la verdad. — — — —

El cliente pregunta directamente a los
demás miembros de la familia que
opinen de él como persona o de sus
conductas. — — — —

El cliente expresa ansiedad de forma no
verbal (por ej., da golpecitos, se agita,
se mueve). — — — —

El cliente se protege de forma no verbal
(por ej., cruza los brazos sobre el pecho,
no se quita la ropa de abrigo o el bolso,
se sienta lejos del grupo, etc.). — — — —

El cliente rechaza o es reticente a la hora
de responder cuando otro miembro de la
familia le habla. — — — —

El cliente responde defensivamente a otro
miembro de la familia. — — — —

El cliente menciona de forma
ansiosa/incómoda la cámara, los
observadores, la supervisión, o los
procedimientos de investigación. — — — —

Puntúe Seguridad para cada miembro
de la familia: −3 −2 −1 0 +1 +2 +3

Sentido De Compartir El Propósito En La Familia:

Miembro De La Familia

Los miembros de la familia ofrecen un acuerdo de compromiso.

    ___   ___   ___   ___

Los miembros de la familia comparten entre ellos una broma o un momento gracioso.

    ___   ___   ___   ___

Los miembros de la familia se preguntan entre ellos sobre sus puntos de vista.

    ___   ___   ___   ___

Los miembros de la familia validan mutuamente sus puntos de vista.

    ___   ___   ___   ___

Los miembros de la familia reflectan-reproducen posturas corporales similares.

    ___   ___   ___   ___

Los miembros de la familia evitan el contacto ocular entre ellos.

    ___   ___   ___   ___

Los miembros de la familia se culpan unos a otros.

    ___   ___   ___   ___

miembros de la familia devalúan la opinión o perspectiva de otros.

    ___   ___   ___   ___

Miembros de la familia tratan de aliarse con el terapeuta en contra de otros miembros de la familia.

    ___   ___   ___   ___

El cliente hace comentarios hostiles o sarcásticos a otros miembros de la familia.

    ___   ___   ___   ___

Algunos miembros de la familia no están de acuerdo entre sí sobre el valor, el propósito, las metas, o las tareas de la terapia, o sobre quien debe ser incluido en las sesiones.

    ___   ___   ___   ___

Puntúe Compartir el Propósito para la familia globalmente:

    –3 –2 –1 0 +1 +2 +3

Note. From *SOATIF–o for clients*, by V. Escudero and M. L. Friedlander, 2002a, Unpublished instrument, pp. 1–5. Copyright 2002 by V. Escudero and M. L. Friedlander. Reproduced with permission of the authors.

Terapeuta

INSTRUCCIONES: Por favor, antes que nada lea detalladamente las definiciones de los siguientes cuatro constructos. Durante la observación de la sesión, marque cada conducta que ocurra. Cuando concluya la sesión, utilice las marcas realizadas para valorar la contribución del terapeuta al Enganche, Conexión emocional, Seguridad dentro del Sistema Terapéutico, y Sentido de Compartir el Propósito. Utilice las directrices del Manual de Entrenamiento para inferir las puntuaciones de escala a partir de los registros de conductas. Observe que los descriptores en itálica reflejan *contribuciones negativas* para el enganche, conexión emocional, compartir el propósito y seguridad.

Utilice la siguiente escala:

–3 = Muy problemática
–2 = Bastante problemática
–1 = Ligeramente problemática
 0 = No reseñable o neutral
+1 = Ligera
+2 = Bastante fuerte
+3 = Muy fuerte

Enganghe En El Proceso Therapéutico:	Seguridad Dentro Del Sistema Therapéutico:
El cliente le ve sentido al tratamiento, se transmite la sensación de estar involucrado en la terapia y trabajando coordinadamente con el terapeuta, que los objetivos y las tareas en terapia pueden discutirse y negociarse con el terapeuta, que tomarse en serio el proceso es importante, que el cambio es posible.	El cliente ve la terapia como un lugar en el que puede arriesgarse, estar abierto a nuevas cosas, ser flexible; sensación de confort y expectación hacia las nuevas experiencias y aprendizajes que pueden ocurrir, de que hay cosas buenas que provienen de estar en terapia, que el conflicto dentro de la familia puede manejarse sin hacerse daño, que no es necesario estar a la defensiva.
Conexión Emocional Con El Terapeuta:	Sentido De Compartir El Propósito:
El cliente ve al terapeuta como una persona importante en su vida, casi como a un miembro de la familia; sensación de que la relación se basa en la confianza, afecto, interés y sentido de pertenencia; de que al terapeuta le importa de verdad y que "está ahí" para el cliente, de que el cliente y el terapeuta comparten una visión del mundo (por ejemplo, que tienen perspectivas vitales o valores similares), que la sabiduría y experiencia del terapeuta son relevantes.	Los miembros de la familia se ven a sí mismos como trabajando en colaboración para mejorar la relación familiar y conseguir objetivos comunes para la familia; sentido de solidaridad en relación con la terapia ("estamos juntos en esto"), de que valoran el tiempo que comparten en la terapia; esencialmente un sentimiento de unidad dentro de la familia en relación con la terapia.

Contribución Del Terapeuta Al Enganghe En El Proceso De Terapia:

El terapeuta explica cómo funciona la
terapia.   _____

*El terapeuta pregunta al cliente acerca qué
quiere hablar en la sesión.   _____

El terapeuta estimula que el cliente defina
sus metas en la terapia.   _____

*El terapeuta pregunta al cliente por su
disposición para hacer una tarea en la
sesión.   _____

*El terapeuta pregunta cuál es la disposición
del cliente para seguir una indicación-
sugerencia o hacer una tarea.   _____

*El terapeuta pregunta al cliente por el
impacto o valor de una tarea asignada
previamente.   _____

*El terapeuta expresa optimismo o señala
que un cambio positivo a ocurrido o
puede ocurrir.   _____

El terapeuta captura la atención del cliente
(por ej. inclinándose hacia delante,
usando el nombre del cliente, dirigiéndose
a él/ella directamente, etc.).   _____

El terapeuta pregunta si el cliente tiene
alguna duda o pregunta que hacer.   _____

El terapeuta elogia la motivación del cliente
para colaborar o para cambiar.   _____

*El terapeuta define metas terapéuticas o impone
tareas o procedimientos sin pedir la
colaboración del cliente.*   _____

*El terapeuta discute con el cliente acerca de la
naturaleza, propósito o valor de la terapia.*   _____

*El terapeuta critica cómo hizo (o por no
hacerla) el cliente una tarea para casa.*   _____

Puntúe la contribución del terapeuta para
Enganche: −3 −2 −1 0 +1 +2 +3

Indica que hay un descriptor similar en la versión del client.

Contribución Del Terapeuta Al Conexión Emocional Con El Cliente:

*El terapeuta comparte un momento
humorístico o un chiste con el cliente.   _____

*El terapeuta expresa confianza o que cree
en el cliente.   _____

El terapeuta expresa interés en el cliente al
margen de la discusión terapéutica
propiamente dicha.   _____

*El terapeuta expresa afecto o toca
afectivamente al cliente dentro de lo
apropiado al contexto profesional (por ej.,
darle la mano, una palmada, etc.).   _____

El terapeuta desvela sus reacciones o
sentimientos personales hacia el cliente o
hacia la situación.   _____

*El terapeuta desvela algún aspecto de su
vida personal.   _____

El terapeuta señala o describe similaridades
con el cliente en sus valores o
experiencias.   _____

El terapeuta expresa explícitamente empatía
(verbal o no-verbalmente) con las
dificultades que sufren los clientes (por
ejemplo, "Se lo duro que debe ser",
"Siento tu dolor", o llorar con el cliente).   _____

El terapeuta normaliza o acoge la
vulnerabilidad emocional del cliente (por
ej., llorar, mostrar sentimientos
dolorosos).   _____

*El terapeuta tiene interacciones hostiles o
sarcásticas con el cliente.   _____

El terapeuta no responde a expresiones de
interés personal o afecto hacia él por parte del
cliente.   _____

Puntúe la contribución del terapeuta para
Conexión Emocional: −3 −2 −1 0 +1 +2 +3

*Indica que hay un descriptor similar en la versión del client.

Contribución Del Terapeuta A La Seguridad Dentro Del Sistema Terapéutico:

*El terapeuta reconoce que la terapia implica aceptar riesgos o discutir cuestiones privadas. _____

El terapeuta proporciona estructura y directrices de confidencialidad y seguridad. _____

*El terapeuta propicia la discusión sobre elementos el contexto de terapia que pueden intimidar al cliente (por ej., equipos de grabación, informes a terceras partes, equipo terapéutico, espejo unidireccional, investigaciones, etc.). _____

El terapeuta ayuda al cliente a hablar sinceramente y a no estar a la defensiva con los demás. _____

El terapeuta intenta contener, controlar, o manejar la hostilidad abierta entre clientes. _____

El terapeuta protege activamente a un miembro de la familia de otro (por ej., de acusaciones, hostilidad, o intrusividad emocional). _____

El terapeuta cambia la conversación hacia algo agradable o que no genera ansiedad (programas de la tele, diversión, elementos de la sala, etc.) cuando parece que hay tensión o ansiedad. _____

El terapeuta pide a un cliente (o subgrupo de clientes) que salga de la sala para quedarse solo con un cliente (o subgrupo) durante una parte de la sesión. _____

El terapeuta permite que el conflicto familiar se escale hacia el abuso verbal, amenazas, o intimidación. _____

El terapeuta no atiende a expresiones claras de vulnerabilidad de un cliente (por ej., llanto, defensividad, etc.). _____

Puntúe la contribución del terapeuta para Seguridad en el sistema terapéutico: $-3 \quad -2 \quad -1 \quad 0 \quad +1 \quad +2 \quad +3$

*Indica que hay un descriptor similar en la versión del client.

Contribución Del Terapeuta Al Sentido De Compartir El Propósito:

*El terapeuta alienta acuerdos de
compromiso entre los clientes.   _____

*El terapeuta anima a los clientes a
preguntarse entre ellos por sus puntos de
vista respectivos.   _____

*El terapeuta elogia a los clientes por
respetar los puntos de vista de los otros.   _____

El terapeuta subraya lo que tienen en
común las diferentes perspectivas de los
clientes sobre el problema o solución.   _____

El terapeuta destaca lo que comparten los
clientes en cuanto a valores, experiencias,
necesidades, o sentimientos.   _____

El terapeuta anima al cliente a mostrar
afecto, interés o apoyo a otro cliente.   _____

*El terapeuta anima a un cliente a pedir
confirmación y opinión (feedback) a
otro/s.   _____

*El terapeuta no interviene (o queda
descalificada su intervención) cuando
miembros de la familia discuten entre ellos
acerca de las metas, el valor, o la necesidad
de la terapia.   _____

*El terapeuta ignora las preocupaciones
explicitadas por un cliente discutiendo
únicamente las preocupaciones de otro
cliente.   _____

Puntúe la contribución del terapeuta para
Sentido de Compartir el Propósito: −3 −2 −1 0 +1 +2 +3

*Indica que hay un descriptor similar en la versión del client.
Note. From SOATIF–o for therapists, by V. Escudero, M. L. Friedlander, and L. Deihl,
2004, Unpublished instrument, pp. 1–5. Copyright 2004 by V. Escudero, M. L.
Friedlander, and L. Deihl. Reproduced with permission of the authors.

SOFTA–O RATING GUIDELINES

After observing the session, the user makes ratings for each of the four dimensions for each participant in the blank spaces provided. The anchors (−3 = *extremely problematic*, 0 = *unremarkable/neutral*, +3 = *extremely strong*) refer to both the frequency of the behavior and its meaningfulness or significance in the session. On the client measure, with the exception of the Shared Sense of Purpose dimension, there are four columns of blank lines next to each indicator, one for each of four family members. (The user labels these columns for each family member.) On the therapist measure, the blank lines are to record tallies or comments. At the end of each section is the 7-point, Likert scale, with the anchors labeled, and blank spaces to record the global ratings. (Note that on the client measure, only one space is provided for the Shared Sense of Purpose dimension, because only one rating is made for the couple or family as a whole.)

The behavioral items are assumed to be indicators of the more global, underlying dimensions, which are defined in more subjective terms (i.e., in terms of the clients' cognitions and affect or the therapist's contributions to each dimension of the alliance). Raters need to use the check marks they made on the individual items to make their overall ratings rather than rely simply on an intuitive sense about each dimension.

It is impossible for a rater to avoid making comparisons of the strength of the alliance across family members while watching the session and marking behavioral indicators. Thus, the rating of each family member is influenced by the ratings of all the other family members. For this reason, the following guideline should be used: The rater should first look at the check marks and decide who in the family seems to be the *least* involved, connected. This person should be rated first, followed by the family member who is the *next least* involved, and so forth. In this way, the family member whose behavior suggests the greatest involvement or commitment is rated last.

To facilitate the process of going from the check marks to the ratings, judges should use the following guidelines for the *Engagement, Safety*, and *Emotional Connection* dimensions:

1. If *no* checks are made in a given dimension, the score should be 0 *(unremarkable)*. This means that the therapist has made no remarks that either contribute to or detract from the alliance. In terms of the family, the client who receives a rating of 0 is viewed as at least moderately aligned (otherwise, he or she would be protesting the therapy or would leave the room). In family therapy, it sometimes occurs that a client does not speak during a given session, particularly if there are many people in the room. If there are no negative or positive indicators and the client does not speak, the rating should be 0.

2. If *only negative* items are checked, the score *must* be less than 0. On the client measure, rate the client as −3 *(extremely prob-*

lematic) only if it is clear that the person is antagonistic to the therapy and demonstrates that antagonism behaviorally—otherwise the score would be a –2 *(moderately problematic)* or –1*(somewhat problematic)*, depending on a decision about how negative the behaviors seem to the judge.

3. If *only positive* items are checked, the score *must* be above 0.

4. If the only positive item is nonverbal (open upper body posture, mirrored body language), the rating should be +1*(somewhat strong)*.

5. A +3 is given *only* if it is clear that the therapist is making a great effort or if the client is *highly* invested in the therapy, as demonstrated by showing a great deal of vulnerability (Safety) or taking a very active part in the therapeutic process (Engagement) or there is clear, important caring demonstrated toward the therapist (Emotional Connection). Otherwise, the score should be a +1 or +2, depending on how positive the behaviors are judged to be. If the client is crying from the heart, for example, the score would probably be a +2 *(moderately strong)*.

6. If there are *both positive and negative* items checked, the rating should either be –1, 0, or +1, depending on an assessment of the balance in frequency or meaningfulness of the checked behaviors. In this case, a 0 means neutral (i.e., that the negative and positive items are judged to cancel each other out).

7. –3 *(extremely problematic)* is given *only* when it is clear that the client is *absolutely not at all* invested in the therapy.

The rater's task is, nonetheless, somewhat subjective. Some behaviors, particularly the nonverbal ones, can occur throughout the session (e.g., "Family members mirror each other's body posture"), whereas most of the other behaviors are likely to occur once or a few times. Here is where the judge needs to decide on the significance or clinical meaningfulness of the behavior. If, for example, a family member "agrees to do homework assignments" once and with minimal enthusiasm, the rating might be +1. If the family member asks for details about the assignment and talks about when, how, and under what circumstances it will be done, the rating might be +2. If the family member is particularly enthusiastic and committed to the assignment, the rating might be +3.

As another example, consider the item, "Client refuses or is reluctant to respond to the therapist." If this occurs once or minimally, the rating would be –1. If the client spends a fair amount of the session refusing to speak, the rating could be –2. If the session is entirely spent this way, the rating would be –3.

For *Shared Sense of Purpose*, one rating is given for the couple or family. Raters should be aware that this dimension refers to a shared sense of purpose *about the therapy*, not about the family in general or the presenting problem. In other words, a couple might enjoy each other's company a great deal yet have very different views on the value of therapy for improving their relationship. Alternately, everyone in the family might agree that the teenage son has a problem; this agreement reflects a shared sense about what the problem is, but not necessarily a shared sense of purpose *with respect to the therapy*. The parents, for example, might indicate that the focus of therapy should be the son's misbehavior, but the teen might state that the therapy is a complete waste of time or that he thinks the therapist should focus on his parents' strictness and his father's alcoholism. In this case, the sense of unity within the family with respect to the therapy is not optimal.

On the client measure, raters should use the following guidelines to go from the behavioral ratings to the overall rating for *Shared Sense of Purpose*:

1. Judges first need to see how many family members have positive and negative items checked.
2. If there are *no* items checked *for any family member*, the rating should be 0 (i.e., *unremarkable*). As with the other ratings, the assumption is that there is at least a moderate sense of purpose within the family if everyone is there and is not showing any behavior indicative of a poor alliance.
3. If there is *at least one positive* item *and no negative* items checked *for every family member*, the rating should be at least +1, and could be +2 or +3, depending on the rater's judgment of the number and meaningfulness of the checked items.
4. If there is *at least one negative* item for *only one family member and no positive items checked for anyone*, the rating should be –1 or –2, depending on the judgment of just how negative the behavior is in the session.
5. If *two or more family members* have *negative* items checked, the rating should be –3 or –2.
6. If there are *both positive and negative* items checked for *any one family member*, the judgment should either be –1, 0, or +1, depending on an assessment of the balance in frequency or meaningfulness of the checked behaviors. In this case, a 0 means *neutral* (i.e., that the negative and positive items are judged to cancel each other out).
7. If there is a major disagreement between family members expressed in the session about the value of therapy or what is going to be accomplished there, the rating should be –3, *even if* no other negative items are checked.

Note. Adapted from the *System for Observing Family Therapy Alliances (SOFTA–o) Training Manual—Revised*, by M. L. Friedlander, V. Escudero, L. Heatherington, L. Deihl, et al., 2004, unpublished manuscript. Available from http://www.softa-soatif.net. Adapted with permission of the authors.

Date: _____ **Rates:** _____

Tape #:_____

Family Member	Rater #1	Rater #2	Rater #3	Rater #4	Consensus
Engagement					
_____	____	____	____	____	_____
_____	____	____	____	____	_____
_____	____	____	____	____	_____
_____	____	____	____	____	_____
_____	____	____	____	____	_____
_____	____	____	____	____	_____
Safety					
_____	____	____	____	____	_____
_____	____	____	____	____	_____
_____	____	____	____	____	_____
_____	____	____	____	____	_____
_____	____	____	____	____	_____
Emotional Connection					
_____	____	____	____	____	_____
_____	____	____	____	____	_____
_____	____	____	____	____	_____
_____	____	____	____	____	_____
_____	____	____	____	____	_____
Shared Sense of Purpose					
Entire Family	____	____	____	____	____

Comments/Concerns:

APPENDIX B:

SOFTA–s (Client and Therapist) and SOATIF–s (Client and Therapist)

SYSTEM FOR OBSERVING FAMILY THERAPY
ALLIANCES—SELF-REPORT (SOFTA–S)

Client Version

Evaluate the following phrases and indicate your level of agreement by circling the appropriate number:

	Not at all	A little	Moderately	A lot	Very much
1. What happens in therapy can solve our problems.	1	2	3	4	5
2. The therapist understands me.	1	2	3	4	5
3. The therapy sessions help me open up (share my feelings, try new things . . .).	1	2	3	4	5
4. All my family members who come for therapy want the best for our family and to resolve our problems.	1	2	3	4	5
5. It is hard for me to discuss with the therapist what we should work on in therapy.	1	2	3	4	5
6. The therapist is doing everything possible to help me.	1	2	3	4	5
7. I feel comfortable and relaxed in the therapy sessions.	1	2	3	4	5
8. All of us who come for therapy sessions value the time and effort we all put in.	1	2	3	4	5
9. The therapist and I work together as a team.	1	2	3	4	5
10. The therapist has become an important person in my life.	1	2	3	4	5
11. There are some topics I am afraid to discuss in therapy.	1	2	3	4	5
12. Some members of the family don't agree with others about the goals of the therapy.	1	2	3	4	5
13. I understand what is being done in therapy.	1	2	3	4	5
14. The therapist lacks the knowledge and skills to help me.	1	2	3	4	5
15. At times I feel on the defensive in therapy.	1	2	3	4	5
16. Each of us in the family helps the others get what they want out of therapy.	1	2	3	4	5

Note. From SOFTA–s, by M. L. Friedlander and V. Escudero, 2002, Unpublished instrument, p. 1. Copyright 2002 by M. L. Friedlander and V. Escudero. Reproduced with permission of the authors.

Therapist

Evaluate the following phrases and indicate your level of agreement by circling the appropriate number:

	Not at all	A little	Moderately	A lot	Very much
1. What happens in therapy can solve this family's problems.	1	2	3	4	5
2. I understand this family.	1	2	3	4	5
3. The therapy sessions are helping family members to open up (share feelings, try new things . . .).	1	2	3	4	5
4. All of the family members who are coming for therapy want the best for the family and to resolve their problems.	1	2	3	4	5
5. It is hard for me and the family to discuss together what we should work on in therapy.	1	2	3	4	5
6. I am doing everything possible to help this family.	1	2	3	4	5
7. Family members feel comfortable and relaxed in the therapy sessions.	1	2	3	4	5
8. All of those who come for therapy sessions value the time and effort the others put in.	1	2	3	4	5
9. The family and I are working together as a team.	1	2	3	4	5
10. I have become an important person in this family's life.	1	2	3	4	5
11. There are some topics that the family members are afraid to discuss in therapy.	1	2	3	4	5
12. Some members of the family don't agree with others about the goals of the therapy.	1	2	3	4	5
13. What this family and I are doing in therapy makes sense to me.	1	2	3	4	5
14. I lack the knowledge and skills to help this family.	1	2	3	4	5
15. At times some family members feel on the defensive in therapy.	1	2	3	4	5
16. Each person in the family helps the others get what they want out of therapy.	1	2	3	4	5

Note. From *SOFTA–s*, by M. L. Friedlander and V. Escudero, 2002, Unpublished instrument, p. 1. Copyright 2002 by M. L. Friedlander and V. Escudero. Reproduced with permission of the authors.

SISTEMA DE OBSERVACIÓN DE LA ALIANZA TERAPEÚTICA EN INTERVENCIÓN FAMILIAR (SOATIF–S)

Cliente

Valore las siguientes afirmaciones y rodee con un círculo:

	Nada	Poco	Algo	Bastan	Mucho
1. Lo que hacemos en terapia puede solucionar nuestros problemas.	1	2	3	4	5
2. El terapeuta me comprende.	1	2	3	4	5
3. Las sesiones me sirven para abrirme (por ejemplo: expresar sentimientos o probar cosas nuevas).	1	2	3	4	5
4. Los que venimos a terapia queremos conseguir lo mejor para nuestra familia y resolver los problemas.	1	2	3	4	5
5. Resulta difícil comentar con mi terapeuta lo que hay que hacer en terapia.	1	2	3	4	5
6. El terapeuta está haciendo todo lo posible por ayudarme.	1	2	3	4	5
7. Me siento cómodo/a y relajado/a en las sesiones.	1	2	3	4	5
8. Todos los que venimos a terapia valoramos el esfuerzo y el tiempo invertido por los demás aquí.	1	2	3	4	5
9. Siento que estoy trabajando en equipo con el terapeuta.	1	2	3	4	5
10. Considero que el terapeuta se ha convertido en una persona importante para mí.	1	2	3	4	5
11. Hay algún tema del que no me atrevo a hablar en terapia.	1	2	3	4	5
12. Algunos miembros de la familia consideran que sus objetivos son incompatibles con los de los demás.	1	2	3	4	5
13. Entiendo el sentido de lo que se hace en terapia.	1	2	3	4	5
14. Al terapeuta le faltan conocimientos y capacidad para ayudarme.	1	2	3	4	5
15. A veces estoy a la defensiva en las sesiones.	1	2	3	4	5
16. Todos en la familia intentamos ayudar a que los demás consigan en terapia lo que necesitan.	1	2	3	4	5

Note. From SOFTA–s, by M. L. Friedlander and V. Escudero, 2002, Unpublished instrument, p. 1.
Copyright 2002 by M. L. Friedlander and V. Escudero. Reproduced with permission of the authors.

Terapeuta

Valore las siguientes afirmaciones y rodee con un círculo:

	Nada	Poco	Algo	Bastan	Mucho
1. Lo que hacemos en terapia puede solucionar los problemas de el/los cliente/s.	1	2	3	4	5
2. Comprendo a esta familia.	1	2	3	4	5
3. Las sesiones les sirven a los clientes para abrirse (por ejemplo: expresar sentimientos o probar cosas nuevas).	1	2	3	4	5
4. Los que vienen a terapia quieren conseguir lo mejor para su familia y resolver los problemas.	1	2	3	4	5
5. Resulta difícil comentar conmigo lo que hay que hacer en terapia.	1	2	3	4	5
6. Estoy haciendo todo lo posible por ayudar a esta familia.	1	2	3	4	5
7. Creo que los clientes se sienten cómodos y relajados en las sesiones.	1	2	3	4	5
8. Todos los que vienen a terapia valoran el esfuerzo y el tiempo invertido por los demás aquí.	1	2	3	4	5
9. Siento que estoy trabajando en equipo con mis clientes.	1	2	3	4	5
10. Creo que me he convertido en una persona importante para mis clientes.	1	2	3	4	5
11. Hay algunos temas de los que los clientes no se atreven a hablar en terapia.	1	2	3	4	5
12. Algunos miembros de la familia consideran que sus objetivos son incompatibles con los de los demás.	1	2	3	4	5
13. Los clientes entienden el sentido de lo que se hace aquí.	1	2	3	4	5
14. Me faltan conocimientos y capacidad para ayudar a esta familia.	1	2	3	4	5
15. A veces los clientes se muestran a la defensiva en las sesiones.	1	2	3	4	5
16. Todos en la familia se ayudan entre sí para conseguir en terapia lo que necesitan.	1	2	3	4	5

Note. From *SOFTA–s*, by M. L. Friedlander and V. Escudero, 2002, Unpublished instrument, p. 1. Copyright 2002 by M. L. Friedlander and V. Escudero. Reproduced with permission of the authors.

SCORING GUIDE (SOFTA–S AND SOATIF–S, CLIENT AND THERAPIST VERSIONS)

Engagement	
Item #	Score
1	
*5	
9	
13	
TOTAL	
Emotional Connection	
2	
6	
10	
*14	
TOTAL	
Safety	
3	
7	
*11	
*15	
TOTAL	
Shared Sense of Purpose	
4	
8	
*12	
16	
TOTAL	
TOTAL SCORE	

*Items with asterisks (5, 11, 12, 14, and 15) must be inversely scored, so that 5 = 1, 4 = 2, 2 = 4, and 1 = 5.

APPENDIX C:

Constructions of Problems Scale and Summary Profile

Directions: We would like to know your own opinions about what the problem or situation is that has brought you or your family here. Would you kindly use the space below to describe the problem or situation and also what you think the causes of it are.

_____

_____

_____

_____

_____

_____

_____

_____

_____

_____

_____

_____

_____

_____

NEXT, the following questions each state a possible cause of the problem situation. For each question, consider how much that is or is not a cause of the problem you just wrote about above. Simply read the question and check the circle that best describes your opinion regarding that particular cause.

Example: to what extent is this problem caused by the stresses of modern living? Checking this circle would mean that you view the problem as somewhat caused by the stresses of modern living.

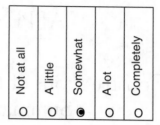

	Not at all	A little	Somewhat	A lot	Completely	
	O	O	◉	O	O	Example

	Not at all	A little	Somewhat	A lot	Completely	
1	O	O	O	O	O	To what extent is this a family problem (vs. an individual problem)?
2	O	O	O	O	O	Is this problem caused by circumstances in the environment which are beyond the control of the people involved (e.g., accident, laid off from job, etc.)?
3	O	O	O	O	O	Does this problem result from the way two or more people in the family relate or communicate with each other?
4	O	O	O	O	O	Are you to blame or at fault for this problem?
5	O	O	O	O	O	Is some other family member to blame or at fault for this problem?
6	O	O	O	O	O	Is this problem related to certain family events or situations that occurred in the family in which you were raised?
7	O	O	O	O	O	Is this problem caused by your own physical illness or condition?
8	O	O	O	O	O	Is this problem caused by the physical illness or condition of a family member other than yourself?
9	O	O	O	O	O	Is this problem caused by the way two (or more) people behave together in a "vicious circle" (e.g., the more the wife nags, the more her husband withdraws and the more he withdraws the more she nags, or the more a brother teases his sister, the more she tattles, and the more she tattles, the more he teases her)?
10	O	O	O	O	O	Is this problem a matter of bad luck?
11	O	O	O	O	O	Is someone in the family other than yourself responsible for the cause of this problem?
12	O	O	O	O	O	Is this problem due to family members not seeing things from one another's point of view?
13	O	O	O	O	O	Is this problem due to the genetic makeup of someone in the family other than yourself?

14	O	O	O	O	O	Is this problem solvable?
15	O	O	O	O	O	Is this problem caused by the mental disorder of someone in the family other than yourself?
16	O	O	O	O	O	Is the problem caused by how family members other than yourself think about, or view, the situation?
17	O	O	O	O	O	Is this problem due to the personality traits of a family member other than yourself?
18	O	O	O	O	O	Is this problem caused by your own mental disorder?
19	O	O	O	O	O	Is this problem related to family events or situations that occurred in previous generations, i.e., things that happened when your parents or grandparents were growing up?
20	O	O	O	O	O	Is this problem due to your personality traits?
21	O	O	O	O	O	Do you have any power or control over resolving this problem?
22	O	O	O	O	O	Is this problem due to your genetic makeup?
23	O	O	O	O	O	Is this problem caused by how you think about, or view, the problem?
24	O	O	O	O	O	Do family members other than yourself have any power or control over resolving the problem?
25	O	O	O	O	O	Are you responsible for the cause of this problem?
26	O	O	O	O	O	Is this problem caused by your attitude?
27	O	O	O	O	O	Is this problem caused by the attitude of someone in the family other than yourself?

Are there any other causes of the problem that are not listed above? If so, please list them here.

_____

_____

_____

Note. From "Assessing Individual Family Members' Constructions of Family Problems," by L. Heatherington, M. L. Friedlander, B. Johnson, R. M. Buchanan, L. E. Burke, and E. M. Shaw, 1998, *Family Process, 37*, pp. 167–187. Copyright 1998 by Blackwell Publishing. Reprinted with permission.

Name _____

Date _____

Summary Profile

	1 Family problem	2 Environment	3 Communication	4 Blame-self	5 Blame-other	6 Family of origin	7 Physical illness-self	8 Physical illness-other	9 Vicious cycle	10 Bad luck	11 Responsible-other	12 Different point of view	13 Genetics-other	14 Solvable	15 Mental disorder-other	16 Thinking-others'	17 Personality-others'	18 Mental disorder-self	19 Previous generations	20 Personality-self	21 Power–control-self	22 Genetics-self	23 Thinking-self	24 Power–control-other	25 Responsible-self	26 Attitude-self	27 Attitude-other
Completely 5	·	·	·	·	·	·	·	·	·	·	·	·	·	·	·	·	·	·	·	·	·	·	·	·	·	·	·
A lot 4	·	·	·	·	·	·	·	·	·	·	·	·	·	·	·	·	·	·	·	·	·	·	·	·	·	·	·
Somewhat 3	·	·	·	·	·	·	·	·	·	·	·	·	·	·	·	·	·	·	·	·	·	·	·	·	·	·	·
A little 2	·	·	·	·	·	·	·	·	·	·	·	·	·	·	·	·	·	·	·	·	·	·	·	·	·	·	·
Not at all 1	·	·	·	·	·	·	·	·	·	·	·	·	·	·	·	·	·	·	·	·	·	·	·	·	·	·	·

REFERENCES

Ackerman, N. W. (1966). *Treating the troubled family*. New York: Basic Books.

Alexander, J. F., & Parsons, B. (1982). *Functional family therapy*. Monterey, CA: Brooks/Cole.

Alexander, J. F., Robbins, M. S., & Sexton, T. L. (2000). Family-based interventions with older, at-risk youth: From promise to proof to practice. *The Journal of Primary Prevention, 21*, 185–205.

Alexander, L. B., & Luborsky, L. (1987). The Penn Helping Alliance Scales. In L. S. Greenberg & W. M. Pinsof (Eds.), *The psychotherapeutic process: A research handbook* (pp. 325–356). New York: Guilford Press.

American Psychological Association, Division 44/Committee on Lesbian, Gay, and Bisexual Concerns Joint Task Force. (2000). Guidelines for psychotherapy with lesbian, gay, and bisexual clients. *American Psychologist, 55*, 1440–1451.

Andersen, T. (Ed.). (1991). *The reflecting team: Dialogues and dialogues about the dialogues*. New York: Brunner/Mazel.

Anderson, C. (2003). Cassandra notes on the state of the family research and practice union. *Family Process, 42*, 323–329.

Andolfi, M., & Angelo, C. (1988). Toward constructing the therapeutic system. *Journal of Marital and Family Therapy, 14*, 237–247.

Ariel, J., & McPherson, D. W. (2000). Therapy with lesbian and gay parents and their children. *Journal of Marital and Family Therapy, 26*, 421–432.

Asay, T. P., & Lambert, M. J. (1999). The empirical case for the common factors in therapy: Quantitative findings. In M. A. Hubble, B. L. Duncan, & S. D. Miller (Eds.), *The heart and soul of change: What works in therapy* (pp. 33–56). Washington, DC: American Psychological Association.

Bachelor, A., & Horvath, A. O. (1999). The therapeutic relationship. In M. A. Hubble, B. L. Duncan, & S. D. Miller (Eds.), *The heart and soul of change: What works in therapy* (pp. 133–178). Washington, DC: American Psychological Association.

Barnard, C. P., & Kuehl, B. P. (1995). Ongoing evaluation: In-session procedures for enhancing the working alliance and therapy effectiveness. *The American Journal of Family Therapy, 23*, 161–172.

Bean, R. A., Perry, B. J., & Bedell, T. M. (2001). Developing culturally competent marriage and family therapists: Guidelines for working with Hispanic families. *Journal of Marital and Family Therapy, 27*, 43–54.

Beck, D. F., & Jones, M. A. (1973). *Progress on family problems: A nationwide study of clients' and counselors' views on family agency services*. New York: Family Service Association of America.

Beck, M., Friedlander, M. L., & Escudero, V. (in press). Three perspectives of clients' experiences of the therapeutic alliance: A discovery-oriented investigation. *Journal of Marital and Family Therapy*.

Bennun, I. (1989). Perceptions of the therapist in family therapy. *Journal of Family Therapy, 11*, 243–255.

Berg, I. K., & Miller, S. D. (1992). *Working with the problem drinker: A solution focused approach*. New York: Norton.

Bibring, E. (1937). Therapeutic results of psychoanalysis. *International Journal of Psychoanalysis, 18*, 170–189.

Bischoff, R., & McBride, A. (1996). Client perceptions of couples and family therapy. *American Journal of Family Therapy, 24*, 117–128.

Blanck, G., & Blanck, R. (1979). *Ego psychology II: Psychoanalytic developmental psychology*. New York: Columbia University Press.

Bordin, E. S. (1979). The generalizability of the psychoanalytic concept of the working alliance. *Psychotherapy, 16*, 252–260.

Bordin, E. S. (1994). Theory and research on the therapeutic working alliance: New directions. In A. O. Horvath & L. S. Greenberg (Eds.), *The working alliance: Theory, research, and practice* (pp. 13–37). New York: Wiley.

Boscolo, L., Cecchin, G., Hoffman, L., & Penn, P. (1987). *Milan systemic family therapy*. New York: Basic Books.

Bourgeois, L., Sabourin, S., & Wright, J. (1990). Predictive validity of therapeutic alliance in group marital therapy. *Journal of Consulting and Clinical Psychology, 58*, 608–613.

Bowen, M. (1976). Theory in the practice of psychotherapy. In P. Guerin (Ed.), *Family therapy: Theory and practice* (pp. 42–91). New York: Gardner.

Bradley, B., & Furrow, J. L. (2004). Toward a mini-theory of the blamer softening event: Tracking the moment-by-moment process. *Journal of Marital and Family Therapy, 30*, 233–246.

Brown, L. S. (1996). Ethical concerns with sexual minority patients. In R. P. Cabaj & T. S. Stein (Eds.), *Textbook of homosexuality and mental health* (pp. 897–916). Washington, DC: American Psychiatric Press.

Brown, P. D., & O'Leary, K. D. (2000). Therapeutic alliance: Predicting continuance and success in group treatment for spouse abuse. *Journal of Consulting and Clinical Psychology, 68*, 340–345.

Brown-Standridge, M. D., & Piercy, F. P. (1988). Reality creation versus reality confirmation: A process study in marital therapy. *American Journal of Family Therapy, 16*, 195–215.

Butler, M. H., & Wampler, K. S. (1999). Couple-responsible therapy process: Positive proximal outcomes. *Family Process, 28*, 27–54.

Carroll, J., & Wyatt, G. K. (1990). Uses of humor in psychotherapy. *Psychological Reports, 66*, 795–801.

Cauce, A. M., Domenech-Rodriguez, M., Paradise, M., Cochran, B. N., Munyi Shea, J., Srebnik, D., & Baydar, N. (2002). Cultural and contextual influences in mental health seeking: A focus on ethnic minority youth. *Journal of Consulting and Clinical Psychology, 70*, 44–55.

Christensen, L. L., Russell, C. S., Miller, R. B., & Peterson, C. M. (1998). The process of change in couples therapy: A qualitative investigation. *Journal of Marital and Family Therapy, 24,* 177–188.

Cline, V. B., Mejia, J., Coles, J., Klein, N., & Cline, R. A. (1984). The relationship between therapist behaviors and outcome for middle- and lower-class couples in marital therapy. *Journal of Clinical Psychology, 40,* 691–704.

Cohen, P., & Hesselbart, C. (1993). Demographic factors in the use of children's mental health services. *American Journal of Public Health, 83,* 49–52.

Coleman, H. L. K., Wampold, B. E., & Casali, S. L. (1995). Ethnic minorities' ratings of ethnically similar and European American counselors: A meta-analysis. *Journal of Counseling Psychology, 42,* 55–64.

Colson, D. B., Cornsweet, C., Murphy, T., O'Malley, F., Hyland, P. S., McParland, M., & Coyne, L. (1990). Perceived treatment difficulty and therapeutic alliance on an adolescent psychiatric hospital unit. *American Journal of Orthopsychiatry, 61,* 221–229.

Coulehan, R., Friedlander, M. L., & Heatherington, L. (1998). Transforming narratives: A change event in constructivist family therapy. *Family Process, 37,* 17–33.

Coyne, J. P., & Pepper, C. M. (1998). The therapeutic alliance in brief strategic therapy. In J. D. Safran & J. C. Muran (Eds.), *The therapeutic alliance in brief psychotherapy* (pp. 147–170). Washington, DC: American Psychological Association.

DeJong, P., & Berg, I. K. (1998). *Interviewing for solutions.* Pacific Grove, CA: Brooks/Cole.

De Rubeis, R. J., & Feeley, M. (1990). Determinants of change in cognitive therapy for depression. *Cognitive Therapy and Research, 14,* 469–482.

de Shazer, S. (1984). The death of resistance. *Family Process, 23,* 79–93.

de Shazer, S. (1985). *Keys to solutions in brief therapy.* New York: Norton.

de Shazer, S. (1988). *Clues: Investigating solutions in brief therapy.* New York: Norton.

Diamond, G. M., Liddle, H. A., Hogue, A., & Dakof, G. A. (1999). Alliance-building interventions with adolescents in family therapy: A process study. *Psychotherapy, 36,* 355–368.

Diamond, G. S., & Liddle, H. A. (1996). Resolving a therapeutic impasse between parents and adolescents in Multidimensional Family Therapy. *Journal of Consulting and Clinical Psychology, 65,* 481–488.

Diamond, G. S., & Liddle, H. A. (1999). Transforming negative parent–adolescent interactions: From impasse to dialogue. *Family Process, 38,* 5–26.

Diamond, G. S., & Siqueland, L. (1995). Family therapy for the treatment of depressed adolescents [Special issue]. *Psychotherapy, 32,* 77–90.

Diamond, G. S., & Siqueland, L. (1998). Emotion, attachment and the relational reframe: The first session. *Journal of Strategic and Systemic Therapies, 17,* 37–49.

Diamond, G. S., Siqueland, L., & Diamond, G. M. (2003). Attachment-based family therapy for depressed adolescents: Programmatic treatment development. *Clinical Child and Family Psychology Review, 6*, 107–127.

DiGiuseppe, R., Linscott, J., & Jilton, R. (1996). Developing the therapeutic alliance in child–adolescent psychotherapy. *Applied and Preventative Psychology, 5*, 85–100.

Doehrman, M. J. (1976). Parallel processes in supervision and psychotherapy. *Bulletin of the Menninger Clinic, 40*, 9–104.

Dore, M. M., & Alexander, L. B. (1996). Preserving families at risk of child abuse and neglect: The role of the helping alliance. *Child Abuse and Neglect, 20*, 349–361.

Dozier, R. M., Hicks, M. W., Cornille, T. A., & Peterson, G. W. (1998). The effect of Tomm's therapeutic questioning styles on therapeutic alliance: A clinical analog study. *Family Process, 37*, 189–200.

Eltz, M. J., Shirk, S. R., & Sarlin, N. (1995). Alliance formation and treatment outcome among maltreated adolescents. *Child Abuse and Neglect, 19*, 419–431.

Epstein, L., & Feiner, A. H. (Eds.). (1979). *Countertransference*. Northvale, NJ: Jason Aronson.

Escudero, V., & Friedlander, M. L. (2002a). *SOATIF–o for clients*. Unpublished instrument. Available from SOFTA Web site, http://www.softa-soatif.net

Escudero, V., & Friedlander, M. L. (2002b). *SOATIF–s*. Unpublished instrument. Available from SOFTA Web site, http://www.softa-soatif.net

Escudero, V., & Friedlander, M. L. (2003). El sistema de observación de la alianza terapéutica en intervención familiar (SOATIF): Desarrollo trans-cultural, fiabilidad, y aplicaciones del instrumento [System for Observing Family Therapy Alliances (SOFTA): Cross-cultural development, reliability, and instrument use]. *Mosaïco, 25*, 32–36.

Escudero, V., Friedlander, M. L., & Deihl, L. (2004). *SOATIF–o for therapists*. Unpublished instrument. Available from SOFTA Web site, http://www.softa-soatif.net

Escudero, V., Friedlander, M. L., & Deihl, L. (2005, August). *Identifying therapist contributions to the family therapy alliance*. Poster to be presented at the 113th annual conference, American Psychological Association, Washington, DC.

Fadiman, A. (1997). *The spirit catches you and you fall down*. New York: Farrar, Straus & Giroux.

Feeley, M., DeRubeis, R. J., & Gelf, L. A. (1999). The temporal relation of adherence and alliance to symptom change in cognitive therapy for depression. *Journal of Consulting and Clinical Psychology, 67*, 578–582.

Firestone, A., & O'Connell, B. (1980). Does the therapeutic relationship matter? A follow-up study of adherence and improvement in family therapy. *Australian Journal of Family Therapy, 2*, 17–21.

Fisch, R., Weakland, J. H., & Segal, L. (1982). *The tactics of change: Doing therapy briefly*. San Francisco: Jossey-Bass.

Fishman, H. C. (1988). *Treating troubled adolescents: A family therapy approach*. New York: Basic Books.

Flaskas, C. (1989). Thinking about the emotional interaction of therapist and family. *Australian and New Zealand Journal of Family Therapy, 10*, 1–6.

Flaskas, C., & Perlesz, A. (1998). The return of the therapeutic relationship in systemic therapy. In C. Flaskas & A. Perlesz (Eds.), *The therapeutic relationship in systemic therapy* (pp. 1–12). London: H. Karnac.

Florsheim, P., Shotorbani, S., Guest-Warnick, G., Barratt, T., & Hwang, W. (2000). Role of the working alliance in the treatment of delinquent boys in community-based programs. *Journal of Consulting and Clinical Psychology, 29*, 94–107.

Framo, J. (1970). Symptoms from a family transactional viewpoint. In N. Ackerman (Ed.), *Family therapy in transition* (pp. 125–171). Boston: Little, Brown.

Framo, J. (1992). *Family-of-origin therapy: An intergenerational approach*. New York: Brunner/Mazel.

Freud, S. (1940). The dynamics of transference. In J. Strachey (Ed. & Trans.), *The standard edition of the complete psychological works of Sigmund Freud* (Vol. 12, pp. 122–144). London: Hogarth Press. (Original work published 1912)

Freud, S. (1959). Future prospects of psychoanalytic psychotherapy. In J. Strachey (Ed. & Trans.), *The standard edition of the complete psychological works of Sigmund Freud* (Vol. 20, pp. 87–172). London: Hogarth Press. (Original work published 1910)

Friedlander, M. L. (2000). Observational coding of family therapy processes: State of the art. In A. P. Beck & C. M. Lewis (Eds.), *The process of group psychotherapy: Systems for analyzing change* (pp. 67–84). Washington, DC: American Psychological Association.

Friedlander, M. L., Ellis, M. V., Raymond, L., Siegel, S. M., & Milford, D. (1987). Convergence and divergence in the process of interviewing families. *Psychotherapy: Theory, Research, Practice, and Training, 24*, 570–583.

Friedlander, M. L., & Escudero, V. (2002). *SOFTA–s*. Unpublished instrument. Available from SOFTA Web site, http://www.softa-soatif.net

Friedlander, M. L., Escudero, V., & Guzmán, M. (2002). International exchanges in family therapy: Training, research, and practice in Spain and the U.S. *The Counseling Psychologist, 30*, 314–329.

Friedlander, M. L., Escudero, V., Haar, N., & Higham, J. (2005, June). *Introducing the SOFTA–s (self-report version of the System for Observing Family Therapy Alliances)*. Poster session presented at the annual conference of the Society for Psychotherapy Research, Montreal, Quebec, Canada.

Friedlander, M. L., Escudero, V., & Heatherington, L. (2001). *SOFTA–o for clients*. Unpublished instrument. Available from SOFTA Web site, http://www.softa-soatif.net

Friedlander, M. L., Escudero, V., Heatherington, L., Deihl, L., Field, N., Lehman, P., McKee, M., & Cutting, M. (2004). *System for Observing Family Therapy Alliances (SOFTA–o) training manual—revised*. Retrieved September 28, 2005, from http://www.softa-soatif.com/docusofta/softa%20insturments/manuales/Softa_CodingManual.pdf

Friedlander, M. L., Escudero, V., Horvath, A. O., Heatherington, L., Cabero, A., & Martens, M. (in press). System for Observing Family Therapy Alliances: A tool for research and practice. *Journal of Counseling Psychology.*

Friedlander, M. L., & Heatherington, L. (1989). Analyzing relational control in family therapy interviews. *Journal of Counseling Psychology, 36,* 139–148.

Friedlander, M. L., Heatherington, L., Johnson, B., & Skowron, E. A. (1994). "Sustaining engagement": A change event in family therapy. *Journal of Counseling Psychology, 41,* 438–448.

Friedlander, M. L., Heatherington, L., & Marrs, A. (2000). Responding to blame in family therapy: A narrative/constructionist perspective. *American Journal of Family Therapy, 28,* 133–146.

Friedlander, M. L., Highlen, P. S., & Lassiter, W. L. (1985). Content analytic comparison of four expert counselors' approaches to family treatment: Ackerman, Bowen, Jackson, and Whitaker. *Journal of Counseling Psychology, 32,* 171–180.

Friedlander, M. L., Lehman, P., McKee, M., Field, N., & Cutting, M. (2000, August). *Development of the Family Therapy Alliance Observer Rating Scale.* Paper presented at the annual conference of the American Psychological Association, Washington, DC.

Friedlander, M. L., Lehman, P., McKee, M., Field, N., Cutting, M., Escudero, V., et al. (2001, November). *The alliance in couples and family therapy: Initial stages in the development of an observational rating system.* Paper presented at the conference of the North American Society for Psychotherapy Research, Puerto Vallarta, Mexico.

Friedlander, M. L., Talka, K., Haar, N., Higham, J., Martens, M., & Deihl, L. (2003, November). *Construct validity of the SOFTA/SOATIF: Incunabulae.* Paper presented at the biannual conference of the North American Society for Psychotherapy Research, Newport, RI.

Friedlander, M. L., Wildman, J., Heatherington, L., & Skowron, E. A. (1994). What we do and don't know about the process of family therapy. *Journal of Family Psychology, 8,* 390–416.

Friedman, M. (1985). *The healing dialogue in psychotherapy.* New York: Jason Aronson.

Gaston, L., & Marmar, C. R. (1994). The California Psychotherapy Alliance Scales. In A. O. Horvath & L. Greenberg (Eds.), *The working alliance: Theory, research, and practice* (pp. 85–108). New York: Wiley.

Gehart, D. R., & Lyle, R. R. (2001). Client experience of gender in therapeutic relationship: An interpretive ethnography. *Family Process, 40,* 443–458.

Gelso, C. J., & Carter, J. (1985). The relationship in counseling and psychotherapy: Components, consequences, and theoretical antecedents. *The Counseling Psychologist, 13,* 155–244.

Gelso, C. J., & Carter, J. (1994). Components of the psychotherapy relationship: Their interaction and variation during treatment. *Journal of Counseling Psychology, 41,* 296–306.

Gelso, C. J., & Hayes, J. (2002). The management of coutertransference. In J. C. Norcross (Ed.), *Psychotherapy relationships that work: Therapist contributions and responsiveness to patients* (pp. 267–283). London: Oxford University Press.

Gelso, C. J., & Mohr, J. J. (2001). The working alliance and the transference/countertransference relationship: Their manifestation with racial/ethnic and sexual orientation minority clients and therapists. *Applied and Preventative Psychology*, *10*, 51–68.

Gibney, P. (1998). To embrace paradox (once more, with feeling): A commentary on narrative/conversational therapies and the therapeutic relationship. In C. Flaskas & A. Perlesz (Eds.), *The therapeutic relationship in systemic therapy* (pp. 99–107). London: H. Karnac.

Goldfried, M. R. (1982). Resistance in clinical behavior therapy. In P. L. Wachtel (Ed.), *Resistance* (pp. 95–113). New York: Plenum Press.

Goldfried, M. R., & Eubanks-Carter, C. (2004). On the need for a new psychotherapy research paradigm: Comment on Westen, Novotny, and Thompson-Brenner (2004). *Psychological Bulletin*, *130*, 669–673.

Goldfried, M. R., & Wolfe, B. E. (1996). Psychotherapy practice and research: Repairing a strained relationship. *American Psychologist*, *51*, 1007–1016.

Goolishian, H., & Anderson, H. (1992). Strategy and intervention versus nonintervention: A matter of theory. *Journal of Marital and Family Therapy*, *18*, 5–15.

Gottman, J. (1994). *What predicts divorce*. Hillsdale, NJ: Erlbaum.

Gray, J. (1992). *Men are from Mars, women are from Venus: A practical guide for improving communication and getting what you want in relationships*. New York: HarperCollins.

Green, R.-J., & Herget, M. (1991). Outcomes of systemic/strategic team consultation: III. The importance of therapist warmth and active structuring. *Family Process*, *30*, 321–336.

Greenberg, L. S., & Johnson, S. M. (1988). *Emotionally-focused therapy for couples*. New York: Guilford Press.

Greenson, R. (1967). *The technique and practice of psychoanalysis*. New York: International Universities Press.

Guerin, P. J., Fogarty, T. F., Fay, L. F., & Kautto, J. G. (1996). *Working with relationship triangles: The one-two-three of psychotherapy*. New York: Guilford Press.

Gurman, A. S., & Kniskern, D. P. (1978). Research on marital and family therapy: Progress, perspective and prospect. In S. L. Garfield & A. E. Bergin (Eds.), *Handbook of psychotherapy and behavior change: An empirical analysis* (2nd ed., pp. 817–901). New York: Wiley.

Haley, J. (1973). *Strategies of psychotherapy*. New York: Grune & Stratton.

Haley, J. (1976). *Problem-solving therapy*. San Francisco: Jossey-Bass.

Hall, G. C. N. (2001). Psychotherapy research with ethnic minorities: Empirical, ethical, and conceptual issues. *Journal of Consulting and Clinical Psychology*, *69*, 502–510.

Hanish, L. D., & Tolan, P. H. (2001). Patterns of change in family-based aggression prevention. *Journal of Marital and Family Therapy*, *27*, 213–226.

Hardham, V. (1998). Embedded and embodied in the therapeutic relationship: Understanding the therapist's use of self systemically. In C. Flaskas & A. Perlesz

(Eds.), *The therapeutic relationship in systemic therapy* (pp. 71–89). London: H. Karnac.

Hardy, K. V., & Laszloffy, T. A. (2002). Couple therapy using a multicultural perspective. In A. S. Gurman & N. S. Jacobson (Eds.), *Clinical handbook of couple therapy* (pp. 569–593). New York: Guilford Press.

Hartley, D., & Strupp, H. H. (1983). The therapeutic alliance: Its relationship to outcome in brief psychotherapy. In J. Masling (Ed.), *Empirical studies of psychoanalytic theories* (Vol. 1, pp. 1–37). Hillsdale, NJ: Erlbaum.

Hathaway, W. L., Scott, S. Y., & Garver, S. A. (2004). Assessing religious/spiritual functioning: A neglected domain in clinical practice. *Professional Psychology: Research and Practice, 35*, 97–105.

Hayes, J. A., McCracken, J. E., McClanahan, M. K., Hill, C. E., Harp, J. S., & Carozzoni, P. (1998). Therapist perspectives on countertransference: Qualitative data in search of a theory. *Journal of Counseling Psychology, 45*, 468–482.

Heatherington, L. (1989). Toward more clinically meaningful research: Taking context into account in coding psychotherapy interaction. *Psychotherapy, 26*, 436–447.

Heatherington, L., & Friedlander, M. L. (1990a). Applying task analysis to structural family therapy. *Journal of Family Psychology, 4*, 36–48.

Heatherington, L., & Friedlander, M. L. (1990b). Couple and Family Therapy Alliance Scales: Empirical considerations. *Journal of Marital and Family Therapy, 16*, 299–306.

Heatherington, L., & Friedlander, M. L. (2004). From dyads to triads and beyond: Relational communication in individual and family therapy. In V. Escudero & E. Rogers (Eds.), *Relational communication: An interactional perspective to the study of process and form* (pp. 103–129). Mahwah, NJ: Erlbaum.

Heatherington, L., Friedlander, M. L., & Greenberg, L. S. (2005). Change process research in couples and family therapy: Methodological challenges and opportunities. *Journal of Family Psychology, 19*, 18–27.

Heatherington, L., Friedlander, M. L., Johnson, B., Buchanan, R. M., Burke, L. E., & Shaw, E. M. (1998). Assessing individual family members' constructions of family problems. *Family Process, 37*, 167–187.

Heatherington, L., Friedlander, M. L., & Johnson, W. L. (1989). Informed consent in family therapy research: Ethical dilemmas and practical problems. *Journal of Family Psychology, 2*, 373–385.

Hedges, L. E. (1992). *Interpreting the countertransference.* New York: Jason Aronson.

Helmeke, K. B., & Sprenkle, D. H. (2000). Clients' perceptions of pivotal moments in couples therapy: A qualitative study of change in therapy. *Journal of Marital and Family Therapy, 26*, 469–483.

Henggeler, S., & Borduin, C. (1990). *Family therapy and beyond: A multisystemic approach to treating the behavior problems of children and adolescents.* Pacific Grove, CA: Brooks/Cole.

Henry, W. P., & Strupp, H. H. (1994). The therapeutic alliance as interpersonal process. In A. O. Horvath & L. Greenberg (Eds.), *The working alliance: Theory, research, and practice* (pp. 51–84). New York: Wiley.

Hoffman, L. (1981). *Foundations of family therapy*. New York: Basic Books.

Hoffman, L. (1991). *Relational systems work: Family therapy in a different voice*. Unpublished manuscript.

Horvath, A. O. (1994). Empirical validation of Bordin's pantheoretical model of the alliance: The Working Alliance Inventory perspective. In A. O. Horvath & L. S. Greenberg (Eds.), *The working alliance: Theory, research, and practice* (pp. 109–130). New York: Wiley.

Horvath, A. O., & Bedi, R. P. (2002). The alliance. In J. C. Norcross (Ed.), *Psychotherapy relationships that work: Therapist contributions and responsiveness to patients* (pp. 37–69). New York: Oxford University Press.

Horvath, A. O., Friedlander, M. L., Symonds, D., & Gruter-Andrews, J. (2003, November). *Perspectives of alliance in couples therapy: Contrasting the "lived" and the "observed" relationship*. Paper presented at the bi-annual conference of the North American Society for Psychotherapy Research, Newport, RI.

Horvath, A. O., & Greenberg, L. S. (1986). The development of the Working Alliance Inventory. In L. S. Greenberg & W. M. Pinsof (Eds.), *The psychotherapeutic process: A research handbook* (pp. 529–556). New York: Guilford Press.

Horvath, A. O., & Greenberg, L. S. (1989). *The working alliance: Theory, research, and practice*. New York: Wiley.

Horvath, A. O., & Symonds, B. D. (1991). Relation between the working alliance and outcome in psychotherapy: A meta-analysis. *Journal of Counseling Psychology, 38*, 139–149.

Housgaard, E. (1994). The therapeutic alliance—A conceptual analysis. *Scandinavian Journal of Psychology, 34*, 67–85.

Imber-Black, E. (1993). Secrets in families and family therapy: An overview. In E. Imber-Black (Ed.), *Secrets in families and family therapy* (pp. 3–28). New York: Norton.

Jacobson, N. S., & Margolin, G. (1979). *Marital therapy: Strategies based on social learning and behavior exchange principles*. New York: Brunner/Mazel.

Johnson, L. N., Wright, D. W., & Ketring, S. A. (2002). The therapeutic alliance in home-based family therapy: Is it predictive of outcome? *Journal of Marital and Family Therapy, 28*, 93–102.

Johnson, S. M., & Talitman, E. (1997). Predictors of success in emotionally focused marital therapy. *Journal of Marital and Family Therapy, 23*, 135–152.

Keith, D. V., Connell, G. M., & Connell, L. C. (2001). *Defiance in the family*. Philadelphia: Routledge.

Kerr, M. E., & Bowen, M. (1988). *Family evaluation*. New York: Norton.

Kiesler, D. J. (1966). Some myths of psychotherapy and the search for a paradigm. *Psychological Bulletin, 65*, 110–136.

Kiesler, D. J. (1983). The 1982 interpersonal circle: A taxonomy for complementarity in human transactions. *Psychological Review, 90*, 185–214.

Kim, E. Y.-K., Bean, R. A., & Harper, J. M. (2004). Do general treatment guidelines for Asian American families have applications to specific ethnic groups? The case of culturally-competent therapy with Korean Americans. *Journal of Marital and Family Therapy, 30*, 359–372.

Kiresuk, T. J., Smith, A., & Cardillo, J. E. (1994). *Goal attainment scaling: Applications, theory, and measurement.* Hillsdale, NJ: Erlbaum.

Klein, M. (1946). Notes on some schizoid mechanisms. *International Journal of Psychoanalysis, 27*, 99–110.

Klein, N. C., Alexander, J. F., & Parsons, B. V. (1977). Impact of family systems intervention on recidivism and sibling delinquency: A model of primary prevention and program evaluation. *Journal of Consulting and Clinical Psychology, 45*, 469–474.

Knobloch-Fedders, L. M., Pinsof, W. M., & Mann, B. J. (2004). The formation of the therapeutic alliance in couple therapy. *Family Process, 43*, 425–442.

Knobloch-Fedders, L. M., Pinsof, W. M., & Mann, B. J. (in press). Therapeutic alliance and treatment progress in couple psychotherapy. *Journal of Marital and Family Therapy.*

Koot, H. M., & Verhulst, F. C. (1992). Prediction of children's referral to mental health and special education services from earlier adjustment. *Journal of Child Psychology and Psychiatry and Allied Disciplines, 33*, 717–729.

Krupnick, J. L., Sotsky, S. M., Simmens, A., Moyer, J., Elkin, I., Watkins, J., & Pilkonis, P. A. (1996). The role of alliance in psychotherapy and pharmacotherapy outcome: Findings in the National Institute of Mental Health treatment of depression collaborative research program. *Journal of Consulting and Clinical Psychology, 64*, 532–539.

Kuehl, B. P., Newfield, N. A., & Joanning, H. P. (1990). A client-based description of family therapy. *Journal of Family Psychology, 3*, 310–312.

Ladany, N., Friedlander, M. L., & Nelson, M. L. (2005). *Critical events in psychotherapy supervision: An interpersonal approach.* Washington, DC: American Psychological Association.

Laird, J. (2000). Gender in lesbian relationships: Cultural, feminist, and constructionist reflections. *Journal of Marital and Family Therapy, 26*, 455–467.

Lax, W. D. (1991). The reflecting team and the initial consultation. In T. Andersen (Ed.), *The reflecting team: Dialogues and dialogues about the dialogues* (pp. 127–142). New York: Brunner/Mazel.

Levant, R. F., & Philpot, C. L. (2002). Conceptualizing gender in marital and family therapy research: The gender role strain paradigm. In H. A. Liddle, D. A. Santisteban, R. F. Levant, & J. H. Bray (Eds.), *Family psychology: Science-based interventions* (pp. 301–329). Washington, DC: American Psychological Association.

Liddle, H. A. (2002). *Multidimensional family therapy: A treatment manual.* Rockville, MD: Center for Substance Abuse Treatment.

Liddle, H. A., Dakof, G., & Diamond, G. (1991). Adolescent substance abuse: Multidimensional family therapy in action. In E. Kaufman & P. Kaufmann (Eds.), *Family therapy approaches with drug and alcohol problems* (2nd ed., pp. 120–171). Boston: Allyn & Bacon.

Liddle, H. A., & Schwartz, S. J. (2002). Attachment and family therapy: Clinical utility of adolescent–family attachment research. *Family Process, 41*, 455–476.

Lipman-Blumen, J., Handley-Isaksen, A., & Leavitt, H. J. (1983). Achieving styles in men and women: A model, an instrument, and some findings. In J. Spence (Ed.), *Achievement and achievement motives* (pp. 151–204). San Francisco: Freeman.

Little, M. (1951). Countertransference and the patient's response to it. *International Journal of Psychoanalysis, 32*, 32–40.

Long, J. K., & Serovich, J. M. (2003). Incorporating sexual orientation into MFT training programs: Infusion and inclusion. *Journal of Marital and Family Therapy, 29*, 59–67.

Lu, Y., Lum, D., & Chen, S. (2001). Cultural competency and achieving styles in clinical social work: A conceptual and empirical exploration. *Journal of Ethnic and Cultural Diversity in Social Work, 9*, 1–32.

Luborsky, L. (1994). Therapeutic alliances as predictors of psychotherapy outcomes: Factors explaining the predictive success. In A. Horvath & L. Greenberg (Eds.), *The working alliance: Therapy, research, and practice* (pp. 38–50). New York: Wiley.

Luborsky, L., Crits-Cristoph, P. Alexander, L., Margolis, M., & Cohen, M. (1983). Two helping alliance methods for predicting outcomes of psychotherapy: A counting signs vs. global rating method. *Journal of Nervous and Mental Disease, 171*, 480–491.

Luepnitz, D. A. (1988). *The family interpreted.* New York: Basic Books.

MacKinnon, L. K. (1998). *Trust and betrayal in the treatment of child abuse.* New York: Guilford Press.

Madsen, N. C. (1999). *Collaborative therapy with multi-stressed families.* New York: Guilford Press.

Mamodhoussen, S., Wright, J., Tremblay, N., & Poitras-Wright, H. (2005). Impact of marital and psychological distress on therapeutic alliance in couples undergoing couple therapy. *Journal of Marital and Family Therapy, 31*, 159–169.

Marmar, C., Gaston, L., Gallagher, D., & Thompson, L. (1989). Alliance and outcome in late-life depression. *Journal of Nervous and Mental Disease, 177*, 464–471.

Martin, D. J., Garske, J. P., & Davis, M. K. (2000). Relation of the therapeutic alliance with outcome and other variables: A meta-analytic review. *Journal of Consulting and Clinical Psychology, 68*, 438–450.

McElroy, L. P., & McElroy, R. A. (1991). Countertransference issues in the treatment of incest families [Special issue]. *Psychotherapy, 28*, 48–54.

Meyer, B., Pilkonis, P. A., Krupnick, J. L., Egan, M. K., Simmens, S. J., & Sotsky, S. M. (2002). Treatment expectancies, patient alliance, and outcome: Further analyses from the National Institute of Mental Health Treatment of Depression Collaborative Research Program. *Journal of Consulting and Clinical Psychology, 70*, 1051–1055.

Minuchin, S. (1974). *Families and family therapy.* Cambridge, MA: Harvard University Press.

Minuchin, S., & Fishman, C. (1981). *Techniques of family therapy*. Cambridge, MA: Harvard University Press.

Minuchin, S., Montalvo, B., Guerney, B. G., Jr., Rosman, B. L., & Schumer, F. (1967). *Families of the slums*. New York: Basic Books.

Minuchin, S., Rosman, B., & Baker, L. (1978). *Psychosomatic families: Anorexia nervosa in context*. Cambridge, MA: Harvard University Press.

Morrow, S. L. (2000). First do no harm: Therapist issues in psychotherapy with lesbian, gay, and bisexual clients. In R. M. Perez, K. A. DeBord, & K. J. Bieschke (Eds.), *Handbook of counseling and psychotherapy with lesbian, gay, and bisexual clients* (pp. 137–156). Washington, DC: American Psychological Association.

Muir, J. A., Schwartz, S. J., & Szapocznik, J. (2004). A program of research with Hispanic and African American families: Three decades of intervention development and testing influenced by the changing cultural context of Miami. *Journal of Marital and Family Therapy, 30,* 285–303.

Muran, J. C., & Safran, J. D. (1998). Negotiating the therapeutic alliance in brief psychotherapy: An introduction. In J. D. Safran & J. C. Muran (Eds.), *The therapeutic alliance in brief psychotherapy* (pp. 3–14). Washington, DC: American Psychological Association.

Myers, I. B., & McCaulley, M. H. (1985). *Manual: A guide to the development and use of the Myers-Briggs Type Inventory*. Palo Alto, CA: Consulting Psychologists Press.

Nathan, P. E., & Gorman, J. M. (1998). *Treatments that work*. New York: Oxford University Press.

Neill, J. R., & Kniskern, D. P. (Eds.). (1982). *From psyche to system: The evolving therapy of Carl Whitaker*. New York: Guilford Press.

Nelson, B. A., & Stake, J. E. (1994). The Myers-Briggs Type Indicator personality dimensions and perceptions of quality of therapy relationships. *Psychotherapy: Theory, Research, Practice, and Training, 31,* 449–455.

Nichols, M. P. (1987). *The self in the system*. New York: Brunner/Mazel.

Nichols, M. P., & Schwartz, R. (2004). *Family therapy: Concepts and methods* (6th ed.). Boston: Allyn & Bacon.

Norcross, J. C. (2002). Empirically supported therapy relationships. In J. C. Norcross (Ed.), *Psychotherapy relationships that work* (pp. 3–16). Oxford, England: Oxford University Press.

Oetzel, K. B., & Scherer, D. G. (2003). Therapeutic engagement with adolescents in psychotherapy. *Psychotherapy: Theory, Research, Practice, and Training, 40,* 215–225.

O'Hanlon, W. H., & Weiner-Davis, M. (1989). *In search of a solution: A new direction in psychotherapy*. New York: Norton.

Palmer, R., & Bor, R. (2001). The challenges of intimacy and sexual relationships for gay men in HIV serodiscordant relationships: A pilot study. *Journal of Marital and Family Therapy, 27,* 419–431.

Patterson, G. R., & Forgatch, M. S. (1985). Therapist behavior as a determinant for client noncompliance: A paradox for the behavior modifier. *Journal of Consulting and Clinical Psychology, 53*, 846–851.

Piercy, F. P., Laird, R., & Mohammed, Z. (1983). A family therapist rating scale. *Journal of Marital and Family Therapy, 9*, 49–59.

Pinsof, W. B. (1994). An integrative systems perspective on the therapeutic alliance: Theoretical, clinical, and research implications. In A. O. Horvath & L. S. Greenberg (Eds.), *The working alliance: Theory, research, and practice* (pp. 173–195). New York: Wiley.

Pinsof, W. B. (1995). *Integrative problem-centered therapy*. New York: Basic Books.

Pinsof, W. B. (1999). *Family Therapy Alliance Scale—Revised* (Unpublished document). Evanston, IL: The Family Institute.

Pinsof, W. B., & Catherall, D. (1986). The integrative psychotherapy alliance: Family, couple, and individual therapy scales. *Journal of Marital and Family Therapy, 12*, 137–151.

Pinsof, W. B., & Wynne, L. C. (2000). Toward progress research: Closing the gap between family therapy practice and research. *Family Process, 26*, 1–8.

Pittman, F. (1987). *Turning points: Treating families in transition and crisis*. New York: Norton.

Postner, R. S., Guttman, H. A., Sigal, J. J., Epstein, N. B., & Rakoff, V. M. (1971). Process and outcome in conjoint family therapy. *Family Process, 10*, 451–474.

Prinz, R. J., & Miller, G. E. (1994). Family-based treatment for childhood antisocial behavior: Experimental influences on dropout and engagement. *Journal of Consulting and Clinical Psychology, 62*, 645–650.

Quinn, W. H., Dotson, D., & Jordan, K. (1997). Dimensions of therapeutic alliance and their associations with outcome in family therapy. *Psychotherapy Research, 7*, 429–438.

Rait, D. S. (1995). The therapeutic alliance in couples and family therapy: Theory in practice. *In Session: Psychotherapy in Practice, 1*, 59–72.

Rait, D. S. (1998). Perspectives on the therapeutic alliance in brief couples and family therapy. In J. D. Safran & J. C. Muran (Eds.), *The therapeutic alliance in brief psychotherapy* (pp. 171–191). Washington, DC: American Psychological Association.

Raue, P. J., & Goldfried, M. R. (1994). The therapeutic alliance in cognitive–behavior therapy. In A. O. Horvath & L. Greenberg (Eds.), *The working alliance: Theory, research, and practice* (pp. 131–152). New York: Wiley.

Raymond, L., Friedlander, M. L., Heatherington, L., Ellis, M. V., & Sargent, J. (1993). Communication processes in structural family therapy: Case study of an anorexic family. *Journal of Family Psychology, 6*, 308–326.

Real, T. (1990). The therapeutic use of self in constructionist/systemic therapy. *Family Process, 29*, 255–272.

Reynes, R. L., & Allen, A. (1987). Humor in psychotherapy: A view. *American Journal of Psychotherapy, 41*, 260–270.

Ritter, K. Y., & Terndrup, A. I. (2002). *Handbook of affirmative psychotherapy with lesbians and gay men*. New York: Guilford Press.

Robbins, M. S., Turner, C. W., Alexander, J. F., & Perez, G. A. (2003). Alliance and dropout in family therapy for adolescents with behavior problems: Individual and systemic effects. *Journal of Family Psychology, 17,* 534–544.

Rogers, C. R. (1951). *Client centered therapy*. Cambridge, MA: Riverside Press.

Rose, E. M., Westefeld, J. S., & Ansely, T. N. (2001). Spiritual issues in counseling: Clients' beliefs and preferences. *Journal of Counseling Psychology, 48,* 61–71.

Rosenberger, E. W., & Hayes, J. A. (2002). Therapist as subject: A review of empirical countertransference literature. *Journal of Counseling and Development, 80,* 264–270.

Ryan, D., & Carr, A. (2001). A study of the differential effects of Tomm's questioning styles on the therapeutic alliance. *Family Process, 40,* 67–77.

Safran, J. D., & Muran, J. D. (1996). The resolution of ruptures in the therapeutic alliance. *Journal of Consulting and Clinical Psychology, 64,* 447–458.

Safran, J. D., & Muran, J. C. (2000). *Negotiating the therapeutic alliance: A relational treatment guide*. New York: Guilford Press.

Santiago-Rivera, A. L., Arredondo, P., & Gallardo-Cooper, M. (2002). *Counseling Latinos and la familia: A practical guide*. Thousand Oaks, CA: Sage.

Santisteban, D. A., Szapocznik, J., Perez-Vidal, A., Kurtines, W. M., Murray, E., & LaPerrire, A. (1996). Efficacy of intervention for engaging youth and families into treatment and some variables that may contribute to differential effectiveness. *Journal of Family Psychology, 10,* 35–44.

Satir, V. (1964). *Conjoint family therapy*. Palo Alto, CA: Science and Behavior Books.

Saunders, S. M., Howard, K. I., & Orlinsky, D. E. (1989). The Therapeutic Bond Scales: Psychometric characteristics and relationship to treatment effectiveness. *Psychological Assessment: A Journal of Consulting and Clinical Psychology, 1,* 323–330.

Scharff, D. E. (1989). Transference, countertransference, and technique in object relations family therapy. In J. S. Scharff (Ed.), *Foundations of object relations family therapy* (pp. 421–445). Northvale, NJ: Jason Aronson.

Scharff, D. E., & Scharff, J. S. (1987). *Object relations family therapy*. Northvale, NJ: Jason Aronson.

Searles, H. (1963). Transference psychosis in the psychotherapy of schizophrenia. *International Journal of Psychoanalysis, 44,* 249–281.

Sells, S. P., Smith, T. E., & Moon, S. (1996). An ethnographic study of client and therapist perceptions of therapy effectiveness in a university-based training clinic. *Journal of Marital and Family Therapy, 22,* 321–342.

Selvini-Palazzoli, M., Boscolo, L., Cecchin, G., & Prata, G. (1978). *Paradox and counterparadox*. New York: Jason Aronson.

Serovich, J. M., & Mosack, K. E. (2000). Training issues for supervisors of marriage and family therapists working with persons living with HIV. *Journal of Marital and Family Therapy, 26,* 103–111.

Sexton, T. L., & Alexander, J. F. (2003). Functional Family Therapy: A mature model for working with at-risk adolescents and their families. In T. L. Sexton, G. R. Weeks, & M. S. Robbins (Eds.), *Handbook of family therapy: The science and practice of working with families and couples* (pp. 323–350). New York: Brunner Routledge.

Sexton, T. L., Ridley, C. R., & Kleiner, A. J. (2004). Beyond common factors: Multilevel-process models of therapeutic change in marriage and family therapy. *Journal of Marital and Family Therapy, 30,* 131–149.

Sexton, T. L., Robbins, M. S., Hollimon, A. S., Mease, A. L., & Mayorga, C. C. (2003). Efficacy, effectiveness, and change mechanisms in couple and family therapy. In T. L. Sexton, G. R. Weeks, & M. S. Robbins (Eds.), *Handbook of family therapy: The science and practice of working with families and couples* (pp. 229–262). New York: Brunner Routledge.

Shapiro, R. J. (1974). Therapists' attitudes and premature termination in family and individual therapy. *Journal of Nervous and Mental Disease, 159*(2), 101–107.

Shelef, K., Diamond, G. M., Diamond, G. S., & Liddle, H. H. (2005). Adolescent and parent alliance and treatment outcome in multidimensional family therapy. *Journal of Consulting and Clinical Psychology, 73,* 689–698.

Shields, C. G., & McDaniel, S. H. (1992). Process differences between male and female therapists in a first family interview. *Journal of Marital and Family Therapy, 18,* 143–151.

Shields, C. G., Sprenkle, D. H., & Constantine, J. A. (1991). Anatomy of an initial interview: The importance of joining and structuring skills. *American Journal of Family Therapy, 19,* 3–18.

Sigal, J., Barrs, C., & Doubliet, A. (1976). Problems in measuring the success of family therapy in a common clinical setting: Impasse and solution. *Family Process, 15,* 225–233.

Slipp, S. (1984). *Object relations: A bridge between individual and family treatment.* New York: Jason Aronson.

Slipp, S., Ellis, S., & Kressel, K. (1974). Factors associated with engagement in family therapy. *Family Process, 13,* 413–427.

Sluzki, C. E. (1975). The coalitionary process in initiating family therapy. *Family Process, 14,* 67–77.

Sluzki, C. E. (1992). Transformations: A blueprint for narrative changes in therapy. *Family Process, 31,* 217–230.

Smith, J., Osman, C., & Goding, M. (1990). Reclaiming the emotional aspects of the therapist–family system. *Australian and New Zealand Journal of Family Therapy, 11,* 140–146.

Snyder, D. (1999). Affective reconstruction in the context of a pluralistic approach to couple therapy. *Clinical Psychology: Science and Practice, 6,* 348–365.

Speed, B. (1996). You cannot not relate. In C. Flaskas & A. Perlesz (Eds.), *The therapeutic relationship in systemic therapy* (pp. 108–122). London: H. Karnac.

Sprenkle, D. H., & Blow, A. J. (2004). Common factors and out sacred models. *Journal of Marital and Family Therapy, 30,* 113–129.

Sterba, R. (1934). The fate of the ego in analytic therapy. *International Journal of Psychoanalysis, 15*, 117–125.

Stevenson, C. (1993). Combining quantitative and qualitative methods in evaluating a course of family therapy. *Journal of Family Therapy, 15*, 205–224.

Stewart, P. (1964). *Jacobellis v. Ohio, 378 U. S. 184, 197 (1964)*. Retrieved September 28, 2005, from http://laws.findlaw.com/us/378/184.html

Stiles, W. B., & Snow, J. S. (1984). Counseling session impact as viewed by novice counselors and their clients. *Journal of Counseling Psychology, 31*, 3–12.

Strupp, H. H. (1973). The interpersonal relationship as a vehicle for therapeutic learning. *Journal of Consulting and Clinical Psychology, 41*, 13–15.

Suen, H. K. (1988). Agreement, reliability, accuracy, and validity: Toward a clarification. *Behavioral Assessment, 10*, 343–366.

Suh, C. S., O'Malley, S. S., & Strupp, H. H. (1986). The Vanderbilt Psychotherapy Process Scale (VPPS) and the Negative Indicators Scale (VNIS). In L. S. Greenberg & W. M. Pinsof (Eds.), *The psychotherapeutic process: A research handbook* (pp. 285–323). New York: Guilford Press.

Symonds, B. D. (1998, June). *A measure of the alliance in couple therapy*. Paper presented at the annual conference of the International Society for Psychotherapy Research, Snowbird, UT.

Symonds, B. D., & Horvath, A. O. (2004). Optimizing the alliance in couple therapy. *Family Process, 43*, 443–455.

Szapocznik, J., & Kurtines, W. M. (1989). *Breakthroughs in family therapy with drug abusing and problem youth*. New York: Springer.

Szapocznik, J., Perez-Vidal, A., Brickman, A., Foote, F. H., Santisteban, D. A., Hervis, O., & Kurtines, W. M. (1988). Engaging adolescent drug abusers and their families in treatment: A strategic structural systems approach. *Journal of Consulting and Clinical Psychology, 56*, 552–557.

Szapocznik, J., & Williams, R. A. (2000). Brief strategic family therapy: Twenty-five years of interplay among theory, research and practice in adolescent behavior problems and drug use. *Clinical Child and Family Psychology Review, 3*, 117–134.

Tichenor, V., & Hill, C. E. (1989). A comparison of six measures of working alliance. *Psychotherapy: Therory, Research, and Practice, 26*, 195–199.

Tomm, K. (1987). Interventive interviewing: Part II. Reflexive questioning as a means to enable self-healing. *Family Process, 26*, 167–184.

Tracey, T. J., & Kokotovic, A. M. (1989). Factor structure of the Working Alliance Inventory. *Psychological Assessment, 1*, 207–210.

Turnell, A., & Edwards, S. (1999). *Signs of safety: A solution and safety oriented approach to child protection casework*. New York: Norton.

Vogel, E. F., & Bell, N. W. (1960). The emotionally disturbed child as the family scapegoat. In N. W. Bell & E. F. Vogel (Eds.), *A modern introduction to the family* (pp. 382–397). Riverside, NJ: Free Press.

Waldron, H. B., Turner, C. W., Barton, C., Alexander, J. F., & Cline, V. B. (1997). Therapist defensiveness and marital therapy process and outcome. *American Journal of Family Therapy, 25*, 233–243.

Wampold, B. E. (2001). *The great psychotherapy debate: Models, methods, and findings.* Mahwah, NJ: Erlbaum.

Watson, J. C., & Greenberg, L. S. (1988). The alliance in experiential therapy: Enacting the relationship conditions. In A. O. Horvath & L. Greenberg (Eds.), *The working alliance: Theory, research, and practice* (pp. 153–172). New York: Wiley.

Watzlawick, P., Beavin, J., & Jackson, D. (1967). *Pragmatics of human communication.* New York: Norton.

Watzlawick, P., Weakland, J. H., & Fisch, R. (1974). *Change: Principles of problem formation and problem resolution.* New York: Norton.

Weingarten, K. (1992). A consideration of intimate and non-intimate interactions in therapy. *Family Process, 31,* 45–59.

Werner-Wilson, R. J., Price, S. J., Zimmerman, T. S., & Murphy, M. J. (1997). Client gender as a process variable in marriage and family therapy: Are women clients interrupted more than men clients? *Journal of Family Psychology, 11,* 373–377.

Westen, D., Novotny, C. M., & Thompson-Brenner, H. (2004). The empirical status of empirically supported psychotherapies: Assumptions, findings, and reporting in controlled clinical trials. *Psychological Bulletin, 130,* 631–663.

Whitaker, C. A., & Keith, D. V. (1981). Symbolic-experiential family therapy. In A. S. Gurman & D. P. Kniskern (Eds.), *Handbook of family therapy* (pp. 187–225). New York: Brunner/Mazel.

White, M., & Epston, D. (1990). *Narrative means to therapeutic ends.* New York: Norton.

White, M. B., Edwards, S. A., & Russell, C. S. (1997). The essential elements of successful marriage and family therapy: A modified Delphi study. *American Journal of Family Therapy, 25,* 213–231.

Winnicott, D. W. (1949). Hate in the countertransference. *International Journal of Psychoanalysis, 30,* 69–74.

Wynne, L. C. (1965). Some indications and contraindications for exploratory family therapy. In I. Boszormenyi-Nagy & J. Framo (Eds.), *Intensive family therapy* (pp. 289–322). New York: Harper & Row.

Wynne, L., Ryckoff, I., Day, J., & Hersch, S. (1958). Pseudo-mutuality in the family relationships of schizophrenics. *Psychiatry, 21,* 205–220.

INDEX

Complementary personality styles, 94–95
Conflict
    among professionals, 245–247, 253–254. *See also* Misalliances among professionals
    in therapy "hostage" relationship, 200
    management for safety, 119
    of power, 216–217
    between presenting problem and hidden problem, 220–224, 225
    in split alliances, 164–165
    therapeutic alliance and, 11–12
Confidentiality. *See* Safety
Constructionist theory 128
    on alliance, 33, 147
    and reflecting teams, 128
    shared sense of purpose and, 128
    therapist attitude in, 89
Constructions of Problems Scale (CPS)
    to enhance shared sense of purpose, 139–140, 303–305
    questionnaires and graphic profile, 303–306
Cooperation, resistance vs., 72–74
Couple Therapy Alliance Scale, 23, 24
Countertransference
    awareness of for therapeutic advantage, 235–236
    case examples. *See also* Ellison family
        Boyd family, 237
        Stacy, 234–237
    classic view of, 229–230
    contemporary definition of, 231
    defined by analytical family therapists, 232, 233
    emotional connection with therapist and, 234, 240
    engagement in the therapeutic process and, 239–240
    frequency of occurrence, 231
    in families with incest, 234
    individual and systemic manifestations, 237–239
    middle ground in, 230–231
    negative emotions in, 238
    object relations view of, 16
    as overidentification, 238
    personal issues, touching on, 235
    projective counteridentification and, 238
    and racial/ethnic differences, 183

    as reaction to child abuse, 234
    research on, 230, 231, 232, 235, 238
    safety within therapeutic system, 241
    scapegoating, 232
    shared sense of purpose within family, 241–242
    as "suction" of therapist into family system, 229
    as window into covert emotional processes in the family, 229
"Customer" therapy relationship, 199

de Shazer, S., 73
Diamond, G. S., 28
Diehl, L., 35, 72, 88, 110, 126
Diversity
    acculturation and, within family, 183–184
    case illustrations
    cultural, 179–187
    cultural tradition and safety, 119–120
    with deaf clients, 183
    of family structures, 191–196
        adoption, 192
        divorce and feelings of shame and failure, 193
        remarried family and shared sense of purpose, 194–196
        infertility and child from previous relationship, 191–193
    gender, 187–188
    with HIV serodiscordant couples, 190
    with language, 183
    race and ethnicity, 180–183
    religion, 186–187
    religion and ethnicity, 180–183
    safety and, 119
    sexual orientation, 188–191
    social class, 184–186
Divorce potential, as zero-sum problem, 225

Ellison family case illustration
    countertransferential identification with, 237–238
        emotional connection with therapist and, 240
        engagement in therapeutic process and, 239–240
        experience of, 238
        projective identification and, 231
        shared sense of purpose and, 240–241